T0354463

SINCE
GOD
IS FOR US

SINCE
GOD
IS FOR US

We Are More
Than Conquerors

DR. RANDALL ODOM

iUniverse®

SINCE GOD IS FOR US
WE ARE MORE THAN CONQUERORS

ESV

Unless otherwise indicated, all scripture quotations are from The Holy Bible, English Standard Version® (ESV®). Copyright ©2001 by Crossway Bibles, a division of Good News Publishers. Used by permission. All rights reserved.s

iUniverse books may be ordered through booksellers or by contacting:

iUniverse
1663 Liberty Drive
Bloomington, IN 47403
www.iuniverse.com
1-800-Authors (1-800-288-4677)

ISBN: 978-1-5320-6091-5 (sc)
ISBN: 978-1-5320-6093-9 (hc)
ISBN: 978-1-5320-6092-2 (e)

Library of Congress Control Number: 2018912535

Print information available on the last page.

iUniverse rev. date: 10/19/2018

Contents

Foreword

I cannot speak about your life, but in mine, there have been times that I have needed a passage of Scripture only to find myself at a loss. My mind couldn't focus on a verse or a passage that seemed to give words of comfort in a difficult situation. As a pastor, there have been times in hospital rooms where someone was close to death, in a family's home after a tragic accident or in the streets of Camiri, Bolivia talking through an interpreter with a lady named Fatima who just found out she had cancer. So, after much prayer and searching the Bible, I have a go-to passage. It is Romans chapter 8. What a powerful chapter of God speaking to His children. It can settle a disturbed spirit, heal a broken heart, comfort those in need and challenge us when we seem stuck.

This is also the chapter that my friend, Dr. Randall Odom, chose to cover in this book. I have known Dr. Odom, his wife Deborah and their children for several years. He pastored for over 40 years and, through those years, he also was able to use Romans chapter 8 to minister to others. But, in this book, he talks about how it has ministered to him. He covers the truth of us being under no condemnation in Jesus Christ because we are God's adopted children; what a beautiful picture of the Father's love for us and the passage ends with there being no separation between us and God's love.

I hope you will learn and grow as you read *Since God Is For Us*. I know it will bless you as it has blessed me.

Blessings to follow…
Pastor Lee Pigg, D. Min.
Sr. Pastor, Hopewell Baptist Church
2018 President of the NC Baptist State Convention

Acknowledgments

I want to thank Deborah, my dear wife, for her patience in listening to me constantly talk out each chapter of this book and for her excellent counsel to me as I was writing this book.

I also want to thank Mrs. Dawn Shaver and Mrs. Mary Pope for being so gracious as to proofread the original draft of this book to eliminate as many mistakes as possible. They did a wonderful job and if there are any remaining mistakes they are attributable to me alone.

I want to thank Rev. Randy Seiver who, when we were both Bible college students (he was a senior and I was a sophomore), took me under wing and informally mentored me in the great doctrines of the Word of God. He helped to ground me in the passionate, in-depth study of the Word of God with a view to ascertaining the meaning of a passage of Scripture with precise accuracy. That discipline and mindset has been of great help to me in the proper study of the Word of God in general and in the writing of this book in particular.

I would like to thank the staff and members of Hopewell Baptist Church, Monroe, North Carolina, for their gracious acceptance of my wife and me and their continued encouragement to me in the writing of this book.

Finally, I would like to thank Mike and Dee Dimitri (two very dear Christian friends and coworkers in the Lord's kingdom) for their continued encouragement of me to write this book and for their gracious participation in enabling it to become a reality.

"Unto the King of the ages, immortal, invisible, the only God, be honor and glory forever and ever. Amen" (1 Timothy 1:17).

Dedicated to:

Deborah Odom, my best friend and the love of my life. She is my coworker in the service of the Lord and she is a woman of great integrity and deep spirituality – faithful in every way and a constant source of encouragement and support. An excellent wife whose "price is far above rubies."

Michael and Dee Dimitri, my dear Christian friends, and my faithful coworkers in the cause of Christ.

Dedicated to

Introduction

THE PARADIGM FROM THE PAST

A Bold Champion For God

Boldly and brazenly he stood with powerful legs spread wide glaring at the Jewish troops. He stood tall like an invincible pillar of solid stone with unmistakable raw power and strength. Totally persuaded that he was the epitome of soldier-like strength and all wrapped up in his own self-importance Goliath repeated his confident dare as he arrogantly bellowed his bold challenge to Israel's trembling warriors. "Who will come out and face me? "Who dares to take his life in his hands and compete with me in a man-to-man battle of life and death?"

There is no doubt about it. Goliath was an awesomely frightening and terrible giant. He was immense and he was standing right there looming over lesser men in a menacing and threatening way mocking Israel's manhood and her army. Goliath was anxious to make quick work of Israel's top soldier and so gain the glory and notoriety that he felt was due him for his professional and preeminent killing ability.

Only one Israelite was fearless enough to face him in battle. He was a young boy who had volunteered to be the sole representative of Israel against this awesome and fearful giant. He was the only one who dared take up the challenge of the terrible champion of the Philistines and Goliath was insulted that Israel would send out a mere boy to face him. When the two opponents drew closer together David could, no doubt, clearly see the beads of sweat glistening off the Giant's massive, muscular body and feel the sheer force of his daunting persona.

The giant was a staggering nine – foot – six inches tall. He was a fierce and fearful fighting machine. Goliath was brimming with bravado – a proud, proven and powerful killer of men eager and ready for his next conquest. It may be difficult for us to imagine a human being who stands 9'6" tall. Just the other day I was pulling through the drive-thru lane at a local Arby's restaurant. As I neared the window to pay my bill, I noticed that the overhang, high above me, had a sign on it that informed drivers that the clearance, at that point, was 9'6". I tried to imagine a real man standing there whose head would bump against that high overhang. He was a giant of a man, wearing bulky battle armor and dedicated as a killing machine for his fellow soldiers. It would have been an awesome sight – a truly frightening scenario. Goliath was a proud, mammoth, bloodthirsty warrior hungry for glory facing off with a young man who had no weapon in reach except a sling and five smooth stones that he had picked up for ammunition.

Where were the soldiers of Israel? Why were they not stepping forward to take up the challenge of Goliath? The reality was that the soldiers of Israel were terrified.

Fear is a powerful thing. A few years ago, I was helping a friend shingle the roof of his house. The roof had an extremely steep pitch and I was standing on the roof without any support or safety gear. Right in the middle of the job I was suddenly overcome with a feeling of overwhelming fear that I was going to fall. The fear was paralyzing and immobilizing. No amount of encouragement or rationalizing could induce me to take even one step more on that roof. The roof was not an exceptionally high distance from the ground but, still, I found myself frozen in place and terribly fearful of slipping and falling. Fear had taken over and was controlling me. I was humbled and embarrassed and yet could not make myself budge an inch. Can you imagine that kind of fear? Have you ever experienced it? It was a terror beyond description and that is just a small portion of the feeling that the Israelite soldiers must have felt when contemplating the frightening challenges of Goliath, the giant. I imagine the Israelite soldiers must have felt a similar but highly amplified terror when contemplating the very real challenges of Goliath.

"All the men of Israel, when they *saw the man (Goliath)*, fled from him and were much afraid" (1 Samuel 17:24). (*parentheses mine*).

The soldiers of Israel were terrified because they were primarily concerned with their own welfare. Their passion for God dwindled and virtually evaporated in the face of the terrifying giant who threatened their lives. Fear had captivated their hearts and minds causing them to doubt whether God was with them and for them. Perhaps, they feared, God had abandoned them. Fueled by these super strong emotions (a dwindling passion for God and a lack of confidence in the fact that God was for them and with them) they could not bring themselves to stand up and step forward to fight for the cause of God. They were helpless and hopeless soldiers. They cowered and cringed with cowardice.

Imagine a sports stadium filled with jeering, bloodthirsty soldiers eager to see the enemy humiliated and defeated. It is likely that the armies of the Philistines were chanting their enthusiastic support for their giant who represented them while they also were vociferously yelling taunts at David and the Jewish army. The cacophony of noise created by their emotional yelling and chanting would only have added to the spectacle and the high-pressure tension of the moment. This terrifying giant had mockingly taunted and challenged Israel's soldiers for days on end and they were all immobilized and paralyzed with fear and trepidation at the thought of facing up to this mammoth military force of nature in a one-on-one battle to the death. No one dared to risk his life facing such a powerful and bloodthirsty giant of a man.

The fearsome giant was bedecked with protective military armor and was carrying an enormous spear whose massive pointed head weighed 16 pounds. Goliath's armor bearer went before him a few yards, as was the custom, to provide him with an extra level of defensive protection. Even the oversized, bigger than life, king of Israel (Saul) was humiliatingly immobilized by an overwhelming fear in the face of this gigantic soldier – a fear approaching sheer humiliating panic.

Have you ever smelled the scent of fear? Years ago, when "Deacon Jones," one of the, "fearsome foursome," of the Los Angeles Rams football team was being interviewed by a sportscaster. Deacon Jones said that you could smell fear down on the scrimmage line when the, "fearsome foursome," were on the field.

When interviewed, soldiers who had participated in the Allied invasion of Europe on D day testified that you could smell fear among the invading young men who were about to step out on the defended and contested French beaches (totally exposed to horrendous, amassed Nazi defensive fire). The sheer panic and terror of the moment emitted the awful scent of fear.

Young David knew perfectly well what he was up against. Yet undaunted, the intrepid young man stepped up all alone, without protective armor, to face off with this frightening, larger-than-life, giant in a winner take all life-and-death fight. Certainly, the world would not have given promising odds to the challenger in this seeming colossal mismatch. But God is not concerned with height measurements, previous experience in battle or muscle girth when He wants to score a victory for His glory.

Christianity stands in constant need of more David–like champions for Christ. The question is, what factors were they that enabled David to step forward and stand up for God and God's people when others cringed in fear and failed to do so?" Since David knew that God was empowering and protecting him, that knowledge and assurance made all the difference. God was on his side.

David Was Properly Prepared

David really had two things going for him. First, he had a consuming passion for God. He loved God and sought to glorify God and to promote His cause. In the Psalms David expresses his love for God and passion for God over and over. He was a man after God's own heart. He loved God supremely and passionately. Second, David was persuaded, beyond a doubt, that God was with him and for him. In fact, David had a rock-solid confidence and assurance that God was for him and with him. Think about it. It would make no sense for David to volunteer to fight this giant behemoth of a warrior if he were doing so merely in his own relatively puny strength without God's help. Instead, David understood that the hand of God was upon him, he understood that God was with him, and that God was for him.

David had some previous history with God. As a child or youth David received a clear indication that God's hand was upon him. David had experienced God's hand upon him when he defended his father's sheep against ravenous predators. When conversing with Saul (the king of Israel) David said to him, "Your servant used to keep sheep for his father, when there came a lion or a bear, and took a lamb from the flock, I went after him and struck him and delivered it out of his mouth. And if he arose against me, I caught him by his beard and struck him and killed him. Your servant has struck down both lions and bears, and this uncircumcised Philistine shall be like one of them, for he has defied the armies of the living God." Then David said, "The Lord who delivered me from the paw of the lion and from the paw of the bear will deliver me from the hand of this Philistine." David had also experienced the hand of God upon him when Samuel had anointed him to be the future king of Israel. These facts buttressed David's confidence in the fact that God was for him. We, too, as believers are informed by the Word of God that God is with us and for us. The more practical experiences that we have with God, the more our faith will be strengthened in this truth. This will give the believer increased confidence and provide him with unusual boldness to stand up for God against the enemies of God.

"Having heard that from David, Saul said to David, "Go, and the Lord be with you" (I Samuel 17: 37 – 44.)

David was completely persuaded that God was with him and for him. Not only was this true in terms of past scenarios but it was also true in this present conflict. David also unquestionably believed that God would be with him and help him throughout his entire life and that ultimately God would secure David's place in heaven. He could confidently write, "Surely goodness and mercy shall follow me all the days of my life, and I shall dwell in the house of the Lord forever" (Psalm 23:6). This same confidence can be shared by every true believer.

THE PRACTICAL IMPORTANCE

Why Is It Necessary to Know Confidently That God Is With You?

Why have I started this book by recalling to the reader the David and Goliath episode? It is because we, as believers, can utilize this event as a paradigm through which to view our Christian experience. David was certain and secure in the fact that God was for him and this empowered him to show courage and do great things for God. The same can be true of every Christian.

If we do not have a burning passion for God, indeed, if we do not confidently and assuredly know that God is with us, our lack of passion and doubt will serve to undercut our ability to serve God effectively.

Personally, I do not think that I could carry on in the ministry of the Lord's work effectively and wholeheartedly if I thought that were I to slip that God would abandon me. If I was not persuaded that God is unconditionally for me and that He will always be for me I would be more concerned and worried about the permanence of my salvation than I would be with doing ministry for the Lord. That is why the Word of God continually declares and reinforces the concept that, "Since God is for us… Who can be against us?" God wants His children to know that He is wholeheartedly and unconditionally for them and always will be.

The Spiritual Armor of God

In the book of Ephesians chapter six, the Apostle Paul is very clear about the fact that all believers will find themselves embroiled in spiritual warfare. Like David, we are often thrust into the fight without prior expectation. Though David could not find any military armor that fit him God provides the perfect armor for every true Christian. To be successful in resisting the devil and in standing firm in the face of our spiritual adversary, God has provided a complete set of spiritual armor for our spiritual success. Paul describes this armor using the common figure of a Roman soldier. His readers would have been keenly aware of what a Roman soldier's armor looked like since the Roman soldiers were everywhere present at all times.

Thankfully, God does not expect the Christian, as a spiritual soldier, to stand against our spiritual giant without adequate spiritual armor to win the battle. Furthermore, God is intent that we know that He is for us so that we can be empowered and enabled to be successful soldiers for the cause of God.

In Ephesians 6:10 – 17, the Apostle Paul identifies six different aspects of the armor of a Roman soldier and uses those as teaching tools for helping Christians understand something about their spiritual armor.

The Belt of Truth

First, he describes the, girdle/belt of truth. In this case, the word "truth," probably indicates truthfulness and sincerity.

The Roman soldier normally wore a free-flowing tunic that covered most of his body. The tunic could easily become entangled with his legs and trip him up in the heat of battle. Consequently, Paul is saying that the Christian warrior needs to tuck his "tunic" under his belt and cinch it up. Paul's point is that the Christian warrior needs to keep himself unencumbered and fully prepared to be committed to do immediate spiritual battle. The tucking of the tunic into the belt signified the soldier's serious intent to engage in immediate combat.

Breastplate of Righteousness

Second, the Apostle Paul mentions the breastplate of righteousness. In Jewish thinking the heart was the seat of thinking. "For as he thinks in his heart, so is he…" (Proverbs 23:7 KJV). The Intestines (or bowels) were considered the seat of emotion. The breastplate was intended to cover and protect the torso and in particularly, the mind and emotions. Paul describes this breastplate as one of righteousness. Righteousness is to govern our thinking and our emotions and thus consequently our conduct as Christians. We are to live righteous lives because our minds and emotions are given over to think on and love righteousness even as God is righteous. As the Bible says, our Shepherd leads us in paths of righteousness for His name's sake. The Christian soldier is exposed to danger if he does not shroud himself in living righteousness. Since God is for us, however, He provides us with this necessary righteousness as a "breastplate" to protect us as we battle for the truth.

Armored Footwear

Third, the Apostle Paul points out that, since God is for you, the Christian warrior wears shoes that are shod with the preparation of the gospel of peace. By this Paul is not, as some have contended, referring to the believer's evangelism of lost sinners. He is rather underscoring the fact that the true Christian warrior is firmly grounded in a relationship with God which guarantees that he is at peace with God through the work of Jesus Christ our Lord and Savior. "Therefore, since we have been justified by faith, we have peace with God through our Lord Jesus Christ" (Romans 5:1). The apostle speaks of these shoes as characterizing the "readiness given by the gospel of peace." In Roman military culture the soldier would often wear shoes that were studded with nails to ensure that he would not slip and slide on hillsides while fighting the enemy. He needed to be firmly grounded so that he could stand and resist the onslaught of his adversaries. This is what Paul has in mind. He is encouraging the Christian soldier to make sure that he is grounded in a relationship of eternal and secure peace with God through faith in the Lord Jesus Christ. Being confident that he is firmly grounded in a relationship of peace with God the believer is then able to be totally devoted to the spiritual battle. A person who has doubts about their fundamental relationship with God will suffer from unsure footing and a lack of absolute confidence that God is for them and with them.

Note that Paul refers to all three of these pieces of armor as armor that the Christian has already put on. He says, "Having put on…" This phrase is indicating that the armor has been put on once and for all. It is not an ongoing, repetitive process.

The Shield of Faith

The *fourth* piece of spiritual armor is described as, "the shield of faith, with which you can extinguish all the flaming darts of the evil one." The Roman soldier had access to two different types of shields. One was round like a garbage can lid with two leather straps on the back into which the soldier would slide his arm. This shield was highly movable and made of thick leather covered with pieces of animal bone or metal. The other primary shield that the Roman soldier had access to was more like a small door. It was about two and a half feet wide and four or five feet high. Normally, those soldiers carrying this type of shield would occupy the front ranks of the Army. They would stand shoulder to shoulder planting their shields on the ground and forming a solid wall of armor that sometimes stretched as far as a mile in length. This phalanx was a formidable defense against an attacking adversary. Behind this assembled wall of shields the Roman archers would launch their arrows while being protected. The adversary would often counter by coating their arrows in pitch and lighting them on fire just before they shot them. The shields were intended to provide an impervious wall of protection for the Roman troops against such attacks. This is the kind of shield that Paul is referring to in his description of spiritual armor in Ephesians 6. Since God is for you He provides you with the shield of faith to protect you and defend you.

The Helmet of Salvation

Fifth, the Apostle Paul speaks of the necessity of the Christian warrior putting on the, "helmet of salvation." Some have mistakenly interpreted this as Paul saying that the Christian warrior needs to be saved. However, Paul has already spoken of the Christian warrior, his commitment to truth, his grounding in the gospel of peace, and his use of the shield of faith. Therefore, the Christian warrior is already saved and does not need to be saved again. What then is the helmet of salvation?

For additional insight into the meaning of this term we have but to consult the Apostle's writings in I Thessalonians 5:8. There the Apostle speaks of the helmet of the hope of salvation. The reference to hope, regarding the helmet, points us to the future and speaks of our anticipation of our ultimate and complete salvation. Hope looks forward with anticipation.

Of course, the helmet was an instrument of armor intended to protect the Roman soldier's head in battle. Primarily, it was worn to protect the soldier against the blows of the enemy's broadswords. These were swords that were double-aged and ranged from three to four feet in length. The adversary would grip the handle of the sword, raise it high above his head, and proceed to slash downward at the Roman soldier's head. The helmet was intended to help deflect a possible blow to the head. It is clear, from the passage in Ephesian 6:6, as well as the passage in I Thessalonians 5:8, that the helmet is related to salvation but what part of salvation is in view?

Often, when we refer to salvation today, we are actually talking about conversion. Salvation, however, comes in three phases. The Christian is saved from the guilt and condemnation of sin through faith in Jesus Christ. This is referred to as justification and occurs when the sinner trusts by faith alone in Jesus Christ alone as their Lord and Savior. Then the justified sinner (now a Christian) is progressively saved from the power and negative influence of sin so that they are enabled to live a righteous and godly life becoming more and more conformed to the image of Jesus Christ. This is called sanctification. Lastly, there is a third phase of salvation which we refer to as glorification. This is when God finally takes us to be with Himself and perfects us, thus, freeing us from the very presence of sin. This final phase of salvation is what Paul has in mind when he refers to, "the helmet of salvation." He is referring to the believer's ultimate hope and salvation. Since God is for you, He provides you with the helmet of salvation which protects your strong and abiding hope of eternal glory.

How do I know this to be true? Consider Paul's words in 1 Thessalonians. There, Paul is referring to the end times and to the coming of the Lord Jesus Christ. He is contrasting those who live in darkness with the believer who lives in light. In this passage, he writes, "But since we belong to the day, let us be sober, having put on the breastplate of faith and love, and for a helmet the hope of salvation. For God has not destined us for wrath, but to obtain salvation through our Lord Jesus Christ..." (1 Thessalonians 5:8 – 9).

Notice, the helmet of salvation, according to the Apostle Paul's letter to the Thessalonians, has to do with our *hope* of salvation. The Bible constantly tells us that we are saved in hope. In Romans 8:24 – 25, Paul makes this abundantly clear and he refers to our "groanings" as we look forward to our certain hope of being delivered from the very presence of sin – (Romans 8:23). When John wrote his first epistle he said that all Christians are saved in hope and he wrote in 1 John 3:1 that everyone, "who has this hope in him…" will go on purifying himself even as his Lord is pure. Here, when referring to our hope, John is speaking of our ultimate glorification… Every Christian has this hope, which is what Paul was talking about when he referred to the "the helmet of the hope of salvation." In addition, the Apostle Peter called it a living hope (1 Peter 1:3). Since God is for you, he fills you with a certain confident "hope" in your ultimate salvation.

Someone has said that a person can live without food for several weeks, without water for three or four days, but one cannot live without hope for even a few minutes. God is for us and with us, therefore, we have a settled and confident hope in our ultimate and complete salvation.

The Sword of the Spirit Which is the Word of God

The Roman soldier employed two very different kinds of swords in battle. One was the broadsword which was three to four feet in length and double-edged. It was used for smashing and wild, thrashing cuts. The soldier would grasp the handle of the sword, raise it above his head, and swing the sword in a vicious arc of power and destruction. The other sword used by the Roman soldier was more like a dagger. It was twelve to eighteen inches long and was used for up–close combat where finesse was needed. This is the sword that the Apostle Paul is referring to in Ephesians 6.

Further, Paul refers to the sword of the Spirit as being the Word of God. Often the word for "word" is the Greek word *logos,* which is a somewhat general term for "Word." It can also refer to something of a profound nature as in John 1:1, "In the beginning was the Word and the Word was with God and the Word was God…" In Ephesians 6, however, Paul employs a completely different word when referring to the, "word" of the

Lord. There he uses the Greek word, *"rhema."* This refers to a specific statement or passage of Scripture. In other words, the Apostle Paul is saying that the believer must be schooled and adequately prepared to use specific statements of Scripture in both a defensive and offensive manner in the battle against Satan.

A perfect example of this kind of spiritual battle is recorded for us in Matthew chapter four, when our Lord Jesus Christ was tempted by Satan in the wilderness. Each time he was tempted, Jesus responded with a specific passage of Scripture in defending himself against Satan's attacks. I encourage the reader to look up this portion of Scripture and see how Jesus used specific passages from the book of Deuteronomy as he contended with Satan. Since God is for you He has provided you with the sword of His Word so that you can use the truth of God skillfully in your warfare with Satan.

Satan wants to destroy our hope and so defeat our efforts at living a successful Christian life. Therefore, we must wear the helmet of the hope of salvation along with the other pieces of spiritual armor. Indeed, we must put on the whole armor of God. In addition, Satan would far rather have us to be entangled with worry over our own relationship with God than being focused on resisting his efforts to attack us. It is vital that we as Christians have a solid confidence and assurance regarding our saving relationship with God. With the broadsword Satan constantly whacks away at our passionate hope and our confident assurance. How does he go about doing this?

Some Samples of Satan's Methods Of Discouraging Christians

Our spiritual adversary has many learned and devious techniques that he uses to attack our hope in Christ. Among these are discouragement, doubt, distraction, and disobedience. He knows that if he can sever the nerve of our certain hope and assurance of God's presence and support that he will be able to keep us out of the conflict with him and thus remove us as a serious threat to his efforts.

Sometimes he seeks to discourage Christians even in the aftermath of spiritual successes. Consider the case of Elijah. Elijah was victorious in his stance for God against the prophets of Baal, but soon thereafter, found himself discouraged and dejected. We are never immune from the danger of discouragement. Elijah was particularly discouraged because he falsely thought that he was the only person still living faithfully for God. Sometimes, Satan will seek to convince us that everyone else has abandoned their faith and we are all alone. How discouraging that would be! We must remember that God always has His remnant of believers who are faithfully serving him.

Satan sometimes seeks to discourage us when we see other Christians struggling under severe hardships. He seeks to discourage us through doctrinal confusion by causing us to believe wrongly about God and His plan for our lives. Satan sometimes discourages us not through a single blow but through a death by a thousand cuts. Often, it is not the massive blow that takes away our hope. Instead, it is the constant, never-ending nibbling away at our faith and hope. To return to the metaphor, it is one little slash after another that finally takes their cumulative toll on the Christian. None of these cuts are fatal in themselves, but it is the cumulative effect that takes its toll over time. Another way he discourages us is by the straying of other Christians who we have invested ourselves in to help them to grow in Christ. It is discouraging to watch them veer off the path of righteousness and truth and live rebellious, ungrateful lives despite our most sincere efforts to help them spiritually.

Sometimes we become discouraged because of unanswered prayer. For example, it can be discouraging when we have been praying for an unsaved husband or wife who continues to reject the gospel or for a child who refuses to follow the ways of the Lord as he has been taught. Discouragement can also come from the bewildering barrage of numerous and varied troubles and struggles in life constantly bombarding us. It sometimes comes, as well, when it seems that the rough road ahead will go on indefinitely with no end in sight. We can also be discouraged by taking on more in life than we think we can handle. That is, we feel like we have bitten off more than we can chew. Satan has no limits to the ways he uses to discourage God's children.

At one time in the past, I kept honeybees. I liked the Italian three banded kind. I would often put on my bee "outfit", light my "smoker" and go up to examine one of the "supers" (square boxes of bees). Inside each "super" were many frames which the bees worked on to produce honeycomb and honey. There were literally thousands upon thousands of bees at work at any given time. Each bee had his designated project and I was always amazed at how effective they were in their work.

I learned that to keep the bees working diligently, I needed to place a few "frames" in the super to give them something to aspire to. If I did not put these frames in the, "super," the bees would become lethargic and stop working concluding that they had finished their job and that there was no more to do. On the other hand, if I put too many new frames in the "super" at one time the bees would become discouraged and would also stop working. Too much of a workload discouraged them even though they were, by nature, diligent workers.

Christians can become discouraged when they take on too much or when they think that they must work at something that they cannot see a successful conclusion to. They lose hope and Satan would like nothing more. Since God is for us He carefully manages our life in such a way as to help us minimize discouragement and to keep us encouraged and productive in our spiritual journey.

With discouragement often comes doubt. Where is God when I call upon Him and He does not seem to answer? Can I trust the Bible? Does God really care about me? Am I really saved or just living under the illusion of salvation? Satan bombards us with doubts created by the false claims of pseudoscience, the misrepresentations of mass media, the secularization of education, etc.

Satan also distracts us. The master distractor is constantly working to distract the Christian. He wants to keep Christians from keeping their eyes on the hope of their salvation. To combat this tactic of Satan we need to be more like the postle Paul, who wrote, "Not that I have already obtained this or am already perfect, but I press on to make it my own, because Christ

Jesus has made me his own. Brothers, I do not consider that I have made it my own. But one thing I do: forgetting what lies behind and straining toward what lies ahead, I press on toward the goal for the prize of the upward call of God in Christ Jesus. Let those of us who are mature think this way..." (Philippians 3:12 – 15a).

Unfortunately, sometimes Christians act like toddlers who can be distracted easily by a new shiny toy. Satan often works with baby steps when distracting Christians from their hope in Christ. He leads them to place their hope on something more temporal and material or in some erroneous, mystical belief system. He is a master of "incrementalism". He cleverly shifts our attention one degree at a time until we lose focus on our hope and become vulnerable in the day of battle. Let the Apostle Paul be our example. Consider his words to the Corinthians, "So we do not lose heart. Though our outward self is wasting away, our inner self is being renewed day by day. For this light, momentary, affliction is preparing us for an eternal weight of glory beyond all comparison, as we look not to the things that are seen but to the things that are unseen. For the things that are seen are transient, but the things that are unseen are eternal" (2 Corinthians 4:16 – 18).

Paul is telling us that God is for us and therefore we are not to become distracted by the things of this world whether they are temptations or trials. Instead, we are to keep our focus concentrated on our hope which is rooted in Christ Jesus. This is remarkably difficult to do in a world which is constantly hawking the desirability of acquiring the next new "thing." We must not be conformed to the world's way of thinking but constantly being transformed by the renewal of our minds through the Word of God.

Satan seeks to damage or destroy our hope through discouragement, doubt, distraction and even disillusionment. Sometimes, Satan also seeks to dampen our hope through tempting us to be out right rebellious and disobedient toward God.

When believers disobey God, they quench the work of the Holy Spirit in their lives and thus the fires of our hope grow dimmer. Satan would like nothing more than to convince Christians that they can sin against God and get away with it. He would like to convince Christians that God is an indulgent, weak-willed parent who will allow His children to be disobedient without chastening them. Nothing could be farther from the truth. We must remember the words of Scripture, "Be sure your sins will find you out." "Do not be deceived: God is not mocked, for whatever one sows, that will he also reap" (Galatians 6:7). Disobedience damages our subjective feeling of hope and places us under the chastening hand of a loving but insistent God.

In referring to the, *"helmet of salvation,"* and, *"the helmet of the hope of salvation,"* Paul was speaking of our confident hope that we will, by God's grace and with God's help, win the good fight of faith and most certainly live in the house of the Lord forever. How is all this possible? Because God is with us and God is for us! That is what David knew and that is what we need to know. Take it to the bank, since God is for you, you will be more than a conqueror.

David's Two Keys to Success

David was fueled by two attitudes that helped him to be successful against Goliath. *First*, he had the attitude of a passion for God and His glory. *Second*, David possessed the attitude of a confident assurance that God was with him and for him. These twin attitudes instilled in David a confident boldness enabling him to personally stand up and step forward to do the work of God and to fearlessly fight the enemies of God. Consider his words as he responded to the threats and taunts of Goliath the giant, he said to the Philistine, "You come to me with a sword and with a spear and with a javelin; but I come to you in the name of the LORD of hosts, the God of the armies of Israel, you have defied" (1 Samuel 17:45).

David's passion for God and confident persuasion and assurance that God was with him and for him enabled him to boldly stand up and defend the cause of God even in the face of overwhelming odds. The same will be true of us when we practice those same two attitudes.

David knew that since God was for him, it was simply irrelevant who was against him – even if his opponent was a giant. All other factors were beside the point. It was Jesus who said that if one had faith comparable in size to a tiny mustard seed that it would prevail against the mountain, because true faith is aligned with the will of a sovereign, omnipotent God. God is greater and more powerful than all.

David also knew that there was another far more formidable giant on this particular field of battle that day – a much larger and more powerful giant than anyone could imagine, a giant who is always, without fail, victorious. God is a "giant" who is always successful. David knew that God was there with him and in that light Goliath was not a major concern. God would defeat him. David believed in the certainty that, "If God is for us, who can be against us?"

The Spark That Ignited a Fire

Interestingly, the Bible says that those previously panic stricken and immobilized soldiers in the Israelite army were suddenly transformed and emboldened by David's action. In fact, we read, "and the men of Israel and Judah rose with a shout in pursuit of the Philistines…" (1 Samuel 17:52). Not only did they rise up and pursue the Philistines but they devastated their pagan army and plundered their camp. The entire tenor of the war changed because of the action of one young man who was passionately zealous for the glory of God and absolutely persuaded that God was with him and for him.

As New Testament Christians, we stand in need of the same things that enabled David to be a champion for God. We need to have a passion for God and a confident persuasion and assurance that God is with us and for us. Fueled by these two factors we need to stand up and step forward to defend the cause of God. Perhaps God will use our faithful actions to turn the tide of battle in His direction for His glory.

There are giant problems confronting us from every direction. If we fail to embody the things that motivated David we will fail in the face of these giant problems. If, however, we embrace the truths that motivated David we too can be champions for the cause of God.

Great assurance can be ours. Great things are possible. Great giants can be slain. Great mountains can be moved. Great changes can take place in our lives. All of this is possible *since God is for us* – and because He is, we can win against our enemies.

What If It Had Been Different?

Now, imagine for a moment David in a different scenario altogether. The same giant looms in front of him but David is unsure as to whether God is with him and for him. David fears that some past sin of his will now cause God to forsake him leaving him to fight the fearsome giant alone. David is gripped with uncertainty and fear, unsure of his standing with God, unsure of his ability to face the giant in battle, and unsure as to whether he will be able to keep his doubts under control and continue to live up to the course of action that he had set himself upon. The key word in David's thoughts is now UNCERTAINTY. The key attitude controlling David would be A FEARFUL LACK OF ASSURANCE which would undercut David's ability to trust God.

Imagine, again, another scenario altogether. In this scenario, David is not a believer at all. He thinks he is and has convinced himself (and many others) that he is a bona fide believer in God. But, in reality, David has mindlessly followed the errant spiritual course that his religious teachers and peers have recommended to him. He has lived his life contenting himself with mere external formalized religion.

Imagine that this David of our imagination has no real heart commitment to God. He knows about God but he doesn't really know God. He understands some of the biblical teaching regarding the attributes of God but he has never personally submitted himself to the Lordship/kingship of God's authority and trusted God as his Savior.

In this fictitious scenario David now presumptively goes up against Goliath with the illusion that God is for him and with him. He recklessly assumes that God is going to be there taking care of him simply because he has dabbled in religion. In this scenario David is in great jeopardy and is foolishly placing himself in a dangerous situation. In reality, he is without God. David, for all his confidence, has no real reason to think that God is for him and with him. In fact, David is facing the giant alone in his own strength.

This book, "Since God is for us", has been written with a view to encouraging true Christians by the solid fact that God is with us. God is always for us and because of that we can enjoy spiritual success now and look forward to enjoying heaven for eternity. We need not fear the world's giants, "Since God is for us."

As we work our way step-by-step through the rich teaching of Romans chapter eight you will become fascinated and staggered by the depth of God's love for you. By reading, "Since God is for us" you will be amazed regarding the rich provisions that He has made for you and your security in Christ. Paul's intention in writing Romans chapter eight, is that the truths of this chapter should forever remove every worry and concern that you might have regarding all of life's circumstances. God loves you. God is for you in every circumstance and in the face of every giant. God is with you. Therefore, we are more than conquerors!

THE PAIN OF MANY CHRISTIANS

Tormented Christians

Some Christians can't bring themselves to live like Christian champions in the shadow of David's example. Why? They can't be totally engaged for God because they are tormented and distracted with uncertainty and a lack of assurance regarding their own eternal salvation. They are fearful and questioning and this hampers their willingness to step out and serve God with boldness and assurance. On the other hand, other people have falsely assumed that God is somehow committed to their well-being even though they have not personally surrendered to His authority and trusted in His salvation. They are superficially convinced that regardless of their lack of real heartfelt commitment God is, nevertheless, standing ready to ensure their victory over every obstacle in life.

These scenarios describe too many professing Christians.

Romans chapter eight is a great passage of Scripture that can be used to eliminate these last two scenarios in the life of any and every reader and this book, "Since God is for us" will clearly explain this tremendous section of Scripture to you. God wants His children to have a genuine sense of security and assurance, but He only wants this for His genuine children. He does not want His children to be disturbed and hindered by uncertainty and needless questioning of their status with Him. Neither does He want the false believer to be deluded with a pseudo-conversion that is not genuinely saving in nature. God wants His dear children to have a consuming passion for Him and to know confidently and assuredly that He is for them and that they can stand up and step forward with confidence as they serve Him.

God's being with us is not merely a formal, feeling–less display of familiarity but it is a very real, loving, intimate and personal commitment to each Christian.

There is an interesting story about Gen. Douglas MacArthur, the military hero of years ago.

Gen. MacArthur was highly thought of and was regarded as a consummate leader. In fact, I, personally, have a tremendous admiration for the military genius that he was. However, he also had a reputation for being a cold fish personally. Because of this, his public relations people came up with a creative idea. They proposed to gather together a contingent of veterans that were preselected for the purpose. In the middle of the review by MacArthur they would have him turn and feign recognition of a particular enlisted man who had served under him during the war.

"It will be a tremendously moving human moment," the advisor said to MacArthur. "Out of hundreds of men lined up for your inspection, you suddenly pick out a single individual, call him by name, and recall past campaigns." MacArthur agreed to go along with the plan.

So, they set up the inspection and chose their veteran. The lucky soldier would be unaware that he'd been singled out for the honor. They went through the Army records, found out everything about the fellow and figured out precisely where he would be standing when MacArthur marched through the ranks. To be on the safe side, they arranged for an aide to nudge MacArthur discreetly when he was directly in front of the proper soldier.

It all went off like clockwork. MacArthur saluted the veterans, the veterans saluted MacArthur. The general began his march along the lines of soldiers. At the right moment, the aide gave MacArthur the nudge.

MacArthur halted. He turned and looked at the man who was standing stiffly and at attention. When he was directly in front of the man he boomed, "Jones! We served together on Corregidor. You are Cpl. Jones. I remember you."

Jones looked startled for a moment. Then he looked closely at the general. Finally, he replied somewhat quizzically: "MacArthur?" – (James in Charleston, West Virginia Gazette 7/2/91).

Gen. MacArthur got his bubble burst that day. It served him right. His allegiance and love for this soldier was artificial. God's love for us, however, is real and pure. It is vibrant.

Arnold Prater, in his book 'YOU CAN HAVE JOY!' tells about a man in a little English village named John Deckard. He was a clerk in a textile factory. A modest quiet man, he lived in an ordinary little house at the edge of town with his wife and his six-year-old son, Rob. Like thousands of Englishmen every morning John put on his plain tweed suit, got on his bicycle, and rode to work.

Returning home at five in the evening, he would work in his garden until supper time. Then he spent a quiet evening with his pipe and family.

He was a very ordinary man living what most people would call a very ordinary life.

But John had one claim to fame. For five consecutive years he had won the blue ribbon in the village garden show with his prize rose. It had gone on so long that people had come to expect it. John Deckard's prize Rose would win, and that was that.

Behind his house was his rose garden. When he returned home each evening, he would put on his coveralls and spend his time out there with his roses. Some said he had more than just "a way with flowers." Some say he mothered them, that he talked to them, and that they understood what he said.

This year, deep in his own heart, John Deckard knew that he would again win the blue ribbon, for this year his rose was truly a rose among roses. Never had he seen such perfection in a flower. This was his masterpiece and he watched it grow daily. It was his pride and joy.

The show was on Saturday and he planned to transplant the rose to a pot early in the morning. But while he was at breakfast, the tragedy happened. His little son Rob burst into the kitchen and chatting excitedly he rushed to the table and cried, "Look daddy, look what I have for you!"

And in his grimy little hand, half its petals gone, its head drooping, was John Deckard's prize Rose.

That afternoon, visitors to the garden show were astonished when they came to John Deckard's entry. For in a flower pot he had thrust a stick, and attached to it, at the very top, was a picture of his little son, Rob. When the judges heard what happened they gave John Deckard an honorary blue ribbon. Some said that the Rose that was not a rose was the finest he had ever grown. God's love is like that..." – (Arnold Prater, "You Can Have Joy!," Atlanta, Georgia: Lay Renewal Publications)

God's love for us is like that of John Deckard for his son. It is unconditional and giving. His commitment to us is voluntary and it is not contingent upon anything in us as believers. God's love for us is compassionate and forgiving. He is with us and for us in every way for our good!

God is not for us merely in some formalized pretense, but God is, in reality, for us. He is for us passionately, purposely, powerfully, perpetually and personally. He has committed Himself to us for our well-being.

God is for us lovingly, unconditionally and sacrificially.

THE PAULINE TOUR

The Apostle Paul Leads Us on a Fascinating Tour

The Bible is the inspired, infallible, inerrant, authoritative Word of God. Nothing else in this world is as unchanging and accurate as the Word of God. Look at the mountains and you think of them as the index of stability. It seems that they are unchanging and fixed but the truth is erosion and other natural factors are constantly altering even the mountains. Today, in Hawaii an active volcano is dramatically changing the landscape of the big Island. The earth, including the mountains, is constantly changing. Think of the earth itself. It is Terra Firma and always the same-or is it? The truth is that because of deviations in the earth's rotation, the stars appear to shift positions over time. The earth does not constantly remain pointed to the same direction. The scientific terms are precession and nutation. Because the earth bulges around the equator from its rotation, the gravitational pull of the sun and moon is heaviest around the equator and causes a slight wobble to the earth's spinning axis. You no doubt have seen the same phenomenon in a spinning top when you have observed it wobbling in its spinning motion due to gravity. This is called precession, and when it occurs with the earth it traces a circular cone in space every 25,800 years. Nutation, or nodding, is a small but irregular movement that swings the celestial pole 10 seconds away from the smooth precession of a perfect circle so that it makes a U-shaped circle every 18 .6 years.

That means that sometime in the distant future *Polaris* will no longer be the North Star. Today, and for generations past, travelers have used *Polaris* (the

North Star) as the fixed point by which to navigate because they believed that the earth was firmly fixed in its place and permanently unmovable. But as *Polaris* drifts away (or more accurately, as the earth changes its orientation) another star will move into position above the North Pole in approximately 345 years. Hundreds of years before the time of Christ, the vernal equinox (spring equinox) (equinox means "equal night"—it is where the sun intersects the celestial equator from south to north thus making it a reference direction for angular distances as measured from the equator) passed through the constellation *Aries*. Because of precession, however, the vernal equinox is now in Pisces and is advancing toward *Aquarius*.

Are you totally confused yet? What's the point of all of this? Merely to point out that even the earth is in the process of changing. Nothing is totally stable and certain except the Word of God. It never changes and is always accurate. Why? Because, as Paul told Timothy, "All Scripture is breathed out by God and profitable for teaching, for reproof, for correction, and for training in righteousness, that the man of God may be complete, equipped for every good work" (2 Timothy 3:16 – 17).

The Word of God is more sure than human reason, human experiences or human senses (2 Peter 1:19). It endures forever (1 Peter 1:25). It is trustworthy in every detail (Matthew 5:18). It never changes and is eternal (Isaiah 40:8). Our Lord Jesus Christ Himself said, "Heaven and earth will pass away but my words will not pass away" (Matthew 24:35). The Bible is the unchanging, accurate standard of truth (John 17:17). It is to the Bible, then, that we must turn for our answers regarding spiritual matters and for our guidance and understanding. God has graciously given us His infallible, unchanging word for our benefit. Oh, how He loves you and me! God is for us.

As the Apostle Paul takes us on a journey through Romans chapter eight of the Bible we can begin to see more clearly how deeply God loves us. We also see how lovingly, wisely, and powerfully He has provided for our every need. This book, "Since God is for us," will serve to help explain each step of the tour that the Apostle Paul takes us on. God is, indeed, for us and we will gain more and more appreciation for that fact and develop an unshakable confidence in it as we study Romans chapter eight together. Indeed, the reader will benefit from an increased insight into this full and completely perfect package of salvation that God has blessed us with. That increased knowledge will only be enhanced as we study Romans chapter eight using this book. "Since God is for us". Furthermore, the more we gaze into this passage the more we will gain a fuller understanding of the depths of God's great love for us and the more we will feel a reciprocal, loving, passion for God. As we grow in understanding of God's colossal sacrifice and absolute commitment to us, as believers, our hearts will be stirred and inflamed to love God more passionately than we have ever loved Him before. That is one great benefit of studying Romans chapter eight. It stokes the fires of our passion for God providing us with that first key element necessary to be a David–like soldier for God. Furthermore, in Romans chapter eight the Apostle Paul takes us on a step-by-step tour of the provisions that God in His grace gives us to ensure our absolute security for all of eternity.

This Pauline tour takes us through eleven separate specialized provisions that our loving God has made for true believers in the process of securing their absolute salvation for eternity. The Apostle Paul begins the tour with the fact that for the Christian there is now "no condemnation" – no condemnation now and no condemnation ever! Then, step-by-step, the apostle reveals to us the many wise and perfect provisions that God has lovingly made to guarantee our ultimate security in salvation. His final revelation to us in Romans chapter eight is that we, as believers, have the divine promise of God that there will be "no separation" of us from the love of God which is in Christ Jesus. God's love for us is not conditional and it is eternally unchanging.

Each of the eleven crucial steps that Paul takes the reader through in Romans chapter eight is like an overlook which provides us with a new and different perspective on the subject of God's work in our salvation and our assurance. While studying Romans chapter eight, we will be privileged to travel with Paul and to stop at each overlook to examine our wonderful salvation from a new and different perspective. This process will enlarge our understanding of God's wonderful work in our salvation and reaffirm in our hearts and minds that our God is glorious in His loving grace and Almighty power. When the tour is over as guided by this book, "Since God is for us" the Christian reader will have been exposed to a tremendous, panoramic, understanding of their absolute security in salvation made possible because of God alone. In the course of this theological/biblical tour, Paul will introduce us to and explain eleven specific ways in which God secures and promotes the ultimate salvation of the one who trusts in Christ alone for his salvation. In this book "Since God is for us" I will spend one chapter explaining each one of these eleven truths that Paul shares with us in Romans chapter eight and I have also inserted an additional chapter at the very beginning of the book which will give you, the reader, strong reasons why you should not hesitate to learn what God has for us in Romans chapter eight.

In this chapter, God shows us repeatedly how committed He is to us. Since God is for us, we can rejoice in the absolute confidence that we can have in the security of our salvation. These two things (a burning passion for God and an absolute persuasion that God is for us) will enable us to be like David who fearlessly faced up to the enemies of God with a supernatural courage and commitment.

The glorious truth is, as true believers in Christ, it doesn't really matter who or what is against us—since God is for us! This book, "Since God is for us" is going to describe and explain many of the ways in which God is for us as believers. We all face giants of one sort or another. Without God these things frighten and intimidate us. Since God is for us, however, we can live life enjoying the full confidence that we are eternally secure in the Lord and that we can face life's large problems without fear. Since God is for us, we can face all the difficulties of life caused by sin. The believer needs to fully understand and wholeheartedly embrace the awesome reality that the Almighty God is for us. This is imperative! Take heart, dear believer, the victory is ours. Our weaknesses and frailties will not hinder our ultimate salvation. Why? We are more than conquerors because God is for us.

Some Christians, as has been stated, suffer from a lack of assurance of the ultimate success and certainty of their salvation. They fear that some giant obstacle or latent personal weakness may ultimately defeat them before they can finally receive their ultimate inheritance in heaven. Like David, however, they must learn to face the prospect of real giants and yet rely completely with absolute confidence on the power and purpose of God and His personal commitment to ensure their ultimate salvation in heaven.

Romans chapter eight was written by the Apostle Paul and inspired by God, among other reasons, to address the issue of the believer's absolute security in Christ and to underscore without a doubt that God is for the believer. Nothing could be more certain than the fact that God will do whatever is necessary to safeguard His children and guarantee their ultimate salvation in heaven. He is 100% committed to His children. He has promised. He is for us! Therefore, we are more than conquerors through Him who loved us.

C. H. Spurgeon had this to say about Micah 2:13. *"The breaker is come up before them."*

> "In as much as Jesus has gone before us, things remain not as they would have been had he never passed that way. He has conquered every foe that obstructed the way. Cheer up now you fainthearted warrior. Not only has Christ traveled the road, but he has slain your enemies. Do you dread sin? He has nailed it to His cross. Do you fear death? He has been the death of death. Are you afraid of hell? He has barred it against the advent of any of His children; they shall never see the gulf of perdition. Whatever blows may be before the Christian, they are all overcome. They are all in alliance, but their teeth are broken; there are serpents, but their fangs are extracted; there are rivers but they are bridged and made fordable; there are flames, but we wear that matchless garment which renders us imponderable to fire. The sword that has been forged against us is already blunted; the instruments of war which the enemy is planning to use against us have already lost their point. God has taken away in the person

of Christ all the power that anything can have against us. The Army may safely march on and you may go joyously along your journey, for all your enemies are conquered beforehand. What shall you do but march on to take the prey? They are beaten, they are vanquished; all you need do is to divide the spoil. You shall, it is true, often engage in combat; but your fight will be with the vanquished foe. His head is broken; he may attempt to hinder you, but his strength shall not be sufficient for his malicious design. Your victory shall be easy, and your treasure shall be beyond all count.

"Proclaim aloud the Savior's fame,

Who bears the "Breakers" wondrous name;

Sweet name; and it becomes Him well,

Who breaks down earth, sin, death, and hell."

(C. H. Spurgeon, *Morning and Evening*, McDonald Publishing Company, McLean, Virginia 22102, page 474)

THE POTENTIAL: IT IS HUGE

Dear Christian, since God is for you, like David your personal potential and spiritual possibilities are enormous. Your eternal security is absolute and guaranteed by God. God has graciously gifted and equipped every believer with a rich and ongoing, eternal salvation which includes spiritual riches that are almost incomprehensible. Don't you want to more fully understand and appreciate what God has, is, and will do for you as the object of His great love? In His Word, God has graciously revealed a portion of those riches to His children so that we can begin to understand, apply and delight in the good things of God even now. Unfortunately, most Christians are unaware of the powerful resources of God working on their behalf.

When I was much younger I owned a beautiful, sporty looking car that I was exceedingly proud of. It had a white Landau roof, white leather interior, mag wheels, a shifter on the floor, bucket seats, a very large and powerful motor, etc. The car was loaded with all kinds of accessories. The only thing that I did not really like about the car was that, in hot weather, the air conditioning system was slow to cool the interior down. I put up with the slow air-conditioning because I liked the car so much. Then one day, while I was fooling around with the instruments on the instrument panel and I was scanning the owner's manual I learned that there was a way to adjust the air conditioner so that it operated with forced air and provided an immediate thrust of cool air for cooling down the car. I had no idea that this option was available even though I had owned the car for over a year. Once I learned how to engage the forced air aspect of the air conditioner I was even more pleased with the car.

Many Christians are thankful to be saved but unaware of the vast resources, the untapped potential and the dynamic power involved in their salvation. When the believer studies the Word of God correctly a world of additional delights becomes apparent. I had owned the car that I spoke of in the above illustration for over a year. I had looked at the instrument panel each time I entered the car. I had no idea that there was more to those controls on the instrument panel than I had realized. It was my fault. I had simply neglected to carefully read the instruction manual. Have you carefully read God's instruction manual to us as believers?

THE PURPOSE OF GOD

Let God's Purpose For You Grip You

Dear Christian, there are many things that God has given us and is doing for us in our lives so that we can slay the giant obstacles arrayed against us and be champions for Christ. This is, no doubt, what the Apostle Paul had in mind when he wrote to the Ephesians and said, "I do not cease to give thanks for you, remembering you in my prayers. I keep asking that the God of our Lord Jesus Christ, the Father of glory, may give you the

Spirit of wisdom and of revelation in the knowledge of Him, having the eyes of your hearts enlightened, that you may know what is the hope to which He has called you, what are the riches of His glorious inheritance in the saints, and what is the immeasurable greatness of His power toward us who believe, according to the working of His great might that He worked in Christ when He raised Him from the dead and seated Him at His right hand in the heavenly places, far above all rule and authority and power and dominion, and above every name that is named, not only in this age but also in the one to come" (Ephesians 1:16 –21).

Paul's desire was for the Ephesians to have an enlarged understanding of and enlarged experience of the great riches and the depth of the salvation which God had blessed them with. He wanted them to more fully realize that there was much more in terms of vast spiritual resources available to them than they might have realized. Furthermore, he wanted them to know just how rich they were in Christ and just how much enormous power and potential they had in Christ as believers. Paul wanted them to have a fuller understanding of the hope of their calling and of their vast inheritance in Christ. He knew that if God were to enlighten their hearts and open their minds to see and appreciate these truths that their passion for God would be greatly enhanced and their persuasion of God's constantly being with them and for them would enable them to live bold, successful Christian lives.

This enlarged and expanded understanding of the riches of their salvation would motivate and equip them to live in light of these great truths and to strive to experience their full spiritual potential for the glory of God. God wants us to live up to our potential as His sons and daughters in Christ and He wants us to feel totally secure and confident in our safety and ultimate salvation in Christ as we do so. This is also why the Apostle Paul in writing to the Ephesians concluded one of his prayers for them with the following words:

"Now to him who is able to do far more abundantly than all that we ask or think, according to the power at work within us, to him be glory in the church and in Christ Jesus throughout all ages, forever and ever. Amen" (Ephesians 3:20 – 21).

Some Amazing Success Stories

Our Lord Jesus Christ employed a common technique in His teachings to enable people to grasp and understand spiritual truths. He would often refer to things in the natural world that they were familiar with such as the sowing of seed by a farmer, the management of investments, etc. to draw analogies from these things to the spiritual principles which He wanted to teach his hearers.

I am going to borrow a page from our Lord's playbook. I want you as a Christian to understand the enormous potential that you have in Christ. I don't want you to be like the panic stricken and immobilized troops of Israel quaking in fear in the face of the giant. I want you to be like David who was filled with passion for God and absolutely confident that God was for him and with him. I want you to see that such a David – like life can be true of you, as well. I want you to get a sense of the potential that God has made available to you in the spiritual realm and then take advantage of that to achieve spiritual strength and enormous growth in grace that, perhaps, you had never thought possible for yourself.

Real life illustrations, even in the normal world of culture, business and economics can provide us with incredible, true examples of those who have and do experience levels of success that they once thought impossible and unattainable – life stories of people who have transitioned from personal poverty to prosperity beyond imagination abound everywhere. These real-life stories do not immediately translate to the spiritual realm but, like the teaching of our Lord Jesus Christ, my point is these same kinds of things are possible in the spiritual dimension of life, for every Christian. We simply need to study prayerfully what God has revealed to us about our wonderful salvation and the spiritual riches that are ours in Christ and then take full advantage of the truth that God has revealed to us. The twin truths of the believer's enormous potential for spiritual success coupled with their enduring assurance and confidence in their eternal security in Christ dominate this glorious eighth chapter of Romans.

To help you, the reader, visualize and relate to the reality that one may tap into hidden personal potential enabling unimaginable levels of success, I offer the following examples in the realms of economics and present world achievements:

Howard Schultz

Howard Schultz grew up in a housing complex for the poor. In an interview with the British tabloid *Mirror,* Schultz says: "Growing up I always felt like I was living on the other side of the tracks. I knew the people on the other side had more resources, more money, and happier families. And for some reason, I don't know why or how, I wanted to climb over that fence and achieve something beyond what people were saying was possible. I may have a suit and tie on now but I know where I'm from and I know what it is like." Schultz ended up winning a football scholarship to the University of Northern Michigan and went to work for Xerox after graduation. Shortly after that, he took over a coffee franchise called Starbucks, which at the time had only 60 shops. Schultz became the company's CEO in 1987 and grew the coffee chain to more than 16,000 outlets worldwide. Today his net worth is estimated at $2,000,000,000.

Oprah Winfrey

Oprah Winfrey was born in poverty. She became the first African-American TV correspondent in Nashville. Winfrey was born into a poor family in Mississippi, but won a scholarship to Tennessee State University and became the first African-American TV correspondent in the state at the age of 19. In 1983, Winfrey moved to Chicago to work for an AM talk show which would later be called "The Oprah Winfrey Show." After many successes in television and movies Oprah Winfrey's net worth stands at $2.9 billion.

John Paul DeJoria

John Paul DeJoria, the man behind a hair—care empire, once lived in a foster home and in his car. Before the age of 10, DeJoria, a first generation American, sold Christmas cards and newspapers to help support his family.

He was eventually sent to live in a foster home and even spent some time in a gang before joining the military.

With a $700 loan, DeJoria created John Paul Mitchell Systems and sold the shampoo door–to–door while living in his car. His net worth now stands at $4 billion.

Ralph Lauren

Ralph Lauren was once a clerk at a Brooks Brothers clothing store. Lauren graduated high school in the Bronx, New York. He started in college but later dropped out of college to join the Army. It was while working as a clerk at Brooks Brothers that Lauren questioned whether men were ready for wider and brighter designs in ties. The year he decided to make his dream a reality, 1967, Lauren sold $500,000 worth of ties. He started Polo the next year. Today his net worth stands at $7.7 billion.

These are almost unbelievable rags to riches stories which are, nevertheless, true. They happened to real people. Their success seemed to be impossible and not available to them but they all gained tremendous success.

The potential for spiritual success is enormous and it is available to what may seem the most unlikely of people. The same kind of incredible success and amazing achievement is available to you as a genuine believer in Christ in the spiritual realm. Since God is for you and you are a "child" of the living God the level of your spiritual attainments can be much greater than you ever thought possible.

What are two critical elements necessary to enable you as a Christian to be courageous in the face of life's difficulties and for you to experience your full potential in Christ? They are a consuming passion for God and an absolute confidence and persuasion that God is for you in a personal and practical way. These are the twin traits that enabled David in his courageous conflict with the threatening giant.

What does Romans chapter eight have to do with these two critical needs that we have as Christians? In Romans chapter eight we will see

God displayed by the Apostle Paul in such a way that our hearts will be enraptured by Him and our passion for Him will be enhanced. Paul will display God as our constant and strong helper, as our sovereign King, and as the one who guarantees our absolute security and assurance in salvation. Paul will show us how much God loves us and that He will always love us. God will be depicted as our generous Father and extravagant benefactor. These and other aspects of God's character and conduct will be portrayed for the reader so that you as a Christian reader will be more and more consumed with a passionate love for and awe of our great God. In this book, "Since God is for us", I will explain and help you to understand the eleven specific ways that the Apostle Paul highlights in Romans chapter eight concerning how God is for us in our salvation. I will explain how God has been for us by sending His son to be the propitiatory sacrifice for our sins. I will also explain how God is presently for us by giving us the ministry of the Holy Spirit to enable and encourage us as believers in Christ. Furthermore, I will show the reader how God will continue to be for us throughout all eternity and will continue to love us in Christ. Romans chapter eight will provide us with an absolute confidence in the fact that God is with us and for us. Consequently, being motivated by a consuming passion for God and thoroughly convinced that God is for us this will immeasurably enable us to live like David – to live courageous lives for God. Since God is for us, we are more than conquerors. That is the key thought permeating all of Romans chapter eight. You will be greatly benefited from the study of this chapter and each time you are confronted with a giant problem you will be able to view it from the perspective of faith by first saying, "Since God is for us/me…"

The Need of Many Christians

I am concerned that many Christians are unnecessarily living in spiritual poverty when they could be enjoying the treasures of abundant grace. I am concerned that many Christians are secretly wrestling with doubts and fears concerning their ultimate salvation and safety on their journey to heaven. I am further concerned that the majority of Christians are only skimming along superficially on the surface and are not really understanding, appreciating, and utilizing the full knowledge of the many facets of their salvation in Christ. They have yet to grasp the awesome fact that God is for them in every possible way.

Since God is for the Christian, it is vital that believers come to understand, appreciate, and fully utilize the riches that are ours in the wonderful salvation achieved for us by our saving union with Christ. To do so will dispel doubts and quiet fears of dying. To do so will thrill the soul, expand our Christian understanding, honor our God, and enable us to grow deeper in our love for God, for our Lord Jesus Christ, and for the Holy Spirit.

Those who are saved by God's grace through faith in the Lord Jesus Christ experience many trials in this world of sin. We sometimes suffer for the cause of Christ. Our Lord Jesus Christ warned us that it would be so. We struggle with sin to live free of it. We are often misunderstood and abused. Satan is our adversary and the world system is constantly trying to either seduce us into sin or squeeze us into its sinful pattern of thinking and living. Indeed, we face many challenges as Christians but we must never forget what a wonderful and permanent salvation we have been granted in Christ. Furthermore, we must never forget the tremendous power that is ours through the Holy Spirit. Since God is for us, we can tap into a world of spiritual riches, power, and delight. Isn't that what you want?

I am convinced that the believer needs to understand and fully appreciate the fullness and security of the salvation that they have in Christ. This will enable each believer to fully rejoice in the wonderful salvation provided in Christ and it will enable us to worship God with increased ardor. It will also empower each believer to live for God with renewed commitment and boldness.

Like David, two key things are necessary for you as a Christian to live boldly for God and to defend the cause of God. First, you need to have a passion for God that exceeds any measure of selfishness and self-preservation that you might have. Second, you need to have an absolute persuasion and confidence that God is for you and with you.

As I have stated, in Romans chapter eight the Apostle Paul takes the reader on a spiritual tour highlighting the wonderful provisions that God has made for the absolute assurance and salvation of each true Christian. In this chapter, Paul shows us God in all His grace and power. He displays God as sovereign and wise. It reveals that God is actively working on our behalf so that all things work together for our good and that He loves us deeply and eternally even to the point of adopting us and making us coheirs with Christ. God is displayed by the Apostle Paul in numerous ways in all His infinite beauty so that the believer's passion for God is enhanced and enlarged. Next, the Apostle Paul systematically explains numerous, incredible things that God is doing, has done, and will do to guarantee the absolute assurance of true believers for eternity. It is as if Paul takes the reader on a guided tour of this great subject. In Romans chapter eight, Paul emphasizes to us that since God is for us we can have absolute confidence in His ability and willingness to safeguard and empower us.

Don't you want more passion for God and confidence that God is for you? I know you do. Understanding, appreciating, and meditating on this wonderful salvation and the incredible involvement of the Holy Spirit in your life will encourage you as you make your journey through this world. It will help you to have increased courage and unflinching determination in your spiritual life. It will fill you with wonder for and increased gratitude to the triune God. It will cause you to love your Savior more deeply and to grow in your love for those who have been saved by our Savior. It will motivate you to expand and enlarge your capacity to worship God in more fullness, in light of who He is, and what He has done for you in your wonderful salvation. It will instill within you a burning hope for the coming day when all true believers will be completely free of sin and in the presence of our Savior. When you face life's trials you will do so with a more confident understanding and a rock-solid confidence knowing that the Holy Spirit is helping you in your weakness to be more than a conqueror in Christ. You will compare whatever hardships you face in your difficult times to the wonderful salvation that you have in Christ and the glorious things that await you in heaven. You will be able to say with the Apostle Paul, "I consider that our present sufferings are not worth comparing with the glory that will be revealed in us" (Romans 8:18).

A Personal Plea~A Heartfelt Invitation

If you are still an unsaved sinner and have not yet trusted in Jesus Christ alone as Lord and Savior, I invite you to go on this spiritual journey with me as we explore the incredible riches of salvation revealed in Romans chapter eight. As they are explained in, "Since God is for us", think deeply about what they would mean to you were you to trust in Christ. Travel with me as we seek to understand the ironclad guarantee and assurance of the believer's salvation in Christ. I also invite you to personally examine yourself as you examine this wonderful salvation revealed by the Apostle Paul in Romans chapter eight. Yes, if you are not yet a Christian, I invite you to examine the precarious position that you find yourself in without Christ and then I urge you to trust from your heart in Jesus Christ as your Lord and Savior believing that He died on the cross to suffer in the place of sinners like you, He was buried, and was raised from the dead on the third day. He has also ascended to heaven and will one day return for His dear children. Meanwhile, He invites/commands you to turn away from your sins and turn to Him, trusting Him as both your Lord and Savior.

1

NO HESITATION
A Word Of Counsel And Encouragement

Before we begin the actual study of Romans 8 and the many facets of the believer's salvation, I would like to encourage you to think with me regarding why you should engage in this study to begin with. I know that your time is, no doubt, at a premium and is limited. I know that there are many voices clamoring to have your attention and many who promise certain benefits to you if you will but go in their direction, benefits that most often never actually materialize. Perhaps you have even become somewhat jaded and defensive regarding another person asking you to spend time and effort in something new. I want to assure you that this book, which highlights the truth that God is for you, is a personally worth–while and practically beneficial study for you to dig deeply into. The spiritual dividends to you will be enormous. You will not be disappointed or let down.

No true Christian should hesitate for a moment to plunge in and spend time in this tremendous teaching of God's Word. Yet, some do. They consider that their time is too limited and wonder if they have the time to spend studying the rich truths regarding God's salvation of believing sinners. They hesitate because they wonder if the effort spent will be worth it, perhaps they even wonder whether they have the aptitude to successfully pursue such a study. They hesitate to commit themselves and this hesitation grows into perpetual procrastination which results in putting off the study of salvation indefinitely. When this happens, the believer is the loser—he who hesitates is the loser. Hesitation must be forcefully overcome. Hesitation will rob you of the understanding and enjoyment of spiritual treasures which could otherwise be yours. Do not hesitate! The book of Romans was a book written to a local congregation of Christians. It was not primarily written for theological scholars, but for sincere believers in Christ. It was written to be understood by both male and female, slave and free, young and old. Dear reader, don't shrink back from the serious study of these truths because you may think yourself to be unqualified and too weak theologically to understand and be benefited by them. Since God is for you He will help you learn these wonderful truths and apply them to your life for your good and His glory.

This book "Since God Is For Us" is not a book of entertainment but it is a book aimed at the edification of the reader.

I believe that our understanding of salvation is often far too superficial and we should never hesitate to grow deeper and more understanding in the things that are ours through God's grace. Why do you need to understand what God has done for you as a Christian in a fuller and deeper way? It is not merely so that you can be intellectually stimulated in some form (in a mere academic way), but it is so that you can better live up to your potential as a Christian and enjoy the full assurance of your absolute security in Christ – right now. Since God is for you – take heart. Since God is for you who can be successful against you?

THE PRICELESS TRUTH OF GOD

The Most Beautiful Chapter In The Bible

Romans chapter eight has often been called the greatest or one of the greatest chapters in the Bible (James Boice, *Romans* (Baker), 2:781; Martin Lloyd Jones, *Romans: The Law: Its Functions and Limits (Zondervan), p. 258)*. The Swiss commentator Godet pointed out that it begins with "no condemnation" and ends with "no separation." Another commentator added that in between there is "no defeat."

The Holy Spirit

As I read and studied this chapter over and over and meditated on its tremendous teaching in the preparation for the writing of this book, I was impressed with the fact that the essential ministry of the Holy Spirit comes into remarkably clear focus in this chapter. When talking about the ministry of the Holy Spirit, Paul does not talk about speaking in "unknown languages," or "visions and miracles." Rather, he zeros in on the practical but powerful workings of the Holy Spirit in relation to the believer's salvation. In fact, in this chapter alone, the Holy Spirit is mentioned nearly twenty times. Let me encourage the reader to read through Romans chapter eight and highlight each mention of the Holy Spirit. Whereas in the previous seven chapters of Romans, the Apostle Paul makes only one reference to the Holy Spirit (Romans 5:5). In this eighth chapter of Romans, Paul saturates his teaching with repeated references to the Holy Spirit and His ministry in the life of the believer. The dynamic person and power of the Holy Spirit in our lives makes all the difference in the world. As a believer, His presence and power are in your life right now. The Holy Spirit is busy applying the benefits of the work of Christ to each believer. Romans chapter eight will help you to understand more clearly the ministry of the Holy Spirit in your life. You will come to understand that since God is for you, every possible problem that you face will be successfully overcome in His power.

Imagine going quail hunting. You are enjoying the quiet, peaceful, solitude of casually strolling down a remote, country trail with your shotgun in hand searching for quail. All is silent around you except for the normal, peaceful sounds of the surrounding woods. Then, suddenly and without warning, a covey of quail unexpectedly launches itself into the air and flies up noisily in frantic flight just ahead of you. There are a great number of them and their sudden appearance shocks and startles you. You marvel at their unexpected appearance and in their abundance when moments ago you were totally unaware of their presence. You will not soon forget the feeling of such an experience. It is dramatic and personal.

Romans chapter eight reminds me of that experience. As I said, prior to this chapter the Holy Spirit and His ministry is mentioned in the book of Romans only one time, Romans 5:5, but in this eighth chapter, His ministry is suddenly highlighted over and over. It flies in our face wherever we look. It is everywhere all at once. The change is remarkable and the constant repetition of His person and work stands out dramatically.

What is the point of all this? Why does the Apostle Paul deliberately bombards the reader with references to the person and work of the Holy Spirit in the life of the believer? The richness of this chapter is beyond measurement. According to the Apostle Paul, the focus on the Holy Spirit and His ministry in our salvation is key to understanding and unlocking the riches of God's teaching regarding our salvation in Christ and our absolute security as Christians. In reading and contemplating the riches of this chapter and what it teaches about our personal salvation one will continually encounter the person and the work of the Holy Spirit and be transported higher and higher in spiritual thought and worship until he concludes the chapter with a crescendo of confident and exuberant praise to the God who is our wonderful Savior. The Christian, therefore, should not merely dangle his toe in the shallow end of the theological pool but rather plunge in wholeheartedly and without hesitation into the depths of God's riches for us in Christ. You will be glad that you did.

In many ways, Paul's letter to the church at Rome is the supreme pinnacle of Scripture. Martin Luther called it "the clearest gospel of all." John Calvin wrote, "If a man understands it (Romans) he has a surer road opened for him to the understanding of the whole Scripture." William Tyndale, in his preface to his commentary on Romans, wrote that Romans is, "The principal and most excellent part of the New Testament, and most pure "Euangelion," that is to say, glad tidings and that we call gospel, and also a light in a way in and to the whole Scripture." It was said of Jonathan Edwards that his doctrine was all application, and his application was all doctrine. The book of Romans is like that, as well

As Romans is the pinnacle of Bible truth, Chapter eight of Romans is the supreme peak of the book of Romans. The Puritan commentator Edward Elton wrote, "As the honeycomb, most full of heavenly sweetness and soul comfort... Our conceits and apprehensions of comfort are but dreams, till we attain some true feeling of God's love to us in Christ Jesus poured out and shed abroad in our hearts by the Holy Ghost given to us: that once gained, it fills our hearts with joy unspeakable and glorious, and it makes us more than conquerors... And where do we find this ground of comfort more plainly and pithily deciphered than in this chapter? (Epistle Dedicatory before *The Triumph of a True Christian Described*, Elton's exposition of Romans 8).

This eighth chapter of Romans probes the unfathomable depths of the gospel and completely sweeps the reader off his feet with a majestic display of God's powerful, wise, and wonderful salvation. Do not hesitate to make

Romans chapter eight a major portion of your study of Scripture. You will not be disappointed in the time that you spend in this wonderfully rich, enlightening and inspiring passage of Scripture. This is a transforming chapter for all of those who study it seriously. It will forever change the way you view your salvation and your Savior – it will completely change your life. "Since God is for us" has been written to guide you through this wonderful chapter. If your desire is to know God better and understand your salvation more thoroughly then you will be delighted with your study of Romans chapter eight. Don't hesitate to make Romans chapter eight the focus of your attention and study. Not only will you not be disappointed by doing so, you will be surprisingly enthralled and enriched by it. Moreover, you will be thoroughly convinced that the Almighty God of the universe is for you.

Romans chapter eight is also an exceedingly practical and helpful chapter of Scripture. If you struggle with sin and guilt, read Romans chapter eight. If you are going through struggles and trials, read Romans chapter eight. If you are struggling with how to pray, if you are awkwardly wrestling with a chronic absence of assurance in your salvation, if you are experiencing smothering dullness in your ability to worship God, read Romans chapter eight.

I am totally convinced that in faithfully studying this tremendous chapter of Scripture, you will come to an increased appreciation of our incredibly wonderful salvation and in doing so you will fall more deeply in love with our wonderful Savior. Its truths will help you in a number of different ways as a Christian. Your study of it and increased understanding of it will liberate and lift you to spiritual heights that you have not known before. "Since God is for us" will be your handy tool to help you to understand this chapter and to explain the rich and encouraging truths contained in it.

My desire is that by reading and carefully studying the following pages of this book, "Since God is for us" you will be guided and helped in your personal understanding of this great chapter and the tremendous truths that it contains and explains. In studying this biblical chapter and this book ("Since God is for us") you will be aided greatly in your Christian walk. Don't allow any hesitation to study Romans chapter eight to become an obstacle to achieving what God wants for you in your Christian walk

I have specifically chosen to focus the contents of this book ("Since God is for us") on the eighth chapter of Romans because it is an unparalleled masterpiece of explanation concerning the glorious subject of our wonderful salvation. Interestingly, Romans chapter eight does not contain one single commandment but it is filled with motivation for engaging God (the living and true God) in keenly exuberant, knowledgeable, and heartfelt worship and service. The German Pietist Philip Spener said that "If the Bible were a ring then Romans is the precious stone in the setting and chapter eight would be the "sparkling point of the stone." (F. Godet, *Commentary on Romans, Kregel, p. 295*)

THE PLAN

The Plan/Design of This Book ("Since God is for us")

The design and structure of this book, "Since God is for us," is very simple. Following some initial introductory remarks, I have included a chapter entitled, "NO HESITATION". In this chapter, I encourage the reader not to hesitate to engage in a serious study of Romans chapter eight and "Since God is for us". In this chapter, I also provide the reader with several suggested reasons why he should not hesitate to carefully study this material. Following this initial chapter, there are eleven succeeding chapters devoted to the examination and clear explanation of the wonderful truths of Romans chapter eight.

"Since God is for us," is NOT intended to be an exhaustive commentary on the book of Romans chapter eight. Instead, I have deliberately extracted the core teaching of the chapter and its various arguments to underscore the certain absolute security of the true believer in Christ. In that light, this book is selective and thematic. It was written with a specific focus and intent. For those who desire a more thorough commentary on this chapter I recommend that you consult some of the excellent commentaries that exist on the book of Romans.

Imagine walking across a pasture and suddenly coming on an unexpected brilliantly colored patch of wildflowers. You stop and examine the beautiful flowers and then you select eleven of the most beautiful ones to pick and arrange into a bouquet for the one that you love.

In a similar fashion, Romans chapter eight contains beautiful and varied aspects and explanations of our wonderful, eternal salvation in Christ. The last eleven chapters of "Since God is for us" is the beautifully arranged bouquet of the various aspects of the salvation which God has lovingly provided for the ones that He has determined to save. After studying this book, the reader will forever have the image of this beautiful, biblical bouquet of the loving grace of God in Christ implanted in their mind and on their heart.

THE PLAN FOR READING "SINCE GOD IS FOR US"

How Should You Read This Book?

How should you read this book ("Since God is for us") on Romans eight? I would have liked to have written this book with short, concise chapters which would have facilitated ease of reading for the reader. I simply could not find a way to do that while at the same time effectively including the material that the reader needs to understand drawn from this chapter of Romans. In that light, I would suggest that the reader set a pace for reading and studying this book that suits their own personality and time constraints. Break down the pages of a given chapter of this book into smaller sections for reading purposes. Read each individual section one at a time in a progressive movement through the chapters of the book. After reading a particular section, mark your location in the book and spend time meditating on that section that you have read to ensure that you understand it and its implications for your spiritual life. The next time you are able to read in the book, proceed to the next section that you have marked out which would be the next section after the one that you previously read and follow the same pattern. In this way, you will be able to proceed through the entirety of the book in bite-size pieces – baby steps.

It was May 31; about 200 powerful animals were lined up in Frankfort, New York ready to begin one of the most spectacular races that any of them would ever be involved in. At the time, the USA was gripped with Bicentennial fever and citizens nationwide were possessed with a patriotic passion. They wanted to engage in some project that heralded their love for the United States and their pride in their nation. Americans have always loved our land. We sing, "This land is your land, this land is my land…" We delight in our country from sea to shining sea.

During the bicentennial celebrations millions gathered to watch the Freedom Train. This was a traveling train that chugged through 48 states. There were also nautical parades as ships of all kinds sailed up the coast, flags flying proudly in celebration of the bicentennial. At the same time, railroad companies even gave their regular trains new paint jobs of red, white, and blue so that the people could see them as they crisscrossed America.

In the midst of this bicentennial fervor, two horse–loving salesmen from the Midwest dreamed up the idea of staging the *Great American Horserace*. This race offered Americans a more historically authentic nationalist experience. It was fashioned after the early European settlers who, at the time, lacked trains and automobiles. These early settlers traveled by horseback.

The route for the race incorporated portions of the Oregon Trail, the Pony Express Trail and, even a portion of the fatal trail taken by the doomed Donner party. The race was to extend 3500 miles over 14 weeks. It was a race that was farther and longer than any organized race in anyone's memory.

The people of America caught the vision and eagerly looked forward to *The Great American Horserace*.

By the start of the race, 91 teams were lined up and raring to go. The riders were from different walks of life. Both the humans and their mounts alike represented a diversity of demographics. The youngest was an 18-year-old Country–Western singer from Oregon and the oldest was a 69-year-old horse trader from Tennessee. There were medical people (chiropractors, pediatricians, nurses, etc.), farmers, cowboys, and at least one university president.

The horses, themselves, made up a magnificent collection of rare horse flesh and exotic breeding. There was a horse who was a direct descendent of a magnificent Russian lineage. Iceland sent ten high–born horses who trained for months prior to the race in the high-altitude atmosphere of San Francisco. France sent over dozens of riders to support the race and all of them were dressed like the Marquee De Lafayette's soldiers. Other countries, including Australia, Denmark, and Japan also provided impressive horses and riders. The one thing that everyone was sure of was that some special breed would take home the win. After all, these steads were bred to perfection. There were Arabian stallions with arched neck and strong – boned bodies that were expected to win by almost all observers. But, there were also Icelandic horses, famous for their smooth gait and magnificent Viking pedigrees. There were the tall Irish thoroughbreds and there were colorful Appaloosas.

And then there was Lady Eloise and Lord Fauntleroy (LeRoy for short). These were two mules bred and owned by Viril Norton who was a steeplejack and life – long horse enthusiast who lived in San Jose, California. Among the many rivals, Norton, and his backup mule, Lady Eloise were, by far, the least likely to win the race.

Norton (who was then 54 years old) had spent his Wyoming youth breaking wild horses so he knew horses. Yet, Norton had an absolute confidence in the ability of his mules to win this august race. The race would move along an extensive route which was grueling and full of rough terrain. The elevation changed constantly. It was estimated that only 25% of the entries would finish the race. When Norton's neighbor at the starting campsite lost her horse due to an injury just a few days before the race started, he even talked her into borrowing another of his mules named "Deacon." She was reluctant but had little choice if, indeed, she wanted to participate in this race.

And so, they were off. Every day the race was less of a frenzied neck – in – neck sprint and more of a prolonged marathon. The pace was slow and grueling. Both horses and riders got extremely tired, injured, or just disenchanted with it all. Some favored mounts fell out of the race altogether.

Even Lady Eloise suffered an injury but Leroy plodded along with determination and stamina.

Norton and Leroy were the 31st team to cross the finish line in the presence of cheering spectators at the state fair in Sacramento. It would take a while before the organizer calculated everyone's ride time, tacked on any penalties, and then declared a winner. When the final count came through, it was Norton's mule team by a landslide. With 315.47 total hours in the saddle Norton had bested the second Place Arabian who had clocked in at 324. 6 Hours.

Everyone was shocked except Norton who was already grinning at the finish line. Norton picked up his $25,000 prize money and for the rest of his life referred to himself as The Great American Horseman. Leroy went on to live out the rest of his days in a green pasture in California.

As you will recognize, this is a real life, version of the fictional story of the tortoise and the hare. It is also an illustration of the fact that the spiritual race is usually not won by the pedigreed person or the seemingly unbeatable stallion. The spiritual race is not a sprint but it is a long, grueling, marathon. The spiritual race is won by those who maintain a steady forward pace as they continue to plod along continually putting one foot ahead of the other while never, ever giving up.

That is how you should plan to read this book. Be a *Leroy* kind of Christian reader. The perseverance is more important than the pace.

There was a time when I would read books one after the other with great speed because, being in school, it was required of me to do so. I found it to be like drinking out of a fire hydrant. Great quantities of material were coming my way and I was desperately trying to assimilate and retain as much as I could while the rest of this deluge of material merely washed past me. I have come to learn, however, that it is much better to read a good book thoroughly and thoughtfully and to spend quality time with it. You will not be disappointed in the time that you spend and the effort that you expend to master the contents of this book ("Since God is for us"). It will be knowledge that stays with you for a lifetime and benefits you many times over in your spiritual life.

NOTE: At the end of each chapter I have included some questions under the title, "Bringing it Home." These questions are intended to help you reflect on what you have read and know that you have understood the teaching of the chapter. This section will also help you to apply the teaching of the chapter to your life. These questions can be used as the foundation and catalysts for group discussions, as well. They will continually emphasize and underscore for you that God is, indeed, for you.

SOME OF THE REASONS YOU SHOULD NOT HESITATE TO STUDY ROMANS CHAPTER EIGHT AND "SINCE GOD IS FOR US"

Why do you need to grow deeper in your understanding of this subject? Why should you be all that concerned with studying the truths of Romans chapter eight? In other words, you might be hampered with a halting feeling of hesitation. You might be asking, "Why spend the time and effort necessary to gain a more full and complete understanding of what God is doing and will do in my life as a Christian? Isn't the fact that you have simply trusted in Christ for salvation enough? There are a number of reasons why you should not hesitate to involve yourself in a serious study of Romans chapter eight. Indeed, you should wholeheartedly apply yourself to gaining a clear understanding of the truths of this chapter. Some of the reasons for doing so are:

SUGGESTED REASON 1: THE WONDERFUL PRACTICAL BENEFITS

The answer to the question, "Isn't just being a believer in Christ enough for every Christian?" The answer might be, "Enough for what?" Simply trusting in Christ by faith is enough to ensure that you have a place in heaven, but it is not enough to ensure that you can fully appreciate, take practical advantage of, and find satisfaction from the salvation that you now have. Nor is it enough for you to have a fuller joy and more complete understanding of what God has done and is doing in your salvation. Just being saved is not enough to adequately equip you to successfully face doubts, fears, obstacles and the various conflicting emotions that you may experience as a Christian.

I am reminded of a story of a shipwreck. Two passengers managed to get into a lifeboat and to get the lifeboat into the water after the ship had run aground on a jagged reef and was sinking. They immediately began paddling toward the shore. One of the two was frantic, worried, fearful, and at his wits end. The other one was calm, confident, and focused on rowing the boat to the shore. The frantic passenger, having experienced the recent shipwreck, was convinced that the lifeboat would also be defective and that they would end up in the water struggling to fend for themselves to survive – perhaps, to keep from drowning. The calmer passenger had spent some time becoming acquainted with the structure and ability of the lifeboats and he had absolute confidence in the little boat's ability to take them safely to the shore. The question often asked is, "Which of the two passengers in the lifeboat was the safer?" The obvious answer is that neither was safer than the other. Both passengers were in the same boat and headed in the same direction. One passenger, however, confidently enjoyed the trip with a sense of assurance while the other passenger, though just as safe, was miserable and fearful during the whole journey because of his fears and lack of assuring confidence in the boat.

Likewise, the Christian who has only a rudimentary knowledge of salvation will be safe in their salvation. They will, however, often be filled with fear and doubts which destroy their sense of joy.

This could all be different if they were only more informed and more insightful. The study of Romans chapter eight and "Since God is for us" will give the believer the assurance and confidence that they need to experience the full joy of their salvation and to know that the incredibly powerful, biblical God is for them.

Gaining a fuller understanding of the truths of Romans chapter eight will give you a deeper confidence in your absolute security as a believer in Jesus Christ. Isn't that what you desire? It will remove every lingering doubt and haunting suspicion that something may be lacking and overlooked that might jeopardize your ultimate salvation and security with God. The frightening specter of possible condemnation will be forever removed when you gain a clearer understanding of the work that Jesus has done for you. "There is therefore now no condemnation to those that are in Christ Jesus..." (Romans 8:1a). The idea is that for the believer there is never, ever again any condemnation possible. The informed believer will no longer feel helpless and at the mercy of his sinful nature but will fully appreciate (from the truths of Romans chapter eight) that God has changed him by His grace in a dynamic and powerful way and that the Holy Spirit is actively involved in effectively helping him to resist and overcome sin. These truths will cause the true believer to find great delight in the Lord and in the salvation which God is accomplishing in him and for him. For the believer God is at work in their lives in a powerful and effective way.

From Romans chapter eight we will learn that salvation does not merely hinge on the believer's strength or stamina. Salvation is being carried on by the Almighty God who dwells within the believer to ensure its completion and perfection.

The practical value of learning these truths is wonderful indeed. Knowing them will interject the dynamic of great delight and a settled confidence into one's Christian walk. Believers will be moved to a greater love of God, a greater delight in God, and to a greater level of joy in their Christianity.

C. H. Spurgeon touched on this truth when he wrote his comments on Psalm 37:4, ("*Delight thyself also in the Lord.*") Spurgeon wrote concerning this passage:

> "The teaching of these words must seem very surprising to those who are strangers to vital godliness, but to the sincere believer it is only the inculcation of a recognized truth. The life of the believer is here described as a DELIGHT in God, and we are thus certified with the great fact that true religion overflows with happiness and joy. Ungodly persons and mere professors never look upon religion as a joyful thing; to them it is service, duty, or necessity, but never pleasure or delight. If they attend to religion at all, it is either that they may gain thereby, or else because they dare not do otherwise. The thought of DELIGHT in religion is so strange to most men, that no two words in their language stand further apart than "holiness" and "delight." But, believers who know Christ understand that delight and faith are so blessedly united, that the gates of hell cannot prevail to separate them. They love God with all their hearts, find that His ways are ways of pleasantness, and all His paths are peace. Untold blessings do the saints discover in their Lord, that so far from serving Him from custom, they would follow Him though all the world cast out His name as evil. We fear not God because of any compulsion; our faith is no fetter, our

profession is no bondage, we are not dragged to holiness, nor driven to duty. No, our piety is our pleasure, our hope is our happiness, our duty is our delight.

Delight and true religion are as allied as root and flower; as indivisible as truth and certainty; they are, in fact, two precious jewels glittering side-by-side in a setting of gold.

> *"'Tis when we taste Thy love*
> *Our joys divinely grow,*
> *Unspeakable like those above,*
> *And heaven begins below."*

C. H. Spurgeon, *(Morning and Evening,* McDonnell Publishing Company, McLean, Virginia, 22102 ISBN 0 – 9 1 7 0 0 6 – 26 – 7, page 332.)

Christians, who are relatively ignorant of the truths revealed in Romans chapter eight, are to that extent, strangers to the delights that Spurgeon is referring to. Those, however, who understand and appreciate these truths, will experience a tremendously increased delight in God and in their salvation. What a wonderful, practical benefit! Isn't that what you desire in your Christianity?

SUGGESTED REASON 2: THE WELFARE OF OUR CHILDREN AND GRANDCHILDREN

A sad and frightening reality is that 40% – 50% of our GOOD students from GOOD families and GOOD youth groups in GOOD churches are walking away from their profession of faith in Christ when they go to college or merely leave home. A nationwide study with 11,000 teens, from 561 congregations representing 6 different denominations yielded some eye-opening results. Only 12% of youth have a regular dialogue with their mom on faith/life issues. Only 1 out of 8 talks with mom about faith. Only 1 of out of 20 talks with dad about their faith/life issues.

Parents must get serious about being involved in the spiritual training of their children. Furthermore, dear parents, just being "saved" with a cursory knowledge of biblical truth is not enough to equip you to adequately and fully impress the truths of God upon your children. You need to have more than merely a cursory, superficial understanding of exactly who God is and how the triune God has and is securing your salvation for all eternity. A vague, foggy, and undefinable, "know–so" kind of relationship with your salvation is substandard and inefficient when you are seeking to clearly teach and encourage your children in the way of God. At best, it will tend to produce the same kind of vague attachment to religion in your children that you have. At worst, your children will see through the shroud of haziness and reject the message of salvation altogether because they have never really understood it in detail.

Of all the attitudes a parent can adopt, the worst surely is to say, as so many do: "I'm not going to force religion on my children. I'm going to let them make up their own minds when they are old enough." So, in the meantime, during their impressionable years the world relentlessly and creatively forces its views upon them, seducing them, intimidating them and entertaining them. Meanwhile, godless teachers and unsaved companions relentlessly mold and fashion their tender minds and hearts in godless thinking. No, dear parent, remember that God holds parents accountable for the spiritual instruction of their children. After all, the average church only has 40 hours in a given year to influence the life of a child for the Lord Jesus Christ. On the other hand, the average parent has 3000 hours per year to influence their child's life in the right direction. Therefore, don't hesitate to engage in the study of Romans chapter eight and "Since God is for us" so that you will be more effectively prepared to understand and explain the truths of God and His salvation to your children. Then, don't hesitate to impress these truths upon your children when you learn them. Consider that if your children are not taught the things of God effectively by you and because of that do not become genuinely saved you will have (humanly speaking) unintentionally contributed to their eternal damnation. I know that is not what you want to happen. I know that you love your children. But love must be demonstrated in a practical and personal way to do everything possible to ensure that one's children will clearly understand and embrace the gospel of Jesus Christ for their salvation.

God intends for parents to bridge the generation gap, age after age, by the personal, persistent and intelligent teaching of the Word of God. The Word of God becomes the connecting factor linking the generations together in both love and truth. The result that we hope for and aim at is that our children's minds and hearts will be so dramatically given over to God and that they will be committed to God for a lifetime. We desire for them to set their hope in God and wholeheartedly keep His commandments. It all begins when the parents love God deeply and walk with Him in devotion and obedience. Then, in the context of a strong spiritual walk with God the parents are prepared to perpetually teach their children the things of God in a practical and personal way.

In this way God desires for parents to be an integral part of a spiritual chain reaction. The truth held and practiced by parents will become the truth held and practiced for generations to come. This is not merely adhering to family tradition but each generation recognizes and holds to the truth of God because it is the truth. This becomes the legacy of each generation.

If there is a breakdown in this line of communication, chaos, ignorance, indifference to God and other sins will assert themselves so that the next generation becomes a stubborn, faithless and rebellious one because of the power of indwelling sin and the incredible pressure of the world system. Furthermore, a giant rift will occur in the relationship between the Christian parent and the non-Christian child.

Toward the end of the 19th century there emerged in Europe a man who did more than any other single individual to pave the way for the coming Antichrist. This man's name was Friederich Nietzsche. He was born into the home of a clergyman and both his father and mother came from a long line of Protestant ministers. His father died when he was still young and the boy grew up in a home dominated by women – a mother, a sister, a grandmother, and aunts. By the time he was 12 he had rejected the Orthodox Christianity of his parents and blasphemously redefined the Trinity as God the father, God the Son, and God the Devil. This twelve-year-old boy was beginning to take the first tragic steps in what would be a lifelong rebellion against God and his home. His philosophies were radical, violent, and disastrous for him and for the society in which he lived. In the end, he died a lunatic. But, his teachings led directly to Nazism and the horrific concentration camps of World War II. His book, *"The Will to Power,"* had a tremendously powerful influence on men like Adolph Hitler. Nietzsche taught that Christianity was "the one great curse... the one great moral blemish of mankind." Nietzsche hammered away at the lie of lies: "God is dead! God is dead! God is dead!" He called openly for the abolition of all morality. His most famous and diabolical work was, *"The Antichrist."* This book called upon the world to recognize its true god (Satan) and fall at his feet.

At the time of his death, Nietzsche had been locked up in a madhouse. At that time, one astute observer pinned this couplet:

"God is dead." (Signed) Nietzsche
"Nietzsche is dead." (Signed) God

How could a man born into a Christian family with such rich Christian heritage turn out so heretical and horribly rebellious to God? Among other reasons, there was a failure of the parents in the home to communicate and instill the truths of God in the heart of their son. The history of Israel is replete with examples in the Old Testament of this same scenario playing itself out with equally devastating results. Parents need to take seriously their responsibility to teach their children the clear truths of God's Word. That is precisely why Moses wrote the following to the Israelites:

"Hear, O Israel: the Lord our God, the Lord is one. You shall love the Lord your God with all your heart and with all your soul and with all your might. And these words that I command you today shall be on your heart. You shall teach them diligently to your children, and shall talk of them when you sit in your house, when you walk by the way, and when you lie down, and when you rise. You shall bind them as a sign on your hand, and they shall be as frontlets between your eyes. You shall write them on the door posts of your house and on your gates.... When your son asks you in time to come, "What is the meaning of the testimonies and the statutes and the rules that the Lord our God has commanded you?" Then you shall say to your son... (Deuteronomy 6:4 – 9, 20 – 21a).

Notice that the spiritual formation of our children, humanly speaking, begins with the spiritual attitude and walk of the parents. The parents are commanded to love God with all their heart and soul and might. This is the beginning point of a successful spiritual ministry with one's children.

Children learn by example as well as by precept and instruction. In some ways spiritual thinking and spiritual attitudes are as much caught as well as they are taught. Parents must provide the right kind of example during the child's life so that when they undertake to instruct their children in the ways of the Lord that instruction will ring true and be reinforced by the real-life love of the parents for God.

Example alone, however, is not enough. Parents must be the principal spiritual educators of their children. In the text just cited, parents are told to instruct their children personally, perpetually, practically (in the normal course of life), and in a plurality of different ways (visual, conversational, etc.). It is the responsibility of the parent to live out the spiritual life and to lead their children into the same path by employing constant attention to achieving the spiritual formation of their children for the glory of God.

For our children to be able to follow God faithfully they must have first become serious students of the Word of God for themselves. Who is to be their example and primary teacher? Dear parent, you are! Their primary spiritual teaching is not the responsibility of the church but it is the primary responsibility of the parents. The parents must teach their children by example, by inundating them with biblical truth, by diligently and perpetually conversing with them about God's truth, by encouragement and correction, with insight, loving concern, and understanding.

One cannot effectively teach what one does not clearly understand. That is one reason why the truths of Romans chapter eight are so valuable and beneficial to every Christian parent. Understanding these spiritual truths will enable parents to communicate these truths accurately, clearly, and persuasively to the next generation.

Therefore, whether you are currently a parent, you have hopes of one day being a parent, you are a grandparent, or you would like to be able to have a ministry equipping parents and children in the things of God, then you should not hesitate to jump into this study of Romans chapter eight and "Since God is for us," with both feet and a ready heart. In fact, when parents do so, they are laying the groundwork for their children to teach the same truths to their children (the grandchildren.) And so, the line of communication regarding the truths of God will go on unbroken bringing with it the safeguards, salvation and sustained understanding of the Bible. This fact alone, should remove any hesitation that you might have in spending whatever time is necessary studying and understanding the rich and relevant truths of this fantastic portion of Scripture.

You may remember that Ephraim was one of the twelve tribes of Israel. There was a time when Ephraim held a vital, dynamic faith, grounded in the Word of God and in the God of the Word. When Ephraim broke the chain of spiritual indoctrination, they no longer retained the heart to serve and sacrifice for God. They became a stubborn and rebellious generation whose heart was not stead–fast, their spirit was not faithful to God. "The Ephramites, armed with the bow, turned back on the day of battle. They did not keep God's covenant, but refused to walk according to His law. They forgot His works and the wonders that He had shown them" (Psalm 78:8–11). Consequently, Ephraim ended up suffering at the hand of the just judgment of God. Parents, if you don't indoctrinate your children as God commanded you to do so you are setting them up to be a stubborn and rebellious, self-centered generation who will face defeat and disgrace because they no longer have a dynamic faith in God rooted in biblical doctrine.

At the end of the 19th century, spiritual revival swept through the mining villages of South Wales. Whole communities turned to God. The face of society changed. Tavern keepers went bankrupt, and prisons were virtually emptied. Life in the mines, harsh and tough though it undoubtedly was, was for the most part, made more pleasant by a new spirit of kindness and godliness among the miners. The reaction of the people to the Holy Spirit of God was dramatic and undeniable.

One humorous reality was that the mules that were used to pull the carts which carried the coal had to be retrained because they had become accustomed to commands laced with profanity. The mules now stood confused and without comprehension when the commands were given to them by the newly saved miners who sought to issue them commands without the use of profanity. The change in the moral and spiritual climate of Wales was dramatic. There was, however, one major flaw. There was no father to son spiritual chain reaction. Children were not indoctrinated carefully and fully into the biblical truths that their parents had experienced so powerfully. Parents were absorbed in their own experience of spiritual renewal to the point that they forgot to focus on instilling these powerful truths in their children. As a result, one can travel up and down those same Welsh villages today and see little or no evidence that this was a land once blessed powerfully by the Holy Spirit in revival. By and large the children have abandoned biblical teaching and opted for whatever ideology has presented itself as an alternative to Christianity.

What happens to the nation which fails to pass on its spiritual heritage to its children? "Give ear, O my people, to my teaching; incline your ears to the words of my mouth! I will open my mouth in a parable; I will utter dark sayings from of old, things that we have heard and known, that our fathers have told us. We will not hide them from their children, but tell to the coming generation the glorious deeds of the Lord and his might, and the wonders that he has done. He established a testimony in Jacob and appointed a law in Israel, which he commanded our fathers to teach to their children, that the next generation might know them, the children yet unborn and arise and tell them to their children, so that they should set their hope in God and not forget the works of God, but keep His commandments; and that they should not be like their fathers, a stubborn and rebellious generation, a generation whose heart was not steadfast, whose spirit was not faithful to God. The Ephraimites, being armed and carrying bows, turned back on the day of battle. They did not keep God's covenant, and refused to walk according to His law. They forgot His works and His wonders that He had shown them" (Psalm 78:81– 11). What a tragedy! The sad thing is, this tragedy could have been avoided. What parent wants that guilt on their conscience? I am certain that you do not.

It is the responsibility and privilege of each Christian parent to pass on and impress upon their children the clear and full teaching of God. If we do, we have every reason to hope that God will use these truths for the salvation of our children. If we don't, there will be a breakdown in biblical understanding in the next generation, leading them to a refusal to walk in the ways of the Lord and fight the good fight of faith.

How can parents possibly teach their children about salvation, in all its fullness, unless they first apply themselves to coming to a deep, clear, and accurate understanding of these truths for themselves? Why should you want to take in the rich truths of Romans chapter eight? One reason is for the welfare and sake of your children and grandchildren. This strong motivation should remove any hesitation on your part. You need to be equipped and actively involved in communicating these precious truths.

SUGGESTED REASON 3: THE PERSONAL WORK OF DISCIPLESHIP AND EVANGELISM

Our Lord Jesus Christ has commanded us to be busy about the work of personal evangelism and discipleship. The true believer is likely aware of what has been called, "The Great Commission" found in Matthew 28:19 – 20. In this passage our Lord Jesus Christ said, "As you're going into the world teach all nations, baptizing them in the name of the Father, and of the Son, and of the Holy Spirit. Teaching them to observe all things that I have commanded you, and lo, I am with you always, even to the end of the ages. Amen."

Notice, that the task of evangelizing people does not, in itself, fulfill the great commission. The great commission requires that we, as true believers, also disciple Christians in all the things that our Lord commanded. Not only are they to be informed about these things, but we are to teach them to "observe" all these things in their personal, Christian, life. Discipleship is a very real responsibility for every Christian. In Ephesians 4 the Apostle Paul described how our Lord Jesus Christ ascended to heaven and gave gifts to men. The gifts that he mentions are particularly related to ministering the Word of God. "And he gave some, apostles; and some, prophets; and some evangelists; and some pastors/teachers" (Ephesians 4:11).

What was the purpose for our Lord giving these gifts to men – these gifts that relate to the use of the Word of God? Paul answers that question in the next verse. He writes, "to equip the saints for the work of ministry, for building up the body of Christ, until we all attain to the unity of the faith and of the knowledge of the, Son of God, to mature manhood, to the measure of the stature of the fullness of Christ, so that we may no longer be children, tossed to and fro by the waves and carried about by every wind of doctrine, by human cunning, and by craftiness and deceitful schemes. Rather, speaking the truth in love, we are to grow up in every way into him who is the head, into Christ, from whom the whole body, joined and held together by every joint with which it is equipped, when each part is working properly, makes the body grow so that it builds itself up in love" (Ephesians 4:12–15).

Notice, according to the Apostle Paul, every member and part of the body of Christ is to be actively building up each other in Christ likeness. Every Christian is responsible to be involved in the work of discipleship just as we are to be involved in the work of evangelism. Every true Christian has the privilege of serving God in this way. No Christian is exempt.

Furthermore, no Christian can begin to adequately carry out their responsibility as a disciple maker of others without first equipping himself with a thorough knowledge of the Word of God. How can you teach someone else what you, yourself, do not know? Pursuing this study of Romans chapter eight and "Since God is for us" will go far in developing a Christian's ability to understand, appreciate, and communicate accurately the truths of God which God will use to save and conform the one being discipled into a more perfect likeness of Jesus Christ.

SUGGESTED REASON 4: THE WORSHIP AND GLORY OF GOD

In addition, you might ask, "What other benefits will I personally gain from a deeper knowledge of this wonderful subject?" I hesitate, in some ways, to approach the motive for this study on those grounds alone. People today are often totally self–centered and tend to think only about what's in it for them personally. Many so-called Christians have been persuaded to seek and embrace a cultural creation of a counterfeit Christ which teaches that our Lord exists to serve their needs and desires.

These people believe that He is to be sought after merely as a means to further realize their human pleasure, potential and prosperity. Although they would not admit it, they tend to think that the Lord Jesus is to be viewed as a kind of celestial, spiritual bellhop. Whatever one desires, he merely calls upon Christ to meet that desire. This is the philosophy behind the "name it and claim it" practice of some who believe that God's role is to await their desires and then to eagerly grant them. Is it loneliness, poverty, boredom, peace of mind, physical health, money, etc.? It is taught that, in many practical ways, the believer is sovereign and the Lord and Savior Jesus Christ is the servant of the believer, then he dispenses His blessings as He acquiesces to the professing Christian's prayers and demands. Calling upon the name of Jesus, they set their focus on some desired possession and, "Name it and claim it." Self–gratification and self-promotion are key motives in the so-called "Christianity" of many modern-day professing Christians.

This teaching is totally at odds with the teaching of the Bible which calls upon those seeking salvation to "deny themselves," and "to take up their cross daily and follow Christ". The Bible teaches when a person is saved they are freed, from the bondage of slavery to sin, to willingly take their place as slaves to Jesus Christ. The goal and purpose of a slave is to seek to do the will of the master and to prove productive and pleasing to him. It is not to pursue his or her own selfish desires by manipulating the master into helping him to do so. Salvation is ultimately about God rather than about man.

We receive many wonderful benefits from salvation because of the tender mercies and goodness of our master, but it is primarily the master's glory that we are to be consumed with. It is all about God – His glory and His worship! Yet, in today's world some have fabricated a "false gospel" that places man at the center of salvation essentially making man sovereign. God is viewed as the one who is intended to serve man and further man's desires. In effect, men worship themselves and seek their own glory. This distortion of the gospel message, conditions some to constantly be asking the question, "What is in it for me?" According to the Bible, the sinner comes to Christ in faith for salvation with an attitude of surrender and submission and with a view to serve Jesus Christ as Lord. Again, salvation is all about God not all about us. His desires are to be fulfilled by us rather than our desires fulfilled by Him. His glory is to be sought after. That is why the Apostle Paul wrote, "Therefore whatsoever you do, whether you eat, or drink, or whatsoever you do, do it all for the glory of God" (I Corinthians 10:31).

Is It All About You?

I am reminded of a song that Carly Simon sang some years ago entitled, *You're so vain*. She sang, "You're so vain. *You probably think this song is about you don't you, don't you"* The essence of the song described a person who cared only for himself. His entire life was about him. This person was a self-centered, self – consumed and self–conceited "vain" person.

As Christians, we can rejoice in the blessings and teachings of Scripture regarding those things that God has graciously done for us and in us. Nothing is wrong with that. But we must never stop at that point. The bigger picture, and the more proper picture, is to see God in all His glory and power in His work of salvation and to worship Him wholeheartedly. Not only does the creation declare the glory of God but so does the salvation of the believer by the free grace of God. God said that he would not share his glory with another. Everything that God did or does is for His own glory. Jesus perfectly pursued the glory of God during His earthly ministry. The Apostle Paul counseled Christians, "Whether you eat or drink or whatever you do, do so for the glory of God" (1 Corinthians 10:31). What is man's purpose? The answer is simple and yet profound. The Westminster Catechism teaches our purpose is to glorify God and to enjoy Him forever. If one is not pursuing the glory of God and enhancing his ability to bring God more glory and to worship Him in fullness that person has missed the mark regarding his purpose in life.

As we study Romans chapter eight and *"Since God is For Us,"* and grow deeper in our understanding of God's work in our salvation, we will have a greater capacity to glorify God and to worship Him. This is true because we will have an enhanced understanding of God's tremendous grace and goodness toward us in Christ. We will see more fully that salvation is really the work of God from beginning to end. God did for us and does for us what we could not do and cannot do for ourselves. God changed our position of guilt to one of justification and forgiveness by providing the necessary propitiation for our sins and then providing us with the faith to trust in that payment made by our Lord Jesus Christ. God changed and is changing the bent of our minds and hearts so that we now hunger and thirst for righteousness instead of sin. God insured that we, in our salvation, would never be left alone and vulnerable in this world of spiritual hostility. To ensure that this would be a reality, God caused us to be indwelt by the omnipotent Holy Spirit. When we are confused and do not know what to pray for, God, the Holy Spirit, prays for us feelingly and effectually. God is providentially at work ensuring that all things, no matter what they are, will work out for our ultimate good and for His own glory. Why does God do all of this for us? Because God loves us, God has loved us from all eternity and will love us for all eternity. God has committed Himself to our eternal well-being and is at work causing all things to work together for our good and for His own glory. God is for us! God has called us, justified us through Christ and will most certainly glorify us. It Is God who declares us to be righteous based on the righteous provision that He has made for us in Jesus Christ. God loves us and nothing can separate us from the love of God which is in Christ Jesus. Let the believer never forget that their salvation is really the work of God. Without this knowledge and understanding we would be unable to utilize these truths of Romans chapter eight to bring glory to God's name, to have complete confidence in the absolute security of our ultimate salvation, and to worship God in a manner worthy of His person and work. So, one major benefit of growing deeper in our understanding of God's work in our salvation as taught in Romans chapter eight and as explained in "Since God is for us" is that it will enhance and expand our ability to worship God in fullness and to bring Him more glory. It's all about God in the final analysis. That is precisely the emphasis that I sought to focus on and teach in, "Since God is for us". I hope that this truth radiates from every page of "Since God is for". In the final analysis, it is all about God!

SUGGESTED REASON 5: THE WEALTH OF SPIRITUAL HELPS

There are several other valuable benefits for the believer who digs deeply into this rich passage of Scripture. First, the believer who studies this passage of Scripture will be filled with an immense, consuming gratitude toward God and an ever-increasing love for God. Those who know little of what is actually involved in their salvation, appreciate it with less gratitude than others. Our Lord Jesus Christ spoke and said, "Those who are forgiven much, love much, those who are forgiven little, love little." The idea is that the fullness of our personal perception regarding how much we are forgiven in salvation versus a scant understanding of such will have a proportionate effect on how much we love God and how much we are grateful to God for forgiving us and delivering us from sin unto salvation. If we wrongly assume that we are only slightly sick due to sin and facing only the remote possibility of divine judgment, then our deliverance from this condition will be appreciated to a lesser degree than if we understand our divine deliverance from the dire straits, spiritual death, utter helplessness, and the certain reality of facing a horrendous punishment in hell due to our sin. Understanding how much God has done for us will dramatically increase our passionate love for Him.

Romans chapter eight will clearly reveal to the believer the depths and fullness of his forgiveness. The benefit will be a proportionate increase in one's personal gratitude towards and love for our precious Savior. This will be accompanied by a willing desire to serve and sacrifice for the one who has loved us so greatly and caused us to love Him. The Apostle Paul continually reveled in the fact that though he was an ardent, violent, and committed sinner against God (Jesus Christ) and the church of Christ, nevertheless, God chose to save him and forgave him from all his sins. Further, God chose to use him to bring glory to His name and the message of salvation to lost sinners by employing him in the gospel ministry. Paul was filled with overwhelming gratitude toward God and an unquenchable love for God which motivated him to ever-increasing levels of joyous service to and sacrifice for his God. The knowledge of where he had once come from and how God had graciously delivered him in love and forgiveness through Christ overwhelmed and motivated him. In fact, Paul, regarding his motive for his ministry, asserted, "The love of Christ controls us…" In the context of this passage it is probably better to assume that the Apostle Paul is referring to the love of Christ for him and not to his love for Christ. Paul never forgot the overwhelming truth of how much Christ loved him in spite of the fact that he was so undeserving of that love. The understanding of these truths will have the same effect on you as a believer. Isn't that what you want? This truth is taught in Romans chapter eight and in "Since God is for us."

In the book of the Revelation, Jesus is depicted as walking among his churches and reviewing them. When he surveyed the church at Ephesus He commended them for their hard work but He rebuked them because they had left their first love. How easy it is for Christians to get caught up in the activities of religion and yet lose the ardor of their affection for God, and to forget how much God in Christ loves them. Has this ever happened to you? Jesus said that the greatest commandment is captured in the thought of loving God with all our heart, mind, soul, and strength. Does this describe your current condition? If you need to rekindle your passionate love for God in Christ, and restore your understanding of how much God loves you in Christ, Romans chapter eight will serve you well in that worthy pursuit.

Are You Absolutely Sure That You Are Saved and That You Are Going to Heaven?

Do you ever find yourself suffering from doubts and a lack of settled assurance regarding your eternal salvation? In the Sermon on the Mount, our Lord Jesus Christ described the following scenario: He described many people who will come to Him at the time of judgment saying, "Lord, Lord, have we not prophesied in your name and have we not done many wonderful works in your name?" And then Jesus said that He would say to them, "Depart from me you workers of iniquity, I never knew you." Do you sometimes feel fearful and haunted by the thought that you may possibly be among that number? Is there a lurking fear that such might happen to you on the final Day of Judgment? Are you wracked with this underlying fear, doubt and a lack of settled assurance regarding your final salvation knowing that on that final day of judgment there are no second chances or do overs? Do you sometimes wonder if God really does love you in a personal and saving way – and how much – and for how long? Do you sometimes question whether God is really for you? Do you ever feel that God has somehow abandoned you and left you alone to fend for yourself in your Christian walk – or that he might do so? Do you fear that some accusation about some sin that you have committed in secret will surface when you are standing before God and that this will destroy the credibility of your salvation? Do you fear that your innate weakness will be confronted by some overwhelming problem that will overcome you and keep you from ultimately being saved? If so, you will profit greatly from a clear and accurate understanding of the teaching of God in Romans chapter eight.

Further, are you puzzled by the fact that so many seem to make a profession of faith in Christ and claim to be Christians but live lives that are dominated by sin? What should you make of this? All these topics, and others, are addressed by the Apostle Paul in Romans chapter eight.

Indeed, some Christians have contented themselves with merely going through the motions of organized religion. These professing Christians see no reason to get beyond a superficial understanding of God and a weak, lukewarm commitment to serve God. Are you one of those Christians who find yourself just going through the motions without feeling a passionate love for God? Have you lapsed into this kind of monotonous, mundane, and meaningless kind of Christianity? I urge you; do not be among that number.

Are you merely going through the motions of your professed Christianity? I hope that you are determined not to do so?

Do you want to know God more and to know more deeply about God's love for you in your salvation, then understanding the truths of Romans chapter eight and this book, "Since God is for us" will enhance your ability to do so and give you added confidence to serve God, to rejoice in God, to gratefully worship God, to grow in the likeness of God, and to experience the benefits of a more full understanding of the salvation that God is working in you and for you – All of this, while learning to love God more fully, while living to bring God the glory due to His name. This being true, there should be NO HESITATION AT ALL on your part to study and learn the truths of Romans chapter eight as explained, in detail, in this book, "*Since God Is For Us.*"

SUGGESTED REASON 6: A KEY TO UNDERSTANDING OTHER BIBLICAL TRUTH

Christianity is a religion of the truth. The truth of God is revealed to us in the Bible. The Word of God is a light to direct our way in this world. The truth of God counsels us and corrects us when we stray from the proper path. The truth of God nourishes us, cleanses us, inspires us, and informs us. It forms the basis, and foundation of our faith. The Word of God performs many other essential functions for the true believer. It is essential to one's growth and godliness and protection against spiritual error. The truth of God is not, however, effective simply because it has been read or recited in some ritualistic form. The truth of God is only as effective as it should be when it is clearly understood, embraced by faith and obeyed. That being the case, it is imperative that the child of God gains a clear and accurate understanding of the truth of God.

Our faith, when rightly understood, can only take us as far as the truth of God leads us. Imagine a locomotive with incredible power ready to charge forward but without the necessary rails and tracks to support it. All the potential locked up in the locomotive would be ineffective. The truth of God forms the foundation of our faith like the rails form the foundation for the locomotive to move forward. It is, therefore, tremendously important for the child of God to understand the Word of God. No portion of God's Word is richer and full of biblical truth than Romans chapter eight and this book, "Since God is for us," is dedicated to explaining these rich truths to the reader with accuracy and simplicity.

Unlocking the Truth of God

In the 18th century Egypt and all things Egyptian were the absolute rage in Europe. In 1799 Napoleon's French army launched a military expedition into Egypt. They were at war with Britain and intended to fight the British Army on Egyptian soil. Along with his army, Napoleon took some experts in ancient Egyptian history. While digging fortifications and setting up reinforcements for a French fort, one of his soldiers (Pierre – Françoise Bouchard) discovered a granodiorite stele inscribed with three versions of a decree issued at Memphis, Egypt in the year 196 BC during the Ptolemaic dynasty. It was issued on behalf of King Ptolemy V. There were three distinct lines of inscriptions on the dark gray fragment of the stele. It was a fragment of a larger stele but upon extensive searching for the rest of the stele no additional fragments were found. The top line of the stele was composed of Egyptian hieroglyphs. The middle line was composed of demotic text. The final line was composed of classical Greek text.

Up until this time no one could interpret Egyptian hieroglyphs. They were a locked revelation and could not be understood. They appeared to be mysterious and undecipherable etchings of people and things but were unintelligible to the "modern" experts attempting to decipher them. The discovery of this fragment (named the Rosetta Stone because it was discovered near the city of Rosetta) opened the possibility of interpreting the heretofore mysterious hieroglyphs. Since the experts were familiar with classical Greek they could read the bottom line of the stele and compare it to the other two lines. Understanding the Greek text opened the door for understanding the Egyptian text.

Likewise, understanding the truths of Romans chapter eight will, to a large measure, unlock and open many other passages of Scripture which otherwise might seem hidden and mysterious in terms of their meanings. Romans chapter eight is a key text in understanding the triune God, justification by faith, the work of the Holy Spirit, the providence of God, the believer's ultimate redemption from sin, the intercession of Jesus Christ, the love of God, the calling of God, etc. By understanding the truths of Romans chapter eight an exciting world of biblical truth is unlocked and opened to the true believer. It is my ardent desire in, "Since God is for us," to help unlock many of these wonderful truths for the reader. Because of the beneficial value of these truths the true believer should not have a moment's hesitation when contemplating the benefit of studying and understanding Romans chapter eight.

The Need For Serious Investigation

This book, "Since God is for us," is dedicated to those who share that passion to know God and the things of God more thoroughly. There is no downside to digging deeply into the truths of Romans chapter eight. I want you to know, however, that you will need to exert personal effort and demonstrate a hunger and thirst for these truths for them to have their maximum, positive, impact on your life. You will have to put your thinking cap on and really think. Consider the words of the Old Testament wise man:

"My son, if you receive my words and treasure up my commandments with you, making your ear attentive to wisdom and inclining your heart to understanding; yes, if you call out for insight and raise your voice for understanding, if you seek it like silver and search for it as for hidden treasures, then will you understand the fear of the Lord and find the knowledge of God. For the Lord gives wisdom; from His mouth comes knowledge and understanding" (Proverbs 2:1–6).

I am reminded of a story I heard about a farmer and his wife who lived in Oklahoma on a hardscrabble piece of land and labored to eke out a meager living from their toil and sweat as they worked the land. One day, a well-dressed man drove up to their house and offered the farmer a substantial sum of money for his land. This man was a petroleum engineer and claimed that he believed that significant oil reserves existed underneath the surface of the farmers land. The farmer refused to entertain any thought of parting with his land at any price.

Years passed and eventually the farmer grew sick and died. His, now aged, widow was left to try to fend for herself and to provide for herself financially. She was no longer young or physically able to do farm work. She had, however, kept the business card of the man who had driven up years before and who had talked to her husband about purchasing their farm. She hoped that he might still be interested in her land.

She called him on the phone and invited him to come out and meet her in anticipation of selling her property to him. The man agreed to come and he did so. When, however, he talked to the aged widow and saw her plight, he proposed that they become partners in the exploration and drilling for oil on her property instead of him merely purchasing the land from her with a one-time payment. In doing so, she could potentially make much more money by partnering with him. She agreed and before long his men discovered the oil that he always thought lurked below the surface. They began pumping it out of the ground and selling it. Before long the previously impoverished widow was wealthy beyond her wildest imaginations.

By digging deeply below the surface of her farm she had acquired a treasure of riches. It had always been there but she had not availed herself of it. Likewise, by digging into the depths of Romans chapter eight, through the use of this book, "Since God is for us," the Christian will acquire a heretofore unknown treasure of spiritual riches.

I hope that I have not unduly wearied, you, the reader by listing some of the important reasons for why you should seek to understand the precious truths of Romans chapter eight. These previously mentioned benefits will be yours as you apply yourself to this study. In addition, you will begin to see God in a much clearer and sharper focus and understand more fully how thoroughly He has designed your salvation so that every contingency has been taken care of for you. Indeed, the gloriously loving God is for you!

God bless you as you read these pages and carefully scrutinize the sparkle on the diamond. God bless you as you come to understand more fully the myriad of benefits and treasures that come to us through our incredible salvation – made secure to us by our wonderful God. Let there be no hesitation on your part to wholeheartedly engage in this study. May God bless you as you ask and answer the life changing question, "If God is for us, who can be against us?"

This chapter of Scripture is filled with incredible insights regarding many aspects of God's bringing about salvation in our lives as Christians. As I write this book, I will try to take time to stop and inspect each major truth with care just as the Apostle Paul presented it to the Roman church. I will seek to do so without becoming bogged down in the minutia of detail. Don't hesitate to take your own notes. Don't hesitate to expand your study based on thoughts that may be triggered in you by this study. Let there be no hesitation.

What are the major truths that the Apostle Paul reveals to the reader in Romans chapter eight? The various chapters of this book will identify, examine, and apply the individual truths that the Apostle Paul highlights in Romans chapter eight.

BRINGING IT HOME

1. Why is it profitable for the individual Christian to understand the truths of Romans chapter eight? Identify some of the benefits.

2. When the Christian reads Scripture, should they primarily see themselves as the center of attention or should they see God as the primary focus of attention? Why?

3. Read through Romans chapter eight and ask yourself if God is actively involved in the life of the Christian today or is He distant and removed from our day-to-day struggles? How do you know? How does your understanding of this impact your worship and your attitude about the things of life?

4. What is God's ultimate purpose in our salvation apart from His own glory? How do you know and what difference does this make in the way you think about your life?

5. Will the individual Christian need to get serious and be committed to diligent study as he investigates the truths of Romans chapter eight? How do you know? Are you prepared to pursue this course of action with heartfelt determination and desire?

2

Because God is for you, there is –

NO CONDEMNATION

Due to Sin –

Romans 8:1–4

"There is therefore now no condemnation for those who are in Christ Jesus. For the law of the Spirit of life has set you free in Christ Jesus from the law of sin and death. For God has done what the law, weakened by the flesh, could not do. By sending His own Son in the likeness of sinful flesh and for sin, He condemned sin in the flesh, in order that the righteous requirement of the law might be fulfilled in us, who walk not according to the flesh but according to the Spirit" Romans 8:1–4

The Apostle Paul begins our tour of God's perfect salvation for believers by affirming and asserting that the one who is in Christ Jesus (the true believer) is not and will never be condemned and suffer the judicial payment for their guilt and sin. This is the foundation of everything else that the Apostle Paul will say in this chapter. This book, "Since God is for us" will help to explain just how God accomplished our freedom from condemnation.

"There is therefore *now no condemnation* to those who are in Christ Jesus." The words, "no condemnation" should fill us with a personal sense of overwhelming relief and profound gratitude.

Understanding the Structure of the Passage

Godly commentators disagree at times concerning the main subject of the first few verses of Romans eight. Some contend that Paul is speaking about justification (the declarative act of God whereby He declares believers to be righteous in His sight based on the imputed righteousness of Jesus Christ, received by faith alone). While others think that Paul is speaking about the believer's sanctification (the process by which God changes the believer's life in a practical way so that he becomes more and more like the Lord Jesus Christ. After much study, I am convinced that the flow of thought indicates that Paul is dealing with justification through most of this paragraph (Romans 8:1–4a), but then Paul switches his focus to sanctification at the end of the first paragraph of Romans 8 (verse 4). He is intent on highlighting the believer's security in Christ and freedom from condemnation, while at the same time defending his teaching from the false accusation of his critics who accused him of promoting licentiousness. Note that verses 2 and 3 both begin with "for." In verse 2, Paul explains what he said in verse 1, which clearly deals with justification. Verse 2 is intended primarily to explain justification. Verse 3 further explains verse 2. The first half of verse 4 is the result of justification (no condemnation). The last half of verse 4 describes the change in lifestyle and an alteration of the conduct of those who have been justified and thus freed from condemnation. This is where the Apostle Paul changes gears and makes the transition from justification to sanctification.

Paul, in describing those who are justified, declares that they do not walk according to the flesh, but according to the Spirit. In this way, Paul underscores both justification and sanctification regarding the true believer in Christ. The point is that they are always inseparable. Those who are genuinely justified by God are also sanctified.

The Grading Process

When I was a young man in school, I experienced different teachers who would grade according to different methods. Some would grade according to the numerical method. The top grade was 100 points. Each aspect of the paper assigned was given a certain number of points.

Grammar, spelling, factual accuracy, logical flow of thought, neatness, etc. were all assigned a numerical value. Deductions from the 100-point total were taken away according to weaknesses and flaws in any of the specified areas. Other teachers graded according to another form of measurement. This provided much more leeway. An "A" would be 94 – 100. A "B" would be 85 – 94. A "C" would be 75 – 84. A "D" would be 70 – 74. Any grade less than this would constitute an "F" or failing grade. Then, there were those teachers who chose to grade on a curve. The highest scoring performance by a student equated to an "A" or 100%. Using that as the standard, each of the other students was graded according to the curve – how they compared with the top score.

God, however, does not grade according to a curve. He does not grade in a general, loose fashion. God's grading scale is precise, inflexible and He requires that we score 100% (no flaws or weaknesses) to qualify for heaven. The specific payment for any and all sin requires spiritual and eternal death. There are no exceptions. God cannot be manipulated into taking any course of action other than that described. Neither will the pleading or excuses of sinners prevail upon Him to change His standard of grading. He cannot do otherwise because He is infinitely holy and just.

A Relevant Illustration

Think of the concept revealed in Romans 8:1–4 as a legal case brought against a criminal. The long, dreaded wait was over. All the court trials and appeals were now finished. The verdict in court each time was the same – GUILTY. The prisoner knew in his heart that he was indeed guilty of gross crimes but he had held out hope that his brilliant lawyers could find a way, a loophole in the law, to save him from execution. Nothing, however, had worked. He now stands condemned and faces the inevitable...execution.

His mind is held captive by the coming time of his execution and he can now think of nothing else but the execution chamber. Nothing else occupies his thoughts except a flurry of regrets over a misspent life. He has acted criminally and it was not the first time he had done so. He regrets his actions but knows that he would likely return to his life of crime if given the chance. Why was he this way?

That final moment which had seemed so distant and far away has now become imminent and inevitable. The authorities finally come for him a few moments before the exact time of his scheduled execution. He is wearing rubber sandals and baggy prison garb. There is an extreme somberness in the air and an overpowering sense of burden on his shoulders. Normally, in such fearful circumstances he would sweat profusely with nervousness but the palms of his hands are now bone dry, his throat is dry and parched, his heart feels constricted, and his mind has virtually given up all hope as he faces the final, fateful, footsteps to the executioner's chamber.

The chaplain is busy trying to give him last-minute comfort and guidance but the prisoner cannot listen and comprehend. His mind is numb – paralyzed with gripping fear. He knows that he deserves what he is going to get and that makes it all the worse. There is no hope for him – it is all over! He is condemned! Not only does he fear the moment of death but he also fears what might come after death. He has heard some talk about a place called hell and he knows that if anyone ever deserved to go there, it is him.

Condemnation is a hauntingly powerful word. It is a frightening and final word. The Bible reveals that all human beings are condemned sinners and held accountable to God (Romans 3:19). "What shall we conclude then? Are we any better? Not at all! We have already made the charge that Jews and Gentiles alike are all under sin. As it is written, "There is no one righteous, not even one; there is no one who understands, no one who seeks God. All have turned away; they have together become worthless; there is no one who does good, not even one" (Romans 3:9–12.) The Bible reveals that the punishment for sin is death, "for the wages of sin is death..." (Romans 6:23a). Divine and eternal condemnation hangs over the head of every sinner and every human being is a sinner. The Bible says, "Whoever believes in the Son has eternal life, but whoever rejects the Son will not see life, for God's wrath remains on him" (John 3:36). Note that the righteous wrath of God already rests upon the sinner (every unsaved sinner) and merely awaits the day of ultimate execution. The Apostle Paul mentioned that unsaved sinners have and do experience the riches of God's kindness in this life along with His patience and tolerance. They experience these things and yet take them for granted and continue to reject God refusing to repent of their sins. They love their sins and are committed in their hearts to continue to sin against God. Then Paul wrote the following words: "But because of your stubbornness and your unrepentant heart, you are storing up wrath against yourself for the day of God's wrath, when His righteous judgment will be revealed. God will give to each person according to what he has done" (Romans 2:5 – 6).

Unsaved sinners, all unsaved sinners, are condemned. There are no appeals, no slick lawyers, and there is no hope. As Dante wrote about sinners who die in their sin and enter hell, "Abandon hope all ye who enter here". No, the living sinner is not yet in Hell, but his condemnation is absolutely certain if something does not drastically change his situation.

The Good News & The Bad News

The Bible is a book of good news. That good news, however, can only best be understood and appreciated when viewed against the dark backdrop of the reality of sin and condemnation. The Bible teaches both truths. Human beings are sinners by virtue of their representation by Adam..." (Romans 5:16). "By the trespass of the one man, death reigned through that one man..." (Romans 5:17). The result of one trespass was condemnation... "For just as through the disobedience of the one man the many were made sinners..." (Romans 5:18, 19). The judgment of God followed one sin and brought condemnation "Consequently just as the result of one trespass was condemnation to all men..." (Romans 5:18). Because we are represented in Adam we are counted as sinners before God and apart from Christ, have no hope.

Human beings are also sinners because they are born with a sin nature derived originally from Adam and transmitted through the human race like some malignant, deadly disease. It is transmitted by each and every birth. Human beings are not merely influenced by sin but they are rooted in sin and dominated by sin.

Furthermore, sinners relish sin. They seek out new ways to sin. Sin permeates and corrupts and degrades and damns every individual. The tragic reality is that sin places us under the power of Satan and exposes us to the righteous wrath of God. All sinners await, "a certain terrifying expectation of divine judgment, "and the fury of a fire which will consume [God's] adversaries" (Hebrews 10:27).

Human beings are sinners by virtue of their representation in Adam and they are sinners by virtue of being born with a sin nature. We are also sinners by personal choice and habit. We choose darkness rather than light and perform evil deeds that our depraved natures inevitably crave and create. We are not reluctant criminals but we "drink iniquity like water". Our Lord Jesus Christ said, "Men love darkness rather than light because their deeds are evil." Lost sinners would like to minimize and play down their propensity to pursue sin but God's Word contradicts this notion. The Bible is like the black box behind the veil of sinful man's spiritual ignorance and self – justifying arrogance.

The Bible reveals the true nature and mechanisms of man's sin. The biblical record is clear. The lost sinner is totally culpable and unquestionably guilty before God. Because of sin, the unsaved person has no future to look forward to except eternal damnation in hell – he is condemned. That is the incredibly dark backdrop and it is only when one understands and believes these facts that the "good news" of the gospel of Christ becomes precious.

A Glimpse of Hell

When I was a young boy, my father worked at an electric power plant. On one occasion he took me on a short personal tour of the facility. Among the features of the plant there was the boiler. When we arrived at the boiler he put a protective helmet and face shield on me and then he opened a small access door into the raging inferno which was the boiler. The flames were unbelievably and indescribably intense. The scene was unforgettable. He then told me that he didn't know exactly what hell would be like but that he always imagined that it would burn with much greater and fiercer intensity than even that boiler. I'm not sure exactly what hell will be like either but that memory has been implanted and engraved on my mind ever since. Hell is a real place of eternal anguish and torment. It is a place of outer darkness where there will be weeping and gnashing of teeth (Matthew 8:12). It is a place without hope and without help. It is the certain future of every sinner who is not saved by the Lord Jesus Christ – every person who is condemned. That is the horrible stark reality! Frighteningly, that is what condemnation involves.

An Infidel's Regret

Think of Francois Marie Arouet, better known as Voltaire. He died in France on November 21, 1694. He was 83 and he died after a prolonged indulgence in sinful pleasure overtaxed his strength. His shriveled and wrinkled body had once been a well-known sight in the glamorous courts of Europe. He had surrounded himself with people of humor, personal interest stories, literary power, etc.

"My trade," said Voltaire, "is to say what I think." And he did a lot of thinking, a lot of talking, and a lot of writing. In fact, he wrote 99 volumes of material including prose, novels, and articles along with some 8,000 letters written to the famous people of the day. One of his works has been translated into more than 100 languages. He was extremely profane. Censors banned his books and closed the places where he publicly shared his works and yet the sinful populace of Paris thronged to them and enthusiastically memorized his most stinging lines.

Fourteen years after his death godless French revolutionaries brought Voltaire's' body back to Paris and laid him out as if he were a triumphant god. They placed his body on the ruins of the Bastille. They also made him their "patron saint." A quarter of a million people eagerly crowded between lines of guards to pay homage to Voltaire's remains. Finally, his body was given a state burial in the French Pantheon.

In the waning days of his life, Voltaire had a stroke and knew that he only had a very short time to live. Consequently, he sent for a priest and desperately sought reconciliation with the church. All his arrogance and pride had faded away. Of course, reconciliation with Rome is not the same as reconciliation with God. Still, not realizing this, he desperately sought to renounce his infidelities to give some comfort to the anguish of his soul. His unbelieving friends sought to prevent him from recanting his writings, but he simply cursed them and turned them out on the street. He prepared a written recantation and signed it before witnesses. But it was too late. Voltaire had spent away the day of grace. There was no hope for him in God. He was condemned and facing eternal retribution. He knew it and he felt it deep in his soul.

For two long months the wretched man was tormented with such agony of soul that he was seen to gnash his teeth and rage against God and man. At other times, he would cry and weep as he turned his face to the wall and he would cry out: "I must die – abandoned by God and man." As the conclusion of his life drew near his nurse declared: "Not for all the wealth of Europe would I see another infidel die." There was no help for him in God!

Not every unbeliever dies in this fashion but the thought of certain anguish of soul and hopelessness should deeply move condemned sinners to seek salvation in Christ rather than being consigned to experience the certain and horrible realities of hell. Some unbelievers will, in fact, confidently step into eternity with a fictitious "know–so salvation" only to shockingly find out that they have been deceived and are not equipped to meet God in their sin. What a frightening prospect!

A Brighter Prospect

Thankfully, there is another reality which is just as certain but far more hopeful and encouraging. The Apostle Paul writes about it in the first few verses of chapter eight of Romans.

"Therefore, there is now no condemnation for those who are in Christ Jesus..." (Romans 8:1).

Two Things of Note

Two things stand out in the first part of these verses. The first is the *logic* of the passage and the second is the *lifting of condemnation* cited in the passage.

The Logic – The word "for or therefore" brings us into the realm of a logical argument and introduces a conclusion based on what has been previously stated. Most likely the Apostle Paul is referring to a conclusion based on his teaching of the first seven chapters of Romans. He has demonstrated that all human beings are sinners and are condemned by a righteous God. He has declared that God set forth His Son as the only perfect and acceptable sacrifice of atonement (propitiation) for sin. He has directed sinners to the only means of personal salvation (saving faith alone in Jesus Christ alone) and he is depending upon the fact that his readers have embraced this salvation. With that in mind, the Apostle Paul now delivers some tremendous news to his readers, and he uses the word "for or therefore" to connect their thinking to what has been previously stated. This is a logical consequence or result, "therefore". That is also why the Apostle Paul includes the word "now". There is therefore "now" – Now that you have received Jesus Christ as your Lord and Savior by faith alone. He also uses the word "now" to indicate that the lifting of the verdict of condemnation is a present reality for the believer. We are saved now.

What results from having pursued this course of action of trusting in Jesus Christ alone by faith alone as our Lord and Savior?

The Lifting of Condemnation -There is therefore now no condemnation... The Greek word *katakrima* (condemnation) appears only in the book of Romans and though it relates to the sentencing for a crime, its primary focus in Romans is on the penalty that the verdict demands. The penalty of condemnation with its inevitable conclusion of suffering in hell as a defiant breaker of God's law. Whereas condemnation is all the unsaved sinner has to look forward to, the tremendous news is, that for Christians there is now no condemnation.

The word *ouketi* (no) carries the idea of complete and utter cessation. Jesus paid the believer's debt of sin and releases him "from all unrighteousness" (1 John 1:9). Not only so, but Jesus also imputes to each believer His own perfect righteousness: "For by one offering He [Christ] has perfected for all time those who are sanctified" (Hebrews 10:14; 2 Corinthians 5:21).

He also shares His vast inheritance with those who come to Him in faith (Ephesians 1:3, 11, 14). For the believer in Christ there has been a complete and fascinating change wrought by God in His grace. The believer is now freed from the fear of condemnation and will never again be subject to it. The previously poverty-stricken sinner is now rich with the blessings of Christ. He who was guilty is now declared righteous in God's eyes. This is the fascinating reality – the good news. It is all because of God's amazing grace in Christ. Indeed, God is for us!

Dear believer, is this not an incredible truth that will move you to worship God enthusiastically and fully with great humility, awe and gratitude?

But how could this wonderful salvation and deliverance from condemnation and sin's dominion become a reality? What made it possible?

It is important for us to be accurate about what the Bible teaches on the subject. Too many read their own interpretation into the Bible rather than allowing it to speak clearly and accurately for itself. Allow me to illustrate:

I once heard Ravi Zacharias speaking on answering life's toughest questions. He said that years ago there used to be a prominent commercial on television. It started out with a picture of the universe and it asked, "How old is the earth? How many miles do you think it is between the planets and the stars, etc.?" It talked about how many thousands of light years it would take to get between planets and stars then it asked the viewer, "How did it all get here?" The idea seemed to be to raise the viewer's awareness of the many tough questions that exist in life. Then the commercial made an immediate, unexpected, transition to softer questions like, "Do you like pizza?", "What is your favorite color?" Finally, and suddenly the screen went completely black with new age music playing in the background. At that point, a motorcycle appeared in the middle of the screen. A single statement also appeared on the screen with the motorcycle. It simply read YAMAHA. Then it said, Yamaha may not be the answer but at least it isn't another question."

It is important however, that we continue to seek for insightful answers to the right questions and that we diligently search the Bible for these correct answers. In doing so, we must make sure that our understanding of the Bible is accurate and correct.

I am reminded of a story I heard years ago of a young man named Sam who was being questioned at his ordination. The questioner conducting his ordination examination asked Sam if he knew the parable of the Good Samaritan and, if so, would he be kind enough to share that parable with them. The young man said, of course, and then he proceeded to explain:

"Once there was a man traveling from Jerusalem to Jericho and he fell among thorns and the thorns sprang up and choked him. And the man didn't have any money so he met the Queen of Sheba and she gave him a thousand talents of gold and a thousand changes of raiment. And he got into a chariot and he drove furiously. And when he was driving under a big Juniper tree, his hair got caught in the limbs of the tree and he hung there many days. And the ravens brought him food to eat and water to drink and he ate five thousand loaves of bread and two fishes. One night while he was hanging there asleep his wife, Delilah, came along and cut off his hair and he dropped and fell on stony ground. But he went on and it began to rain and it rained for forty days and forty nights. And he hid himself in a cave and lived on Locust and wild honey. One day he went along the road until he met a servant who said, "Come take supper at my house." But, he said, "No, I won't because I have taken a wife and I must go home. But the servant went down to the highways and the hedges and compelled him to come in. After he finished supper he went on down to Jericho and when he looked up he saw that old Queen Jezebel sitting up high in a window and she laughed at him he said, "Throw her down from up there," and they threw her down. And he said, "Throw her down again." And they threw her down seventy times seven. And of the fragments that remained they picked up twelve baskets full not counting women and children. And they said, "Blessed are the *piece* makers." Now, whose wife do you think she will be on that judgment day?"

This little story points out the reality that it is not enough to be loosely familiar with biblical truth. Instead, it is vital that we learn the truth of the Bible in an accurate manner.

THE REASON

Why do Christians Now Have Real Hope

"Because through Christ Jesus the law of the spirit of life set me free from the law of sin and death" (Romans 8:1b–2).

In the preceding verse the Apostle Paul spoke of being "in Christ". There is therefore now no condemnation to those that are "in Christ Jesus." The real key to every aspect of salvation is the simple yet profound statement of being "in Christ." When we are "in Christ" we are not simply outwardly identified with Him, but we are part of His body. Whatever Christ accomplished we derive the benefits from it by virtue of being "in Christ". We were chosen by God "in Christ"; we are baptized spiritually by the Holy Spirit into Christ. The Apostle Paul wrote "For as in Adam all die, so also "in Christ" all shall be made alive" (1 Corinthians 15:22). In describing Jesus Christ, C. H. Spurgeon commented on Psalm 45:2 in his own uniquely eloquent manner:

"You are fairer than the children of men." He wrote, "The entire person of Jesus is but one gem, and his life is all along but one impression of the seal. He is altogether complete; not only in his several parts, but as a gracious all – glorious whole. His character is not a mass of fair colors mixed confusedly, nor a heap of precious stones laid carelessly one upon another; he is a picture of beauty and a breastplate of glory. In him, all the "things of good repute" are in their proper places, and assist in adorning each other. Not one feature in his glorious person attracts attention at the expense of others; but he is perfectly and altogether lovely.

Oh, Jesus! Your power, your grace, your justice, your tenderness, your truth, your Majesty, and your immutability make up such a man, or rather such a God–man, as neither heaven or earth has seen elsewhere. Your infancy, your eternity, your sufferings, your triumphs, your death, and your immortality, are all woven in one gorgeous tapestry, without seam or rent. You are music without discord; you are many, and yet not divided; you are all things, and yet not diverse. As all the colors blend into one resplendent rainbow, so all the glories of heaven and earth meet in you, and unite so wondrously, that there is none like you in all things; no, if all the virtues of the most excellent were bound in one bundle, they cannot rival you, you are the mirror of all perfection. You have been anointed with the holy oil of myrrh and cassia, which your God has reserved for you alone; and as for your fragrance, it is as the holy perfume, the like of which none other can ever mingle, even with the art of the apothecary; each spice is fragrant, but the compound is divine.

"Oh, sacred symmetry! Oh, rare connection of many perfects, to make one perfection!

Oh, heavenly music, where all parts do meet in one sweet
strain, to make one perfect sweet!"

(C. H. Spurgeon, *Morning and Evening, McDonald Publishing Company,
McLean Virginia 22102 page 346*)

Spurgeon is eloquently highlighting the superlative and unique person
of Christ Jesus the Lord, and the glorious thing is that by the grace of God
the believing sinner is, "in Christ," for all eternity.

The Reason Explained

Notice that the apostle includes the word, "FOR," in his statement at
the beginning of verse two. The word "for" has the meaning of "because"
and it leads us to consider the reason why condemnation is no longer a
reality for believers. Some translations use the word, "Therefore" at this
point. Either way the meaning is the same.

In this passage, the Apostle Paul is discussing and explaining that two
combating laws or principles are competing for control in the sinner. In
this context, Paul is not using the word "law" to refer to the Mosaic Law or
to other divine commandments. He is referring to an operating principle
which is at work. The principle of sin and death and the principle of the
spirit of life are viewed in the context of salvation. Paul uses this same
kind of thinking in Romans 3:27 when he refers to the principle or "law"
of faith. In Galatians 6:2, he also uses the terminology of "law" when he
means a principle. There, Paul is speaking of fulfilling, "the law of Christ"
by which he means the principle of Christ.

In speaking of the "law" of sin and death, Paul is referring to a principle
which is operative in all sinners. "The wages of sin is death…" (Romans
6:23) and when speaking of the "law" of the Spirit of life, the Apostle is
referring to the new principal which operates with the fixedness of a law
(a fixed principle). He is referring to the operation of the Holy Spirit in the
application of the gospel benefits to the believing sinner. He makes that
even clearer later in the chapter. The Apostle Paul is saying that the reason
condemnation is no longer a concern or a threat for the Christian is that
the Holy Spirit has applied the righteousness and works of the Lord Jesus
Christ to the believer (through the gospel), This work of God frees the

believing sinner from the principle of sin and death. The reason we can never be condemned is because we've been set free from the law of sin and death. For the believer, this transaction has already been accomplished – we do not have to strive to get freedom, but rather we only need to stand in the freedom that has been given to us by God. It is like getting on an elevator – you do not have to push your way upward. We are forever free from condemnation and will never again be condemned. We are now (already) freed from sin's power and authority, sin's dominion and sovereignty, and will ultimately be freed from sin's presence and influence.

We, as believers in the Lord Jesus Christ, will never experience the eternal punishment of sin because we have been set free from that fearful reality because of what Jesus Christ did for us – and the Holy Spirit was the divine agent that made this a reality in our lives. What is required of us as sinners? We must turn from our sin in an act of repentance and trust alone in Jesus Christ alone as our Lord and Savior from sin.

There Is a Critical Key

Our wonderful freedom from condemnation was made possible, not only because Jesus Christ died on the cross as our substitute and was raised from the dead, but also because the Holy Spirit stepped in and changed the spiritual balance in our favor by applying the righteousness and benefits of Christ to us. That was the key that made all that Jesus Christ had done for us applicable to our salvation and why the sentence of condemnation no longer applies to the believer. That is why Paul could start out this sentence by saying, "Therefore there is now no condemnation to those that are in Christ Jesus because..."

A Necessary Helper

I was the eldest child of my family. I had a younger brother who I loved very much but who also had the tendency to be a bit mischievous. When we were young, He would do something to antagonize some of the other kids in our neighborhood and then he would come running to me for protection and defense. Often the other kids were too much for him to handle and he feared having to deal with them. His predicament was fearful, often caused by his own actions and they also put him in a hopeless situation that threatened pain and humiliation in the end. That is, until I stepped in to protect him against that which threatened to hurt and harm him. In a much more threatening and fearful way that is how we find ourselves as unsaved sinners. Our problem is self – induced and yet certain to bring us to eternal pain and humiliation. That is, until the Holy Spirit steps in to become our necessary helper. The question remains, however, how does this work?

The Right Method - Substitution

"For the law of the Spirit of life has set you free in Christ Jesus from the law of sin and death. For God has done what the law, weakened by the flesh, could not do. By sending His own son in the likeness of sinful flesh and for sin, He condemned sin in the flesh, in order that the righteous requirement of the law might be fulfilled in us, who walk not according to the flesh but according to the Spirit" (Romans 8:3 – 4).

What is the actual heart of the gospel? It is the fact that Jesus Christ paid the full penalty for sin on behalf of His people (every person who had been chosen by God for salvation and who would ultimately turn from sin and trust in Jesus Christ alone as Lord and Savior) and that, in doing so, He fully satisfied the wrath of God against believing sinners.

At this point, we must focus in more detail on the real heart of the gospel.

Even pagan religions utilize a form of sacrifice in the worship of their creatively imagined, fictitious deities. These fictitious deities are often concocted so that they reflect something of the likeness of the pagan worshipers. Their "deities", then, are merely magnified and exalted forms of themselves. In the pagan's mind these "deities" are often thought to be much like themselves complete with character flaws, pettiness, and a tendency to be quickly angered. The only course of action that the pagan can envision to placate these supposed "deities" is to humor them and try to seek to manipulate them and impress them so that they will be favorably disposed towards them.

In most cases, this calls for sacrifices to be offered to the imagined deity to gain their favor and stave off their wrath. The rule seems to be the bigger the sacrifice the better. The rationale seems to be that the bigger sacrifices are more likely to accomplish the purpose of placating the deity and securing his/her favor. In pagan theology, these supposed gods are often thought to be inclined to be most favorable towards the bigger sacrifices. These imaginary deities are also often thought to be cruel and heartless. The pagan, intimidated by the thought of His cruel and fickle deity, seeks to bribe and manipulate that "deity" by impressive sacrifices – often this results in the greatest/most valuable of all sacrifices – actual human sacrifices. This whole process seems to be a form of crass commercialism and forms the basis of a spiritual bribery system which constitutes what we might call pagan propitiation.

"Propitiation," is a word that means to appease or satisfy the wrath of another.

Propitiation: A Word You Should Know

Both the Bible and pagan religions teach a form of propitiation but they are far different in definition and character. In fact, they are opposites.

In the Old Testament, the concept of propitiation underlies the prescribed rituals of many of the offerings required of Israel. In the New Testament, the "propitiation" word–group appears in four different passages of Scripture that are incredibly important.

1. The first passage is found in the midst of Paul's statement of the rationale of God's justification of sinners. "But now the righteousness of God has been manifested apart from the law, although the Law and the prophets bear witness to it – the righteousness of God through faith in Jesus Christ for all who believe. For there is no distinction: for all have sinned and fall short of the glory of God, and are justified by His grace as a gift, through the redemption that is in Christ Jesus, whom God put forward as a *propitiation* by His blood, to be received by faith. This was to show God's righteousness, because in his divine forbearance He had passed over former sins. It was to show His righteousness at the present time, so that "He might be just and the justifier of the one who has faith in Jesus" (Romans 3:21 – 26).

2. The second passage is part of the explanation in Hebrews regarding the reason behind the incarnation of God the Son. The passage

reads, "Therefore He had to be made like His brothers in every respect, so that He might become a merciful and faithful high priest in the service of God, to make *propitiation* for the sins of the people" (Hebrews 2:17).

3. The third passage where propitiation appears is in John's testimony to the heavenly ministry of Jesus Christ as the intercessor for believers. It reads, "My little children, I'm writing these things to you so that you may not sin. But if anyone does sin, we have an advocate with the Father, Jesus Christ the righteous. He is the *propitiation* for our sins, and not for ours only but also for the sins of the whole world" (1 John 2:1).

4. The fourth and final use of the word *propitiation* in the New Testament is used when John is defining and describing the love of God. "In this the love of God was made manifest among us, that God sent his only son into the world, so that we might live through Him. And this is love, not that we have loved God but that He loved us and sent His Son to be the *propitiation* for our sins" (1 John 2:9 – 10).

Propitiation or Expiation? That Is the Question

Some liberal scholars have sought to eliminate the concept of "propitiation" teaching that wrath and anger have no place in our understanding of God. Unfortunately, their erroneous unbiblical ideas have even made their way into some translations of the Bible. The NEB renders the word propitiation as "remedy for defilement" of our sins; other versions replace the thought of propitiation by the word expiation. Expiation is an action that has sin as its object, but does not focus on the reaction of God against sin. On the other hand, propitiation focuses both on the problem of sin and the condemnation and settled anger of God who righteously reacts to that sin in wrath. In other words, propitiation denotes all that expiation means, as well as including the necessary ingredient of the pacifying of the wrath of God toward sin. It is a far more biblical term.

For those who want to eliminate the idea of the wrath of God toward sin because of a supposed desire to protect God from any association with wrath, they should consider the Apostle Paul's clear line of thought in the book of Romans. There, Paul speaks of the wrath of God as a present manifestation as well as a future reality.

In Romans 1:18 Paul sets the stage for his declaration of the gospel by affirming that "the wrath of God is being revealed from heaven against all ungodliness and unrighteousness of men." In the succeeding verses Paul demonstrates that the wrath of God is already an operative principle in the history of man. It can be seen in the judicial hardening of rebellious, apostate man and is highlighted by the three times repeated phrase, "God gave them up" (Romans 1:24, 26, 28). Then when Paul moves to Romans 2:1 – 16 he once again confronts his readers with the certainty of the wrath of God, "but because of your hard and impenitent heart you are storing up wrath for yourself on the *day of wrath when God's righteous judgment* will be revealed. He will render to each one according to his works: to those who by patience in well doing seek for glory and honor and immortality, he will give – eternal life; for those who are self-seeking and do not obey the truth, but obey unrighteousness, *there will be wrath and fury*" (Romans 2:5 –7).

In Romans chapter three, Paul proceeds in his argument to prove that every man, Jew and Gentile alike, are "under sin" (3:9) *and exposed to the wrath of God* in both its present and future manifestations. It is with this understanding that Paul transitions into the glorious explanation of how *God's wrath can be pacified* and the sinner can be delivered from *the certain wrath of God against sin.*

As astounding as it may seem Paul explains that God has personally undertaken to propitiate Himself on our behalf. We were bereft of hope. We had no sufficient resource or acceptable means of propitiating God's righteous wrath. But God, in His gracious love, designed and implemented a unique and totally sufficient means by which He would propitiate Himself for our sakes.

Unlike supposed pagan deities who demand that men propitiate them, God in His love, has provided a means for His own propitiation which assuages His righteous wrath against sin.

Peace with God

What a wonderful and marvelous God we have! God is a God who lovingly and mercifully undertakes to propitiate Himself to save His people (who were sinners) from His wrath and righteous indignation against sin. That is why the Apostle Paul is able to write in Romans 5:1, "Therefore, since we have been justified by faith, we have peace with God through our Lord Jesus Christ" (Romans 5:1).

What happened? How does this peace with God come about? The wrath of God against us, both present and to come has been satisfied and quenched through the death of Christ on our behalf. God's wrath against sin is not a capricious, fickle, loss of temper, or conceited rage. It is not the same kind of wrath that sinful man feels but it is the righteous, just, reaction of the moral perfection of our holy Creator towards perversity and rebellion.

The Work of God Himself

It must always be remembered that propitiation is entirely a work of God Himself and not in any way a work of man. In fact, the reader of Romans chapter eight should take note of the fact that it is God who is acting on behalf of the believer at every stage of our salvation to secure the believer's complete and ultimate salvation. Salvation is of God. It is accomplished by God on behalf of the sinner. It is entirely to the glory of God!

At this point in Paul's discussion of our salvation as believers we are focused on the work of propitiation. This divine propitiation is prompted by God's great love for sinners, it is carried out in accordance with God's infinite justice and it redounds exclusively to the glory of God. Divine propitiation was designed by God and accomplished by the sacrificial death of Jesus Christ alone. It demonstrates not only God's great love for sinners but also God's immutable righteousness. God could not merely ignore sin. Because of His holy nature it was necessary and inevitable for God to react against sin. He did so, however, in a marvelous display of His love to sinners by giving His own Son as the propitiation and sacrifice for our sins punishing His only begotten Son as our substitute. This is really the heart and core of the gospel.

The gospel is not primarily God's triumphant answer to human, social or emotional concerns. While believers in the gospel may help to bring enormous benefits to the world, the gospel's primary concern is to solve a much deeper problem. The gospel is primarily concerned with man's deepest problem and that is the problem of restoring man's ruptured relationship with his maker caused by sin. It is accomplished through the substitution of Jesus Christ as the propitiatory sacrifice to God for sin/sinners in order that true believers in Christ can have the sentence of condemnation forever lifted and removed from them. Propitiation forms the basis for our reconciliation with God and actually paves the way for additional, tremendous, blessings. Those, however, who in this life reject God will forever be rejected by God and must eternally suffer God's wrath themselves.

Propitiation is God's great gift of peace, forgiveness and hope to lost sinners. The peace that we gain with God as true believers through faith in the Lord Jesus Christ is primarily and fundamentally a new relationship of forgiveness and acceptance – and it stems from the propitiation of God by the sacrificial death of Jesus Christ. Propitiation, among other things, also highlights the infinite glory of God.

In the upper room, after Judas had gone out into the night to betray Jesus, Jesus said, "Now is the Son of Man glorified, and God is glorified in Him" (John 13:31). Our Lord Jesus Christ was facing His imminent death on the cross. He was thinking specifically of the atoning death, the "lifting up" on the cross which Judas had gone to precipitate. Satan had tried to keep Him from accomplishing God's will but Jesus had triumphed over him. Now, in the cross, the glory of God including His wisdom, power, righteousness, truth, and love have been supremely displayed by Jesus Christ in His making propitiation for our sins. Charles Wesley wrote the following beautiful lines and I love them.

> "Bearing shame and scoffing rude
> In my place condemned he stood;
> Sealed my partner with his blood;
> Hallelujah! What a Savior!"

The word "propitiation" only occurs four times in the New Testament, however, the concept is found everywhere in both the Old and the New Testament. The propitiating of God by means of an acceptable sacrifice is the essence of what Jesus was doing when He became our substitute on the cross.

Permit me to include one more piece of hymnody before I conclude this chapter. John Newton, the famous author of *Amazing Grace* also wrote these lines:

> I saw one hanging on a tree
> In agony and blood
> He fixed His languid eyes on me
> As near His cross I stood.
>
> Surely, never till my latest breath
> Will I forget that look,
> He seemed to charge me with His death
> Though not a word He spoke.
>
> My conscience felt and owned the guilt,
> It plunged me in despair.
> I saw my sins His blood had spilt,
> And helped to nail Him there.
>
> Another look He gave which said
> I freely all forgive.
> This blood is for thy ransom paid,
> I died that thou mayest live!

BEFORE WE GO ANY FURTHER...

An Invitation & Strong Encouragement

Do these words ring true in your own experience of faith? It is not too late to trust in Jesus Christ for salvation. If you have not already done so I implore you to act immediately. Run to Christ for safety. Trust Jesus as the propitiation for your sins and as your King and master.

As I write these words, it is September 2017 and hurricane Irma is rapidly descending upon the state of Florida with its savage, unprecedented, record-breaking winds, drenching rains, and flood surges. Gov. Rick Scott has been doing a fantastic job of getting the citizens and resources of Florida situated to successfully endure and survive this meteorological onslaught. He has repeatedly appealed to the citizenry of Florida to take this horrible, murderous storm seriously and to evacuate before it is too late to do so. Now the storm is just about to crash into the mainland of Florida and swallow the entire state in its awful and massive maw. Gov. Scott has ushered one last appeal to those who are still holding out with a view to riding out the storm. He said, This may be your last chance to make a good decision.

I want to address you, the reader, who may not yet have sought refuge in Jesus Christ. Be assured that the inevitable, unprecedented, storm of the wrath of God will descend on all unbelievers. This may be your last chance to make a good decision. Don't pass it up. Don't ignore your danger. Jesus Christ is the only place of safety.

Jesus Christ lovingly and willingly substituted Himself for His sinful and hell deserving people. He paid their entire debt and absorbed the full punishment of God that was due to them. His substitution was not simply a provisionary payment but he was the real, actual, effectual payment that forever secured their salvation. It was a payment that paid the price and secured the salvation of His people.

The Holy Spirit Prepares the Way

But how did the eternal God of the ages acquire a human body to fulfill this role of sacrificial substitution? The answer is found in Matthew's gospel, "Now the birth of Jesus Christ took place in this way. When His mother Mary had been betrothed to Joseph, before they came together she was found to be with child from the Holy Spirit" (Matthew 1:18). There was no divinely acceptable human sacrifice in existence until the Holy Spirit stepped in and changed the picture. He (the Holy Spirit) was instrumental in ensuring the formation of the body of our Lord Jesus Christ.

The Apostle Paul, in Romans 8:3 wrote *"For* what the law was powerless to do..." He uses the word "for" in order to further his logical argument. Each time Paul uses this word "for" in this section of Scripture he is stating another fact or logical step in his argument: *"For* the law of the Spirit of life has set you free in Christ... *"For* God has done what the law, weakened by the flesh, could not do." "For those who live according to the flesh set their minds on the things of the flesh..." *"For* to set the mind of the flesh is death… "*For* the mind that is set on the flesh is hostile to God…" "*For* it does not submit to God's law…" Paul's reasoning is airtight and totally convincing to the unbiased reader. He sets forth his argument with unassailable logic.

Paul's main point is to demonstrate that salvation is impossible by law keeping because of the innate weakness and sinfulness of our fallen character. The law is able to detect sin but not to defeat it. The law sometimes even stimulates the sinner toward sin. Like a bear hibernating in his cave sin lies dormant until the prodding of the law awakens it into action. Then, the sinful, rebellious, nature lashes out against the probing of the law. Paul will, later in this chapter, state that the fleshy mind is hostile to God. It is not subject to the law of God; indeed, it cannot be. The holy law of God, then, sometimes provokes the sinner in such a way that he lashes out in open rebellion to God's holy standards. On the other hand, salvation has been accomplished and provided by God Himself by utilizing the perfect sacrifice of His Son and the powerful ministry of the Holy Spirit. This whole process provides a picture of God's holy character, His deep love and commitment to sinners, His unfathomable wisdom, and His incredible omnipotence. Trusting in your flesh and hoping to be saved is like trusting your weight on a bruised reed. It is hopeless to lean your weight upon it and expect it to hold you up. Because the law is forced to use the weak and sinfully "bruised"/flawed tool of the human being to fulfill God's holy demands. The law could never be perfectly kept by any sinner.

Jesus Christ, on the other hand (by means of the ministry of the Holy Spirit), was virgin born and without sin. During His life on earth He obeyed the law of God perfectly being tempted in all points as we are, yet without sin. He then gave Himself as the perfect, sinless offering for sin on behalf of sinners. God sent His Son into the world for that purpose. According to the writer of Hebrews quoting from "Psalm 40:6 – 8, He sent his Son into the world in the following manner: "Sacrifices and offerings you have not desired, but a body have you prepared for me; in burnt offerings and sin offerings you have taken no pleasure. Then I said, 'Behold I have come to do your will, O God, as it is written of me in the scroll of the book.'" And in another place – "Since therefore the children share in flesh and blood, He Himself likewise partook of the same things, that through death He might destroy the one who has the power of death – that is, the devil" (Hebrews 10:5 – 7, 2:14).

Jesus Christ served as the willing and acceptable substitute for sinners and suffered in their place under the righteous wrath of a holy God who had been rightly offended by the disobedience and rebellion of these selfsame sinners. He vicariously paid for the sins of His people and suffered in their place. That is how God was able to achieve our salvation while still maintaining His righteous and holy standards.

All of this was made possible because the Holy Spirit stepped in and caused it to become a reality. The Holy Spirit was instrumental in producing the body of Jesus Christ so that our Lord could be made in the likeness of sinful flesh to serve as our substitute before God. Notice how careful Paul is in the selection of his words. He speaks of Jesus Christ being in the "*likeness* of sinful flesh." Jesus Christ had every human quality with the exception of sin, therefore, Jesus was made in the "likeness" of sinful flesh. "For our sake He (God) made Him (Christ) to be sin who knew no sin, so that in Him (Christ) we might become the righteousness of God" (2 Corinthians 5:21). God punished sin, but did so in a substitute (the substitute being the Lord Jesus Christ). Comparing the flawed and weak sacrifices of Old Testament animals to the perfect sacrifice of Jesus Christ for sinners on the cross the writer of Hebrews wrote, "For if the blood of goats and bulls, and the sprinkling of defiled persons with the ashes of a heifer, sanctify for the purification of the flesh, how much more will the blood of Christ, who through the eternal Spirit offered Himself without blemish to God, purify our conscience from dead works to serve the living God" (Hebrews 9:13 – 14).

The fact that Jesus Christ died for sinners to save them and protect them from the wrath of God reminds us of the passage of Scripture found in Psalm 91:4 which reads, "He will cover you with His pinions, and under His wings you shall find refuge: His faithfulness is a shield and buckler."

#1 Illustrating God's Sacrificial Protection of Believers

Once, not far from a mission station in the heart of Africa, a brush fire swept through the brush leaving death and desolation in its wake. After the fierce flames had subsided, the missionary took a walk down one of the trails surveying the terrible damage wrought everywhere by the fire. He noticed a nest by the side of a path that he was on. Enthroned on the remains of the scorched nest were the charred remains of a mother bird. Without much thought he kicked the nest with his foot and, to his astonishment, out from under the burned and blackened carcass there were baby chicks – still alive. This was a clear demonstration of a mother's love and ultimate sacrifice for her young. By instinct the mother bird had been moved to give her life for her brood. They had found refuge from the flames beneath her feathers.

In a very similar way, our salvation has been purchased by the willing sacrifice of Jesus Christ who served as our personal substitute shielding us from the flames of God's wrath and suffering them himself. He gave himself for us that we might live. That is precisely why for believers in Christ there is now, "no condemnation."

Hell is a real place. The sinner stands as a child of wrath, under the condemnation of a holy God who is offended at every sin and renders a just judgment. The sinner is condemned. As such, he faces the real pain of hell and the real absence of God. How does the sinner escape this predicament? There is only one possible way: By substitution through Jesus Christ.

#2 Illustrating God's Sacrificial Love For Believers

The story is told of a man who operated a drawbridge. At a certain time, each afternoon, he had to raise the bridge for a ferry boat then lower it quickly for a passenger train to cross that bridge at high-speed a few minutes later. One day the man's young son was visiting his father at work and decided to go down below to get a better look at the ferry as it passed. He was fascinated by the site. He was so fascinated that he did not watch carefully where he was going and fell into the giant gears of the bridge. He became caught in the gears and was helpless to free himself. The father saw what had happened but he knew that if he took time to free his son, the train would plunge into the river before the bridge could be lowered and all the passengers of the train would be killed. On the other hand, if he lowered the bridge to save the hundreds of passengers and crew members on the train, his son would be crushed to death by the gears. When he heard the trains whistle, he knew that it would soon reach the river and he knew what he had to do. He loved his son very much, and he did not know the people on the train at all. The sacrifice of his son for the sake of other people was an act of pure grace and mercy but he sacrificed his son for their sake and well-being.

God's grace and mercy towards sinners is even greater. His willingness to sacrifice the Lord Jesus Christ as the substitute for sinners who deserved nothing but condemnation is more than we could have hoped for. It was on the battlefield of the cross and the tomb that Jesus, the captain of our souls, won the battle and secured our salvation for all eternity. That is why for believers in Christ there is now, "no condemnation."

Prior to Sunday, June 18, 1815, hardly anyone had heard of a place called Waterloo. It was just a tiny village in the vast empire of France, but it was there that the Duke of Wellington on that fateful Sunday in June mastered the armies of Napoleon and changed the entire course of history for all the rest of time. Waterloo! It has assumed an importance in our thinking far larger than its actual size geographically. Why? It is because of what was accomplished there. Such is the nature of the cross and the empty tomb. It is almost inconceivable to think that our Lord Jesus Christ strode upon the battlefield of a sinful world and won our freedom from sin delivering us from its condemnation. But that is exactly what he did! Jesus Christ is the substitute for condemned sinners who will trust Him as their Lord and Savior. What a wonderful Savior! What a wonderful salvation!

None of this would have been possible without the person and work of the Holy Spirit. It was when the Holy Spirit became active in our salvation that the other pieces, necessary for our salvation, fell into place. But there is more – much more.

For millennia people had been waiting for the coming of the Messiah. They waited expectantly for Him to come. When He did come, however, He was largely rejected by all except a relatively small group of people. Finally, the Messiah was here and the disciples didn't want Him to leave. They wanted Him to stay to set up His kingdom and fulfill all prophecy bringing a culmination to all things.

The Promise of the Helper

It was the last evening that Jesus had with the disciples. They were gathered together meeting with the Lord Jesus in the Upper Room before He was taken to be crucified. It was then and there that Jesus said to them in so many words, I'm leaving, I'm going to go away, and you're not going to be able to get to me right now. But I'm going to tell you something, it is to your advantage that I go away. How could it possibly be to their advantage to have Him go away and leave them? They had waited so long for Him to be here and He had finally arrived. Now, He is telling them that He is going away. That would have been disconcerting to say the least. What they did not know, was that the Holy Spirit He was promising to send to them, would be instrumental and vital to them to help them successfully carry on the work of ministry that Jesus had left them in charge of. The Holy Spirit would be given not only to empower the apostles personally but He would also be given in order to convict sinners, regenerate sinners, grant faith and repentance for salvation, indwell and securely seal believers in salvation. In fact, without the Holy Spirit being given there would be no New Testament Scriptures, no New Testament church, no ability for lost sinners to repent and believe in Christ for salvation. What a wonderful salvation! It all is made possible because the Holy Spirit stepped in to apply the work of Jesus Christ to us. That is why for those who trust in Jesus Christ alone through faith alone for their salvation there is now, "no condemnation." Since God is for us he has freed us from the curse of condemnation and has given us the Holy Spirit to ensure that all aspects of our salvation would be accomplished. Hallelujah! God is for us!

The Results

In the epistle to the Romans, Paul has one major theme and that is teaching how sinners can become "righteous" before God through the Lord Jesus Christ alone, by faith alone and how such saved sinners are to live in righteousness. The first key to this process is justification by grace through faith alone based on the person and work of the Lord Jesus Christ alone. Paul is continually saying that the only way that men can be right with God is through faith alone in the Lord Jesus Christ alone. By utilizing this, the only true method of salvation, the law of God is satisfied and at the same time our lives as believers are forever changed by the Holy Spirit. Aren't you thankful that God is for us?

There is Much, Much More

In Romans chapter eight, the Apostle Paul continues his explanation of our freedom from divine condemnation by writing:

"In order that the righteous requirement of the law might be fully met in us, who walk not according to the flesh but according to the Spirit" (Romans 8:4).

The Apostle Paul states that two conjoined things are true of those who have experienced God's salvation in Christ. First, the righteous requirements of the law are fully met in us. Note that this verse that expresses the idea of "might be fully met" is passive in Greek. That is, someone else does it in us. The power for the Christian walk is the Holy Spirit – even though it is still our walk. The Apostle Paul underscores this idea in his letter to the Philippians. There, he wrote "work out your own salvation with fear and trembling, for it is God who works in you, both to will and to work for his good pleasure" (Philippians 2: 12b–13). Second, our lives now take on a different bent and direction and we no longer live according to the sinful nature as the dominant factor in our lives as we once did but now we live according to the Spirit. How is this possible? What rendered this change in us when we were converted? The answer to this question is that The Holy Spirit, through Christ, delivered us from condemnation but He has also changed our heart and the course of our lives in a practical sense.

At this point Paul is making the transition from talking about justification to talking about sanctification. The inevitable result of genuine justification (legal righteousness before God) is sanctification (actual, practical righteousness in life). The righteousness spoken of here, then, is not merely a forensic righteousness (one which successfully takes care of our bad record before God as sinners) but it is also an ongoing practical righteousness "in us" (A type of righteousness which actually transforms our character and conduct in a practical way). Our sanctification as believers is, of course, not yet a perfectly completed righteousness in the sense of making us sinless in our personal walk. It is, however, a personal, practical, powerful, perpetual pattern of righteousness played out in our lives.

It should be pointed out, that God does not free men from their sin for them to go on sinning with abandonment. The phrase "who do not live according to the flesh but according to the Spirit" is not an admonition but an apt statement of reality applicable for all believers. It is not a prescription for the saved person but a description of the saved person. Paul's words here are descriptive and not hortatory (this is not an exhortation to do this). Being "in the flesh" as a pattern of life is simply not a possibility for Christians – they are "in the Spirit." Paul is simply showing the powerful and profound influence of the Holy Spirit on our mind thus determining our choices and desires.

Notice that the Apostle Paul does not say that this is a possible option for true Christians but he indicates that this transition to a life of holiness is a standard reality for all true believers. Being delivered from condemnation is something which is true of all true Christians and the same certainty applies to the fact that we will not live according to the sinful nature but according to the Spirit. He is not merely saying that we ought not to live according to the sinful nature. Instead, Paul is affirming that the true believer will live as a pattern of life according to the Spirit. He is stating that such a kind of conduct is a standard reality for any and every true believer. When the Apostle Paul wrote to the Galatians concerning the nature of true salvation he said, "Who gave himself for our sins, to deliver us from this present evil age according to the will of God and our father: to whom be glory forever and ever, *Amen*" (Galatians 1:4 – 5). Notice that our Lord Jesus Christ intended that his sacrifice for us would deliver us *from this present evil world*. This is God's will. Our deliverance from sin begins right here and right now. Such a practical deliverance from sin is a distinguishing evidence of genuine salvation. The Greek preposition *kata* here represents the standard, "according to the standard of" – flesh or spirit.

How does all this operate? There is an old illustration of dog training: if you are walking the dog down a path and the path is strewn with bones, or if other dogs are around, something in the dog will trigger a response and cause it to be drawn away to the bones or to the other dogs, but a stern "No" from the master will make it possible for the dog to continue along the path (as long as the dog listens and looks up to follow the commands of the master). As Christians our desires and instincts are changed by the Holy Spirit but personal discipline is still required on our part to look to the master and obey his commands. As a rule, however, the Christian lives an overall pattern of life that is one of living in and striving to live in righteousness and walking according to the Holy Spirit's leading. If you are truly a Christian, that's what you do. To be sure, this is not an easy task. As Christians we will wrestle and struggle with sin. Be sure, there will be times when we fail to live righteously and we give into the temptation of sin. But these are temporary aberrations and not the normal pattern of our lives. That is why the Apostle Paul could write, "do not present your members to sin as instruments of unrighteousness, but present yourselves to God as those who have been brought from death to life, and your members to God as instruments of righteousness." Again, "for sin will have no dominion over you, since you are not under law but under grace" (Romans 6:13–14).

Notice, the Apostle Paul clearly states that *sin shall have no dominion over you*. Once again, I want to make it clear that this is a statement of fact for the true believer. Paul is referring to the overall life pattern of the believer. We have been given the spiritual horsepower to overcome sin by means of the help of the Holy Spirit. Sin cannot and will not have dominion over the believer as a way of life.

There are no exceptions. It is true that a Christian will struggle with sin. Hence, the apostles' admonition to offer our bodies as instruments of righteousness and not as instruments of sin. It is also true that the saved person can be overcome by sin for a temporary period of time but not for a lifetime. Those who continue to live in sin (even though they make a profession of faith and join a church) are still unsaved. Much that passes for salvation and spirituality in our superficial culture is spurious. Many who have a "know so" confidence in their salvation may need to go back and check on the reality of it.

Have you trusted by faith alone in Jesus Christ alone for salvation? Have you been genuinely changed by the Holy Spirit? One is not saved by sanctification but sanctification is an inevitable result of being saved. Later in chapter eight of Romans the apostle Pau writes, "For all who are led by the spirit of God are sons of God" (Romans 8:14). The righteous requirements of the law have not only been met for us by Christ but will be met in us as we live according to the Spirit. Sin once condemned us but through Jesus Christ sin is condemned. Once we could not live according to the requirements of the law of God but through the work of the Holy Spirit the requirements of the law of God are fully met in us. Since God is for us He creates us as new creatures in Christ yearning for holiness with a passionate desire to be Christlike.

Psalm 1

In Psalm 1, the psalmist describes the condition of the godly man and then contrasts it to the life and condition of the ungodly man. The description of the godly man is found in Psalm 1:1 – 3. The psalmist pictures the godly man as one who avoids the company and practice of sinners, who meditates and delights in the law of God, and who is spiritually stable, nourished, and fruitful. Having described the godly man, the psalmist now turns to contrast this picture with the ungodly man. This contrasting picture is found in Psalm 1:4 – 6. The psalmist writes, "The ungodly are not so." In the Septuagint version there is a much more targeted way of expressing the double negative of this verse: "not so the ungodly, not so." Unlike the godly man who is likened to a towering tree with roots deep in the soil, nourished by a constant stream of water, the ungodly is likened to the chaff which the wind drives away. The unsaved man is at the mercy of forces he does not see and which he cannot control.

But since God is for us, as believers, our character and conduct are vastly different than that of the person of the world.

In a recent hurricane in the Caribbean a ship found itself in desperate trouble. Its engines malfunctioned and thus it was impossible for the captain to control the bearing of the ship amid the howling winds and tempestuous seas. The ship was caught in the grip of a monster gale.

Imagine if there had been a rocky shore near where the ship floundered. The ship, being driven by wind and tide toward the jagged rocks, gripped by forces beyond its control, would have been headed straight for certain disaster. As it was, the ship sank in the horrendous winds and waves of the hurricane killing all who were aboard it.

Such are the forces at work in the life of the ungodly. They are satanic forces, forces controlled by "the prince of the power of the air, the spirit that is now at work in the children of disobedience." They are sinful forces. By means of the Bible the believer is able to access the black box of spiritual infidelity which is behind the curtain of spiritual ignorance. The Bible teaches the real truth. That at the core, sinful man is depraved and through culture is further directed to be disobedient to or indifferent to God. The unsaved man has been taught error by his education. He has been taught that all men are good at their core – including himself. He has been taught that society is basically good and that all religions are basically the same. What he cannot perceive is that there are invisible forces exerting incredible pressure on him in the direction of sin. These are forces that are driving him toward ungodliness.

The ungodly man flatters himself that he is the master of his own soul, the captain of his own destiny. But it is not so. He's being relentlessly driven. He is as powerless against these incredible forces as the chaff is before the wind. That is how God describes the ungodly.

Not only is the ungodly man driven by the invisible forces of sin and Satan, but he is also doomed to be judged by the holy God for each and every one of his sins. Think about it. If a sinner committed a sin only once each day that would be 365 sins per year or 3,650 sins per decade. Multiply that by the number of years in a lifetime and a tremendous number of sins would have to be accounted for and answered for. In truth, sinners sin many more times than one per day. Adam sinned one time and plunged mankind into a state of death and depravity. Imagine the awesome and frightening gravity of standing before God guilty of thousands of sins. No wonder that the psalmist wrote, "Therefore the ungodly shall not stand in the judgment, nor sinners in the congregation of the righteous" (Psalm 1:5).

The unsaved sinner has no standing and that will become very apparent in the Day of Judgment. He will be summoned to the great white throne only to find that heaven and the earth have fled away. Everything familiar and assuring will be gone. All that he has attempted to build, everything that he has invested his time and talents in, all that the things that he has trusted in, are suddenly gone. He has nowhere to stand. As Jesus warned, he has built his house upon the sand and the awesome judgment of God has swept it all away.

Britain's illustrious Queen Elizabeth launched the ships which smashed the power of Spain and saved England from the Roman Catholic Inquisition. She put Britain on the road to Empire and inaugurated a golden age. She reigned in pomp and splendor for 45 years. Though she claimed to be a staunch Protestant one wonders how much she really knew of the true salvation of God.

The historians tell us that she died, propped up on her throne, a haggard old woman of 70, frantically hanging on to life, desperately fighting off the last enemy. She did not want to be taken by death. Her last words have run down through the centuries of time: "All my possessions for a moment of time." But death came as it always does. There is an appointed time to die. Every person will die in the time and manner appointed by God. No matter how desperately the sinner tries to hang on to this earthly life, death will always come and usher them into an eternity where they have no ability to stand up under the judgment of God. The ungodly are not only driven by unseen forces of sin and Satan but they are also doomed as they face death and the certain judgment of God.

Finally, the ungodly are also damned (Psalm 1:6). "For the Lord knows the way of the righteous; but the wicked shall perish." Notice that God classifies those who are not righteous as being wicked. There are only two ways — two options available to the sinner. As Jesus taught, there is the narrow way that leads to life everlasting and there is the broad way that leads to destruction. There is the way of the cross that leads by Calvary to glory. And there is a way of curse that leads to a lost eternity.

By nature, the ungodly man is on the broad way, the way of the curse. He lives as a condemned person awaiting a certain, fearful, future. Thanks be to God's grace, humanly speaking and with God's enablement, it is possible for a sinner, by a deliberate choice to make the change from one way to the other way. How? We come to Jesus, "the way, the truth, the life," the one who says, 'No man comes to the Father but by Me.' We receive Jesus Christ as our Lord and Savior and become numbered with the godly rather than the ungodly. We are no longer driven but directed. We are no longer doomed but delivered. We are no longer damned but look forward to the delight of heaven. For such people there is now, "no condemnation." To be sure, if any sinner chooses this path it is because of God's drawing and grace. Why do some choose to follow Christ? Because God is for us!

Our Return to Our Initial Illustration

The prisoner finally turned the corner after walking down the long hallway and he entered the execution chamber. The remaining moments left are few. His fears are many. He is strapped down for final, lethal execution and led in his last prayer. Then, just before he is executed the phone on the wall rings. It is the governor and the governor has issued a last-minute pardon for the guilty and condemned prisoner. There is a stay of the execution. In fact, there is a permanent dismissal of the order of condemnation and execution relative to the prisoner.

Can you just imagine the inexpressible joy, the astounding relief, the exhilaration and a sense of overwhelming gratitude that the prisoner would feel upon learning that there is therefore now no condemnation for him?

Allow your imagination to run free for a moment. Let us imagine that the governor is a multi – billionaire. Let us further imagine that he is a man who is incredibly loving and generous. Let us imagine that he not only issues a pardon for the prisoner but he also adopts him into his own family and gives him all the rights of an heir to his vast fortune. I know this sounds fanciful and beyond the possibility of reality but just pretend with me for a moment. Let us also imagine that this governor somehow has the means of radically changing the criminal's heart and mind so that his wicked tendencies are now replaced by a thirst for righteousness. Let us imagine that the criminal is made into a new and positive person, free from guilt and condemnation, filled with thankfulness toward his new benefactor, forever changed in heart, mind, and behavior. He is now deeply grateful and desirous of living a positive life of gratitude and goodness. Wouldn't that be wonderful?

Now, think of your own salvation in those terms – with one critical exception. In the spiritual realm your sins and their penalty must be fully paid for. It is not possible for you merely to be pardoned without such a payment because God is a just God and must punish sin. It is at this point that the entire Trinitarian Godhead undertakes to do that which is necessary to save sinners from condemnation to glorification. God lovingly gives us His son to be our Savior. Jesus Christ lovingly inserts himself into the realm of pain and suffering by bearing the sinners penalty in his own body on the cross. He becomes the believers substitute. The Holy Spirit steps in and makes sure that our salvation is perfectly secured and paid for and that it is applied to us personally and savingly. What a wonderful salvation! What a glorious thing it is that God is for us!

Who do we have to thank for this wonderful salvation and our deliverance from sin and its condemnation? We have the triune God to thank! We have the Lord Jesus Christ to thank for paying our penalty due to our sin.

On the other hand, by way of illustration, I want to point you to a real-life occurrence that took place on July 17, 2017 in Arizona. A family was happily celebrating a birthday near the Gold Springs swimming hole on Saturday afternoon when heavy rains from upstream caused a flash flood to come rushing down the canyon/arroyo and suddenly, without warning it engulfed and swept away the entire family. In a moment death came without warning. Happiness evaporated on the spot. Eternity was entered at an unexpected time but, nevertheless, their condition and state in eternity is permanently fixed forever. Recent brushfires had destroyed all the vegetation along the sides of the river. There was nothing to keep the deluge of water from running unimpeded down into the river. The rainstorm actually occurred eight miles upstream. By the time the unsuspecting family was aware of their danger they merely heard a tremendous roar and looking up saw a forty-foot-wide torrent of water that was six feet high. It was relentlessly rushing directly towards them. As soon as they heard the thunderous roar it was upon them – and it was too late to escape. There was no escape. The torrential rushing water had uprooted trees, dislodged boulders, and swept away everything in its path. There was no escape and at least nine family members died that day. In the aftermath of the raging river dead bodies were strewn everywhere and mud and rocks were left in its wake.

God's judgment for the unsaved will occur somewhat like that. In John's Gospel we read, "Whoever believes in the son has eternal life; whoever does not obey the Son shall not see life, but the wrath of God remains on him" (John 3:36). It is clear from this verse that the wrath of God toward the nonbeliever in Christ already perches over the unsaved person. He is already condemned and only the grace of God withholds the immediate carrying out of the sentence of that condemnation.

I certainly do not mean to imply anything regarding the spiritual condition of those dear people who suffered this great tragedy. I do not know anything about whether they were believers in Christ or not. I'm merely using this current event to illustrate how rapidly and decisively God's wrath will one day descend eternally upon the ungodly.

Paul confronted unbelievers with their defiance of God even despite God's repeated kindness to them and he declares that they were storing up wrath for themselves (the word for storing up means to treasure up or stockpile) This reminds us that there is a coming day when God's righteous judgment will be revealed in all its fierceness and all of this treasured up wrath will come crashing down upon the unsaved without further warning. Like the flood victims, they may hear the roar immediately before the wrath of God is upon them but there will be no escape and no second chances.

Eternity is an awful long time to be wrong. Those condemned will experience the full wrath of a righteous God who will exact retribution upon those who refused to repent. They considered the precious Son of God to be someone that they could be indifferent to and ignore, reject and spurn, and even curse and mock. Perhaps they heard the message of the gospel but merely treated it with indifference and defiance and delayed obeying it for a more opportune time. Such are the condemned and they will remain condemned for all eternity under the Almighty wrath of a righteous God. There will be no end to their condemnation and no second chances. That is a truly frightening perspective! Thank God, for the believer no such frightful future awaits them. Why? We are safe and secure since God is for us. For that one in Christ there is no condemnation – either now or ever.

Aren't you glad that God has not shrouded the precious and powerful gospel of salvation in mystery but has made it abundantly clear and open for all? Are you glad to know that since God is for you, you are safe for all eternity?

There is a story about an English gentleman named Alfie. Alfie could do nothing right. He boggled everything he ever touched. One day in a moment of deep despair and desperation, he tried to take his own life. He failed at that, too. While he was in the hospital, a friend came to visit. The friend asked, "Alfie, why did you do it?" And Alfie responded, "Because there is no good news anywhere. There just can't be any good news anywhere. Because, if there was, surely someone would have come running to me to share it with me." (From a sermon by Eric Ritz)

If you watch the evening news broadcasts you may conclude that Alfie was correct and that there is nothing but bad news. Thankfully, the Bible tells us that there is good news for those who will believe in Jesus Christ as Lord and Savior. This good news is crystal clear and unmistakable.

We are now entering a particularly glorious section of Scripture. Unfortunately, this section of Scripture has also been viewed as being controversial by some and they have suggested repeatedly that preachers and Christians should steer clear of teaching these biblical truths because they might be misunderstood, abused or even found to be offensive to some who hold to an alternative doctrinal position. The Apostle Paul begins this section of Scripture by dealing with God's foreknowledge, God's calling sinners to salvation, God's predestination of those who are elected by Him for eternal salvation, etc. I want to encourage you, the reader, to focus your *entire attention on the explanation of this wonderful section of* Scripture. The story is told of a man who showed up at church with his ears painfully blistered. After the service, his concerned pastor asked, "What in the world happened to you?" The man replied, "I was lying on the couch yesterday afternoon watching a ball game on TV and my wife was ironing nearby. I was totally engrossed in the game when she left the room, leaving the iron near the phone. The phone rang and keeping my eyes glued to the television, I grabbed the hot iron and put it to my ear." "So how did the other ear get burned?" The pastor asked. "Well, I had no more than hung up and the guy called again." (*Country*, October – November 1994, page 45, "overheard at the Country Café," Bill Teweles). Now there, my friend, is a man who was focused. The best way to understand this section of Scripture is to focus your whole attention on it. Rivet your thinking to the specific revelation that the Apostle Paul gives us and you will come away with a clear understanding of this precious part of the perfect package of salvation that God has constructed for us.

There Is No Mystery

God has been very clear regarding the gospel. In fact, the biblical communication regarding the gospel has been crystal clear and unmistakable so that it can be understood by one and all.

NEWSWEEK cited a humorous historical footnote that reveals how easily communications can be garbled. Perhaps you remember that famous speech or remember reading about the speech given by Pres. John F. Kennedy at the Berlin wall in 1963. He ended the speech by saying, "Ich bin ein Berliner." Literally that translates to "I am a Berliner," but according to Newsweek, and the German vernacular it really translates as "I am a jelly doughnut."

I live near Charlotte, North Carolina and I have become interested in North Carolina history. In 1590 John White, who had established a colony on Roanoke Island three years prior, returned to Roanoke Island only to find that the colony had vanished. The only thing left was a carved inscription on a wooden post that read, "Croatoan." God has been very clear regarding the gospel. In fact, the biblical communication regarding the gospel has been crystal clear and unmistakable so that it can be understood by one and all.

Thank God, the way of salvation is not an ongoing mystery. The Bible has clearly revealed that salvation is by God's grace through faith alone in Jesus Christ alone. Salvation is achieved by the acceptable blood sacrifice of Jesus Christ for sinners. The Lord Jesus Christ said, "I am the way, and the truth, and the life. No one comes to the Father except through me" (John 14:6). The Apostle Peter also underscored this essential truth when he said, "There is salvation in no one else, for there is no other name under heaven given among men by which we must be saved" (Acts 4:12). There is no mystery about the message of the gospel. We are not left to speculate and guess regarding the method by which God has chosen to save sinners.

One of the greatest minds of all time belonged to Albert Einstein. His theory of relativity gave us the atomic age. He reduced the complexity of the universe to the deceptively simple formula E= MC2. Many books have been written to explain the mysteries of relativity. The theory, however, is not a simple one; it's mathematics are so complex that it is only understood by a small contingent of the scientific community. One person asked if it were true that only three people really understood the subject, a prominent scientist jokingly replied, "I'm trying to think who the third person is."

The tragic reality is that Einstein was insensitive and unreceptive to spiritual truth. Asked by a rabbi if he believed in God, Einstein replied, "I believe in Spinoza's God who reveals himself in the orderly harmony of all that exists, not in the God who concerns himself with fates and the actions of human beings." (*Time* February 1979, page 76). Einstein declared that the universe, "could not operate on chance." But, still, he did not know God. God and the way of salvation remained a mystery to him. For all his brilliance, he missed the most important facts of all, the greatest truths discoverable. There is no real mystery to the nature of the gospel since God has made it abundantly clear, nevertheless, he was blinded by his sin and it remained a mystery to him. He needed to be born again but apparently never was. Are you?

Some agnostics ridicule Christians by pointing to the moral chaos of the world and saying, "if your God made the world, He did a very poor job of it." "It is a mystery to me how anyone with a brain could, therefore, believe in your God."

A simple response to such people could be: Suppose a man bought a complex piece of machinery. When it was installed he was given an operator's manual and warned to read it and to follow the instructions carefully because the manufacturer's liability and warranty would be voided if he did not do so. Instead of following these simple and yet critical instructions and reading the manual, however, he threw it away, saying that he was not going to be told how to run this equipment. So, he went ahead and did it his way. He ended up ruining the machine. Then he blamed the manufacturer for making such a poor piece of junk and charging such an enormous price for it. This is just what men do regarding God. When God made the world, He sent along some instructions as to how things should be done but in arrogance men have refused to read God's manual, the Bible, and follow its instructions. Unsaved people (whether agnostics or whatever) are correct in asserting that things are in terrible shape in this world, but they don't need to blame God. They need to blame themselves. God has removed all the mystery regarding the gospel and salvation. It is man's responsibility to read and follow God's simple instructions to be saved and restored to a right relationship with Him.

If you travel to Hickory, North Carolina you will find street signs that may seem somewhat confusing. For example, you may see the following on various streets signs: 7th Avenue Pl., NW, 7th Avenue NW, 7th St., Drive SE, 7th Street Court, and so on. These are all completely different streets. In 1951, city leaders divided Hickory into four quadrants and began renaming its roads to make addresses easier to find on a map. If you get one letter or number wrong, however, it may well take you to places in Hickory that you never knew existed.

God, however, has not confused us with a conundrum of changing directions regarding how to be saved. He has not shrouded salvation in mystery and intrigue. God has clearly revealed to sinners the fact that they must be saved but God also has clearly revealed exactly and precisely how they must be saved. What a gracious God! What a wonderful salvation he has granted us in freeing us from the condemnation of sin! Since God is for us we can never be condemned.

The End Will Surely Come

Some people foolishly postpone seeking after God and salvation thinking that their lives will somehow go on without end and they will not have to answer for their sinfulness. What a foolish assumption. The statistics are overwhelmingly impressive. One out of one person dies. Death is inevitable just as facing God in judgment is inevitable.

In Charlotte, NC there is a neighborhood known as Myers Park. It is a beautiful section of the city. Back in 1916 it was a treeless cotton farm that sat just outside the city limits. At that time, a young landscape architect just out of Harvard came to town. His name was John Nolen and he was a disciple of Frederick Law Olmsted who designed the grounds of Biltmore estate, Central Park in New York, and Boston's Emerald Necklace park system. The developer of Myers Park, George Stevens, gave Nolen carte blanche when it came to creating something different on the farm of Jonathan Springs Myers. Consequently, Nolen drew up a plan for sweeping roadways and side–streets that curved to match the gentle topography. He varied the size of the lots and filled the area with ample green spaces of grass and trees. It was Nolen's dream to fill his neighborhood with young oaks that would grow up to majestically tower over the stately homes and spacious streets below.

In 1916, workers plucked trees from creek beds and delivered them on carts pulled by mules to transport them to Myers Park. There they were planted upright along the roadways, in the wide medians, in front yards, and along empty green spaces. All kinds of trees were planted (Elm, tulip, etc.) but the predominant tree used was the Willow Oak. The Willow Oak would grow to be tall and elegant, well-suited to thrive even in a city environment. Its small leaves would not clog the drainage and so it was deemed perfect for Myers Park.

Over time, people moved into Myers Park and the trees slowly grew. Meanwhile, Charlotte's city limits pushed outward. Myers Park eventually became an affluent neighborhood with beautiful mansions and towering trees. Today the stately Willow Oaks tower above the houses and yards and streets of Myers Park. They form a lush tunnel of green beauty with their branches reaching out to touch each other enclosing the streets below in a sort of natural, verdant umbrella. It is a beautiful area to drive through. Looking at the beautiful trees which are a key ingredient of Charlotte's attractiveness one would think and hope that they will go on living forever. Sadly, such is not the case. The lifespan of a Willow Oak is about one hundred years. They are even now in the process of reaching the extended limit of their lifespan and already there is a natural thinning-out process taking place among the beautiful canopy of trees in Myers Park.

Everything on this earth has a lifespan. Every child born is figuratively tattooed at birth with the words, "mortal," on his forehead. It is appointed unto man once to die and then to stand before God in judgment. As I have previously stated, what many sinners do not realize is that they are living on borrowed time. Indeed, they have already been condemned by their sin and God's justice demands that they pay for it eternally. It is only the present patience and grace of God that currently withholds the execution of the sinner's condemnation. God is being patient and long-suffering while He continues to graciously offer the unbelieving sinner salvation from his dire predicament. But for the true believer the sentence of condemnation has been removed already and forever through Christ. No true believer will ever be condemned. "There is therefore now no condemnation for those that are in Christ Jesus…"

Those who are sport fans have undoubtedly noticed those big Scripture signs at significant sporting events: the Super Bowl, Monday Night Football and Baseball, golf tournaments, the Olympics, the Indy 500, etc. in bold letters the signs read "JOHN 3:16," "II COR. 5:17," or "ROM 5:8" These large signs pop up on bedsheets hanging from the upper decks, behind home plate, near professional golfers as they putt, and even on posters beside the Miss America Pageant runway.

The signs are the work of a man named Rockin' Rollen Stewart; his wife, Margaret; and a friend, William King. They drive approximately 55,000 miles per year and speak to numerous religious groups. They receive support from law officers which they then use to buy tickets from scalpers to gain admittance to the sports events. Then, with a handheld television, they get in line with the right camera. It seems that Rollen Stewart was once addicted to alcohol and drugs. The addiction was so bad that it was choking the life out of him. Indeed, his life fell apart! When the Lord saved him, he started pursuing every biblical avenue that he knew. One Sunday morning he was watching a worship service on TV. While watching the service, he was struck with the idea that he could take the Word of God to the world using TV. He needed to figure out a way that he could do it free of commercial costs and what he came up with was this ministry that I have previously described.

It's true that Rockin' Rollen's method of communicating the good news is not the same as mine or perhaps yours but you have to admire his determination.

God has made the gospel message crystal clear and entrusted its communication to the world to his people.

Rollen was quoted in *PEOPLE* magazine saying, "We are evangelists who want to get everyone to read the Book, and we reach millions."

We need to get the "Good News" to the unsaved world!

No wonder Christians revel in and celebrate their full and total freedom from all condemnation through Christ Jesus their Lord. When you meditate on the fact that God is for you does this not kindle within you a strong passion and love for that God who has secured your freedom from condemnation and has secured your ultimate glory in heaven? Does this not also give you an added sense of confidence in the fact that God is for you regardless of what circumstances of life you may be called upon to face?

Consider the words of the hymn writer who wrote many years ago regarding this very subject:

"THERE IS A FOUNTAIN FILLED WITH BLOOD" By William Cowper

> There is a fountain filled with blood,
> Drawn from Emmanuel's veins,
> And sinners plunged beneath that flood,
> Lose all their guilty stains…"

Thank God, with me, there is now, "no condemnation for those that are in Christ Jesus." Hallelujah!

BRINGING IT HOME

1. Have you experienced this wonderful freedom from sin and sin's condemnation? Would you like to? Then look to Christ by faith alone and embrace Him as your Lord and Savior. Trust in Him and obey Him.

2. How has your worship of God been affected by the gratitude that ought to attend one who has been powerfully, graciously, and eternally delivered from condemnation to a consecrated life of godliness and an eternity filled with the riches of God?

3. Do you consistently share the "good news" of this wonderful salvation with others who have yet to experience it? What are some of the key elements that you must keep in mind when you share the gospel with the unsaved?

4. What part does each of the three members of the Trinitarian Godhead play in the salvation of lost sinners? What difference does it make in your thinking and feeling to know that God is for you?

WHAT A WONDERFUL SALVATION WE HAVE!
THERE IS NOW "NO CONDEMNATION FOR
THOSE WHO ARE IN CHRIST JESUS."

3

Since God is for Us there is

NO DOMINATION

Romans 8:5–9a

"For those who live according to the flesh set their minds on the things of the flesh, but those who live according to the Spirit set their minds on the things of the Spirit. To set the mind on the flesh is death, but to set the mind on the Spirit is life and peace. For the mind that is set on the flesh is hostile to God, for it does not submit to God's law, indeed, it cannot. Those who are in the flesh cannot please God" (Romans 8:5 – 9a).

The Apostle Paul moves us, his readers, along in our tour of our wonderful salvation. He continually emphasizes that this wonderful and perfect salvation that we have as believers has been accomplished for us entirely by the perfect and powerful work of our gracious God. Every stage of our salvation is accomplished by God alone. Because of this, we can rest assured that our salvation is perfect and it is being powerfully worked out in our lives. In this second stop along the tour the apostle tells us that God has not only freed us from the condemnation of sin but God has also changed our fundamental nature so that we now have the mindset (bent of mind) to seek the things of the Spirit rather than the things of the flesh. The salvation that God grants those in Christ, changes our character and conduct enabling us to live in such a way as to please God.

This passage introduces us to the subject of sanctification. Perhaps no other biblical doctrine has been more ignored in today's culture than that of sanctification.

In Galatians 4:19–20 the Apostle Paul expresses his perplexity and deep concern for the churches of Galatia.

Paul had devoted his life, at great risk, to establish the churches in Galatia. He had preached the gospel to them and they had received the true gospel by faith. He had established Christian churches in this formally pagan environment. Like a pregnant woman, Paul had endured the agonies of ministering the gospel to them until they finally believed and had been born into the kingdom of light. Paul had labored intensely to see that happen. The Galatians are now not only God's children but also, in a very real way, Paul's children. Now, because of their vacillating, double-minded erring from the proper path, Paul feels like a mother who is unnaturally being subjected to the travails of labor, once again, to see Christ formed in the Galatian Christians.

Those to whom he wrote were Christians. They had begun in the Spirit (Galatians 3:1). Heretical teachers, however, had adversely influenced them and they were stalled in their spiritual progress.

Paul is feeling pain and perplexity as he contemplates how to see Christ formed in them again. He says that he would like to come and interact with them personally and perhaps more tenderly than his written communications allowed him to do.

These Christians are a great burden on the apostle's heart because his earnest desire is to see Christ formed in them and that component of their salvation is desperately lacking. What they lacked was a full and robust sanctification.

Sanctification is a glorious word. This theological/biblical word is familiar to most Christians. It means to be separate. Holy is a synonym of sanctification. The idea is that the Christian is separated from the world and sin and separated unto God and righteousness. The doctrine of sanctification has become unpopular in our time.

In recent years there has been a resurgence of interest in the biblical doctrine of election. The divine sovereign selection of sinners to salvation before the foundation of the world is a very precious truth which has been embraced wholeheartedly by many in our day. Praise God for that!

The wonderful doctrine of justification by faith is also a very popular and much emphasized biblical truth. The fact that sinners are saved from their sin by faith in Jesus Christ alone is a truth often heard from the pulpits of our churches.

Occasionally, though not nearly as often as we might like, the biblical truth of glorification is highlighted in our churches. The glorious hope of heaven where we will live in a world of joy, worship, love, and service to God is not taught enough but it is referred to from time to time.

But, the present-day church seems to be mute when it comes to the subject of sanctification. Nothing is more important for us to understand, however, than this work of sanctification. And yet the truth of sanctification is commonly treated with indifference and it is ignored by many preachers. The fact is, some preachers even attack the concept of sanctification. Most, however, just ignore it.

Sanctification is what defines the work of the Spirit in our lives. In terms of time, it comes between justification and glorification. Whereas divine election took place before the foundation of the world, and justification takes place at a point in time when we believe in Christ, and glorification is yet future– sanctification covers the entire scope of our lives from the moment we believe until the time that we are taken to heaven. If there is any doctrine/truth that we ought to know, understand, and be totally committed to it is the doctrine of sanctification. This is what Paul was referring to when he said, "For those who live according to the flesh set their minds on the things of the flesh, but those who live according to the Spirit set their minds on the things of the Spirit. For to set the mind on the flesh is death, but to set the mind on the Spirit is life and peace. For the mind that is set on the flesh is hostile to God, for it does not submit to God's law; indeed, it cannot. Those who are in the flesh cannot please God. You, however, are not in the flesh but in the Spirit, if in fact the Spirit of God dwells in you. Anyone who does not have the Spirit of Christ does not belong to him" (Romans 8:5-9).

Sanctification relates to all the other doctrines of Scripture that describe our salvation. God has chosen us to be holy. He has predestined us to be holy and conformed to the image of Jesus Christ. As our justification was accomplished when the Holy Spirit gave us faith to believe so our sanctification is accomplished by the powerful work of the Holy Spirit. In terms of our glorification, that will be the time when we are perfectly sanctified and free of sin. Sanctification is therefore directly connected with every stage of our salvation.

God did not declare us to be righteous only to be indifferent as to whether or not we actually live righteously.

As we consider the subject of sanctification as it is discussed in our text allow me to suggest that we briefly look at it under six headings. They are:

1. The Meaning
2. The Miracle
3. The Main Importance
4. The Means
5. The Missing of the Mark
   A. Sanctification
   B. Justification
6. The Major Goal

1. *The Meaning* – We have already pointed out that sanctification means separation and is synonymous with being made holy.
2. *The Miracle* - I well remember what my life was like prior to being saved. I had no inclination toward spiritual matters. I indulged in sin wholeheartedly. I valued material things over spiritual things. I had a general distaste or indifference for the things of God. The Bible was never consulted and prayer was only resorted to as a means to try to acquire some earthly pleasure or to escape some difficult situation. Then God saved me.

The immediate result was dramatic. God changed my heart and mind. Whereas I once ignored or rebelled against God now I yearned to understand God's will so that I could submit to God. Whereas I once ignored the Bible, now I wanted to constantly read and understand it. Whereas I previously plunged into sin wholeheartedly, I now viewed sin with distaste and hungered and thirsted after righteousness. Now, I valued spiritual things more than material things. Prayer came as natural as breathing and my prayers were less self-centered and more concerned with the glory of God.

A miracle of grace had taken place in my life separating me from what I had once been and separating me to God.

This kind of miracle can be seen in the life of the Apostle Paul. In short order, Paul was transformed from a hater of Christ to a lover of Christ. He was changed from a rabid persecutor of Christians to a real lover of Christians. America will of grace had taken place in Paul's heart.

That is what Paul is talking about in our text. He is saying that all of those who are genuinely saved and free of condemnation are also genuinely changed and free of the domination of sin. In other words, they are being sanctified. Not only does God impute His righteousness to the believer, but He also imposes His righteousness to the true believer

All who have been saved can attest to the fact that God performed a miracle of grace in their lives which dramatically changed them from the inside out. Just as God ordained our justification as believers so He ordained our sanctification as well. Most Christians are familiar with Ephesians 2:8–9. But, it is instructive to go on and read the next verse. In verse 10 the apostle continues his thought regarding salvation by grace and he says "We are his workmanship/masterpiece created by God…. Notice that those who are saved are saved by grace. They are not saved *because* of good works, but they are saved *for* good works. In fact, Paul says that God has ordained that those who are saved by grace will walk in good works. This is sanctification and it is ordained for the Christian as surely as is justification.

3. *The Main Importance of Sanctification-* Allow me to merely cite some of the passages in the Bible that point out the main importance of sanctification.

    A. 1 Thessalonians 3:12–13 "And may the Lord make you increase and abound in love for one another and for all, as we do for you, so that He may establish your hearts blameless in holiness before our God and Father.

    B. 1 Thessalonians 4:3–4 "For you know what instructions we gave you through the Lord Jesus, for this is the will of God, your sanctification: that you abstain from sexual immorality; that each one of you know how to control his own body in holiness and honor, not in the passion of lust like the Gentiles who do not know God."

C. 2 Thessalonians 2:13 "But we ought always to give thanks to God for you, brothers beloved by the Lord, because God chose you as the first fruits to be saved, through sanctification by the spirit and belief of the truth."

D. Titus 2:14 "For the grace of God has appeared, bringing salvation for all people, training us to renounce ungodliness and worldly passions, and to live self-controlled, upright, and godly lives in the present age…"

E. Hebrews 12:14 "Strive for peace with everyone, and for the holiness without which no one will see the Lord."

4. *The Means of Sanctification*-The Lord Jesus Christ prayed in John 17:17 "Sanctify them in the truth. Your word is truth." It is obvious, from this verse, that God's Word is a tool that we use to develop our sanctification but how does this process operate? Are we sanctified by reading the commandments over and over? Or are we sanctified if we merely work up enough willpower and exercise enough discipline to force ourselves to obey the commandments of God? Is that how sanctification works?

Salvation is a work of the Holy Spirit. Justification is a work of the Holy Spirit but not without means. We are justified by means of faith in Christ. Likewise, sanctification is a work of the Holy Spirit but not without means. We are sanctified by means of loving obedience to the Word of God and to the Lord Jesus Christ. This obedience is not merely a matter of raw discipline but it is a matter of real delight. Our Lord said, "If you love me keep my commandments. Whoever keeps my commandments loves me."

Sanctification comes from learning to love Christ more and, in light of that love, to obey Christ more fully. The more we love Christ, the more we will pursue obedience to His commandments and be sanctified.

The unconverted don't love Christ. In fact, they are hostile to Christ and, if pressed, they will indicate that they actually hate Christ and the things of God. Romans 8:7 reads "For the mind that is set on the flesh is hostile to God, for it does not submit to God's law; indeed, it cannot."

When we think of sanctification we must not think of it in terms of half measures. We must not ask ourselves how much sin we can get away with and still be okay. Sanctification involves our vision of Christ's perfect life as our supreme role model. It involves our earnest desire to pursue this kind of sanctification that our Lord Jesus Christ evidenced. It is when we desire to be conformed to the image of Jesus Christ that sanctification really begins to take hold.

Obedience to God's will is that which marked the life of Jesus Christ. He willingly obeyed the Father and He, among all human beings, is the most sanctified of all people. He denied Himself and delighted to do the will of God.

How does one grow in love to Christ to become more obedient? "And we all, with unveiled face, beholding the glory of the Lord, are being transformed into the same image from one degree of glory to another. For this comes from the Lord who is the Spirit" (2 Corinthians 3:18).

As we continue to gaze on the glory of the Lord, the Holy Spirit uses this constant vision as a means to help us to be transformed to increasing levels of glory. This is sanctification. This is what we must do to be sanctified. This constant gazing on God's glory will move us to repent of our sin and to aspire to be more like Christ in holiness.

5. *The Missing of the Mark*
   A. Sanctification

There was a time in the history of the church when preachers preached on holiness and sanctification regularly. They preached on virtue and resisting sin. They called Christians to walk in holiness and it mattered to people how you lived and how you thought and how you talked and how you conducted yourself in such a way as to honor and glorify the Lord.

Sadly, that is seldom true in today's church. The emphasis on holiness, godliness and sanctification is fast disappearing from popular Christianity. Some popular preachers never speak of sin and never call Christians to a life of real holiness. They studiously avoid talking about separation from the world, self-denial, and resisting the temptation to sin. Instead, the contemporary church now offers God up as the one who is waiting to fulfill everyone's desires. People are encouraged to seek God for the fulfillment of the longings of their selfish hearts and this new concept is being repackaged as "spirituality."

Churches are accommodating the message of the gospel to the world so that the things of the world are incorporated into the church. In that way, the church has become full of people attempting to satisfy the longings of their fallen human hearts in the name of religion. Consequently, the church looks more and more worldly, more people centered and more likely to import the sinful culture, the fashion of the world, and the value system of the world into its embrace.

Consider the following along this line of thought: In his unsaved condition the lost sinner is dominated by the desire to sin. Those who have made a superficial, spurious decision for Christ are still dominated by sin. After the Los Angeles riots, Steve Futterman of CBC radio broadcasted an interview he had with one of the many looters. One man had been interviewed among the many people who had looted a record store. When asked what he has stolen, the man replied, "Gospel tapes, I love Jesus." ("Quotes and Comments," *The United Church Observer*, September 1992, p. 48).

By contrast, the church is supposed to look like Christ in the world. Yet, the church of today is fraught with sordid scandals, theological/ biblical errors, and people who have a lukewarm, lackluster attachment to external or emotionalized religion.

In times past, the church was God centered. It was Christ centered. People trusted God for the growth of the church rather than resorting to slick marketing techniques. Churches opposed sin and worldliness of every type.

New churches today to often tend to be non-theological and non-biblical. They are emotionally driven, sociologically minded and purveyors of modern psychology in the place of biblical truth. Further, many churches have exchanged transcendence for imminence. God is no longer revered and extolled but rather He is regarded as a friend and or lover. Worship has been redefined as a mindless musical stimulation that is specifically designed to grow a crowd (as opposed to a church).

This whole trend began when churches adopted the prevailing philosophy of the world called humanism. Man was seen as the center and main focus of everything. The human being and his needs and wants were to be catered to and fulfilled as the greatest good. This mindset appealed to many people but particularly to the youth. Along came the 60s and this era fueled the burgeoning desire for absolute, immediate gratification and self-fulfillment. It, for the first time, caused churches to fervently seek to accommodate the selfish, self-indulgent, immoral, hedonistic people of that day. Churches, in turn, seeking to keep the young people in church began to tailor their ministries and messages in such a way as to tap into this prevailing humanistic mindset. Nothing could have been more unpopular than to have emphasized sanctification and holiness. Driven by this errant principle the church missed the mark. No longer could the church be serious, thoughtful, scriptural and God honoring in its preaching. No longer could the confrontation of sin be tolerated. The call to sanctification, holiness and separation from the world went silent because it was offensive to those sitting in the pews.

The result was devastating. Sanctification was all but forgotten.

5. The Missing of the Mark
   B. Regarding Sanctification

It is glorious to celebrate our justification and it is also glorious to anticipate our glorification. It is exhilarating to contemplate the doctrine of election. We, however, currently live in the realm of the operating doctrine of sanctification. We need to give more consideration to the important subject of sanctification. Once, sanctification was prominent in the church. It needs to be prominent once again.

6. The Main Point of Sanctification

As with everything related to our salvation the ultimate goal is the glory of God. Particularly, however, God is working out our salvation in such a way as to cause us to be conformed to the image of His Son Jesus Christ. Sanctification is that progressive process which causes us to become less and less attached to sin and more like the Lord Jesus Christ. The main point of sanctification is to glorify God by our being conformed to the image of Christ. In pursuing this course, we both please God and we become living testimonies of God's saving grace to the world.

This dramatic change is brought about by God alone and occurs in the life of every true Christian. Whereas once we were helplessly and even willingly dominated by sin, we are no longer under the dominion of sin.

I was reading recently about the island nation of Guam. Guam now has an almost insoluble problem – snakes. There are between 6,000 and 12,000 snakes per square mile in Guam. The slithering problems often reach lengths of 8 feet or longer and they have wiped out 70% of Guam's native species of birds.

This problem, however, is actually a man-made problem. There was a time when Guam had no snakes at all. During World War II, however, the Brown tree snake was evidently imported from Australia, New Guinea, and the Solomon Islands as a stowaway in military naval shipments. The snakes multiplied prodigiously and now Guam has no way to get rid of the snakes. The island is dominated by these slithering menaces.

The Bible teaches us that man has always carried a snake problem with him ever since the fall in the Garden of Eden. Sin was introduced to our world by man and it grew to such proportions that it now dominates mankind. Interestingly, we have discovered a way to harness the wonderful energy of the atom but then we misuse it to create destructive bombs of enormous proportions. We discover a way to extract from nature cures for various ailments and then we use those "cures" to produce addictive drugs. We contaminate everything that we touch because we walk in the darkness of sin. It is a problem that we introduced into our own world and yet now we are suffering under its deadly dominion. How can we be free from the controlling dominion of this incredible problem?

Romans chapter eight highlights the person and work of the Holy Spirit and His instrumental part in our salvation.

In this next section of Scripture Paul will continue to emphasize the indispensable and vital role of the Holy Spirit. This emphasis in the section of Paul's writing in Romans chapter eight that we are currently focused on can best be understood by using the following outline:

In this next section of Scripture Paul will continue to emphasize the indispensable and vital role of the Holy Spirit. This emphasis in the section of Paul's writing in Romans chapter eight, that we are currently focused on, can best be understood by using the following outline:

I. THE FOCUS ON THE HOLY SPIRIT

II. THE FOCUS ON THE HOLY SPIRIT AS IT RELATES TO THE CHANGE OF THE BELIEVER'S NATURE

Her pregnancy captured the attention of much of the world. When was the baby going to be born? Would we be able to see the birth? Then it happened. April, the 15-year-old giraffe gave birth to her baby in a pen at the Harpursville, New York Animal Adventure Park where she lives with her mate, Oliver. The pregnancy had lasted for 15 months captivating thousands of people who kept up with her by means of the Internet. After weeks of anticipation, April the giraffe finally gave birth to a baby calf—a male. The birth was covered on Livestream and witnessed by over 1.2 million viewers. It occurred on April 21, 2017 at 10 AM. When she finally gave birth the calf's front hooves came out first, followed by his snout. Then the rest of him emerged. The calf stood on its wobbly legs for the first time while mom helped her baby steady itself.

My curiosity was piqued by the coverage of the birth of this giraffe. The giraffe seems like a strange and homely creature in appearance; his or her movements seem awkward and peculiar and when it comes to giraffe childbirth things seem even stranger.

I did some reading about the birth of giraffes. It seems that a giraffe's childbirth is very interesting. The moment of birth finally comes after the long gestation period. After months of anticipation viewers are not disappointed. In one account that I read a calf, a plucky male, hurtled forth, falling ten feet and landing on his back. The mother giraffe gives birth to its young standing up, and the distance from the birth canal to the ground is about ten feet. Can you imagine this? I am six feet tall and if I stretch my arms upward I may be able to touch an eight and one-half foot ceiling. The calf, however, falls out of its mother ten feet above ground and lands on his back. It may lay there for a few moments, and then, it scrambles to get its legs underneath it so that it might take a look around and check out the world it has just entered.

When the calf emerges, the mother lowers her head so that she can clearly see her newborn. She stands there towering directly above the baby calf. Then surprisingly the mother swings her great, long leg outward and boots her newborn calf into the air. The calf sprawls head over heels across the ground, puzzled and protesting. After all, the young calf has experienced enough trauma already. That action by the mother giraffe might seem cruel and strange but she wants him to get up – and if he doesn't get up, she's going to do it again. Often, the mother giraffe is forced to repeat this process again and again. Finally, the newborn calf will stand up, on its own, for the first time. It will struggle to maintain its balance on its wobbly and spindly legs. Then, she (the mother giraffe) will kick her newborn calf off its feet again. She wants it to remember how it got up so that it can repeat the process the next time it becomes necessary to do so.

Sometimes God deals with us the same rough way. If we're uninformed as to God's methods and purposes, these actions can seem cold and even cruel. After all, we fight and struggle to get our feet under us, and as soon as we gain some stability it seems like they are just kicked out from under us again. God is intent on enabling us to get up successfully after each fall so that helplessness and sin will not dominate us and keep us from moving forward in life as we should. He is going to do whatever it takes to keep us from being dominated by sin and rendered helpless and impotent.

Since God is for us, He does not stop with merely freeing us from the condemnation of sin but He totally re-creates us as new creatures in Christ. In our new found spiritual state we hunger and thirst for righteousness. In regeneration God changes our hearts and minds and then we are indwelt by the Holy Spirit and guided by the Word of God so that we can be holy as God is holy. God takes us out of the "miry clay" and off the wayward path and places our feet on the narrow path that leads to life everlasting. He orients us to set our focus on things above and not on things of the earth. As Christians, we are dramatically changed from what we once were without Christ.

Nature is full of illustrations that can be used to illustrate spiritual truths. Consider the case of the monarch butterfly. These are beautiful creatures of God. Each autumn the monarch butterflies who reside in the northern United States make a massive migration to the warm climate of Mexico to escape the winter cold. Can you imagine the millions and millions of monarch butterflies all flying southward with an intent and purpose to arrive in Mexico for the warm weather?

It is as if Mexico is in their DNA. It is remarkable to note how God has created that desire in them to motivate them to fly thousands of miles for their safety and survival. The illustration becomes even more dramatic when we focus our attention on a single monarch butterfly. I will call this butterfly, Butterfly A. Butterfly A flies down to Mexico for the winter and when the winter is over Butterfly A sets out to follow the same course only in reverse direction to return to its original destination. Along the way going north, Butterfly A lays eggs and then moves on. During the course of the return flight, Butterfly A dies. The eggs that were laid hatch and mature and the butterflies that come from them instinctively begin to fly north along the same path as their predecessors did. They fly north with a special dead reckoning accuracy but before they can reach their ultimate destination they, too, die. They, too, have been laying eggs all during their relentless trip north and throughout the trip their eggs hatch and the butterflies that come from them also mature. In time, these butterflies, which now constitute the third-generation, finally reach their ultimate destination in the northern states. Not one of these third-generation monarch butterflies has ever been to Mexico. There is no single butterfly that has previously made the trip. There is not a single one who has a firsthand knowledge of the way to Mexico so that they can serve as the guide for the others when it comes time for the annual migration the following year. Yet, when autumn comes these third-generation butterflies point themselves in the direction of Mexico, as if they had access to a GPS, and they fly there for the winter.

When God grants the sinner new birth He re-orients the once lost sinner so that built into their spiritual DNA there is an insatiable desire for and pursuit of God, the things of God, and heaven. Our spiritual DNA is programmed in this way so that we are no longer dominated by sin but we are constantly pressing toward the things of God.

This is where the critical ministry of the Holy Spirit comes to our aid. Without the ministry of the Holy Spirit salvation would be just wishful thinking. In fact, without the ministry of the Holy Spirit there could be no real salvation. It was necessary for the Holy Spirit to step in and help us. That's what the Lord Jesus Christ was trying to explain to His apostles when He told them that He was going away but that He would send them another comforter to take His place in their lives. The word *"another"* carries a very specific meaning in Greek. It means, "another of the same kind or essence." Our Lord is saying that the Holy Spirit is deity just as He is deity. The Holy Spirit is lovingly and vitally concerned with the welfare of true believers just as Jesus is concerned with their welfare. Since God is for you He ensures that through the ministry of the Holy Spirit you will become more and more freed from sin and more and more identified with holiness.

It may seem utterly impossible to you that the Almighty God of the universe would go to such great lengths to save you from your sin. Go out and stand looking at the nighttime sky and contemplate the vast multitude of that tremendous expanse and then ask yourself, "Who am I? How could it be even remotely possible that I could become the recipient of God's eternal love and salvation?" Allow me to illustrate how the seeming impossible can become a reality:

In case you didn't already know this little tidbit of wonderful trivia... On July 20, 1969, as commander of the Apollo 11 lunar module, Neil Armstrong was the first person to set foot on the moon. His first words after stepping on the moon: "That's one small step for man, one giant leap for mankind," were televised to earth and heard by millions.

But, just before he reentered the lander, he made the enigmatic remark, "Good luck, Mr. Gorsky."

Many people at NASA thought it was a casual remark concerning some rival Soviet cosmonaut. However, upon checking, there was no Gorsky in either the Russian or American space programs. Over the years, many people questioned Armstrong as to what the, "Good luck, Mr. Gorsky" statement meant, but Armstrong always just smiled. On July 5, 1995, in Tampa Bay, Florida, while answering questions following a speech, a reporter brought up the twenty-six-year-old question about Mr. Gorsky to Armstrong. This time he finally responded because his Mr. Gorsky had just died, so Neil Armstrong felt he could now answer the question. Here's the answer to "Who was Mr. Gorsky?":

In 1938, when Neil Armstrong was a kid in a small Midwestern town, he was playing baseball with a friend in the backyard. His friend hit the ball, which landed in his neighbor's yard by their bedroom window. His neighbors were Mr. and Mrs. Gorsky. As young Neil Armstrong leaned down to pick up the ball, he heard Mrs. Gorsky shouting at Mr. Gorsky. "Sex! You want sex?! You'll get sex when the kid next door walks on the moon!" Neil Armstrong's explanation broke the place up and was confirmed by his family as a true story. The meaning of Neil Armstrong's comment, "Good luck, Mr. Gorsky," finally came out.

I don't mean to be indiscreet. I'm merely relating the story as told by astronaut Neil Armstrong in order to point out that what might seem utterly impossible can become a reality. Who would have thought, in that day, that a man would walk on the moon? More specifically, who would have thought that the neighborhood kid next door would be the one to do it? It seems impossible that the Almighty, eternal creator God would go to great lengths to rescue a rebellious sinner from sin, doesn't it? Yet, the impossible becomes possible.

Who would have ever thought that the Almighty God of the universe would go to such lengths to save rebellious and depraved sinners like ourselves? Yet, that is exactly what He did and does. The believer, therefore, is encouraged by the fact that because God is with us, "All things are possible." Salvation is impossible apart from God but it is absolutely certain when we trust in Christ and live in obedience to God through faith in the Lord Jesus Christ. The believer's salvation, sanctification, and security are not mere wishful thinking but they are a concrete reality brought about by the grace and power of our sovereign God. Since God is for you He is leading you, instructing you, encouraging you, correcting you, loving you, forgiving you, defending you, to assure you that He is for you and your ultimate salvation is absolutely guaranteed.

I. THE FOCUS ON THE HOLY SPIRIT

I am convinced that one of the great needs of today is to refocus in a biblical way on the ministry of the Holy Spirit. The Holy Spirit has been misrepresented, ignored, insulted, and dishonored by the church. We need to disassociate ourselves from the spurious claims of miracles, visions, and material prosperity supposedly brought about by the Holy Spirit and we need to refocus our thoughts in a biblical way on the person and ministry of the Holy Spirit in the true light of Scripture. The Apostle Paul highlights some of the saving work of the Holy Spirit in the eighth chapter of the book of Romans. He mentions the Holy Spirit nearly twenty times in this chapter.

The Real Person of the Holy Spirit

The Holy Spirit is a real person. The Holy Spirit is not merely an influence or impersonal power. He is the third member of the Trinity, equal in every way to the other two members of the Trinity.

Consider some of the characteristics of personhood that the Bible teaches that the Holy Spirit possesses. He loves and communicates with Christians. He teaches, guides, comforts, and corrects them; He functions with mind, emotion, and will. He can be lied to, grieved, quenched, tested, resisted and blasphemed. The Bible speaks of his omniscience, omnipotence, and omnipresence. He is holy and possesses divine glory. He comforts and functions as an advocate. He intercedes for the Saints. He was fully active in the creation of the world and in our new birth as well as with many other activities. He indwells believers and functions in a number of different ways in their lives.

Today's church, in general, has largely misrepresented the Holy Spirit and His work. This is particularly so in charismatic circles. Paul's words in Romans chapter eight go far to rectify that problem. In the Bible the Holy Spirit is referred to as the eternal Spirit, the generous Spirit, the Spirit of wisdom, the Spirit of counsel, might, understanding, and knowledge, the Spirit of God, the Spirit of holiness, the Spirit of Christ, the Spirit of the Son, the Holy Spirit, the Spirit of truth, the good Spirit, the Spirit of glory, the Spirit of grace, the seven – fold Spirit, the Spirit of the Lord, the Comforter, the Power of the Most High (Luke 1:35). Without the work of the Holy Spirit salvation would be impossible. The Holy Spirit is the power (ruach – violent force) of God. He is a person with all the attributes of a person and equal in every way to the other members of the Trinity. Our salvation is possible only because the Holy Spirit stepped in and insured that it would be so.

The Charismatic Fiasco

In the last century the charismatic movement or Pentecostal movement has been the fastest growing form of religion in the world. Modern-day professing Christianity is really made up of three distinct types of professing believers. There are those involved in Roman Catholicism.

There are those involved in Protestantism. Then there are those involved in the Pentecostal charismatic element.

The latter or third group purports to be a movement of the Holy Spirit and it has been pervasive and highly successful in gaining adherents. In the year 1900 there were no Pentecostals or charismatics but a few years ago the latest statistics indicated that there are now over 500 million. This movement has permeated mainline denominations as well. Since 1960 when it launched itself into mainline denominations from an Episcopal church in California it has been dynamic in its growth.

This movement deals recklessly with the interpretation of Scripture and poses a dramatic danger to the welfare of the church. It dishonors the Holy Spirit and His work by distorting it. Whereas the Bible teaches that the ministry of the Holy Spirit is to point people to Jesus Christ and to help them to understand and appropriate the things of Christ. The contemporary focus on the Holy Spirit in these circles is anything but what the Bible declares His ministry to be. The current fixation with the Holy Spirit revolves around supposed ecstatic utterances, prayer languages, miracles of healing, material prosperity, etc.

Much of modern-day professed Christianity, in these circles, focuses on the Holy Spirit Himself rather than on Jesus Christ. People claim to want to be baptized by the Holy Spirit, filled by the Holy Spirit, enlightened by the Holy Spirit, led mysteriously by the Holy Spirit's private communications, etc. The Holy Spirit becomes the center of their attention. The Holy Spirit is the one who is sought after rather than Jesus Christ. The experience of the Holy Spirit is thought of as the supreme evidence of spirituality. This is all a radical distortion of what the Bible tells us the ministry of the Holy Spirit is to be like.

The Triune God is For Us!

The Apostle Paul refocuses our attention on the true person and work of the Holy Spirit in Romans chapter eight. According to Paul, the entire Trinity is involved in our wonderful salvation. The Father planned our salvation. The Son procures our salvation. But the Holy Spirit steps in and produces our salvation. One day you became convicted over your sinfulness and convinced of the sinlessness and sufficient sacrifice of

Jesus Christ. Why? The answer is found in John chapter 16 where Jesus predicted that the Holy Spirit would come and convict the world of sin and righteousness and judgment. One day your entire perspective and personal desire changed regarding God. Why? Because you were regenerated or born again by the Holy Spirit (John 3:3–8). The Holy Spirit was even involved in your justification, "You were justified in the name of the Lord Jesus Christ and by the Spirit of our God" (1 Corinthians 6:11).

The Holy Spirit is fully involved in our wonderful salvation. The Holy Spirit convicts the sinner of sin, convinces him of his need for a Savior and that the Lord Jesus Christ is the only perfect Savior, grants faith, regenerates new life, baptizes us into the body of Christ, dispenses gifts to us (1 Corinthians 12), gives us the fruit of the spirit (Galatians 5), illuminates the Word of God to us (1 Corinthians 2:9-13), anoints us (1 John 2:27) so that we don't need a man to teach us because we have an anointing from God that teaches us all things, seals us, empowers us (Ephesians 5:18).

I should also like to point out that the omnipotent Holy Spirit's work is always efficacious. He always accomplishes what He sets out to do. When God chooses to save a sinner, the Holy Spirit ensures that the sinner will be saved. That is why the Apostle Paul could write, "and those whom He predestined, He also called, and those whom He called, He also justified, and those whom He justified, He also glorified" (Romans 8:30). God utilizes the ministry of the Holy Spirit to call us to salvation. That "calling" is always efficacious when God intends it to be so thus all those that are called (in this sense) are justified (declared righteous) and will be glorified. In Ezekiel 36:27 the Bible says that when we are saved, God puts His Spirit within us. He enables us to do things that we would never want to do or be able to do otherwise. Everything changes when the Holy Spirit steps in.

The Father planned and initiated salvation. The Son validated and victoriously secured salvation and then demonstrated it. But the Holy Spirit activates and communicates the salvation of God within you and me. The Holy Spirit frees you from the dominating and damning principle of sin and death and enables you to trust in Jesus Christ by faith and to keep the law of God. He changes your nature and makes you a new person so that you have your mind set on what the Spirit desires rather than on what the sinful nature desired. He transfers you from death to life. He causes you to cry, "Abba Father," and witnesses or testifies with our spirit that we are the children of God and heirs with Christ.

God created the various creatures to inhabit our planet and sometimes we can almost discern spiritual and moral instruction by examining them. Consider the toad, for instance. What an ugly creature it is! It is quite clumsy, covered with warts, etc. In fact, its skin carries a poisonous liquid which it exudes when attacked. His primary weapon of offense is its tongue. It lashes out with an incredibly fast motion almost undetectable by the human eye. But, what is of special interest about the toad is a balloon-like sack attached to its throat. When it wants to announce its presence, it fills this fleshy bag with air which it then forces across its vocal cords, making them vibrate. This is what causes the bellowing noise that one can hear at night near a lake. What a picture of man in his sin! Squat, ugly, poisonous, with a tongue ready to attack and destroy – yet all the while bellowing proudly his presence. Yet, God transforms this disgusting creature (man in sin) into something beautiful. He does so through the work of the Lord Jesus Christ and the ministry of the Holy Spirit. Therefore, sin's dominion can be broken for the true believer. The Holy Spirit breaks us free from sin while changing our nature to one that desires holiness. With this process in play, the Holy Spirit ensures that sin will not have dominion over us.

The Holy Spirit & the Ministry of Jesus Christ

Think of the ministry of the Holy Spirit in the life and work of Jesus Christ. The Holy Spirit was the inseparable companion and indispensable power of Jesus Christ. He was with the Lord Jesus from the womb to the tomb. Luke 1:31 is where it all got started. The angel said to Mary, "You will conceive in your womb and bear a Son and you will name him Jesus. He will be great and will be called the Son of the Most High and the Lord God will give Him the throne of His father, David."

How in the world is that going to happen? Verse 35, "The Holy Spirit will come upon you and the power of the Most High (which is the same thing) will overshadow you so the holy one to be born will be called the Son of God." The Holy Spirit overshadowed or hovered over the birth of Jesus like He hovered over the original creation of the world to turn its formlessness into form. He hovered over Mary to create the Son of God in human form. It was the Holy Spirit who created in the womb of Mary the very human embryo of the Son of God – the God man. From that time forward the Holy Spirit was with Jesus and the grace of God was upon Him. When it came time for His public baptism, we learn that the Spirit of God descended on Him and was His constant companion in a powerful way.

In Mark 1:12 we read that the Holy Spirit led Him (Jesus) to go out into the wilderness for His time of temptation. When it was time to launch His public ministry, we read in Luke 4:14 that He returned to Galilee in the power of the Spirit. His ministry was Spirit empowered. Everything He did, He did by the power of the Holy Spirit (Acts 10:38).

When our Lord Jesus Christ came to the time of the cross and the time to die, the Bible says in Hebrews 9:14, "How much more will the blood of Christ who through the eternal Spirit offered himself without blemish to God." The Holy Spirit empowered Him on the cross. Then in Romans 1:4 we read, "The Spirit raised him from the dead." Everything in His life was Spirit empowered!

The Holy Spirit and His ministry in the life of Jesus Christ was giving us a picture of what a Spirit–powered human being looks like. Jesus is the perfect man because He was fully controlled by the Holy Spirit. The Holy Spirit points us to Jesus so that we can see a perfect man. Jesus, in His life, demonstrated what we ought to be like and in His death, He secured and validated our salvation. In our lives the Holy Spirit is actively working to cause us to be conformed to the image of Jesus Christ. Sanctification is the work of the Spirit by which He shows us Christ and moves us to want to become more like Christ.

It might be helpful to think of the Holy Spirit and His ministry in our spiritual lives as like what the creator is to the physical world. The physical world owes its very existence to the creator. Further, it is sustained, upheld, preserved, and made functional by the creator. Without the creator the world would dissolve into nothingness. In a similar way in the spiritual dimension without the Holy Spirit we would never have been re-created. Further, without the Holy Spirit we could never have been sustained, preserved, upheld, and been made functional. Without the Holy Spirit we would degenerate and dissolve into nothingness.

The Holy Spirit's ministry and resource in the life of the believer is essential and it is also inexhaustible. This ongoing ministry of the Holy Spirit in the life of the believer is a further indication that God is for you and me.

The Pitch Lake

The Pitch Lake, located in Southwest Trinidad, in the village of La Brea, is the largest and most significant pitch Lake in the world, measuring approximately 100 acres, and is estimated to be 76 meters deep in the center. The liquid asphalt is black and viscous.

The lake is thought to have been created when the Caribbean continental plate was forced under another tectonic plate causing oil from deep underground deposits to rise to the surface where it collected in a volcanic crater. Sir Walter Raleigh discovered the Pitch Lake in 1595. It was already known to the natives as the Tierra de Brea, its Spanish name. Sir Walter Raleigh was introduced to the 100-acre lake of black gold by his Amerindian guides. He immediately recognized the potential and began caulking his ships with the tar. The actual mining of the lake started in 1867 and an estimated 10,000,000 tons of asphalt has been extracted since. Tar from the La Brea Pitch Lake in Trinidad has been used to provide high grade road surfaces in over 50 countries. The lake is estimated to contain reserves of around 6,000,000 tons which would last 400 years at the current rate of extraction. Though the lake of tar is being constantly mined, it continually replenishes itself so that there is no perceptible depletion in the available resource.

There is, however, a limit even to this vast resource of tar/asphalt from the Pitch Lake in Trinidad and it will begin to be used up and depleted in the distant future. but since the omnipotent God is for you, there is no limit to the inexhaustible resource of the Holy Spirit in the life of the believer. The Holy Spirit is constantly giving the believer whatever he needs and will continue to do so as long as the needs exist.

Paul is going to focus our attention on the wonderful ministry of the Holy Spirit in this eighth chapter of Romans.

C. H. Spurgeon, commenting on the biblical phrase, *"Oil for the light,"* wrote the following:

> "My soul, how much thou needest this, for thy lamp will not long continue to burn without it. Thy snuft will smoke and become an offense if thy light be gone, and gone is oil if he be absent. Thou hast no oil wells springing up in thy human nature, and therefore thou must go to them that sell and buy for thyself, or like the foolish virgins, thou will have to cry, "My lamp is gone out." Even the consecrated lamps could not give light without oil; though they shown in the tabernacle they needed to be fed, though no rough winds blew up on them they required to be trimmed, and our need is equally as great. Under the most happy of circumstances thou canst not give light for another hour unless fresh oil of grace be given thee."

It was not every oil that might be used in the Lord's service; neither the petroleum which exudes so plentifully from the earth, nor the produce of fishes, nor that extracted from nuts would be accepted; one oil only was selected, and that the best olive oil. Pretended grace from natural goodness, fancied grace from priestly hands, or imaginary grace from outward ceremonies will never serve the true saint of God; he knows that the Lord would not be pleased with rivers of such oil. He goes to the olive – press of Gethsemane, and draws his supplies from Him who was crushed therein. The oil of the gospel of grace is pure and free from lees and dregs, and hence the light which is fed thereon is clear and bright. Our churches are the Saviors golden candelabra, and if they are to be lights in this dark world, they must have much holy oil. Let us pray for ourselves, our ministers, and our churches, that they may never lack oil for the light. Truth, holiness, joy, knowledge, love, these are all beings of the sacred light, but we cannot give them forth unless in private we received oil from God the Holy Ghost."

(C. H. Spurgeon, *Morning and Evening,* MacDonald Publishing Company, McLean, Virginia 22102, page 482.)

II. THE FOCUS ON THE HOLY SPIRIT AS IT RELATES TO THE TRUE BELIEVER'S NATURE

Have you ever watched a football game where one team utterly dominated the other? Not long ago I was watching college football on Saturday afternoon when that very thing happened. I felt sorry for the losing team. I wondered how such a mismatch could have occurred. Then I thought of how perfectly that game pictures what a person's life is like outside of Jesus Christ. In our unsaved condition sin dominates us. We are no match for it. We cannot, in ourselves, win.

But as a Christian, you are no longer like what you once were. You are fundamentally different. If you are a Christian then you are not like what you used to be like before you became a Christian because the Holy Spirit has made you different. The Holy Spirit has freed you from the dominion of sin and translated you into the dominion of Christ and the Lord Jesus Christ is now your King. Your fundamental nature has been changed by the awesome power of the Holy Spirit and you "play" the game of life with increased efficiency and strength enabling you to win over sin.

The reason that I am emphasizing the issue of domination is that this is the core of what Paul is focusing on in our text. He is saying that the unsaved person is dominated and controlled by the flesh whereas the Christian is now dominated and controlled by the Holy Spirit. The two have completely different mindsets. One has the mindset of a sinner whose value system and passionate desires revolve around sin and the world system. The other (the saved person) has been so changed and altered by the saving grace of God through the ministry of the Holy Spirit that his mindset embraces the value system of God and he passionately and personally seeks after obedience to God for the glory of God. The issue is "domination." One lives in the dominion of darkness and the other lives in the dominion of light (the kingdom of the Lord Jesus Christ). This brings us to the need to understand exactly what is involved when we speak of dominion.

Dominion

The word, "dominion," is an interesting word. The state of Virginia is sometimes called, the "Old Dominion." Queen Elisabeth I asked Sir Walter Raleigh to explore and settle the land north of the Spanish held territories around what would become Florida. This happened in 1583. Sir Walter Raleigh did this and named the territory after her, the Virgin Queen (hence – the name Virginia), but in those days, the territory of Virginia ran from the Carolinas to Maine. In 1607, Virginia became the first colony to host a permanent town, which was called Jamestown.

England, and then Britain, as it became known at the beginning of the 16th century, founded its American and Caribbean colonies as private financial enterprises. This meant that one of a number of commercial companies formed and founded the colony, and these colonies were not directly run by the crown or government of Great Britain. Virginia, however, was unique among these colonies in the fact that it was a direct crown colony and was run directly by the British government through a governor.

Later in English history when Charles II ascended to the throne of England he ascribed the title "Dominion of Virginia" (1663) to Virginia. This means that alongside the four original dominions of England, Scotland, Ireland, and France, Charles II was now recognizing Virginia as the fifth dominion. He did this by also putting the coat of arms of Virginia on a shield as one of the four quarters alongside France, Ireland and Scotland.

Virginians added the term "old" to denote the states status as being the oldest crown governed colony in the Americas. The "Old Dominion of Virginia" was from the reign of Charles II onward, considered equal to the other dominions of England and of a higher status than the mere colonies that surrounded it. Hence, the word "dominion," refers to direct domination or rule.

According to the dictionary, "domination," is "the exercise of control or influence over someone or something or the state of being so controlled.";

"Supremacy or preeminence over another; exercise of mastery or ruling power; exercise of preponderant, governing or controlling influence." (Miriam Webster dictionary)

The continent of Europe has never been dominated by any one power. The ancient Romans under Julius Caesar could not subdue the Northern Germanic tribes. Napoleon could not subdue Spain. Though Adolph Hitler was a dominant force in Europe for a temporary period of time, he could not subdue England. Unlike comic book characters, who fantasize about world domination the entire continent of Europe has never been dominated by any one governmental power.

Prior to being saved every sinner, however, is dominated by sin. He or she is enslaved by it, addicted to it, in love with it, and lusting for it. Our Lord Jesus Christ, when conversing with the Jews, said this, "Truly, truly, I say to you, everyone who commits sin is a slave to sin" (John 8:34). The Apostle Paul, when writing to the Romans, wrote, "But thanks be to God, that you who were once slaves of sin have become obedient from the heart to the standard of teaching to which you were committed, and having been set free from sin, have become slaves of righteousness"(Romans 6:17). Once true salvation takes place by the power of the Holy Spirit this old scenario of being a slave to sin changes dramatically. The Apostle Paul declares to the Romans in his letter to them, "For sin will have no dominion over you, since you are not under law but under grace"(Romans 6:14). In this verse the apostle is contrasting our helpless and sinful condition when we were under law (the law could command obedience and holiness but could not enable the sinner to live up to that standard) with our new condition now that we are under grace. In this new condition God gives the saved believer that which he needs to overcome sin and to freely live a godly life. Again, this does not mean that successful Christian living comes easily or without struggles and trials. We are told that the flesh wars against the Spirit and the Spirit against the flesh. We are counseled to set our affections on things above not on things of the earth, and we are told to slay the sins in our life which fight to have dominance over us. There are times when we find ourselves weak and unwilling to strive for that mark of holiness which we know we should be striving for. All of this is a reality in the Christian life. We are at war, not only with Satan and the world system, but with the remaining sin that continues to plague us. The promise of God for this life is not one of perfection, but it is one of a pattern of godly living and holy desires. This stems from a changed heart and is nourished by the indwelling Holy Spirit. It is directed by the Word of God and encouraged by all true believers. Since God is for you, dear one, sin, as a pattern of life, will never dominate you.

There is a popular but distorted gospel that is being propounded today that assures those who would like to become Christians that they can be saved while still living in their sin. Of course, this stripped model of Christianity is presented as a less than optimal option but, nevertheless, a real and viable one. This kind of message, however, is not the gospel of God. God does not save us in our walk of sin but He saves us from our walk of sin. He frees us from the dominion of sin.

Charles Wesley, in one of his hymns, wrote:

> "Long my imprisoned spirit lay,
> fast – bound in sin and nature's night.
> Thine eye diffused a quickening ray,
> I woke – the dungeon flamed with light,
> My chains fell off, my heart went free,
> I rose went forth and followed thee."

The Christian's new sphere of authority and new standard of living will serve to have a powerful witness and effect upon those who observe our Christ-like behavior. All of this is designed to bring glory to the name of God.

Dr. Livingstone, I Presume

The testimony of H. M. Stanley is very much to the point that I am seeking to make. In 1869, the *New York Herald* sent him out to Africa to find David Livingstone who, having won the heart of the world had disappeared in the Dark Continent. Stanley plunged into the interior of Africa searching for him and eventually found him living near Lake Tanganyika. Livingstone was the only other white man within hundreds upon hundreds of miles. Stanley's greeting to Livingstone has gone down in history as the most casual on record, "Dr. Livingstone, I presume."

Livingstone refused to return to civilization with Stanley, so Stanley gave him some supplies and remained with him for about five months. The following is his testimony:

> "In 1871 I went to him as prejudiced as the biggest atheist that London had. To a reporter and correspondent such as I, who had only to deal with wars and mass meetings and political gatherings, sentimental matters were entirely out of my province. But there came for me a long time for reflection. I was out there away from a worldly world. I observed this solitary old man there, and asked myself, "How on earth does he stay here – is he cracked, or what? What is it that inspires him?" Four months after we met I simply found myself listening to him, wondering at the old man carrying out all that was said in the Bible: "leave all things and follow me." But little by little his sympathy for others became contagious; my sympathy was aroused; seeing his piety, his gentleness, his zeal, his earnestness, and how he went quietly about his business, I was converted by him although he had not tried to do it." (*"Dawn"*, December 16, 1929).

The powerful effect of a genuine Christian life which was freed from the dominion of sin and lived in the loving light of righteousness was enormous. It still is.

This freedom from the dominion of sin is not some experience that is reserved for only "*super* saints" but is something which is commonly shared by all true saints. That is why the apostle, though he had never met the Roman Christians in person, could, nevertheless, confidently write, "Sin will have no dominion over you, since you are not under law but under grace" (Romans 6:4). The Apostle John teaches this very same truth when he writes, "Everyone who makes a practice of sinning also practices lawlessness; sin is lawlessness. You know that he appeared to take away sins, and in him there is no sin. No one who abides in him keeps on sinning; no one who keeps on sinning has either seen him or known him. Little children, let no one deceive you. Whoever practices righteousness is righteous, as he is righteous. Whoever makes a practice of sinning is of the devil, for the devil has been sinning from the beginning. The reason the Son of God appeared was to destroy the works of the devil. No one born of God makes a practice of sinning for God's seed abides in him, he cannot keep on sinning because he has been born of God. By this it is evident who the children of God are, and who are the children of the devil: whoever does not practice righteousness is not of God, nor is the one who does not love his brother" (John 3:4 – 10).

This same truth of the Christian being freed in a practical, personal way from the dominion of sin is cited over and over again in the New Testament. Because God is with and for the Christian sin will not have dominion over a true believer. This does not mean that the true believer cannot fall into a temporary period of sin. It does not mean that true believers do not continually wrestle with temptation and sin. It does mean, however, that true believers, because of the indwelling of the Holy Spirit and the dramatic change of their spiritual nature, cannot be dominated as a pattern of life by sin. Salvation ensures not only that there is no longer any condemnation for the true believer but that also there is no domination of the believer by sin. God does not save believers so that they can continue uninterrupted in a life of sin. Since God is for you He will ensure that you are not dominated by sin.

Not only is the true believer set free from the ongoing dominion of sin but He is also set free to glorify God and to thoroughly enjoy Him forever. The true believer's inner nature and fundamental makeup is changed by a mighty work of the Holy Spirit who enables the believer to experience a genuine zeal for God.

A Zeal for God

The true believer's old zealousness for sin is replaced by the Holy Spirit with a deep zealousness for God and the things of God. The classic description of the zeal for God is given by the 19th century preacher Bishop J. C. Ryle. He wrote and I quote him at length:

> "Zeal in religion is a burning desire to please God, to do
> His will, and to advance His glory in the world in every

possible way. It is a desire which no man feels by nature – which the spirit places in the heart of every believer when he is converted – but which some believers feel so much more strongly than others they alone deserved to be called, "zealous," men...

The zealous man in religion is preeminently a man of one thing. It is not enough to say that he is earnest, hearty, uncompromising, thoroughgoing, wholehearted, and fervent in spirit. He only sees one thing, he cares for one thing, he lives for one thing, he is swallowed up in one thing; and that one thing is to please God. Whether he lives, or whether he dies – whether he has health, or whether he has sickness – whether he is rich, or whether he is poor – whether he pleases man, or whether he gives offense – whether he is thought wise, or whether he is thought foolish – whether he gets blame, or whether he gets praise – whether he gets honor, or whether he gets shame – for all this the zealous man cares nothing at all. He burns for one thing, and that one thing is to please God, and to advance God's glory. If he is consumed in the very burning, he cares not for it – he is content. He feels that, like a lamp, he is made to burn; and if consumed in burning, he has but done the work for which God appointed him. Such a one will always find a sphere for his zeal. If he cannot preach, work, and give money, he will cry, and sigh, and pray... If he cannot fight in the valley with Joshua, he will do the work of Moses, Aaron, and Hur, on the hill (Exodus 17:9 – 13). If he is cut off from working himself, he will give the Lord no rest till help is raised up from another quarter, and the work is done. That is what I mean when I speak of zeal in religion (*Practical Religion, 1959, ed., p.* 130)

The Bible commands and commends zealousness. As Christians, we are to be, *"zealous of good works,"* (Titus 2:14). Elijah was "very zealous for the LORD God of hosts" (1 Kings 19:10, 14), and God commended him for his zealousness. The Apostle Paul was a zealous, single–minded, all –out man of God. He lived for one thing only, "For me to live is Christ and to die is gain" (Philippians 1:21). It is sad to see a Christian lose his or her zealousness for God – but it sometimes happens. Sometimes the fires of love and the energy for God grow dimmer then they should be. That does not necessarily mean that the person is not a Christian. Perhaps, all Christians experience some of this "doldrum effect" in their spiritual life at one time or another. It is possible to lose one's "first love" and to become a mere methodical, mundane, mediocre Christian. This should never be a condition in which the Christian is content but this malaise can and does sometimes settle on the Christian's soul.

After our Lord Jesus had cleansed the temple of the moneychangers, His disciples remembered the passage of Scripture that predicted the reason for His action. It reads, "The zeal of your house has eaten me up" (John 2:1).

There is a modern-day distortion of God's real plan of salvation which teaches that true Christians need not be overly concerned with spiritual things and the glory of God but that a superficial, temporary, nod in God's direction will suffice for salvation. It is as if people are being taught that God is privileged to receive the sinner's attention even if it is halfhearted. In reality, God saves people through faith and repentance so that they will be conformed to the image of His Son Jesus Christ. He saves us from sin not in sin. He gives us a zeal for him and a delight in Him. The dominion of sin is broken forever for the true believer by the presence and power of the Holy Spirit. Since God is for you He provides you with the resources to stoke the fires of your spiritual zeal.

Two Kinds of Persons

In the eyes of God there are only two kinds of persons – those who are unsaved and still operate according to the sinful nature and those who are saved and operate according to what the Spirit desires. The Apostle Paul contrasts these two kinds of persons in the following verses:

"Those who live according to the sinful nature have their minds set on what that nature desires; those who live in accordance with the Spirit have their minds set on what the Spirit desires. The mind of sinful man is death, but the mind controlled by the Spirit is life and peace; the sinful mind is hostile to God. It does not submit to God's law, nor can it do so. Those controlled by the sinful nature cannot please God" (Romans 8:5–8).

In all honesty, ask yourself what spirit dominates your thinking and your behavior? According to the Apostle Paul, there are only two basic choices. One's answer to this question reveals whether you have been genuinely saved or else you are still in your sin and condemned. Evaluate yourself with judgment day honesty. Don't allow yourself to be duped into thinking that a superficial decision for Christ or an emotional experience of some type is the critical earmark of true salvation in your life. Either you live according to the sinful nature or you live according to the Holy Spirit. Remember, Paul is not talking about a perfect life but he is referring to a pattern of life. There is no middle ground – or third choice. Thankfully, if after examining your life you conclude that you are still living according to the sinful nature as a pattern of life you can still be rescued from your sin dominated lifestyle by trusting in Jesus Christ alone by faith alone. Although His salvation of sinners cost Christ dearly it is offered to believing sinners freely–received through faith alone.

The, "things of the Spirit," would include, among other things, the pursuit of personal holiness (prompted and guided by the Holy Spirit), a love for the Word of God and a willing submission to its divine authority, a consistent and heartfelt prayer life, a delight in the worship of God, a love for the people of God (and a practical ministry relative to their needs), a desire to help others become Christians through faith in the gospel, etc. The word, "flesh," in our text is most likely referring to more than merely the physical body but it is likely referring to the control of our entire being by the corruption of sin.

The reason that the Apostle Paul emphasizes the Holy Spirit in this chapter is because the Holy Spirit changes the way we think and changes our behavior as Christians thus enhancing our sense of security that we are truly children of God. As a believer, isn't it encouraging to know that God is powerfully working in us? Isn't it comforting and ingratiating to know that even in our weakness God through the Holy Spirit is enabling us to be victors over sin?

The unsaved person lives according to the sinful nature and has his mind set on what that sinful nature desires. This characteristic is true irrespective of gender, age, education, cultural background, race, etc. (Galatians 3:28). The verb (*phroneo*) translated as "their minds set", refers to the basic orientation, bent, and thought pattern of the mind, rather than simply to the mind or intellect itself (*Greek nous*). It includes a person's affections as well as their reasoning capacity. This is talking about how the person is fundamentally wired. By contrast, those who live in accordance with the Spirit have their minds set on what the Spirit desires. The word "minds" is *exactly* the same in both cases. Paul does not say that the mind of sinful man leads to death, but that it is death. The unsaved operate in a world of spiritual death and they are already dead spiritually.

The apostle is not stating a spiritual equation but rather a spiritual reality. People in such an unsaved condition inevitably have their minds set on what the spiritually dead and sinful condition desires. The opposite is true of those who have experienced genuine salvation. They also operate in a given spiritual context but it is a positive one. This has been made possible and not only possible but necessary and a standard reality by the wonderful ministry of the Holy Spirit.

Paul goes on to state another reality. That is, the person with his mind set on the Spirit is a person who has experienced spiritual life and peace with God. That is, this person is a Christian. The drastic change in their fundamental nature gives evidence to the fact that they have trusted in Jesus Christ for salvation and have been made new creatures in Christ. As to the mind of the person who is still set on the things of the sinful nature, it is hostile to God, it does not submit itself to God's law, nor can it do so – it cannot please God. Notice that the unsaved mind is unwilling to submit to God and is also incapable of submitting to God. This is true whether that person is religious or not religious. These factors hold true for all people in every circumstance. If such a person is ever to be saved that salvation must be entirely a work of God's sovereign power and grace. What does this say to the person who thinks he can save himself by doing good works, by keeping the law of God, or by being religious/spiritual? Can the unsaved person actually submit from the heart to the law of God? Can they actually please God? Can they be so controlled in mind and heart that they are willingly in sync with the dictates of a holy God? What insight does this give regarding the motivations of a person who is religious but unsaved? What hope is there for such a person in terms of their eternal salvation?

Consider the words of the Apostle John:

"Do not love the world or anything in the world. If anyone loves the world, the love of the Father is not in him." (1 John 2:15)

"Dear children, do not let anyone lead you astray. He who does what is right is righteous, just as He is righteous. He who does what is sinful is of the devil, because the devil has been sinning from the beginning. The reason the Son of God appeared was to destroy the devil's work. No one who is born of God will continue to sin, because God's seed remains in him; he cannot go on sinning, because he has been born of God. This is how we know who the children of God are and who the children of the devil are: anyone who does not do what is right is not a child of God; nor is anyone who does not love his brother" (1 John 3:7–10).

Not a *Perfection* of Life But a *Pattern* of Life

Obviously, as has already been stated, these verses are referring to a pattern of life not a perfection of life. Just as obviously, they are referring to a stark contrast between the life of an unsaved person and that of a genuinely saved person. The writer is not talking in theory, but in reality. The genuine child of God is no longer dominated by sin.

We have been playing church far too long. We have been reluctant to tell resolved sinners that their salvation is in real question. We have been too concerned with attracting people and too little concerned with preaching the Word of God accurately and boldly. Thank God for those preachers who are faithful to their calling. Thank God for Christians who share the Word of God accurately and lovingly with the unsaved people who they come in contact with in their daily life. The wonderful salvation made possible by Jesus Christ and the work of the Holy Spirit is a salvation which delivers true believers from the domination of sin. We become winners rather than losers! Not only are we freed from the condemnation of sin but we are also freed from the domination by sin. All of this is true because God is alive and powerfully at work in the lives of His children. God is for us!

Dear one in Christ, not only are you free from sin's condemnation but since God is for you, you are also free from sin's domination, as well. Sin shall not have dominion over you. Why? Because the Spirit whose very name is holy will not allow it and He will so move in your heart and life as to cause you to pursue holiness while causing you to flee from sin and to fight against it. The Holy Spirit will continually stoke the fires of your zeal for God as you cooperate with Him in stirring up your own heart to love and serve God passionately. Paul wrote to the Philippian church and he told them to, "Work out their own salvation with fear and trembling" then he added "because it is God who works in you both to will and do of his own good pleasure" (Philippians 2:2 12). In effect, he was saying that we must be active and diligent in working out our own salvation but constantly mindful of the fact that since God is for us He is working within us to give us the will to do so and the ability to do so. We will be successful in our salvation because God is for us.

In his book entitled *God's Righteous Kingdom,* Walter J. Chantry writes,

> "When preachers speak as if God's chief desire is for men
> to be happy, then multitudes with problems flock to Jesus.
> Those who have ill health, marital troubles, financial
> frustration, and loneliness look to our Lord for the desires
> of their hearts. Each conceives of joy in being found in
> health, peace, prosperity or companionship. But in search
> of the elusive happiness they're not savingly joined to Jesus
> Christ. Unless men will be holy, God is determined that
> they shall be forever miserable and damned." (Carlisle,
> Pennsylvania: Banner of Truth, 1980, P. 67)

A Time for Self-Examination

Do you find that this powerful work of the Holy Spirit in delivering you from the dominating influence of sin is evident in your heart and life? This is a key reason why the writer of Hebrews could write and say, "Strive for peace with everyone, and for the holiness without which no one will see the Lord" (Hebrews 12:14).

Don't Be an Actor

Some people have learned to play the part of a Christian so well that they can often pass for the real thing. I remember reading a story on one occasion about Gregory Peck. Gregory Peck was a top movie star in Hollywood and he was in the process of filming the full-length motion picture about the life of Gen. Douglas MacArthur. He was dressed exactly like Gen. Douglas MacArthur dressed and he had schooled himself in the specific mannerisms of Gen. MacArthur so that he could act the part convincingly. In the actor's parlance he was "in character."

While filming this movie Gregory Peck's wife called him in a great sense of urgency. It seems that she had found the perfect house for them and needed him to come to view it before someone else bought it ahead of them. Reluctantly, because he was deeply ingrained in his character and pretending to be Gen. Douglas MacArthur for the camera, Gregory Peck consented to his wife's request. During his lunch hour he had his driver take him to the address that his wife was enamored with. Getting out of the limo dressed in full military regalia he walked into the house to view it. In doing so, he passed several people and each one of them thought that they were in the presence of Gen. Douglas MacArthur. He looked like Gen. Douglas MacArthur, he acted like him, he sounded like him. This must be Gen. Douglas MacArthur! Everyone was duly impressed and convinced that they had seen the great man himself.

There are people who have learned to dress, act, and talk like Christians but who are merely acting the part. Sadly, some of them have been taught that Christianity is a matter of acting in a certain fashion. They have convinced themselves that they are Christians. They are "in character" and others are equally convinced of their Christianity. Christianity, however, is more than excellent acting. It is a vitally transforming experience beginning with a dramatic change of heart and mind which evidences itself in a change of conduct.

Christians do not merely act like they are freed from the dominion of sin but they are freed from sin through faith in Jesus Christ and by the work of the Holy Spirit. Dear one, examine yourself and make sure that you have experienced a genuine spiritual transformation in your heart and mind. Make sure that you are the genuine thing

On April 30, 2018 CNN ran an article by Kara Fox entitled, "French Museum discovers more than half of its paintings are fakes." The Terus Museum in Elne, the southern French village where the painter Etienne Terrus lived was founded in 1994 to commemorate the artistic work of this painter.

Recently, the Mayor of Elne told local TV France 3 that an investigation into the paintings was first launched after some art experts detected some serious discrepancies in the paintings. 82 of the 140 paintings have now been determined to be counterfeits. They are fakes. Currently, an investigation is underway to determine who the counterfeiters were. The selling price of the paintings has diminished precipitously. It seems hard to imagine that this hoax presenting fake paintings as the real thing went on for over 24 years before being detected. Some professing Christians have learned to pass themselves off as the real thing. Sometimes, because of their being taught incorrectly, they may actually think that they are the real thing when, in reality, they are clever fakes rather than real Christians. It is vital for every individual to examine himself in light of Scripture so as to establish whether he is a real Christians or a clever fake.

BRINGING IT HOME

1. How important is the Holy Spirit to your salvation? Name a few things that He does to make your salvation possible.

2. Describe some characteristics that are true of a person whose mind is set on what the sinful nature desires. Describe some characteristics that are true of a person whose mind is set on what the Spirit desires. Which best describes you?

3. Name two or three passages other than Romans chapter 8:5–10 that describe the same concept as mentioned in question number two (that the saved person is a positively changed person who seeks to pursue spiritual things and to avoid sin.) Why is it important to teach this truth to today's church?

4. How can you be sure, from Scripture, that sin will not habitually dominate you if you are a Christian? How does the fact that God is for you affect your answer?

WHAT A WONDERFUL TRUTH – GOD IS FOR YOU!

Remember, by God's grace we, as true believers in Christ, are freed not only from the condemnation because of sin but also from the ongoing domination of sin.

4

Since God is for us there is

NO ISOLATION

For Believers

Romans 8:9–11

"You, however, are not in the flesh but in the Spirit, if in
fact the Spirit of God dwells in you. Anyone who does not
have the Spirit of Christ does not belong to Him. But if
Christ is in you, although the body is dead because of sin,
the Spirit is life because of righteousness. If the Spirit of
Him who raised Jesus from the dead dwells in you, He who
raised Christ Jesus from the dead will also give life to your
mortal bodies through the Spirit who dwells in you."

For the purposes of our study regarding the absolute security of
the believer in salvation, I'm not going to deal with this entire
passage exhaustively. Instead, I want to focus your attention on
the fact that when God saves us He does not leave us spiritually alone and
in isolation. As part of our security package as believers God causes us to
be indwelt by the third member of the Trinity (the Holy Spirit). Were this
not true we would be like stray lambs that are easy prey for a predator. If
this were not true we might get the feeling that we were cut off from God
and left in total isolation in a hostile world.

Thankfully, our gracious God lovingly provides for us so that we will
never be in total isolation and without a helper.

GENERAL OUTLINE

The Control of the Holy Spirit
The Constant Indwelling of the Holy Spirit
The Character and Conduct of righteousness produced by the Holy Spirit

Isolated & All Alone

There was a song sung by a band in the 1960s entitled, "One is the loneliest number." No one wants to be alone. Soldiers fighting in a combat firefight don't want to find themselves isolated and detached from the main body of troops. Such a situation is fearful and dangerous.

It was 1965 and American troops had been deployed to Vietnam. Lt. Col. Hal Moore (he was ultimately to retire as a Lieut. Gen. and destined to live to be nearly 95 years old) was in command of the 1st Battalion, 7th cavalry Regiment. American troops had been attacked and Lieutenant "Hal" Moore and his troops were transported by means of helicopters to the La Drang Valley where the combat had taken place to search out and destroy the enemy. It was the first time that helicopters had been used to transport American troops into a field of battle. They landed on landing zone X-Ray and for the next 34 days they engaged in a campaign involving, among other things, a climactic four-day battle in which 234 Americans died at landing zones X-Ray and Albany in November 1965. Thousands of Vietnamese troops were killed by the American army as the Vietnamese repeatedly attacked and sought to destroy the American forces.

A book was written by Joseph Galloway along with Lieut. Gen. Harold G. "Hal" Moore chronicling this first major battle between American soldiers and regular Vietnamese soldiers. It is titled, "We Were Soldiers Once...and Young". In addition, a 2002 American war film starring both Mel Gibson and Sam Elliott captured and depicted the events of that battle.

In the movie, depicting the actual events of 1965, Lieut. Col. Hal Moore learns that an American base has been attacked, and he is ordered to take his 400 men and decisively deal with the enemy and eliminate the North Vietnamese attackers. All of this, despite the fact that "military intelligence" had no idea of the number of enemy troops awaiting them. In this military action Moore leads a newly created air cavalry unit into the

La Drang Valley to accomplish his mission. After arriving in "The Valley of Death" the American soldiers captured a North Vietnamese soldier and learned from him that the location that they were sent to is the base camp for a veteran North Vietnamese Army division of 4000 men.

As the battle ensued, one of the especially aggressive American army platoons chases after some North Vietnamese soldiers and becomes detached and isolated from the main body of troops. Repeated efforts to rescue them fail. It soon becomes clear that they are totally ISOLATED from the main battalion and virtually surrounded by an overwhelming force of North Vietnamese soldiers that is intent on their destruction.

There was no chance of retreat and the platoon was cut off without any real hope. The movie depicts how frightening and dangerous their plight was as they vainly tried to defend themselves throughout the inky black darkness of night as well as the brightness of day. ISOLATION, in this situation, was an awful and frighteningly dangerous experience. In the end, many of the soldiers in that platoon were killed and only a few survived. For a combat soldier ISOLATION is a terribly frightening and foreboding possibility.

We have all experienced times when we were somewhat isolated, alone, and in need of a friend for support. The Apostle Paul even mentioned this in a letter to Timothy. He lamented the fact that all had deserted him and yet he rejoiced that God stood with him and therefore he was not totally isolated at all. "At my first defense no one came to stand by me, but all deserted me. May it not be charged against them! But the Lord stood by me and strengthened me..." (2 Timothy 4:16 – 17a). Even the Lord Jesus Christ felt the need to keep from being totally isolated. He understood the need for human companionship. He would sometimes take Peter, James, and John with Him on special occasions to avoid being totally isolated and alone. For example, on The Mount of Transfiguration, when the disciples of Jesus (who He had taken with Him for companionship and support) had fallen asleep, God sent Moses and Elijah to accompany and converse with Jesus about His death and His exit from this world. Jesus did not need to feel isolated and alone. Even in the beginning of time God looked upon the first man, Adam, and declared, "It is not good for man to be alone." ISOLATION is never optimal and is sometimes dangerous and deadly. Many other passages in the Bible highlight the advantage of not being isolated and alone. For example, in the book of Ecclesiastes we read, "Two are better than one, because they have a good reward for their toil. For if they fall one will lift up his fellow. But woe to him who is alone when he falls and has not another to lift him up!" (Ecclesiastes 4: 9–10).

ISOLATION (in its ultimate and total sense), however, is never experienced by a true child of God. Since God is for you, as a believer, not only are you free from condemnation and you are free from the dominion of sin over you but you are also insured by God there will never come a time in life when you are ever isolated from Him. For the genuine Christian there is never any total and complete ISOLATION.

The Key Points

Three things point to the wonderful fact that we are never deserted, overlooked or isolated by God. These facets of our passage clearly teach that we are never allowed to become totally isolated in the world and left alone as Christians to fend for ourselves in a hostile spiritual environment. First, true Christians are controlled by the Spirit of God who permanently lives in them. The Holy Spirit is all Powerful and Sovereign. His constant and powerful indwelling of the believer insurers that He is in control of the believer's life and is an on-site protector and comforter. The Holy Spirit does not merely mildly influence the life of the believer but rather every believer is controlled by the Holy Spirit who indwells him. Sometimes, Christians denigrate the person of the Holy Spirit by minimizing the fact that He is the Almighty powerful God. Such an extraordinarily dynamic being indwells each true Christian. No wonder we are protected from Satan's attacks while we are still in his domain. No wonder we can recoup and continually reassert our commitment to God even when we have fallen flat on our faces and have failed to be as faithful as we should have been. No wonder we are continually drawn to the Scriptures and to God from our innermost being. We have the indwelling Holy Spirit to thank for that.

Second, the phrase, "Holy Spirit," identifies a major characteristic of the Spirit's character and person and (holiness) also points to that which the Holy Spirit seeks to produce in the life of the true believer. The adjective "Holy" when understood as one who is totally holy identifies the Holy Spirit with the other members of the deity. It was God the Father who said, "Be holy for I am holy," it was Jesus Christ who was called God's holy child and was described as being, "holy, undefiled, and separate from sinners." In the "Holy Bible," we read about the, "holy Angels," "the holy of holies," and Saints (a term indicating those who are separated unto God in holiness). It follows that the Holy Spirit will produce holy living in God's holy Saints.

Third, the word "lives" (*oikeo*) carries with it the idea of being settled down in one's own home. It does not describe an occasional visitation or even a frequent visitor. Rather, the Spirit of God, in some mysterious way, makes His constant residence and home in the life of every person who trusts in Jesus Christ for salvation. God never leaves His children in isolation and without protection. He constantly indwells them. God never leaves His children at the mercy of a sinful world or an evil devil.

It's Time to Grow Up

Almost every culture on earth practices a ritual (symbolic or otherwise) that marks a young boy's transition from childhood to manhood. Many of these rituals are bizarre and often involve pain and excruciating experiences. Our own culture is somewhat devoid of a significant ritual marking this major transition from childhood to adulthood. Because of that, we have witnessed and are witnessing a continual extension of the age limit marking the distinction between childhood and manhood. In years gone by it might have been assumed that an 18-year-old was at that stage where he was leaving childhood and entering permanently into manhood with all its expectations and responsibilities. His family and friends and community would have understood that he was no longer a child but was now a man.

Accordingly, they would have rightly expected this new man to act like an adult discharging his responsibilities to family and community with maturity and manliness. Without a definite ritual marking this transition in our culture we have witnessed the age of childhood extending beyond age 18 and on into one's 20's. In fact, sometimes individuals who are older continue to view themselves as less than adult and more like children. They Prefer to play and avoid responsibility rather than to grow up–and they act accordingly.

Thus, the age of childhood and its attendant attitudes and actions has now crept into the 30s and sometimes, unfortunately, into the 40s. We are plagued with a society where such people have not grown up and so still act like children expecting to be taken care of by someone else. I saw a picture just the other day of a monument that was jokingly said to be a monument depicting modern-day Americans. The monument was a giant pacifier.

Christians must grow up and think like mature believers. Even though we might want to feel the presence of God without interruption we must continue to trust that He will not isolate us or desert us even in trying times. I have a young grandson who is two years old. He loves his mother and draws a great deal of comfort from her presence. When she leaves the room temporarily he sometimes cries for her. He wants to see her in his immediate presence and to feel the touch of her hand. She is an extremely good mother and even when she is not in the same room with him she loves him and is thinking about him. She would never leave him isolated and alone to his harm. As he grows up, he will come to learn the reality of that. Right now, he is just a small little child and cannot fathom that she still loves him and is carefully watching over him even when he cannot sense her presence.

Christians must learn to grow up and think biblically rather than act and react emotionally. God will never let us become isolated and exposed to danger in this sinful world. Though, at times, we may not sense His presence, God is always with us and will never forsake us.

Never Left Alone

I once read about a ritual that was practiced by a Native American tribe symbolically marking a young boys transition from childhood to adulthood. Every young man was expected to undergo this ritual marking his transition into adulthood so that he could view himself and be viewed by others as a man rather than as a child. This symbolic ritual was also necessary for the young boy to go through for him to be qualified for training as a warrior and for recognition by the tribe as a man. The ritual involved the father blindfolding his young son and then taking him out into the thick, dark, woods at night and sitting him on a wooden stump.

The young man was instructed by his father that he was to spend the entire night sitting alone on that stump without being able to see where he was or what surrounded him. The ritual was designed to be a test of the young boy's courage, endurance, and his ability to control his emotions.

As the night wore on, the young man could hear the sounds of animals moving in the brush. He heard the breaking of twigs and the rustling of leaves. His natural fear was fueled by his imagination so that he envisioned ravenous wolves, bears, and all manner of wild beasts circling him and sizing him up as an easy prey. The night hours seemed to go on forever and the feeling of isolation and loneliness as well as fear seemed to grow worse with each passing moment. The feeling of being alone, totally alone, in the wilderness at night worked on his psyche and his emotions. This was a completely new and frightening experience for the young boy. Yet, despite that, the young man was expected to deal with the terrors of the night without moving off the stump upon which he had been placed by his father. As the sun finally rose in the early morning hours and the birds could be heard singing while a slight breeze filled the air and the night began to ebb away the young man heard footsteps behind him. Frightened beyond belief he tensed up and forced himself to remain still though everything in him told him to bolt away and escape. His father was there and had come to remove the blindfold from the young man's eyes. Little had the young man known, it but his father had actually been sitting just a few feet away from him all night long serving as his protector without saying a word or making the slightest sound. His father was for him, and God is for you and me as our Father.

Sometimes it feels that we are all alone in a dark and terrifying world. We hear the sounds of what we fear will be our imminent hurt and destruction. We feel all alone and isolated, yet we must never forget that God our Father is always with us. He never abandons his children. It was Jesus who said, "I will never leave you nor forsake you – I am with you, always, even to the end of the ages." We have a good, good Father.

The Holy Spirit is perpetually *with* us, and more so, He is permanently and powerfully in us as true believers in Christ. If the Holy Spirit does not indwell a person then that person does not belong to Jesus Christ – which is the case with the unsaved. But, if a person is a true Christian then they are never abandoned and isolated by God. After all, it was our Lord Jesus who told us that He would never leave nor forsake us.

The person who is constantly indwelled by the Holy Spirit and under the control of the Holy Spirit need never think that they are all alone in this world. The Holy Spirit who indwells us will make His presence known and produce in us a sense of reassurance as well as the continued conduct of righteousness. He will empower the believer to produce righteousness in his mortal body and will also empower the believer to new life not only now but also forever (John 6:63; 2 Corinthians 3:6). The Holy Spirit will produce the fruit of the spirit in the life of the Christian (Galatians 5:22 – 23).

It was the Holy Spirit who acted as the divine agent of Christ's resurrection. Just as the Holy Spirit lifted Jesus out of physical death and gave Him life in His mortal body, so the Spirit, who dwells in the believer, gives to that believer new life now and forever including but not limited to the resurrection. Every true Christian should be able to examine himself and see the fruit of the Holy Spirit demonstrated in his life thus giving indication of the Holy Spirit's perpetual presence (Galatians 5:22). Do you have a clear inclination to avoid sin and a powerful passion to please God? Then this is the working of the Holy Spirit in your life as a believer. It is a practical indication that God is for you keeping you in the paths of righteousness for his namesake and for your good.

Not Alone – But Feeling All Alone

Now, I would like to address a common experience shared by many Christians – that of feeling isolated and alone in the world. It is one thing to know objectively that we are never isolated and left alone in this world of sin but that the Holy Spirit is constantly in us. It is another thing to subjectively feel the presence of God or to feel like we have somehow been abandoned by God. I am taking the time to address this subject for the practical benefit of those who may be suffering or will suffer from the feeling of isolation and loneliness.

The Lord Jesus Christ, prior to his arrest and crucifixion, must have felt some of this feeling of lonesomeness and isolation in His own life.

As has been previously pointed out, at one point in the ministry of the Apostle Paul he was also alone and in need of companionship. He wrote to Timothy, "Do your best to come to me quickly, for Demas, because he loved this world, has deserted me..." (2 Timothy 4:9 – 10). He also wrote to Timothy and said, "At my first defense, no one came to my support, but everyone deserted me. May it not be held against them. But the Lord stood at my side and gave me strength" (2 Timothy 4:16 – 17).

Loneliness and isolation are terrible experiences. Prisoners speak of the awfulness of solitary confinement and isolation. It is possible to have the feeling of loneliness and isolation even while being surrounded by people. Paul was feeling the pain of seeming isolation. Indeed, people may desert us and abandoned us as Jesus followers did Him in the garden of Gethsemane. But God will never leave us nor forsake us and isolate us. With this wonderful salvation that we have in Christ – there is no isolation in sin, but the Holy Spirit constantly indwells the believer and seals him until the day of redemption (Ephesians 4: 30). God is always with us and in us regardless of the circumstances that we face. Isolation or seeming isolation and loneliness are very real struggles but they are somewhat mitigated by the sure knowledge that God is always with us and for us. Still, how does a Christian rightly respond to the subjective feeling of being seemingly abandoned by God and isolated from Him?

A Lonely Psalmist

In Psalm 13, David felt isolated and alone. He wrote:

"How long O Lord? Will you forget me forever?
How long will you hide your face from me?
How long must I wrestle with my thoughts
and every day have sorrow in my heart?
How long will my enemies triumph over me?
Look on me and answer me Lord my God.
Give light to my eyes,
or I will sleep In death;
my enemy will say,' I have overcome him,'
and my foes will rejoice when I fall.
But I trust in your unfailing love;
my heart rejoices in your salvation.
I will sing to the Lord, for He has been good to me."

Have you ever felt isolated and alone like this? You pray and God doesn't answer. You try to be patient but God still doesn't answer or show up. You find yourself fearfully and frantically trapped in the dark tunnel and there is no light. You weep and cry in frustration and desperation but God still doesn't answer. You hope for the problem to go away, you hope for a miracle, but God doesn't answer and the pressing problems only continue to grow worse-and you feel more and more alone and isolated. Before long you begin to pray like David prayed, "How long, O Lord will you forget me forever?"

First, consider the context of Psalm 13. David has spent his childhood as a shepherd boy, just one of several sons in a large family. But one day, by the grace of God, David was led to kill the giant Goliath and his life would never be the same again. At first, he was the toast of the nation. Later he was a desperate young man hiding out in caves trying to elude the envious and jealous King Saul who viewed him as a rival for the throne. Saul was bitterly jealous, insecure, and highly temperamental. While the women of Israel celebrated the victory of David over Goliath by singing a new song (1 Samuel 18:7) the lyrics of the song ate away at the egotistical monarch. Saul's predictable response was to grow angry and seek to eliminate David as a threat to his kingdom and kingship. David became a fugitive for eight or nine years and lived a life of a desperate fugitive on the run from Saul. To complicate matters further David was best friends with Saul's son Jonathan and he had also fallen in love with Saul's daughter.

During those eight or nine years of living as a fugitive David had to remain constantly on the move living in forests, deserts, and caves. He could never relax and let down his guard. Finally, he was chased out of the land of Israel and into the territory of the Philistines whose hero he had previously slain (Goliath). The only way David could think of to escape the wrath of the Philistines was to act as if he had lost his mind. Therefore, that is what David did. He dribbled in his beard, scratched his hands on the doors of the city, and performed an Academy award presentation of a person who had completely lost his mind.

Later, David was able to manage to assemble the companionship and protection of 600 of his faithful men and he settled them in a place called Ziklag, where they lived peaceably for 16 months. One day, however, David and his men left on a military mission and when they returned home the city of Ziklag had been burned to the ground by his enemies. All the wives and the children of his soldiers, who had been left behind by their husbands when they went off to battle, had been carried away as captives by the marauders – including David's own family.

David's men were not only grief-stricken but they were filled with fury and anger at David and threatened to stone him to death as if he had caused it all of this to happen. They blamed David for everything – after all, he was their leader.

David was now physically exhausted and emotionally depressed when he wrote Psalm 13. His troubles seemed to be interminable – One after another after another with no end in sight they bombarded him. His life had been an interminable life of constant strain. David was confused, impatient and desperate. He felt isolated and alone. Would the problems never end? Would help never come? Was he totally isolated and alone? Would God never answer him?

If you have felt this way, or are feeling this way now, then take comfort in the fact that David also experienced the same feelings. The two words that seem to stand out in the Psalm are, *"How long?"* The general feeling seems to be one of isolation and desperation. Notice, that in this Psalm David had the feeling of being *forgotten* verse 1, "How long, O Lord? Will you forget me forever? His faith was running on nothing but fumes. Perhaps he believed that God had given up on Him – or perhaps he was at the point of giving up on God. Not only did David feel forgotten but he also felt *forsaken* (verse 1b), "How long will you hide your face from me?" Forgetting someone may be unintentional but forsaking them involves a personal choice. You will recall that on the cross the Lord Jesus Christ cried out, "My God, My God, why have you forsaken me?" Perhaps you have felt this way. David suffered and felt both forgotten and forsaken. Jesus was forsaken on the cross because he chose to become sin's sacrifice on behalf of sinners but because of what he did for us no true child of God will ever be forsaken. Neither David nor any other believer can now be forsaken by God. God turned his back upon His Son so that He would never have to turn his back on you and me.

David not only felt forgotten and forsaken but he also felt frustrated. "How long must I take counsel in my soul and have sorrow in my heart all the day?" (v. 2). Every day, he wrestled with his problems and every night, he tossed and turned and wrestled with them some more. David kept crying out, "How long...?" He was frustrated because of the daily grind and daily silence. Sometimes one of the hardest things to endure is the day–to–day, slow, silence as no help seems to come from God. David was frustrated because of the exalted position of his enemy over him. (v. 2) He was frustrated because of the seeming hopelessness of his situation. He felt forgotten, forsaken, and frustrated – and probably a bit fearful. What would become of him? In short, though he was a child of God, He felt isolated and alone. Have you been there? Are you there now?

It was at this low point, that David has finally sunk to the level of finding spiritual pay dirt. He had become so desperate that his prayer was for God to "give light to my eyes, or I will sleep the sleep of death" (v.3). He felt like he was going to die and needed an infusion of life and light to survive. David was also, at this time, concerned for the glory of God. He prayed that he would not be defeated and that God would not be disgraced by his defeat. He prayed that God would hear him and look upon him in mercy and power. He wanted to sense that God was with him and that he was not isolated and alone in the midst of his problems. His prayer was not a self-help model nor was it a self-seeking model but it was all about God.

Sometimes we will struggle with the subjective feeling of being isolated and alone as we make our journey through life as Christian pilgrims. Sometimes everything will seem to go wrong. We will have the tendency to feel forgotten, forsaken, and frustrated – even fearful. Sometimes God will not answer our prayers immediately. It is at those awful times that we must remember that we are, indeed, constantly being indwelt by the Holy Spirit who has given us life and is continually sustaining us in that life. We are never really isolated and alone. God's love is unfailing (v5). God's salvation is certain (v5b). God's goodness is forever (v6). David resolves to respond to his desperate condition by faith in God. "But I have trusted in your steadfast love; my heart shall rejoice in your salvation. I will sing to the Lord because he has dealt bountifully with me". The Holy Spirit is controlling us, constantly indwelling us, and producing the conduct or behavior of righteousness in our lives. No one or anything can keep Him from being successful in this work of salvation. There is no isolation in sin for the true believer in Christ. As the Apostle Paul wrote, "And I am sure of this, that he who began a good work in you will bring it to completion at the day of Jesus Christ." (Philippians 1:6) – God ensures it!

Furthermore, God not only ensures that we will not be isolated in this world of sin but he also touches our hearts with an overwhelming love causing us to live in a love relationship with Him.

A Testimony

Phil Christiensen and Shari McDonald have written a book about, "The Stories Behind Your Favorite Praise and Worship Songs." (Copyright 2003, Kregell Publishing). In this book, they include a testimonial by Lenny LeBlanc who was dramatically saved by the grace of God. Lenny's previous life had been in the world of secular music, drugs, and self-indulgence.

He was a successful songwriter with one of the world's largest and most influential music labels. Through the 1970s Lenny had been a successful pop artist and seemed to be on top of his world.

Then in 1981, Lenny got a call from a close friend who lived in Florida.

The caller was a big-time drug smuggler and he called Lenny late one night and said, "Lenny, I got saved. I'm going to heaven and I want you to be there with me. Are you saved?" This friend was like an older brother to Lenny, so what he said had weight. The two of them started talking about God even though Lenny was somewhat reluctant to talk about spiritual things. He had no idea what "saved" even meant and he hadn't been inside a church in probably 20 years. After their conversation, his Christian friend sent him a Bible, and Lenny started reading and God graciously started revealing Himself to Lenny.

As the words on the page spoke into Lenny's life, he found himself torn up about the choices he had made in the past. He was eaten up with guilt because he had left his family six or seven years before that, for his career. God started revealing to Lenny how much he needed to know God. The understanding of God's love melted Lenny's heart. He started crying out to God for forgiveness, and soon became born-again right there in his house".

Lenny's friends suggested that he might be losing his mind.

They thought he was nuts and that he was going off on some religious tangent, but Lenny had found the Lord...or, more accurately...God had found and saved Lenny.

At that time, Lenny was signed to Capitol records as a solo artist and had one record left on his contract. As he sat down to write songs for that record, praise and worship – not pop lyrics – fell from his lips.

Every time Lenny would write a song, by the time he got to the chorus it would be about what Jesus had done in his heart. He called his manager in Los Angeles and said, "Do you think they would let me out of my record deal?" He thought Lenny was completely crazy.

Crazy or not, Capitol Records agreed to put Lenny in suspension of his contract – he couldn't record for another label unless they bought out his contract. This was unlikely, since Christian music was still a relatively small industry in 1981. Few Christian record labels could afford to buy Lenny away from Capital.

Forced into an early retirement from the music industry, Lenny – a talented craftsman as well as a musician – made stained-glass. Often, he would get a job creating a window for a church, and the church would ask him to give his testimony to the youth group, sing a song during the Sunday morning service or give a Saturday night concert. At the same time, Lenny was still writing. But his songs were no longer about worldly matters. They were about the things of God! By the time Lenny had written more than a dozen Christian songs, God began to open new doors.

Lenny soon met many of the key figures in Christian music, including Michelle Pillar, who recorded three of his tunes. Two years after he left Capitol records, Capital realized that no one was willing to purchase Lenny's contract. They let him out of the agreement. Now Lenny recorded his own albums, this time for smaller Christian labels. But industry shakeups and financial considerations at the labels often interfered with his releases, leaving a sour taste in Lenny's mouth.

Lenny got really frustrated with the whole industry, thinking that this is the kind of stuff that goes on in pop music. All these Christian artists seem to want was to cross over to pop music where Lenny had originally come from.

Finally, in 1986, Lenny pulled back from the music industry and turned his focus to leading worship at his home in Florence, Alabama. There he noticed a need for more strong praise and worship music.

Back then churches were singing camp meeting songs. They really didn't have any contemporary worship songs. Lenny started asking God, "Would you give me some songs, just for our own fellowship? You know, songs that will relate to our generation?" And so, he started writing worship songs.

Lenny met some of the leaders at Maranatha Music, and they started using some of his songs – as well as his voice – on their projects. In 1998, Lenny recorded a solo worship album for Maranatha. He also provided background vocals on more than 20 of *Integrity Music's* Hosanna albums, and the labels started using several of his songs on various projects. In the early 1990s, Integrity approached him about doing a worship CD for them. When Lenny sat down to write a collection of songs specifically for that project, 1994's Pure Heart, he wrote, "There is None Like You".

Lenny said that he had a deadline and had to write 10 songs, or at least three or four great songs that would eventually make it to the CD. So, one morning he began playing the piano. A lot of times, he would just hum along with the piano, with no real idea what to write about but he was trying to stir up an idea. That morning he started singing. "There is none like you…" It just built from there, and another line or two came for the chorus."

After he had completed the chorus, Lenny took a brief break and thought, "Wow, this could really be something good."

He went back into the studio and sat down at the piano and sang through the chorus a few more times and fine-tuned it. And that's when the new song became crystallized in his heart and mind. He got on his face and started weeping. He couldn't control it. He couldn't believe that God was that good to give him something so beautiful and expressive.

Then Lenny started writing the verse.

After the success of "Pure Heart," Integrity signed Lenny as a solo artist, and he spent time writing songs that were not specifically worship songs. "But even when he wrote the artist–type songs they were always written from a heart of praise.

For five years, Lenny wrestled with the dilemma. What am I? Am I an artist? Am I a worship leader? Although highly skilled and successful in both roles, Lenny ultimately felt the strongest calling in the area of worship.

The second line of, "There is None Like You" says, "no one else can touch my heart like you do." That's where God touched Lenny. There's thousands of ways in which there is a no one like Him, but that's the one way that Lenny wanted to convey in his song. "No one else can touch my heart like you do. I could search for all eternity long to find there is none like you."

Lenny said, "No person, no thanks, no amount of money, no fame, I don't care what you put up against it, it doesn't even hold up." Lenny penned those thoughts in the first lines of his song and continued that theme throughout:

There is None Like You by Lenny LeBlanc
There is none like you
No one else can touch my heart like you do
I could search for all eternity long
And find there is none like you...

These lyrics describe the kind of intimate relationship that exists between true believers and the one true and living God. He loves us and touches our hearts like no one else can. God does not allow us to become isolated in this world of sin nor does He leave us in a state of emotional detachment. Instead, God "woo's" us and amazes us and touches us in our inner being so that we constantly exclaim with love and wonder, "There is none like you." For the true Christian, there is not only no condemnation and no domination by sin but there is also no isolation from God. Since God is with us we have a WONDERFUL SALVATION!

BRINGING IT HOME

1. What were the three points that I mentioned that capture the essence of this portion of the passage of Scripture in Romans chapter 8?

2. Think back to a time when you felt forgotten, forsaken, and frustrated with God. What was the occasion? Were you fearful? What helped you to work your way out of the situation? From what we studied in this chapter, what can you use the next time you face such an isolating and lonely feeling?

3. Is the Holy Spirit vitally interested in producing practical righteousness in the lives of true believers? Is the Holy Spirit interested in doing this in your life? How do you know?

5

Since God is for You there is

NO OBLIGATION

(TO SIN) – Romans 8:12 – 14

"So then, brothers, we are debtors, not to the flesh to
live according to the flesh. For if you live according to
the flesh you will die, but if by the Spirit you put to
death the deeds of the body, you will live. For all who
are led by the Spirit of God are the sons of God."

Bruce Larson writes about a friend of his who is an avid Eagle watcher. Rick takes his family to remote places where they can watch this great bird. On his most recent trip, he witnessed a strange incident. He had his binoculars fixed on a large, old Eagle he had given the name "Boss" because he seemed to be the biggest bird in the valley. Boss was soaring beautifully, catching the thermals and wheeling effortlessly in the sun. Suddenly the bird dove straight down, his eye is on a target invisible to Rick. But when the eagle reached the valley and began to ascend once more, it was obvious that he had gained the prize he was after. A large animal was gripped in his talons. Rick continued to watch, first with fascination, then with growing apprehension. Boss begin to fly crazily and erratically, still gripping his prize. Finally, he wheeled abruptly, crashed headlong into a nearby cliff, and plummeted to the valley floor.

Rick was stunned by this strange turn of events and determined to find out what happened. He marked the place where he had last seen Boss fall and then laboriously began to climb down into the valley to see if he could find him. Rick searched over an hour before he came upon the stricken Eagle with his dad pray still in his grip. The strange events were immediately explained. Boss's prize was a badger, one of the meanest and most ferocious animals alive. The scenario was obvious. Boss had gotten his prize, but the badger was no easy victim. He retaliated by gnawing away the eagle's stomach. Boss's prize was his undoing. (The Presence, San Francisco, Harper & Row, Publishers, 1988, pp. 8-9).

The unsaved person is driven by a sinful nature to pursue sin even at great risk to himself. When presented with the opportunity to sin he feels obligated to pursue it with all his ability. This sense of innate obligation to sin is often his undoing. The believer in Christ is forever freed from this slavish sense of obligation to sin and instead he feels a great sense of gratitude toward the God who saved him and thus he willingly obligates himself to serve is God with total commitment.

As sinners, we used to feel that we had to sin. There was a compulsive desire inside of us driving us to seek fulfillment and pleasure in sin. We were convinced that ultimate happiness or at least temporary pleasures necessitated that we eagerly engage in sinful activity. Our Lord said that men loved darkness rather than light because their deeds are evil. Such a constant craving for sin and its supposed delights comes to control our thoughts, desires, and actions. We are convinced that more sin is the answer to our inner emptiness and so we submit ourselves willingly to its allure until we actually become voluntary addicts to sin. It can and does become a kind of obligation on our part. We feel obliged to tell increasingly bigger and more constant lies to make ourselves look bigger and better. We feel obliged to drink too much and to party too much, etc. We feel obliged to buy things that are beyond our means so that we can impress other people. Our natural tendency toward sin is compounded by the sense of needing to live that way. We can even feel obligated to maintain a certain image at any cost.

When God saves us, He helps us to realize that we are no longer the same kind of person that we once were. We are no longer obligated to sin to scratch our sinful itch. Rather, we are now changed people by the grace of God in Christ. Now, we are deeply obligated to God. Why? Because of God's miraculous deliverance of us from sin's guilt and penalty (condemnation) and from the power that sin once exerted over us (the domination of sin). We owe God so much that we could never repay it but now our continual, willing obligation as Christians is to, with gratitude, live for God with all our hearts.

The songwriter of old wrote:

> "Were the whole realm of nature mine,
> that were a present far too small,
> love so amazing, so divine,
> demands my life, my soul, my all"

"Much Obliged" To the Nth Degree

Years ago, when someone helped another person or did a favor for them, the recipient of the favor was likely to thankfully reply, "Much obliged." The phrase came to be another handy, formal way of saying, "thank you." The earliest quotation for this phrase in the Oxford English dictionary is dated at approximately 1548. This dictionary defines the sense of the phrase "being obliged" as, "to be bound to a person by ties of gratitude; to owe or feel gratitude; to be indebted to a person for something."

This original meaning of the term multiplied exponentially to the Nth degree (which means multiplied as many times as is possible – without conclusion) describes quite well the attitude of the true Christian toward God their Savior. The true Christian, unlike the unsaved person, does not feel any obligation to obey the dictates of sin-quite the opposite.

The believer was once mastered by sin and Satan. He obediently submitted to the things of the world and things of sin. Sin lied to him. Sin devastated his life. Sin increased God's wrath against him Sin contaminated, distorted, misdirected, and burdened him with guilt and shame. Sin placed him under the wrath and condemnation of God. Sin did all of this and yet the lost sinner still felt obligated to continue down the path of sin.

The unsaved sinner dwells on sinful thoughts, pursues sinful pleasures and delights in sinful entertainment. He gleefully associates with and participates with sinful people, prefers darkness (sinfulness) to light, and adamantly defends his sinful practices. He stands constantly ready to obey and submit to any sinful invention. He is under the control of sin even though he fancies himself to be free and fully in charge. The lost sinner is, in fact, obligated to sin by virtue of his inner nature which compels him to continue in sin.

Upon conversion to Christ, that has now all changed. No longer does there exist a sense of obligation to sin, but now there is a loving sense of indebtedness to God (exponentially to the Nth degree) for the great salvation which He has accomplished and is accomplishing for the believer. Sin no longer sits on the throne of the heart dictating and controlling the sinner's attitudes and activities. Sins captivating grip has been broken through the powerful operation of the Holy Spirit in accordance with God's abounding grace in Christ. The Apostle Paul, writing about the death of Christ, wrote, that "He died for all, that they which live should not henceforth live unto themselves, but to Him which died for them, and rose again." Paul listed as one main reason for this dramatic change now being true: "Therefore if any man is in Christ, he is a new creature/creation: old things are passed away; behold, all things are become new" (2 Corinthians 5:15, 17).

Paul wrote to the Ephesians and told the Ephesians that they were once darkness but now that they were Christians they should consider themselves to be children of light. He encouraged them to walk in the light as children of light. A partial line from an old hymn reads "He breaks the power of canceled sin." This is exactly what happens in salvation. The power of sin and our personal sense of willing obligation to pursue it is broken. We, as Christians, are free from sin's power.

When writing to the Romans, Paul employed the imagery of slavery. He wrote, "For in that He (Christ) died, He died to sin once: but in that He lives, He lives unto God. Likewise consider yourself also to be dead indeed unto sin, but alive unto God through Jesus Christ our Lord. Let not sin therefore reign in your mortal body, that you should obey it and its lusts. Neither yield your members as instruments of unrighteousness to sin: but yield yourselves to God, as those that are alive from the dead, and your members as instruments of righteousness unto God. For sin shall not have dominion over you: for you are not under the law, but under grace" (Romans 6:10 – 14). Paul went on in the same context to tell his readers that they had once been willing slaves to sin when they were unsaved, and consequently obligated to obey its commands, but that now, as Christians, they were to be willing subjects to God. The obligation they had before was an obligation to sin. The obligation they have after conversion is a loving and eagerly willing obligation to serve God with love and gratitude.

O to Grace, How Great a Debtor

Robert Robinson, the 18th-century pastor and hymnist, wrote the hymn, "Come Thou Fount of Every Blessing." The theme and lyrics of this hymn highlight the beauty of divine grace. The actual words are based on 1 Samuel 7:12.

Robert Robinson was just a small boy when his dad died. In 18th-century England, there was little in the way of a social welfare system and this meant that he had to go to work at a very young age. Without a father to guide and keep him steady Robert fell in with bad companions.

One day his gang of roughnecks harassed a drunken Gypsy. They poured copious amounts of liquor into her and demanded that she tell their fortunes for free. Pointing her finger at Robert she told him he would live to see his children and grandchildren. For some reason, the words of that Gypsy fortuneteller touched a tender spot in his heart. "If I'm going to live to see my children and grandchildren," he thought, "I'll have to change my way of living. I can't keep on like I'm going now."

Robert Robinson decided to go hear the Methodist preacher George Whitfield. To cover his "weak" urge, he talked the other boys into going with him to heckle the gathering. Whitfield preached on the text, "O generation of vipers, who has warned you to flee from the wrath to come?" (Matthew 3:7). This message greatly disturbed Robert and he was unable to shake the deep sense of the burden of sin that he felt. Indeed, this deep conviction over his sin lasted three years.

Finally, at the age of 20, Robert made peace with God and immediately set out to become a Methodist preacher himself. Two years later, in 1757, he wrote a hymn which expressed his joy in his new faith. Two of the stanzas to that hymn are as follows:

> "Come thou fount of every blessing,
> Tune my heart to sing Thy grace.
> Streams of mercy, never ceasing,
> Call for songs of loudest praise.

Teach me some melodious sonnet,
Sung by flaming tongues above.

O to grace how great a debtor
Daily I'm strained to be!
Let thy goodness, like a fetter,
Bind my wandering heart to thee.
Prone to wander, Lord, I feel it
Prone to leave the God I love.
Here's my heart, O take and seal it
Seal it for Thy courts above.

This is the kind of debt or obligation that the believer feels to God. He feels eternally indebted to the one who loved him and saved him from sin and its devastating consequences.

I am obligated to love my wife and children, yet this obligation is not some kind of onerous burden. It is an obligation that I gladly discharge out of deep love for them. The debt that I feel toward them is not a drag on my emotions but rather a delight to my heart.

One of the greatest hymn writers of all time was Isaac Watts. At the time of Watt's birth, churches in England sang only metrical Psalms led by a cantor. During his lifetime, however, Isaac Watts composed over 600 hymns. One of my favorite hymns by Isaac Watts is *"When I survey the wondrous Cross"* which is a classic example of his theological content in writing. This hymn ends with a climax. I have already quoted the last lines part of which read, "Demands my soul, my life, my all." This hymn is a masterpiece that marks the genius of one man and his influence on millions of singers throughout the ages. As one writer stated, "He successfully built a bridge from psalmody to hymnody and set the church free to create a living body of Christian praise and song." Two of the stanzas of that well-known hymn are of particular note in light of our examination of Paul's contention that as Christians we are, "debtors," or "obligated," out of love and gratitude to willingly serve God from the heart. These two stanzas read:

"When I survey the wondrous Cross

On which the Prince of glory died,
My richest gains, I count but loss,
And pour contempt on all my pride.

Were the whole realm of nature mine,
That were a present far too small;
Love so amazing, so divine,
Demands my soul, my life, my all.

The other stanzas of this hymn are pregnant with powerful biblical and theological truth and imagery but I have chosen to quote these stanzas again to underscore the sense of debt and obligation that the true believer feels toward God for his salvation.

There are some things, of course, that we are obligated to do that we don't look forward to. Perhaps, one such thing is paying our taxes. Another might be paying off debt that we have incurred from overspending. These are obligations that we have that must be met faithfully. As I have already mentioned, there is also the obligation of loving our wife, husband, children, and other family members. These are obligations but they pose no kind of onerous or burdensome feeling in us. Love causes us to want to support and sacrifice for our family. This latter kind of obligation is the kind that the Christian has regarding God's Word, "By this we know that we love the children of God, when we love God and obey His commandments. For this is the love of God, that we keep His commandment and His commandments are not burdensome" I John 5:2 – 3.

"So then, brothers, we are debtors, not to the flesh, to live according to the flesh. For if you live according to the flesh, you will die, but if by the Spirit you put to death the deeds of the body, you will live, for all who are led by the Spirit of God are sons of God" (Romans 8:12 – 14).

Notice the following points drawn from this text:

I. The Mandated Duty
II. The Major Choice – a death and life choice
III. The Meaning
IV. The Manner

I. The Mandated Duty

The Apostle Paul begins in these verses with the words "So then". In the previous 11 verses of chapter 8, Paul has described many wonderful things that are true of one who has been genuinely saved by Jesus Christ through the work of the Holy Spirit. Such a person is no longer condemned, is no longer under the dominion of sin, is never isolated in sin, and they now live a life of peace with God and produce positive spiritual fruit in their lives because their minds and natures have been changed by the Holy Spirit. Now he writes, "So then". Paul also reemphasizes the relationship that he has with his readers and the relationship that they have with God by referring to them as "brothers". "Therefore, brothers…". He next includes both them and himself by saying, "we are…" What is it that they "are" or that they have in common? What common experience do they share? Whatever it is, it forms the basis of a common obligation – but an obligation to whom or to what? Paul writes that we have an obligation (we are debtors) but that it is not to live according to the sinful nature but rather to live according to the Spirit. That is now our duty – the debt that we owe.

We began this book by using David is an example of one who had the courage to stand up and step forward for God in the face of a daunting challenge and a fearful situation. I mentioned that David had two key ingredients in his life that were missing in the lives of the other Jewish soldiers. These two key ingredients enabled him to be a bold and faithful champion for God. These two ingredients were a passionate commitment to God and a personal assurance that God was with him and for him. As we have begun to work through Paul's description of the wonderfully perfect salvation that God has blessed us with, have you begun to increase in your passion for God and are you becoming thoroughly convinced that God is with you and for you? That is the response that you should be having as we examine Paul's vivid description of God's provision of a perfect and guaranteed salvation for believing sinners like yourself.

"You Got To Do It!"

Some time ago a salesperson was attempting to coerce me into signing a contract. That person was extremely arrogant, pushy and rude. Every so often that sales person would point to the contract in question, hold up an ink pen, gesture toward the contract and say, "You gotta sign right here!" "You got to do it!" After each pushy presentation the salesperson would make the same attempt to get me to sign the contract using the same annoying words, "You got to do it." Finally, having just about had enough of this high-pressure technique, I replied, "I don't gotta sign anything – furthermore, I don't intend to". I was under no obligation to sign the contract and had no intention of doing so. As Christians, we are under no obligation to obey sin and should have no intention of doing so.

The story is told of a former black slave who after his emancipation encountered his old master. Evidently, the old master still considered himself to be the supreme voice of authority over this black man who was once his slave. Consequently, he barked out an order to him and, momentarily, conditioned by years of unquestioned obedience and servitude, the black man instinctively started to comply with the command of his old master. Then he realized that the old relationship of master and slave which had once controlled his life no longer existed. Once it had been his duty to obey every command of his old master unquestionably and immediately. Now, no such duty remained. He had been freed from the old relationship that had once enslaved him and was no longer under any obligation to obey the old master.

As Christians, we were once enslaved in sin and dominated by it. We felt obligated to obey its every command. But now, that old relationship has been terminated – it has been changed by the Holy Spirit. We are no longer obligated to sin. Our obligation now is to obey our new Lord and Master Jesus Christ and to do so willingly and freely and fully out of a heart dominated by overwhelming love.

Do You Realize You Are a Willing Slave?

This brings up an interesting and instructive point. Many Christians do not realize that Jesus frees us from bondage under sin and delivers us to a royal slavery that we might be his possession. Those who would be His followers must then be willing also to be his slaves. We are slaves of Christ who is a wonderful and gracious master. When our English Bibles use the word, "servant," it is the word for slave in the original Greek.

This metaphor is used more frequently to refer to Christians in the New Testament than any other.

In today's world and culture, we must realize that Christians have actually volunteered to become the slaves of Jesus Christ. To be sure, we are also sons of God, members of Christ's church, the bride of Christ, the light of the world, etc. In the early church, however, the outside world referred to the believers as "Christians" because of their likeness to Christ and because of their devotion and obedience to Him, Christians referred to themselves as the slaves of Jesus Christ. This sheds great light on what it means to be a real Christian. This also explains how the biblical writers could so easily talk about our obligation to submit to and obey Jesus Christ in everything.

An Important Distinction

We must not confuse the concept of biblical slavery with the abuses of 18th-century slavery that we have become familiar with or the horrendous atrocities of the modern-day slave trade.

Slavery in the days of Paul was quite different. Slavery in that day was not racially motivated. Furthermore, the institution of slavery was a pervasive social structure of the Roman Empire. There were slaves of all ethnicities, ages, and abilities regardless of gender or creed. Roughly one fifth of the Empire's population were slaves – totaling as many as 12 million people at the outset of the first century A.D.

Indeed, some slaves found life to be very difficult because they had poor, harsh masters who mistreated them. This was especially true of those slaves who worked in the mines or on farms. There were also household slaves who received greater honor than other slaves because they worked more closely with their masters. Then there were slaves trained to be teachers, trained to work in the world of medicine, etc. Many slaves had good and generous masters who treated them justly and fairly. They were cared for and valued. Their sole concern was to carry out the interest of their owner. In return, the master cared for their needs and provided for them. If a master was particularly prestigious or powerful in the community his slaves were respected because of their relationship with him. That being said, they were nevertheless someone else's possession and totally obligated to be obedient to their master.

This may all seem repugnant at first sight when we consider that we are the slaves of Christ. But if we think about it in greater detail we will see that the Holy Spirit who indwells us prompts us to have the same desires that Christ has for us. That is why His commandments are not a burden to the believer. We desire the same thing that He desires. We love the same things. We rejoice in the same things. We love our master and our master loves us deeply. We are obligated but that obligation is a delight. The personal obedience to our master is our mandated duty (our obligation) but it is also our most cherished desire.

II. The Major Choice – A Death & Life Choice

The idea that human beings are completely free from obligation is a distortion of the devil. Satan sought to promote this idea to Adam and Eve in the Garden of Eden and so persuaded them to act with complete independence from God. The results were devastating. The truth is, all people, because of the way they are wired inwardly, are obligated either to live in sin or to live according to God's Spirit.

Some decisions that we are called upon to make are less important than others. The decision regarding our personal salvation, however, is a crucial one. The Apostle Paul, in the book of Romans, has already dealt with this issue to a large extent. In Romans chapter 5 the apostle extolled the wonderful grace of God and spoke of its super abounding quality. Where sin abounds, grace does much more abound.

In Romans chapter 6, the apostle anticipates some possible objections to his message of salvation by grace alone. One such objection, is that if grace in its abundance glorifies God by overcoming sin, then why not sin in abundance so that God's grace could be displayed in superabundance and therefore bring much more glory to God.

It is hard to believe that one would reason in this fashion but this is exactly the perverted interpretation taught by some in church history such as the infamous Rasputin. Rasputin was a religious advisor to the Romanov family of Russia in the late 19th and early 20th centuries. He and others like him believed that the more you sin the more God gives you grace and therefore glorifies Himself through that process. In that light, he taught that one should strive to be more than just an ordinary sinner. He or she should seek to be an extraordinary sinner and sin with utter abandonment thus requiring more and more of the grace of God to be demonstrated in his or her life. Throughout church history many people have drifted into extremism like this or in some other form. Some have sought to overcome sin by endless rules and regulations, rituals and religious ceremonies. Others have licentiously used the freedom of grace to espouse ideas of extreme libertarianism and sinfulness. Both are distortions of the true gospel. The Apostle Paul raises the anticipated objection to his teaching of grace that might come from such people and asks, "What shall we say, then? Shall we go on sinning so that grace may increase? (Romans 6:1). He answers this anticipated objection with the strongest possible idiom of repudiation in the New Testament Greek (me genoito). He couldn't have said what he said any stronger – "May it never be!" or "Perish the thought!" "By no means! We died to sin; how can we live in it any longer?" (Romans 6:2).

Paul emphasized the vital identification of each and every believer with the Lord Jesus Christ. True believers are baptized into Jesus Christ (speaking of our spiritual baptism) especially in terms of His death to sin and His resurrection. In this context, the word baptism carries with it the idea of being identified with. In his first letter to the Corinthians Paul spoke of Israel being baptized into Moses (1 Corinthians 10:2). This symbolized the identification and solidarity of the people with Moses as God's spokesman and leader. In terms of the Christian and his identification with Christ, Paul is referring to the historical fact of Christ's crucifixion – His death. Our identification with Christ in his death (through spiritual baptism) is so that we may live a "new life".

The Old & The New Self

Paul is contrasting the "old" self with the "new life." The dualistic view that a Christian has two separate natures is a non–biblical one and such teaching can be very destructive to the child of God. The truth is, our old self was crucified with Christ and identified with Him in His death making way for a new life. To be sure, we still are plagued with remnants of the old sinful nature but the old nature itself has been crucified. To be crucified not only means to suffer extreme pain but it means to experience certain death. Crucifixion is the end of the life of a person and crucifixion is the end of our old nature. The Apostle Paul wrote to the Galatian church and said, "Those who belong to Christ Jesus have crucified the flesh with its passions and desires" (Galatians 5:24). The same apostle when writing to the Colossian church states clearly that the putting off the old self is something that has already and irreversibly occurred. "Do not lie to one another," he says, "since you laid aside the old self with its evil practices, and have put on the new self who is being renewed to a true knowledge according to the image of the one who created him" (Colossians 3:9 – 10).

Why was our old self crucified with Jesus Christ? Paul answers this question for us in Romans 6:6 – 7?

How did Jesus Christ die to sin since He wasn't a sinner? He died to sin in that He died to its penalty by taking upon Himself the sins of all His people and paying for them in full. He met sins legal demand. Christ also died to the power of sin by forever breaking its power over those who belong to God through faith in Him. He also died to sin permanently – once and for all (Romans 6:10). His sacrifice is not replicated. He is not sacrificed afresh as is thought to be done in the Roman Catholic Mass or in any other way.

What resulted from our identification with Christ in His death and resurrection? The answer is that the body of sin is "done away" with. Or as some translations prefer to use the words, "destroyed" or "annulled." This does not mean that sin is eliminated but it does mean that sin as a dominating force has been overcome. Secondly, now we are no longer slaves to sin (Romans 6:7). In our previous life as non-Christians, we had little choice but to obey the dominating sinful influence that dictated our actions and controlled our desires – in that sense, we were obligated to sin. Now that we have become Christians we are forever freed from that dominating influence of sin. We are no longer obligated to sin. Third, we now have a new life Romans 6:4. The word "new" in this text does not mean new in terms of chronological newness but rather new in terms of quality. Our new life has a new and different quality than did our old life. Since God is for you your sense of obligation is forever changed. You are no longer obligated to sin or to serve sin. Out of gratitude you are now obligated to love and serve God.

THE REALITY, RESPONSIBILITY,
& THE RESULTS

Paul has been describing the reality of the believer's being united with and identified with the Lord Jesus Christ in his death and resurrection. Next, he moves to the responsibility which every believer has, as a result of his identification with Christ, and his reception of a new life principle by the Holy Spirit. Paul writes, "In the same way, count yourselves dead to sin but alive to God in Christ Jesus. Therefore, do not let sin reign in your mortal body so that you obey its evil desires. Do not offer the parts of your body to sin, as instruments of wickedness, but rather offer yourselves to God, as those who have been brought from death to life; and offer the parts of your body to Him as instruments of righteousness. (Romans 6:11–13)

Our responsibility is clear. Paul stated in Romans chapter 8:12a, that "we are debtors – we have an obligation. But it is not to the sinful nature, to live according to it. The apostle has highlighted the reality of our identification with Christ and our responsibility as those who are identified with Him. Finally, he turns to the results of our identification with Jesus Christ in His death and resurrection and our reception of a "new" life by the Holy Spirit. What is the inevitable result? The apostle answers this question by powerfully affirming a spiritual truth. "For sin shall not be your master, because you are not under law, but under grace" (Romans 6:14). Paul is not saying that it would be nice if sin were not your master but he is stating an irrefutable fact. The law could not free us from the mastery and domination of sin but grace does. What a wonderful salvation! Our obligation is not to the law, not to sin, not to Satan, not to the world system, but to our new Master who is loving, gracious, merciful, tender, wise and knowledgeable, etc.

The results: The Apostle Paul has approached this subject by explaining to his readers the reality of our identification with Jesus Christ in his death and resurrection, our responsibility as those who have been united with Him through faith, and the inevitable results in the life of one who has been so united to Christ in a saving way (the result of a dramatically changed life in the direction of godliness, holiness, and increased and conformity to the image of Jesus Christ our Lord). Interestingly, all of this has been made possible by the work and ministry of the Holy Spirit in the life of the believer. Because God is for you He has given you the Holy Spirit to be your helper as you live the Christian life.

Next the apostle returns to the generally anticipated objection to grace. He is imagining someone who is saying that if grace is such a grand thing and is always victorious over sin then why not go on sinning. Paul responds to this perverted thought just like he did to the previously anticipated objection (me genoito) – "By no means!" Paul then seeks to relate to his readers by using a common illustration of the day. The Roman world was approximately 1/5 slaves and 4/5 free. The people of that culture were conditioned to understand and function within the parameters of the institution of slavery. It is estimated that a great many in the early church were, themselves, slaves.

Paul wrote to the Romans and reminded them that if a person offers himself to someone to obey that person then they become His slave. That would have been common knowledge and the common experience for the people of his day. He is saying that the same thing holds true in the spiritual realm. You are slaves to the one whom you obey. He goes on to thank God and to commend the Roman believers for having obeyed the gospel (good news) by which they were liberated from sin and made servants/slaves of righteousness (Romans 6:15–18). By way of illustration Paul reminded them of how they had served sin in their previous manner of living when they were "slaves to sin". He asked them to assess the benefit and loss of such a lifestyle in light of what they now know (6:21). And then he encourages them to live with total commitment to the new life that they now have in God which leads to holiness and eternal life. They have been set free from sin to serve God. What a wonderful transition! – What obligation do we now have?

This is the background behind Paul's reasoning in Romans 8:12 when he writes, "Therefore, brothers, we are debtors – we have an obligation – but it is not to the sinful nature, to live according to it."

An Either/Or Option

Paul is saying that we are obligated but that our obligation is to a different master and to a different way of living. What happens if a person makes a profession of faith in Christ and yet continues to live in a manner consistent with their old sinful lifestyle? The apostle answers that question, "For if you live according to the sinful nature, you will die; but if by the Spirit you put to death the misdeeds of the body, you will live" (Romans 8:13). The options are crystal clear. It is an either/or life or death proposition. The apostle is not warning genuine believers that they may lose their salvation and be condemned to death if they fall back into some of the ways of the flesh. He has already assured believers that there is no condemnation left for them because they are in Christ Jesus. He is rather saying that a person whose life is characterized by the way of the flesh (sinfulness) is not a genuine Christian. Sadly, that person who fails or refuses to turn away from his sin by turning to God in repentance by trusting Jesus Christ alone for salvation, is headed for eternal death and separation from God in the torments of hell.

Many in churches today have made a superficial commitment of faith to historical facts or have made a religious response to some emotional trauma, or high-pressured presentation of the gospel, but have never been changed so that they have turned from sin and to righteousness as a pattern of life. They show no signs of repentance or conscious concern for the things of God. They have a general indifference to worship and the fellowship of the saints and must be urged again and again to be faithful to attend church. Yet, they take supposed refuge in the fact that they have technically touched base with God by walking an aisle of invitation, signing a piece of paper, raising their hands at the end of a church service, being baptized, joining a church, giving money, etc. They are not really seeking to put to death the misdeeds of the body and to live according to the leading of the Holy Spirit in the path of holiness.

The fact is, they feel no duty or obligation or desire to do so. These people are not Christians. Some may occupy positions of responsibility and authority. Some may even preach behind pulpits or sing beautifully in church, but they are not Christians. Some may be charter members of the church and respected members of the community, but if they live in sinfulness and not righteousness as a pattern of life then they are not genuine Christians.

I am not setting myself up as the judge of such people. Far be it for me to do so. I'm merely sharing with you what God's Word clearly says. How many fall into this category? We sometimes refer to them as "nominal

Christians" or "carnal Christians". Often at funerals people try to put the best spin on the life of the departed person but, if truthful, they are forced to ask themselves, "Did this person actually display the marks of a true Christian during his lifetime?" Thank God for those who do!

III. The Meaning - Putting to Death the Misdeeds of the Body

Paul describes the life of the true Christian as follows: "By the Spirit you put to death the misdeeds of the body..." (Romans 8:13). Sin will linger long and silently while it waits for its opportunity to break out in open rebellion. Religion can sometimes distract a person from the real issue of personal salvation. Sin must be dealt with—we are obligated to do so. What does it mean to put to death the misdeeds of the body? It means to kill sin! Jesus said, "If you're right eye makes you stumble, tear it out, and throw it from you, for it is better for you that one of the parts of your body perish, than for your whole body to be thrown into hell, and if your right hand makes you stumble, cut it off, and throw it from you; for it is better for you that one of the parts of your body perish, than for your whole body to go into hell" (Matthew 5:29 – 30).

I remember reading the story of U. S. Navy Seal, Bradley Cooper. His life story was also made into a motion picture. Cooper was renowned for eliminating the enemy. In doing so, he was, at the same time, protecting the lives of American Marines. He knew that if he did not kill the enemy that the enemy would kill his fellow combatants. He developed a keen skill and a determined focus on killing the enemy. Sin is a serious matter. We must track it down and kill it without mercy. If we do not kill sin, sin will kill us! That is what God's Word tells us. We should do whatever is necessary to keep ourselves from sinning because if we do not kill sin then we will die. One of the key characteristics of a true child of God is that that person is busy about the business of killing sin in their life. This is the pattern for every true believer. In that sense, we must be ruthless eliminators of every known sin in our lives.

IV. The Manner

How do we, by the Spirit, put to death the misdeeds of the body? Before we deal with that, let me remind the reader that God's people will invariably fall back into sin when their focus is taken away from God and placed upon themselves and the world. That is why we must heed the admonition, "Set your mind on things above not on things that are on earth. For you have died and your life is hidden with Christ in God" Colossians 3:1 – 3. We must constantly be thinking about God and the things of God to stave off the persistent and insidious attacks of sin. Jesus often said, "I must be about my father's business," "the Father makes it rain on the unjust as well as the just," "If God so clothes the lilies of the field..." Jesus was always thinking about God and the things of God – so must we be as well. Regarding the means of putting to death the misdeeds of the body, allow me to suggest some practical things that may be helpful in pursuing this path:

Recognize the remaining presence of sin in your flesh. It oftentimes hides from clear view but is, nevertheless, lurking in the shadows. If you do not recognize that you are still a sinner and will not admit it then you are setting yourself up for destruction. Too often our tendency is to clearly see the sin in the lives of others while being blind to sin in our own life. Every Christian needs to examine himself on a regular basis and deal with the sin that they find there. We must not give sin and opportunity to take root and to grow. Personal sin must be identified early and rooted out by a ruthless determination to eradicate it in our lives.

Rivet your heart and mind on God. The psalmist wrote, "O that my ways may be established to keep your statutes! Then I shall not be ashamed when I look upon all your commandments" (Psalm 119:5 – 6). Think about God, about God's character, about God's actions, about "God's expectations, about God's goodness, and seek after God with all your heart. Rivet your heart and mind on God.

Ruminate, or chew on the Word of God – meditate upon it. The Word of God becomes a searchlight for our lives and by it we see ourselves in a different light than we would have seen ourselves without it. A brief and cursory reading of the word is not enough. One must ponder the principles and consider the application to their life. One must think deeply and continually on the Word of God. The psalmist wrote, "Your Word I have treasured in my heart that I may not sin against you" (Psalm 119:11). The person who is blessed of God is described in the following way: "his delight is in the law of the Lord, and in his law he meditates day and night" (Psalm 1:2).

Regularly engage God in prayer. Acknowledge and confess your sins to God. Ask Him for forgiveness and cleansing. Ask Him to help you make progress in holiness and in your spiritual life. Ask God to further His kingdom and glorify His name by using you as His tool and available instrument. Ask God to make you usable – a clean vessel for the Master's use.

Resolve that you will obey God in everything – obedience should be practiced by all true Christians. We do not wait to the moment of temptation to make up our mind to sin or not but we make that decision far in advance and we persist in our obedience when times are difficult as well as when times are easier. We must be resolved, in our hearts, to obey God regardless of the consequences and possible distractions.

Daniel is a prime example of one who was resolved to obey God regardless of the situation and the possible personal cost to him. Even when ordered by the King to cease praying to God Daniel persisted in obeying God rather than submitting to the earthly authority. He did so knowing that such obedience to God may well cost him his life. This practice will help keep us from giving in to the misdeeds of the body and will propel us forward along the path of righteousness. Resolute determination to be obedient to God is a genuine mark of true salvation and will enable us to be led by the Spirit in putting to death the misdeeds of the body.

The importance of this practice of following the Holy Spirit's leadership and putting to death the misdeeds of the body cannot be overemphasized: "Because those who are led by the spirit of God are sons of God" 8:14. How does the Spirit of God lead Christians? Paul has stated that those who are led by the Spirit of God are the ones who are the sons of God. How do you know you're being led by the Spirit of God? I believe God wants His children to know that they are His children. One of the ways that He makes this known to them is by His leading of them by the Holy Spirit. But how does this work?

How Does the Holy Spirit Primarily Lead Christians?

Let me be quick to say that sometimes a Christian may not *feel* like a child of God. Feelings fluctuate and are affected by a number of different factors. I remember hearing Mark Lowery talk about this subject in one of his comedy routines. He said that he woke up in the middle of the night to go to the bathroom and on his way there, he stumped his toe against the metal frame of the bed. Biting his tongue and hopping around in the dark bedroom seeking some relief from the throbbing pain in his toe Mark said that he did not at that moment feel like a Christian. I'm sure we've all had experiences and/or failings when we did not feel like a Christian. Some people even feel insecure by nature. Circumstances can too often affect the way we feel. Even a chemical imbalance can adversely affect the feelings of a true Christian. True Christians can sometimes feel like anything but a true Christian. The leading of the Holy Spirit is not dependent upon feelings. God saves men and women through faith in Him and He leads us in life through the same mechanism of faith. The Holy Spirit leads God's children in many ways. He is sovereign and can act in whatever way He is pleased to do. But the primary ways by which the Holy Spirit leads Christians are those of the Word of God and the way of sanctification.

A Word About Divine Guidance

The primary means by which God leads and guides His people is the Scripture applied to our living. The Word of God counsels us to be like Jesus Christ in both character and conduct, it counsels us as to how to conduct our family affairs, it counsels us in the area of morals, it counsels us in terms of how to interact with our fellow Christians and how to evangelize and disciple the unsaved, it counsels us as to what to avoid in life and what to seek after, it counsels us in the area of good citizenship, it counsels us in the area of friendship, it counsels us in the area of compassion and benevolence and love, it counsels us in the area of one's work, etc. This is primarily how God guides us through life. Every area and dimension of our lives should be governed by our willing obedience to the Word of God. The Bible is our standard for guidance and direction from God our lives must be directed within the parameters and guidelines of the Bible. God never leads us to violate Scripture.

Christians run into trouble when they are unwilling to think biblically and when they have not disciplined themselves to learn how to think and discern things biblically. Christians must also learn to think ahead and consider the long-term consequences of any decision as well as considering the impact that our decisions may have on others. Christians must not be headstrong and unwilling to accept advice from godly sources. Christians must learn that they sometimes are tempted to make decisions based on inner compulsions and desires which are unwise. They must be careful to be honest with themselves about this. Christians must learn not to be swayed by the personal magnetism of any individual, but rather to consider, with discernment, everyone's comments in such a way as to decipher truth from error. Christians must sometimes learn to wait on the Lord, and to meditate on His Word rather than making quick, knee-jerk, rash decisions. We must realize that God leads according to His own timetable and not according to ours. All of these are principles that the Christian should keep in mind when seeking to be led by God.

One of the biggest errors of our day is sometimes people feel, if they are being genuinely being led by the Spirit of God that the path they take should be an easy one free of problems and obstacles. This, however, does not comport with the teaching of Scripture. Consider that our Lord Jesus Christ was led by the Holy Spirit and yet was tempted of the devil in the wilderness. Further, He went on to experience the criticisms and hardships associated with His ministry on earth, and ultimately suffered the ignominious death of crucifixion. His being led by the Holy Spirit did not mean that His path would be free of problems any more than when we are led by the Holy Spirit is our path guaranteed to be free of problems. Sometimes, like the Lord Jesus Christ or the Apostle Paul or other godly Christians God leads His children through difficult circumstances.

We also have the misconception today that being led by the Holy Spirit means that we feel at peace in our hearts about the path that God is calling us to travel. Consider the example of Jonah. God was leading him to go to Nineveh and yet, Jonah felt no sense of peace about doing so. I have known people who claim that God had given them peace about a certain course of action when that action was clearly unbiblical. In truth, they had already made up their mind as to what course of action they wanted to take and they were merely attaching this religious excuse of God giving them peace to justify and rationalize their decision.

One must remember that the Holy Spirit is the divine agent that moved holy men of God to write the Scriptures. He ensured the inspiration of the Bible. The Holy Spirit is also identified as our teacher. The Holy Spirit is resident and indwelling each and every Christian. When we read, study, memorize, and meditate on the Word of God the indwelling Holy Spirit encourages and empowers our efforts in illuminating the Word of God and enabling us to understand and appreciate the things of God to a greater degree than we could do in any other way. The indwelling Holy Spirit becomes our interpreter and tutor. The psalmist prayed, "Establish my footsteps in your Word, and do not let any iniquity have dominion over me" (Psalm 119:133). When Jesus instructed the disciples on the road to Emmaus the Bible says He did so based on the teaching of the Word of God and then Dr. Luke adds, "Then he opened their minds to understand the Scriptures" (Luke 24:44–45). When the Apostle Paul wrote to the Ephesians he included a prayer that he was praying for them, "I keep asking that the God of our Lord Jesus Christ, the glorious Father, may give you the Spirit of wisdom and revelation, so that you may know Him better. I pray also that the eyes of your heart may be enlightened in order that you may know the hope to which He has called you..." (Ephesians 1:17 – 18). The Word of God illuminated by the ministry of the Holy Spirit is a major way that we are led by the Spirit. The Christian must remember that God does not bless spiritual laziness in His leading of His people by the Holy Spirit. God is not going to lift the lid of our brain and merely pour in the necessary insights that we need to follow Him properly. God is not going to merely take us by the hand and lead us when we could have studied His Word and gained the necessary insight that we need to be led by the Holy Spirit.

Another major way that the Holy Spirit leads Christians is in the way of sanctification. The Holy Spirit not only enables us to understand the Bible but He also empowers us to obey it, in such a way that we are made progressively more sanctified. This is probably what Paul had in mind when he wrote Romans 8:14. The context is one of practical holiness and the pursuit of personal righteousness as opposed to living according to the sinful nature. In that context, the apostle states, "Because those who are led by the Spirit of God are sons of God" (verse 14). God saves people by grace through faith in Him. He then directs us to walk as Christians in the same manner (by faith). We are to walk by faith and not by sight. Whatsoever is not of faith is sin. We are told, "Trust in the Lord with all your heart, and lean not on your own understanding. In all your ways acknowledge Him, and He will make your path straight" (Proverbs 3:5 – 6). God *leads* us along the path of sanctification by means of faith. He leads us when we respond to Him with genuine humility and trust. God resists the proud but gives grace to the humble and when we humbly obey God we are divinely led. We cannot understand the full implications or manner in which God performs His work of sanctification in and through us. We are simply commanded, "Work out your own salvation with fear and trembling for it is God who works in you to will and act according to his good pleasure" (Philippians 2: 12 – 13). In leading us along the path of sanctification God uses people, circumstances, trials, worship, the Word of God, prayer, etc., to move us along the way of holiness and sanctification. Jeremiah acknowledged, "I know, O Lord, that a man's way is not in himself, nor is it in a man's way to direct his steps" (Jeremiah 10:23). Oftentimes, we are unaware of what the Holy Spirit is doing during the time when we are engaged in struggles or just living our daily lives. God is Sovereign and the Holy Spirit sovereignly leads in many mysterious and indecipherable ways. Occasionally, however, God gives us a peek in retrospect at what He was doing in our lives. Often what He was doing was not produced by our own efforts or power or insight but was instead accomplished by a mysterious work of the Holy Spirit as He led us along in the way of sanctification.

God is pleased when His children are willingly subject to the Holy Spirit. In fact, we are commanded to be under the constant control or filling of the Holy Spirit. This is our constant duty and obligation toward God. We should be people of the Word of God and people committed to the way of sanctification. In that way, we know we are being led by the Holy Spirit.

Being led by the spirit of God also brings the true believer great encouragement, assurance and strong hope.

As Christians, we are being constantly and powerfully led by the Holy Spirit to live out the genuine Christian life even to the point of being led through difficult times and difficult decisions. The Holy Spirit will not leave the true child of God but will continue to lead him on to ultimate victory. Therefore, the Apostle Paul could write:

"And I'm sure of this, that He who began a good work in you will bring it to completion at the day of Jesus Christ" (Philippians 1:6).

"Now may the God of peace himself sanctify you completely, and may your whole spirit, soul and body he blameless at the coming of our Lord Jesus Christ. He who calls you is faithful; He will surely do it" (1 Thessalonians 5:23 – 24).

What an encouragement and confidence builder for the true believer to know that because God is for you, as a believer, you are being led by the Holy Spirit to ultimate victory!

Summary

As Christians, are we debtors – are we obligated? Yes, but we are not obligated to the sinful nature. We have been freed from the sinful nature by our wonderful salvation and our wonderful Savior. Does this mean that we are now perfect? Not at all! We still wrestle with the remains of sin but we are no longer dominated by sin. It is much like a mopping up operation after a major battle. The battle has been won and victory is ours through Jesus Christ our Lord and by the power of the Holy Spirit. Yet, there are still pockets of resistance that pose serious and dangerous problems. These must be dealt with. This is the mopping up stage of the operation. Paul's main point in this section of Scripture is that, by the power of the Spirit who dwells in them, Christians are able to live in such a successful spiritual way that they will be able to resist and destroy the dominance of sin in their lives. They will persevere through the many difficult obstacles in their lives. They are no longer obligated to serve in the army of the enemy but are obligated to serve in the army of God. Paul wrote to the Galatians, "For the sinful nature desires what is contrary to the Spirit, and the Spirit what is contrary to the sinful nature. They are in conflict with each other, so that you do not do what you want. But if you are led by the Spirit, you are not under law" (Galatians 5:17–18).

Paul's point is that we have the resource of the indwelling Holy Spirit to keep us from doing what we would otherwise want to do if we were still in our old, sinful self. If we have been saved then we are being led by the Spirit and we are no longer under the law. The law could command us but not enable us to be holy. By contrast, the Holy Spirit is able to make us holy. We are no longer obligated to live in sin but we have been liberated by the Holy Spirit and our debt or obligation is toward God.

When your inner self, or someone else, tries to convince you that you are obligated to sin, just remember that you don't have to sign that contract—you don't have to do anything of the like—furthermore, you don't intend to. You are now under the leadership of the Holy Spirit.

The Strong Influence of Leadership

It is remarkable to note how influential some kinds of leadership are. Sometimes leadership leads us to do the right thing while at other times we can be led in such a way to be self-destructive.

One similarity can be seen between mice and men. None of us wants to die. Self-preservation is one of the strongest instincts in living creatures. And yet high in the Scandinavian Mountains lives a small mouse–like creature that every few years is led to commit mass suicide. The creatures are called Lemmings.

They have given us the phrase, "like Lemmings headed for the sea," for that is what they do. Every few years when their population has grown too large, and the food supply has become too scarce, they leave their burrows and like a mighty army, swarm out of the mountains and rush downward toward the sea. Normally, Lemmings fear and avoid water. During their mass march, however, they brave streams and lakes. They also devour everything in their path.

After running for weeks, the Lemmings finally reach the seashore, and then, row upon row, plunge headlong into the water! For a short time, the frantic rodents remain afloat, but soon the creature's tire, and one by one sink to their doom. These Lemmings are being led by some mysterious leading into a path of self-destruction and death. American Buffalo have also been known to follow their leader as a mass herd over a cliff and to their death. These animals seem to feel obligated to follow their leader regardless of the consequences. In a similar way unsaved people are being led by their sinful nature along a path of self-destruction to inevitable death and eternal torment. When God saves a person, He destroys our relationship with sin as our master and replaces it with Jesus Christ/the Holy Spirit as our master and leader. Just as we were once led effectively, but detrimentally, by our sin nature we are now, as believers, lead effectively and advantageously by the Holy Spirit.

When different parts of the brain are stimulated in a particular way, the behavior of animals can be dramatically affected. One of the most famous examples of this was a feat performed by the researcher José Delgado. Delgado had planted electrodes into the brain of a ferocious bull. He went into a rink with the bull armed only with a red cape and a radio transmitter. He waved his cape, the bull charged, Delgado pressed a button on his transmitter, and the bull came to a screeching halt only a few feet from him, then he calmly wandered away. By stimulating a certain section of the bull's brain, its entire disposition had been changed.

In a spiritual and mysterious way, God reorients the thinking and feeling of the person that He is saving. Consequently, the believer's attitudes and actions are forever changed in a positive way. The presence of sin that twisted and distorted our natures is reset in a proper way by God. He sets our hearts aright in the process of the new birth and thus He changes us permanently into what we should have been without sin. Therefore, we are no longer obligated to follow the dictates of our sinful nature, but are now obligated to live according to the leading of the one who has re-created us in His image and for His glory. SINCE GOD IS FOR US WE HAVE A WONDERFUL SALVATION! In order for us to do this successfully, we must constantly look to and depend upon the Lord himself for our strength to comply with his commands and our obligation to him.

BRINGING IT HOME

1. Explain Paul's comments regarding the obligation of a true Christian.
2. What two pathways or choices are available regarding one's lifestyle? What are the characteristics of each and the end results of each? Is this being taught in our churches today?
3. In what two primary ways does the Holy Spirit lead Christians? Are you being led by the Holy Spirit? How do you know?

GOD IS FOR US – WHAT A WONDERFUL SALVATION!

6A

NO ALIENATION

Since God is for Us, there is No Danger Of Alienation from God

Romans 8:15 – 17

"For you did not receive the spirit of slavery to fall back into fear, but you have received the Spirit of adoption as sons, by whom we cry, "Abba, Father." The Spirit Himself bears witness with our spirit that we are children of God, and if children heirs – heirs of God and fellow heirs with Christ, provided we suffer with him in order that we may also be glorified with him." (Romans 8:15 – 17)

ADOPTION (BIBLICAL) – A GENERAL SURVEY

"Alienation" – Miriam – Webster defines alienation in their dictionary as:

"Withdrawing or separation of a person or a person's affections from an object or position of former attachment: estrangement alienation."

You may not know that the famous Wesley Brothers, John and Charles – who founded the Methodists and influenced so many other Christian groups – had a beautiful, intelligent, and very sensitive sister by the name of Hetty.

Like girls before and since, at age 27, Hetty had become involved with a young man. Against the expressed warning of her father, Samuel,

Hetty ran off with this young man. Even worse, for a while the preacher's daughter lived in sin – a practice looked down on far more 200 years ago than today. The young man did not marry her. Eventually, Hetty returned home brokenhearted and carrying a child.

Hetty wanted to fall at the feet of her disgraced father and beg his forgiveness, but Samuel would not give her that satisfaction. He all but banished her from the family. He refused to have anything to do with her. He forced her to marry a disreputable man who was a drunkard and abused her as well. Hetty pleaded to her father for reconciliation, particularly at the birth and early death of her child, but he would not relent. He went to his grave without ever showing his daughter the slightest sign of mercy or compassion. (Arnold Dallimore, GEORGE WHITFIELD, volume II, Westchester, Illinois: Cornerstone Books, 1979, p. 12.)

The true child of God never needs to fear that he will be alienated from his divine Father. Thankfully, God is gracious, loving, and forgiving in his love and commitment to his children. God's love for us is not only long-suffering but it is eternal and unchanging. His commitment to us is such that a true Christian can never be alienated from God.

Some people feel that certain immigrant groups or ethnic–religious groups are increasingly alienated from the new cultures and populations that they find themselves in due to suspicion, fear, prejudice, etc. No city in the Netherlands is so identifiably Dutch as The Hague. The Binnenhof, the seat of government, is a quaint Gothic fortress which seems to have been lifted out of a Brothers Grimm fairytale. A mile to the west stands the Beaux–Arts Peace Palace, headquarters of the World Court. Yet, not far from this classic, Dutch and world community is a cluster of Turkish teahouses and men and women wearing traditional Turkish garb. They can be seen making their way to a storefront mosque for evening prayers. Often, this Turkish Muslim community feels alienated from the community and country at large. Whose fault is it? That is not an issue that I care to delve into now. My only purpose for mentioning this situation is to underscore the meaning of alienation.

William Burnet, a professor of psychiatry at the Vanderbilt University School of Medicine is an advocate for the inclusion of a new "disease" in the Diagnostic and Statistical Manual of Mental Disorders (the Bible of mental health). This so-called disease is *parental alienation syndrome.*

Burnet describes it as "a mental condition in which a child, usually one whose parents are engaged in a high conflict divorce, aligns himself strongly with one parent, and rejects a relationship with the other parent, without legitimate justification."

What is the downside to including parental alienation syndrome in the DSM? With a minimum of three participants needed to diagnose it, PAS starts to look less like a mental health disorder than something more academic. It assumes that one crazy person (the mother) brainwashes a second crazy person (the child) into telling lies about a third person (the father). This can occur just because a parent has experienced blocked visitation or unreturned phone calls. That, however, does not make it a medical "syndrome." Joan S. Meier, a professor of clinical law at George Washington University School of Law, has explained it this way: "PAS is a label that offers a particular explanation for a breach in relationship between a child and parent, but insofar as that breach could be explained in other ways, is not in itself a medical or psychological diagnosis so much as a particular legal hypothesis."

It is a sad reality of modern culture that previously loving spouses can become alienated from each other. Children can become alienated from parents. Former friends can become alienated from each other. Alienation is a sad reality of life.

There is ethnic alienation, religious alienation, racial alienation, social alienation, financial alienation, political alienation, parental alienation, and among other things – spiritual alienation.

The Apostle Paul wrote: "And you who were once alienated and hostile in mind, doing evil deeds, He has now reconciled in His body of flesh by His death, in order to present you holy and blameless and above reproach before Him" (Colossians 1:21 – 22).

As unsaved sinners we were alienated from the thrice-holy God by our sin. We were cut off, disconnected, estranged, withdrawn, isolated from God and it is only through faith in Christ that we are now reconciled to God instead of being alienated from him.

The question is, "Will we ever experience or can we ever experience this state of alienation from God again?" This is an important question for the Christian. It is a question, that when answered properly, will display the supreme perfection of the salvation which God has designed and is performing in us and for us as believers. The answer to this question will serve to give the true Christian a genuine sense of security and assurance. It will give the Christian a firm conviction that God is with them and will always be with them and for them.

In Romans chapter eight, the Apostle Paul is led by the Holy Spirit to teach us that there is no chance of the believer ever being alienated from God again. Simply put, for the Christian, there is no alienation – ever. One way that the Apostle Paul uses to communicate this endearing truth to us with unmistakable clarity is that he uses the illustration of adoption. To fully appreciate Paul's mindset in this matter we must explore and understand the way in which he viewed the subject of adoption.

The Meaning of Adoption

To better understand the Apostle Paul's thinking when he used the analogy of, "adoption," to illustrate the believer's salvation we will pursue the subject along the following outline:

I. The Record of Adoptions in the Old Testament
II. The Roman Legal System and Adoption
III. The Relevance of Adoption to the Believer's Salvation
    A. The manner of imparting the feeling of adoption
    B. The leading of the Holy Spirit by:
        1. The Word
        2. Revelation
        3. Illumination
        4. The Way – sanctification in holiness
        5. The Liberation by the Holy Spirit
        6. The Loving Assurance by the Holy Spirit

The focus of the Apostle Paul in this passage is on *the spirit of adoption* and the assurance that it brings. Before we can understand the spirit of adoption, however, we must come to a clearer understanding of the actual meaning of adoption itself as understood by the writer and his initial readers. God wants His children to know with certainty and assurance that they are His children and that they are loved and will experience infinite grace and compassion in this secure and close family relationship. To highlight the reality of this privileged relationship, the apostle chooses to insert the idea of adoption into the discussion.

One major benefit of adoption is that it ensures us that we will never be alienated from God. In our wonderful salvation there is never any alienation from God.

If it is asked, "What is a Christian?" One has suggested that a succinct definition of a Christian, is "a Christian is one who has God as his Father." Christianity can be described in many ways but this definition is as good as any.

Some may wonder if this statement is not true of all human beings. We constantly hear liberal theologians and politicians telling the masses that, "We are all God's children." I suppose they mean that all of humanity somehow sustains a relationship with God so that they are His children and He is their Father. Nothing, however, could be farther from the truth. It is true, that every human being owes his existence to God. He is their creator. In that sense, He might be called the Father of the human race somewhat like George Washington might be called the father of our country or Thomas Edison might be called the father of the incandescent light bulb. But if we are talking about a familial relationship with God, He is not the Father of all human beings. Consider the words of Paul when he wrote to the Galatians, "You are all sons of God, through faith, in Christ Jesus... You are all one man in Christ Jesus. And, if you are Christ's, then are you Abraham's seed" (Galatians 3:26). Consider the words of the Apostle John, "As many as received Him, to them He gave power/authority to become the sons of God, even to those that believe on His name: which were born, not of blood, nor of the will of the flesh, nor of the will of man, but of God" (John 1:12). Consider also the Words of Jesus Christ himself, "No man comes to the Father (in other words, is acknowledged by God as a son) but by Me." (John 14:6) – (parentheses mine). In fact, our Lord Jesus Christ made this fact unmistakably clear as recorded by John in John 8:36, 42, 44.

Sonship to God is a gift of grace. Is not a natural son-ship but an *adoptive* son–ship that is in view. We read in the Bible, "God sent forth His Son... To redeem them that were under the law, that we might receive the adoption of sons" And again, "Behold, what manner of love the Father has bestowed upon us, that we should be called the sons of God..." (1 John 3). And again, as true Christians, "We were foreordained unto adoption as sons by Jesus Christ unto Himself" (Ephesians 1:5).

In a very real sense *adoption* enables us to soar to the pinnacle (the very heights) of God's blessings while at the same time underscoring the absolute permanence of our family relationship with God as believers in Jesus Christ.

In Old Testament times, God gave his people a covenant name by which to speak of Him and call upon Him. It was the name Yahweh (Jehovah the LORD). By this name God described Himself as the great "I AM." By this title God meant that He is completely and consistently self-existent and dependent on no one and no thing. He is the cause of all causes and all events. He is sovereign and totally free from all constraints. He stands alone as the only God and there are no others beside him. Israel was to think of their God in those awesome and mysterious ways.

In the Old Testament, more focus is placed on God's holiness than on any other attribute of God. The angelic beings which Isaiah heard and saw in the temple were emphatic in their praise of God by thrice repeating, *Holy, Holy, Holy!*" (Isaiah 6:3). The basic idea intended by the word "holy", when used in connection with God, is the thought of all that separates Him and sets Him apart and makes Him totally different than creatures. It encompasses His absolute purity and majesty. In the Old Testament we find God telling Moses to remove his sandals from his feet in the presence of God because he is standing on holy ground. The temple was constructed with a holy place and the holy of holies. Priests were dedicated with the words holy unto the Lord. Israelites were reminded constantly of their sinfulness and of the holiness of God. Religion largely consisted in "the fear of the Lord."

But in the New Testament the tone changes dramatically. God's holiness remains the same and men are still required to humble themselves before this awesomely holy and sovereign God.

But something has been added. A new ingredient surfaces in the New Testament. In the New Testament we see that believers deal with God primarily as their Father. Father is the name by which the believer is taught to refer to God and call upon God. His covenant name has now become, "Father." God's people now sustain a family relationship with

Him. Christians are His children. They are His sons and heirs. No longer is the stress on the difficulty of drawing near to God, but now through Christ, all of God's children are commanded/invited to come "boldly", lovingly, confidently to their Father. We now pray, *"Our Father, who is in heaven..."* And we are constantly reminded that we are to be like our heavenly Father, that we are to glorify our Father who is in heaven and do only those things that please Him. We are to let our good works shine before men that they may see them and glorify our Father in heaven. We are to be imitators of God as beloved, "children." And on and on I could go.

This tonal change can be clearly seen in the Sermon on the Mount. This sermon does not teach Christian conduct by giving a detailed scheme of rules and requirements in a mechanically precise operator's manual type of instruction. Rather, our Lord teaches us in a broad and general way the spirit and guiding principles and ideals that the Christian must use to steer his course through life.

The reason for this change in method of instruction is because God now deals with us as a Father with his children. In fact, our Lord Jesus Christ stresses that we are to imitate our Father in the way that we live. "I say unto you, love your enemies... in order that you may be children of your Father which is in heaven..." "Be perfect even as your Father which is in heaven is perfect" (Matthew 5:44, 48). Incorporated in the Sermon on the Mount is the primary principle of glorifying the Father. "Let your light so shine before men, that they may see your good works, and glorify your Father which is in heaven" (Matthew 5:16). The Sermon on the Mount also stresses the need to live in such a way to please our heavenly Father. In Matthew 6:1–18, Jesus dwells on the need to be a single-minded God–pleaser. He teaches, "Beware of practicing your piety before men to be seen by them; for then you will have no reward from your Father who is in heaven (6:1). He also tells us not to pray ostentatiously with the idea of being seen and heard by men but rather to go into our "closet" and pray privately knowing that our Father sees us and hears us even in the privacy of that location and will reward us openly. In terms of communicating in prayer our Lord Jesus Christ counsels us to pray, "Our Father..." According to our Lord, prayer is personal rather than impersonal. Prayer should also be free and bold. There needs to be no hesitation in the spiritual child when it comes to his asking his Father for help. We are encouraged by the fact that we are told to, "Ask, and it shall be given you… Everyone that asks receives… If you then, being evil, know how to give good gifts unto your children, how much more shall your Father who is in heaven give good things to them that ask Him?" (Matthew 7: 9 – 11).

In the Sermon on the Mount Jesus also teaches us that our life is to be a life of faith in the Father. "Do not be anxious for your life," says the Lord, "what you will eat, or what you will drink; nor for your body, what you will put on" (Matthew 6:25). As impossible as this may sound we are to do everything that we can in a responsible way to provide for our support in life and then merely trust God by faith to take care of us. After all, God is our Father. "Behold the fowls of the year… Your heavenly Father feeds them. Are you not much better than they" Matthew 7:26. If God cares for the birds who have no family relationship to Him, will He not be more careful to care for His children? The overriding point is, "Do not be anxious, saying, what shall we eat? Or, what shall we drink? Your heavenly Father knows that you have need of these things. But seek first His (your Father's) kingdom and His righteousness, and all these things shall be added unto you" (Matthew 6:31 – 33).

This constant emphasis in the Sermon on the Mount and throughout the New Testament on the Fatherhood of God and the son–ship of Christians is made possible because of the reality of divine adoption which makes every Christian a child of his Father who is in heaven. "For this reason, I bow my knees before the Father, from whom every family in heaven and on earth is named, that according to the riches of His glory He may grant you to be strengthened with power through His Spirit in your inner being…"

Consider the language that the Apostle Paul uses to describe his prayers, (Ephesians 3:14 – 16) and you will understand the clear emphasis of the New Testament on the fact that God is the Father of every true Christian.

I hope that you can clearly see the tonal change from the Old Testament to the New Testament. All of this is attributable to the glorious truth of our divine adoption through Christ.

A formal definition of what adoption means is found in the Westminster Confession (Chapter XII):

"All those that are justified, God vouchsafeth, in and for His only Son

Jesus Christ, to make partakers of the grace of adoption: by which they are taken into the number, and enjoy the liberties and privileges of the children of God: they have His name put upon them, receive the Spirit of adoption, have access to the throne of grace with boldness; are enabled to cry, "Abba, Father"; are pitied, protected, provided for, and chastened by Him, as by a father; yet never cast-off, but sealed to the day of redemption, and inherit the promises, as heirs of everlasting salvation."

That is the nature of the divine son-ship that is bestowed upon believers through divine adoption. Because of adoption, God is the Father of every true believer in Christ in a very special and spiritual way.

The fact that God is our Father underscores His authority. Just as the Lord Jesus Christ was resolutely obedient to the Father's will, even in the most difficult circumstances, so every child of God is to possess that same mindset because our Father exercises His control over the family with absolute authority.

The fact that God is our Father, also tells us that God has strong affections and love for His children. We read in Scripture, "As a father shows compassion to his children, so the LORD shows compassion to those who fear Him" (Psalm 103:13). The fact that He is our Father guarantees that we are able to have fellowship with Him. The fact that He is our Father means that He deserves our honor as well as our love. The fact that He is our Father means that He has personally assumed the responsibility for our protection and provision.

What a wonderful reality! But how did this wonderful relationship come to pass? The answer is that God chose to adopt us into His family. Adoption is the key. Adoption transcends justification. Justification declares that though we have sinned we are, nevertheless, declared free from our sin and viewed as righteous in God's eyes through the work of Jesus Christ. But adoption takes us a step farther. Not only are we declared righteous but we are also granted the right to be God's own child with all the attendant benefits – an heir of God and a co–heir with Christ.

How did this all come about? How does the Bible treat the subject of adoption?

I. The Record of Adoptions in the Old Testament

The practice of adoption was not something commonly legislated by law in Jewish culture. In many cultures adoption was utilized so that a person's family name and resources could be perpetuated after his death. The legal adoption of a male into the family when there was no suitable male heir served the purpose of enabling the family name and family line to be perpetuated in the future. In Jewish culture, however, if a man died without offspring then the "levirate" was practiced. If a man died childless, his wife was to marry the man's brother, and then her oldest son would be counted as the child of the dead man and carry his name and family rights (Deuteronomy 25:5 – 10; Mark 12:18 – 27). Since the Hebrews did not normally practice adoption as other cultures did they knew little if anything of adoption and this may be one reason the word "adoption" (*huiothesia*) is only used five times in the Bible and always in the New Testament – and always in the Paul's church epistles (Romans 8:15, 23; 9:4; Galatians 4:5; Ephesians 1:5). This also may be the reason that Peter and James speak of being born again while only Paul refers to salvation in terms of "adoption." Whereas their ministries were largely focused on Jewish Christians, Paul's ministry largely involved Gentile Christians. That said, however, there are Old Testament examples where adoption, after a fashion, did take place.

The Adoption of Moses – The first record of adoption in the Bible is that of Moses. During a time of great stress, when Pharaoh ordered all the male children of the Hebrews to be slain, Moses' mother placed him in a little waterproof basket/boat and set him in the Nile River among some reeds. Providentially, Pharaoh's daughter came to the river along with her maids to bathe and she saw the little basket with a baby in it. She had her maids retrieve the basket and immediately realized that the tiny infant in the basket was a Hebrew. Nevertheless, she took pity on the helpless infant.

Meanwhile, Moses' sister, Miriam, had been watching events unfold from the nearby riverbank. She stepped forward and offered to find a nursemaid for the child as her mother had instructed her to do. This nursemaid was then paid to take care of Moses and nurse him at her home. Miriam, per the plan, brought her own mother forward for the job. Later, when Moses was a young boy, he was brought to the palace and adopted by Pharaoh's daughter (Exodus 2:1 – 10).

Esther's adoption – Esther's parents had died. She was then adopted by an older cousin named Mordecai. He loved her as a dear child and took special care to look after her welfare (Esther 2:5 – 11).

The Adoption of Mephibosheth – David and Jonathan loved each other dearly and had covenanted to take care of each other's families. Mephibosheth was the crippled son of Jonathan and the sole descendent of Saul. David gave him all the land that had belonged to his grandfather Saul and bestowed tremendous honor on this son of his dearest friend, Jonathan, by having him become a regular guest at the King's table in the palace at Jerusalem (2 Samuel 9:1–13).

It is interesting to compare and contrast these records of adoptions in the Old Testament. Pharaoh's daughter adopted Moses out of sympathy. Mordecai adopted Esther out of a sense of family duty. But David adopted Mephibosheth because of pure and gracious love. David took the initiative and sought out Mephibosheth. Being crippled, he could not render David any meaningful service. His lineage also stemmed from Saul who had sought repeatedly to kill David. Despite this, David adopted him into his family and showered him with honor and gifts that he did not deserve.

Our adoption by God is much like this. God took the initiative and sought us out. We were crippled by sin and corrupted by it so that we were personally unfit for God and His family. Despite that fact, God saved us and blessed us by bestowing on us honor and gifts which we did not deserve. He adopted us, and in so doing, demonstrated that He is for us.

II. The Roman Legal System and Adoption

When we think of adoption today in our culture it is quite different than the way it was perceived in ancient culture.

I have some friends who live in Massachusetts. The man was involved in a horrific automobile accident rendering him a paraplegic and making it impossible for him and his wife to have biologic children. Yet, they had the strongest desire for children and a family. They prayed about what to do, consulted counsel, and began to explore the options relative to adoption. Finally, they decided to adopt a young child from Ecuador, South America.

They went through the tedious process of adoption agencies, and the governmental requirements from both nations involved. They took several trips to Ecuador to facilitate things on site, etc. After much heart wrenching waiting and hoping and praying the day finally arrived when they could fly down to Ecuador and receive their new little baby boy and bring him back to their home in Massachusetts as their own. They were overjoyed. The child was much better off. In fact, I remember that the little child had been hungry so much that when he was finally brought to the United States to their home they could not, at first, feed him enough to satisfy his ravenous appetite. It seemed that he feared that there would be no more food available to him after a meal. Over the years they have enjoyed family life as their child has grown and matured in a love filled family environment. Such is a heartwarming example of adoption. Other than the emotional enjoyment of obtaining their new child they derived nothing from the child himself in terms of material assets or learned skills that might help the family.

I have also met some adopted children (thank God only a few) who were treated as second-class citizens in their adoptive home. Most parents treat their adopted children the same way they do their natural born children but occasionally some selfish parents will be able to have natural born children after they adopt other children and sometimes these adopted children are treated with less intimacy and acceptance as part of the family. Again, this is rare but it does occur. Perhaps that is why some people think that the idea of adoption carries with it a second-class status in the family.

In the Roman culture of Paul's day, however, such was not the case. "Augustus, the first Emperor of the Roman Empire, is possibly the most famous example of adoption in ancient Rome. He was adopted by Julius Caesar to qualify him to become the next Emperor of Rome. Nevertheless, after his adoption, historians referred to him as "Octavian" from 44 BC until 27 BC when he obtained the name "Augustus." Again, Augustus was the adopted son of Julius Caesar.

In ancient Rome, adoption of boys was a fairly common procedure, particularly in the upper senatorial class. The need for a male heir and the extreme expense of raising children in ancient Rome motivated many in the upper classes to utilize "adoption" within the Roman inheritance rules (*Lex Falcida*). Many factors served as strong incentives to have at least one son, but not too many children. Adoption was the logical solution. It also served to cement ties between families, thus fostering and reinforcing alliances. Adoption of girls was far less common. Raising children in ancient Rome was extremely expensive and therefore most Roman families limited the number of children in their families to three. If a male heir was needed to perpetuate the estate, family name, and political tradition of the family then adoption would often be the solution of choice.

In Roman law, the power to give children in adoption was one of the recognized powers of the father. This was called the rule of *paterfamilias*. It was a complicated process and a permanent one. In this process, the adopted son assumed the adoptive father's name, was released from any obligation or any debts incurred during his relationship with his birth family and the act of adoption brought the adopted son into a privileged relationship, heretofore unknown to him. It was a legal transaction and the adoptee was given full access to the adoptive family's resources.

In the Roman Empire, adoption was the most common way of ascending to the throne without use of force. For example, the second Emperor, Tiberius, was the adopted son of Octavius. During the Roman Empire's first 200 years, this tradition of adopting the next successor to become Emperor was commonplace.

It was not unheard of for an adopted son to have greater prestige than the natural born son. A Roman father had absolute sovereignty over his family. If, in his estimation, his children were unworthy to carry on his lineage and manage his affairs as they should be managed he could seek to adopt another child who would better fulfill his wishes.

Generally speaking, a Roman father would seek out a full-grown boy available for adoption who demonstrated the qualities that he desired. This could become a touchy subject when it came to family dynamics. Primarily because, at the point of the father's death, the adopted son would often inherit the father's title, the major portion of the estate, and the right to carry on the father's bloodline. Because of this, the process of Roman adoption involved some carefully prescribed legal procedures.

The actual practice of adoption was conducted in a very formal and legal way. It involved a symbolic sale process whereby the natural father would offer his son for sale to the perspective adoptive father. The adoptive father would buy the son and then sell him back to the natural father. This was repeated twice. Then, the natural father would offer his son for sale to the prospective adoptive father a third time. This time the adoptive father would purchase the son but not offer to resell him again to the natural father. This concluded the transaction and the transfer of the young man from one family to the other was then complete.

It was required that seven witnesses be present to witness this transaction. The reason for this was that in the future when the adoptive father died, if there should be any contesting of the legal right of the adopted son to inherit his new father's resources one or more of the witnesses would then step forward to testify that the young man had been legally and fully adopted with all the rights and privileges pertaining to his new position in his new family.

Roman fathers did not enter into this adoptive process lightly or thoughtlessly. Once the young man was adopted into the new family he could never be disowned or disinherited. He held a permanent status. Under Roman law, his previous life was expunged from the records and he was now considered to be a new person. The young man could now, for the first time, with a sincere and heartfelt authenticity call the new father, "*Abba*" (daddy). The adopted child could have a legitimate sense of absolute security and assurance. No doubt, Paul had that in mind when he wrote to the Roman Christians that they had been adopted by God. That is why he told them that they (and we) can cry out, "Abba, Father."

The word "Abba" is an informal Aramaic term that equates with our English "daddy" or "papa." Jesus used this endearing and intimate word when addressing God as he prayed during His agony in the garden of Gethsemane, "*Abba!* All things are possible for you; remove this cup from me; yet not what I will, but what you will" Mark 14:36.

We can also use terms of endearment and intimacy as we converse with our Father. When we are saved our old life is canceled out and a new, permanent, life as God's adopted child is given to us freely and graciously. We no longer fear sin and death but we are alive to the reality that we are God's secure and loved children—and always will be. Until we get home with God in heaven He has given us the Holy Spirit to be a constant witness to the fact that we are indeed His children.

As a songwriter wrote, "I am His, and He is mine." No doubt, this concept may have been upon Paul's mind when he wrote, "Praise be to the God and Father of our Lord Jesus Christ, who has blessed us in the heavenly realms with every spiritual blessing in Christ. For He chose us in Him before the creation of the world to be holy and blameless in His sight, In love He predestined us to be adopted as His sons through Jesus Christ, in accordance with His pleasure and will – to the praise of His glorious grace, which He has freely given us in the one He loves" (Ephesians 1: 3 – 6).

The wonderful salvation that we have in Christ cannot be entirely captured simply by the word or concept of adoption as wonderful as our adoption might be. Our salvation is so wonderfully full that the Bible utilizes many different words and many different concepts to convey just how wonderful it is and how tremendously full it is. Adoption is a marvelous concept but it is only one of many that the Bible uses to describe the many facets of our fantastic salvation. We are justified, sanctified, and will be glorified. We are loved by God, convicted of our sin by God, redeemed by God, regenerated by God, converted by God, protected by God, led by God, empowered by God, gifted by God, and we will be rewarded by God, etc. Adoption is one of the bright and shining jewels in the crown of our salvation and ensures us that not only are we the children of God through Christ now, but we always will be—there is no alienation in our salvation—because we are adopted. Does this not give you as a Christian reader an added sense of assurance in the security of your salvation? What a wonderful thing it is to know that God is always for us – always!

The Manner – How Does the Holy Spirit Assure Us of our Adoption?

The Holy Spirit assures us of our adoption in three specific ways. First, the Holy Spirit *leads* us. Second, the Holy Spirit *liberates* us in our spirit and our lives. Third, the Holy Spirit *lovingly assures us* that we belong to God.

The story is told of a sea captain who was training a fellow sailor in terms of how to bring his boat into the harbor and stay in the channel of safety. It was nighttime and the sailor was concerned that without the landmarks being visible he might have difficulty navigating the harbor and staying in the channel. The captain of the vessel told the sailor to locate the light blinking along the seashore. Then he pointed out two other lights that were near and located on floating buoys. He instructed the sailor to line the boat up so that the lights would be aligned with each other. Then he said to him, "keep the lights lined up and you will be assured to remain in the channel."

In the passage before us, the Holy Spirit gives us three lights that we are to keep lined up to experience the assuredness that we have been adopted by God and are indeed His children. They are the lights of the *leading* of the Holy Spirit, the *liberating* influence of the Holy Spirit, and *the loving assurance* of the Holy Spirit.

The Holy Spirit leads us to put to death the misdeeds of the body but, the Holy Spirit also leads us, as believers, to pursue the path of biblical love and godliness. The Holy Spirit leads us to love God and obey Him and to love our neighbors.

During the Italian occupation of Ethiopia in the days of Mussolini, Christian believers suffered terrible persecution. In his book, FIRE ON THE MOUNTAINS, Raymond Davis tells of the Holy Spirit prompted, genuine love demonstrated by believers for each other during this period of intense affliction. This Christian love, which is a prominent part of the fruit of the Spirit, made a major impression on unbelievers. For example, the invading army did not make any provision to feed the prisoners in their jails. Instead, they left the responsibility for doing so up to the relatives and friends of the prisoners. One would think that this would have put the Christian prisoners in great jeopardy but, such was not the case. Actually, Christians in prison had no problem in this regard. They were well cared for by friends and family. In fact, so much food was brought to them by fellow believers and church groups that enough remained to feed the unbelieving prisoners also.

This clear and observable love demonstrated by Italian Christians brought many to seek the Lord in salvation. This kind of love was previously unheard of in word of it spread rapidly. Nonbelievers sought out believers to learn more about the Christian faith. When those who were converted in jail were finally released they went back home and shared the message of the gospel with their friends and family and they also began attending the nearest churches to them. (Leslie B. Flynn, *You Don't Have to go it Alone*, (Denver, Colorado: Accent Books, 1881). The Holy Spirit was leading believers to engage in self-denial and to sacrifice generously and lovingly for the welfare of others.

The leading of the Holy Spirit – The Holy Spirit leads us to put to death the misdeeds of the body. He leads us in a myriad of ways to accomplish this end. But primarily, He does so by leading us in the Word of God and by the way of sanctification. I have dealt with this previously in the preceding chapter and ask the reader to refer to that section of the book to refresh his mind regarding how and why the Holy Spirit leads the true child of God. The Holy Spirit's leading in this regard is a marked evidence of the fact that the one being led is a son of God, "because those who are led by the Spirit of God are sons of God" (Romans 8:14). Without the evidence of the ongoing leading of the Holy Spirit directing a person to kill the misdeeds of the body, there can be no assurance of genuine eternal life. Eternal life is more than just quantity in terms of longevity but it is also made up of quality. The life which God gives the true believer is a life that turns away from sin and pursues the path of personal righteousness. The apostle John wrote, "Everyone who sins breaks the law; in fact, sin is lawlessness. But you know that He appeared so that He might take away our sins. And in Him is no sin. No one who lives in Him keeps on sinning. No one who continues to sin has either seen Him or known Him. Dear children, do not let anyone lead you astray. He who does what is right is righteous, just as He is righteous. He who does what is sinful is of the devil, because the devil has been sinning from the beginning. The reason the Son of God appeared was to destroy the devil's work. No one who is born of God will continue to sin, because God's seed remains in him, he cannot go on sinning because he is been born of God. This is how we know who the children of God are and who the children of the devil are: anyone who does not do what is right is not a child of God; nor is anyone who does not love his brother" (1 John 3: 4 – 10).

Could anything be more clear? The modern church, in many cases, has tried to alter the reality of this concept and to convince committed sinners that if they technically touch base with Christ in terms of a mental or superficial decision that they are therefore children of God. They are nominal Christians perhaps—but nevertheless Christians. Nothing could be farther from the truth! Consequently, many churches are filled with unconverted, superficially Christianized people who are convinced that they are heaven–bound. This is a tragedy and a dangerous thing for both the individuals involved and for the church. No one is harder to win to the Lord than those who think erroneously that they do not need to be saved because they have been already "saved," by making a superficial decision for Christ. No church can make genuine, spiritual progress when its membership is filled with unsaved, superficially Christianized people.

The only viable solution to this problem is to return to the clear teaching of the Word of God and insist that an essential mark of genuine salvation is that the professing person is being led by the Holy Spirit to kill the misdeeds of the body. Note that this passage tells us what sin is–it is lawlessness against God (the breaking of God's law). It tells us where sin began. It began with Satan who has been sinning from the beginning. It tells us why Jesus came. He came to destroy the devil's work. It tells us how we can know who has the earmarks of a child of God and who does not. "This is how we know who the children of God are the children of the devil are. Anyone who does not do what is right is not a child of God; nor is anyone who does not love his brother".

In Romans chapter eight, the Apostle Paul does not indicate that the leading of the Spirit is some sort of mystical, mysterious experience. Perhaps you have been exposed to those who are always claiming to have received special revelation from God. This is not what Paul had in mind when he wrote about us being led by the Spirit of God. True Holy Spirit leading has to do with God directing us and empowering us to put to death the misdeeds of the body so that we can become more Christ–like. When this mark or evidence is in the life of the professing person then there is reason to have assurance that they have come to know the Lord in a saving way.

In another place, the Apostle Paul described salvation as something which comes by God's grace through faith alone. It is all a work of God. He then added, "For we are God's workmanship, created in Christ Jesus to do good works, which God prepared in advance (preordained) for us to do" (emphasis mine) (Ephesians 2:10).

The true believer no longer lives according to the flesh and delights in the misdeeds of the body but has been and is being transformed by the grace of God. Paul wrote to Titus, "For the grace of God has appeared, bringing salvation for all people, training us to renounce ungodliness and worldly passions, and to live self-controlled, upright, and godly lives in the present age, waiting for our blessed hope, the appearing of the glory of our great God and Savior Jesus Christ, who gave himself for us to redeem us from all lawlessness and to purify for himself a people of his own possession who are zealous for good works" (Titus 2:11 – 14). The true believer is being taught and led by the Holy Spirit to do good works and to live in righteousness.

BRINGING IT HOME

1. Describe two examples of adoption from the Old Testament Scriptures. Why do you suppose the Old Testament does not refer more frequently to the practice of adoption?
2. How does the "tone" of the Bible change from the tone of the Old Testament to the tone of the New Testament?
3. By what three ways does the Holy Spirit assure us of our "adoption" into the family of God? Briefly describe the ways in which the Holy Spirit leads the true believers.

6B

Since God is for Us there is

NO ALIENATION

from GOD

Adoption and the Believer's Salvation

We have previously noted the work of the Holy Spirit in providing our Lord Jesus Christ with a human body, empowering Him to live a sinless life, enabling Him to offer a perfect sacrifice for sinners, and thus ensuring His resurrection from the dead, applying the gospel to our hearts in such a powerful and effective manner that it delivered us from our defiled, spiritually dead and depraved sinful condition and enable us to become willing and devoted disciples of Jesus Christ through saving faith. We are now underscoring the fact that for those who are in Christ there is never any danger of being alienated from God. In the process of explaining this principle we have noted that the Holy Spirit leads all true Christians to put to death the sinful deeds of the body. The Apostle Paul further drives home the reality of the fact that as adopted children we can never be disenfranchised or alienated from God. Now, I would like to focus our attention more fully on:

The Liberating Influence of the Holy Spirit

The Apostle Paul has told us that the law of the Spirit of life (the Holy Spirit empowered gospel) set us free from the law of sin and death (verse two). He has told us that the true believer has been freed from the dominion of the old nature and liberated from the domination of sin. The true believer has been freed from the mindset of the flesh and given the mindset of the Spirit. The true believer has been freed from the obligation to sin and liberated into a world where he is now obligated out of gratitude and love toward God to live righteously. The true believer is also freed from the spirit of bondage and fear so that he can experience the Spirit of adoption as God's children. Freedom is a key experience for the true child of God. Jesus said, "I tell you the truth, everyone who sins is a slave to sin. Now a slave has no permanent place in the family, but a son belongs to it forever. So, if the son sets you free, you will be free indeed" (John 8:34 36). What a testimony to the fact that God is for you!

Freedom in Christ is a major theme and a major benefit of the gospel. We are familiar with the concept of freedom. From the earliest days of American history when the first settlers left the authoritarian regimes of Europe and came to America and experienced liberty and began to breathe the heady air of freedom we have been a people who highly value freedom. It was Patrick Henry who declared, "Give me liberty (freedom) or give me death!" We are not unfamiliar with slogans like, "Live free or die." We rejoice in freedom and ascribe to the slogan, "The land of the free and the home of the brave." We believe in the freedom of speech, the freedom of the press, the freedom of religion, etc. We rejoice in and sing about our freedom. We fight to defend our freedom. That which distinguishes us from all other people on the face of the earth is our freedom. We understand it, feel it, delight in it, and live in light of it. America is inhabited by the spirit of freedom.

Imagine, for a moment, a person who has lived all their life in the bondage of slavery. Then the time comes when they are purchased out of that slavery or emancipated from it–they are now free. There are no longer any chains and no harsh masters–they are free! They are overwhelmed by their newfound freedom and deeply grateful for it. They rejoice in it and feel the intoxicating spirit of liberty pulsing through them.

When I played football in high school our coach would sometimes have us harnessed to a weight or sled and we would be required to run with this weight dragging behind us. The idea was to build up our leg muscles and increase our running power. When the exercise was over we would be uncoupled from the harness. I remember how weightless I would feel when I was no longer tethered–how unencumbered and light. It felt almost as if I could fly with speed and agility. I was free!

When God saves the believing sinner He breaks him free from the tether of sin and the sinner is no longer harnessed and shackled to that which had encumbered him and dragged him down. He is free! This is not merely a forensic matter but it is also a practical and personal experience. The believing sinner realizes that the load of sin to which he had previously been chained and which was previously causing him to fall short of the glory of God and to walk in the path of destruction is gone. As with Pilgrim in *Pilgrims Progress* the burden of sin is no longer on his back. Though he was speaking of social and political freedom, Dr. Martin Luther King Jr. captured the essence of this spirit when he declared, "Free at last! Free at last! Thank God Almighty, I am free at last!"

The songwriter captured this concept in the words:

"He breaks the power of canceled sin, and sets the prisoner free."

In our passage, this new freedom is juxtaposed against the old bondage of sin. More than that, the believer is rescued from the old *spirit* of bondage and fear. The old *spirit*–the *spirit* of fear is embedded in the heart of all sinners. All unsaved sinners realize that they will one day die and then face God. They may argue against that reality, try to convince themselves and others that it is not true, but in their hearts, they know that there is a God and that they are accountable to this God and unprepared to stand before this God–but that they one day must do so. Therefore, there is fear. The writer of Hebrews wrote:

"Since the children have flesh and blood, He too shared in their humanity so that by His death He might destroy him who holds the power of death – that is, the devil – and free those who all their lives were held in slavery by their fear of death" (Hebrews 2:14 – 15).

It is a fearful thing to fall into the hands of the living God. Jesus told us not to fear him which could kill the body but to fear God who could kill the body and cast the soul into hell. The unsaved sinner cannot free himself from his attachment to sin but, instead, is bound up in the tangled web of sin and facing inevitable and righteous divine judgment. It is a frightening thing to think of standing before an infinitely holy God exposed as an unsaved and rebellious sinner. But it is a wonderful thing to be rescued and liberated from this condition and endued with the spirit of son–ship (based on our adoption by God through Jesus Christ our Lord). Christians are freed from both the bondage of sin itself and the spirit of bondage which brought fear. We are liberated from it by the Holy Spirit! As Christians we know that we are God's sons. God has given us the Spirit of son-ship. As the Bible says, "Now the Lord is the Spirit, and where the Spirit of the Lord is, there is freedom" (2 Corinthians 3:17).

Furthermore, the believer is not merely liberated from the bondage of sin and its attendant fear but the believer is also liberated into the family of God with all its riches and blessing. The recognition and appreciation of this fact comes through the ministry of the Holy Spirit in the heart of the believer. Chapter eight of Romans is filled with this theme. In verses 2 and 3, the Holy Spirit is viewed as freeing us from death, from sin, and from condemnation. In Verse 4, He is empowering us to fulfill the law of God and freeing us from the dominating influence of sin. We are not merely being freed from the curse of the law, but in a more powerful and positive way we are being liberated from sin itself and enabled to fulfill the law. Verses 5–11 teach us that the Holy Spirit is liberating us from our sinful nature–by changing our nature and mindset. Verses 12–13 teach that He is liberating us and empowering us continually for righteousness. Verses 14–17 teach that He is confirming our adoption as sons of God and that He leads us as sons of God. Finally, in the verse now under consideration (verse 17b) we are told that *the Holy Spirit is guaranteeing or securing our future eternal glory which is the ultimate goal* of God. He is liberating us from the spirit of bondage and fear to the confident security of knowing that we are adopted in Christ and coheirs with Christ. Not only does the Holy Spirit sanctify us but He also secures us. Does this not give you, as a believer, an increased sense of passion for God and assurance in your salvation. Does this fact not serve to dramatically increase your gratitude toward and love for the triune God who has made it possible?

Concerning this truth that the Holy Spirit provides absolute assurance and guarantees our salvation the Apostle Paul wrote, "And you also were included in Christ when you heard the Word of truth, the gospel of your salvation. Having believed, you were marked in Him with a seal, the promised Holy Spirit, who is a deposit guaranteeing our inheritance until the redemption of those who are God's possession – to the praise of His glory" (Ephesians 1:13 – 14).

Anyone who tries to tell you that you can lose your salvation simply does not understand salvation and what the Bible teaches about it. After all, the Apostle Paul wrote, "For those God foreknew He also predestined to be conformed to the likeness of His son, that He might be the firstborn among many brothers. And those He predestined, He also called; those He called, He also justified; those who justified, He also glorified" (Romans 8:29 – 30).

Notice that no one is lost in this train of salvation from beginning to end. We are also referred to as having already been glorified. Why? Because God is in control of the entire process none of His people will be lost. The ultimate glorification of every true believer is ensured by God and guaranteed by the ministry of the Holy Spirit" (Romans 8:17).

There is no sense in which salvation is true and real if there is no glorification. In Ephesians 1:3 – 4, the Apostle Paul wrote, "Blessed be the God and Father of our Lord Jesus Christ, who has blessed us with every spiritual blessing in the heavenlies in Christ…" Why did God do this? Paul continues, "He chose us in Him before the foundation of the world that we should be holy and blameless before Him." God's intention and His resolved will is that everyone who is a true believer and therefore a true child of God will be glorified – therefore, we are secure. Jesus said, "No one can come to me unless the Father who sent me draws him, and I will raise him up at the last day" (John 6:44). Everyone who comes savingly to Christ does so because he has been drawn by the Father and that person will inevitably be raised at the last day when believers are glorified. Not one will be lost among that number.

The Holy Spirit is the instrumental means that God uses to draw sinners to Jesus Christ in faith and the Holy Spirit's work in this area is always efficacious and successful. Every true Christian is secured in their salvation by the ministry of the Holy Spirit. True salvation not only forgives us for past sins and empowers us to overcome the present tendency to sin but it also ensures us of our future removal from sin—our glorification.

Regarding Paul's reference to believers sharing in the glory of God, "… that we may also be glorified with Him" (Romans 8:17b), it is important to note that no one could look at the glory of God in the Old Testament. When Ezekiel the prophet saw just a tiny portion of the glory of God he went into something of a trance or a semi-coma. When Isaiah the prophet saw a glimpse of the glory of God he immediately humbled himself and placed a curse on himself. Think of how Paul responded to his meeting with Christ on the road to Damascus. He went blind for a while and his life was forever transformed. The Apostle John experienced a similar vision on the Isle of Patmos, and he was greatly traumatized by the vision of the glory of Christ. People who have not yet been glorified and perfected are not prepared to stand before God. That is one reason why the Holy Spirit is constantly sanctifying us and preparing us to meet God. Ultimately, the Holy Spirit will perfect us in an act of glorification enabling us to stand in the presence of God and to behold His glory–and share in it. "Now if we are children, then we are heirs – heirs of God and coheirs with Christ, if indeed we share in His sufferings in order that we may also share in His glory" (verse 17). What a glorious inspiration for the true child of God! What an affirmation that God has committed himself to our ultimate salvation. Indeed, God is for you and me.

The word, "if", is not intended to express a doubt. It is the word *"ei"* in the Greek. It introduces what is called a fulfilled condition. Perhaps the best way to translate it is by using the word, "since." The Apostle Paul is saying, "Since we are children..."–And how do we know that we are children? Galatians 3:26 reads, "For you are all sons of God by faith in Christ Jesus." We read in John 1:12–13: "Yet to all who received him, to those who believed in His name, He gave the right to become children of God – children born not of natural descent, nor of human decision or a husband's will, but born of God." If you put your faith in Christ Jesus, you are a son of God and if you are son of God then you are an heir of God–a joint–heir with Jesus Christ. James wrote, "Listen my beloved brethren, has not God chosen the poor of this world to be rich in faith and heirs of the kingdom" (James 2:5). In Colossians 1:12, the Apostle Paul wrote, "giving thanks to the Father who has qualified you to share in the inheritance of the saints in the kingdom of light." The same apostle wrote to the Galatians and said that if we belong to Christ by faith then we are children of Abraham (Abraham's seed) and heirs according to the promise (Galatians 3:29). In fact, he wrote in the fourth chapter of Galatians verse 7 that we are no longer considered mere servants but are now full-grown sons and if sons, then heirs of God through Christ.

The Holy Spirit is at work in us moving us step-by-step along the continuum of glory and more and more into the likeness of God until we gaze at the glory of Christ and share in it fully. Every Christian lives in the light of glory, the hope of glory to come. I remember when I was a child that the adults sang a song in church that contained the refrain:

"O that will be, glory for me, glory for me, glory for me."

Consider the words of the Apostle Paul, "And we, who with unveiled faces all reflect the Lord's glory, are being transformed into His likeness with ever increasing glory, which comes from the Lord, who is the Spirit" 2 Corinthians 3:18. The psalmist declared that he would never be satisfied until the time came when he awoke in the likeness of the Lord. Heaven is our great hope because it brings us into the presence of God and the personal likeness of our Lord. The Holy Spirit is the one whose ministry insurers that we will be glorified. What assurance and settled confidence this gives to the true believer! What an antidote to fear and doubt! God is for us!

The psalmist wrote concerning his longing for God, "My heart pants after You as a deer pants after the water brook." In another place the psalmist writes, "Whom have I in heaven but You and there is none upon earth that I desire beside You" (Psalm 73:25). The believer longs for God, to be in the presence of God, to worship God in perfection, to enjoy God and glorify God. We inherit that privilege as children of God and in some mysterious way we are co-inheritors with Jesus Christ. Everything will ultimately be brought into subjection to Jesus Christ and we are co-inheritors with Him. There won't be anything that doesn't belong to us. Can you believe it? The concept is staggering and overwhelming.

In Hebrews 1:2, Jesus describes Himself as the heir of all things. If we are coheirs with Christ that means that we also are heirs of all things. That doesn't mean that all things will be divided up and parceled out to every believer so that we all get a little piece of the whole. It means that every believer gets all of it. In Romans 8:17 we read, "so that we may also be glorified together." Incredibly, we enter into the same glory of Jesus Christ. No wonder the Apostle Paul could write, "For you know the grace of our Lord Jesus Christ, that though He was rich, yet for your sakes He became poor, so that you through His poverty we might become rich" (2 Corinthians 8:9).

The Apostle Paul does not want to misrepresent the believer's path to glory. It is a path fraught with problems and suffering. That is why he wrote,

"If indeed we suffer with him in order that we may also be glorified with him" (Romans 8:17d). As in the beginning of the verse, the word, "if", does not connote a mere possibility but rather underscores an actuality. It can be translated by the word, "because". In a very real way the Apostle Paul is stating that one proof of the believers being glory bound comes through the believer's willingness to suffer on the Lord's behalf. Because if we suffer with Him, we know that we will also be glorified with Him. With all the positive emphasis in this passage of Scripture, this reality of suffering for the Lord really stands out. Suffering for the Lord will be used by God to further conform us to the image of Jesus Christ. It will cause us to long for heaven, to lean in dependence on the Holy Spirit, to find solace and direction in the Word of God, to increase our sympathy for and rapport with other Christians who are also suffering for the Lord, to develop the strength of our faith and to confirm that we are, indeed, children of God. So, if it is sometimes required that we experience opposition, affliction, and suffering all of this is nevertheless a part of the path to glory for the true believer. These sufferings will not keep us from growing in grace but, instead, they will promote growth in us and give us stronger and stronger assurances that we are children of God and are bound for glory.

Let this truth whet your appetite for heaven? Let it cause you to be humbled before God and filled with immeasurable gratitude to God? Let it cause you to exclaim, what a wonderful salvation! What a wonderful Savior! Next, let us note:

The Loving Assurance of the Holy Spirit

First, the Holy Spirit *leads* those who are God's adopted children to kill the misdeeds of the body in an ongoing way. Second, the Holy Spirit *liberates* us from the old spirit of bondage and fear and instills within us the spirit of son-ship. Third, the Holy Spirit *lovingly assures* us that we are children of God.

God wants his children to feel secure in His love. Therefore:

> "The Spirit Himself testifies with our spirit that we are God's children..." (Romans 8: 16).

Unlike what you may have heard about this concept and this passage, Paul is not talking about some kind of still, small, whispery, internal voice that talks to us and tells us that we are children of God. He is not talking about a mystical experience detached from a walk of godliness. More than likely, he had in mind the idea of a Roman adoption and the responsibility that the seven witnesses had of testifying to its validity. Likewise, the Holy Spirit Himself is constantly providing assurance of our divine adoption. The question is, "How does He do so?"

The most likely answer to that question is that the Holy Spirit testifies to the reality of our salvation by producing in us "the fruit of the Spirit" (Galatians 5:22–23) and by causing us to feel deep hatred for sin, a rejection of the world, a deep love for God and other Christians, prayerfulness, a longing for Christ's return and for heaven, etc.

Whenever we find ourselves questioning our salvation, we need to look to the cross of Christ and then to the work of the Holy Spirit in our lives. We are Christians because of what God has done for us and in us. Indeed, there is a subjective element in our assurance but it is based on objective reality. We are not saved simply because we feel saved. Further, we are not unsaved simply because we may have doubts at times. Our feeling must be based on objective truth. The Apostle John touches on both areas when he writes:

"Little children, let us not love with mere word or with tongue, but in deed and truth. We shall know by this that we are of the truth, and shall ensure our hearts before Him..." (1 John 3:18 – 20a).

John is saying that our assuredness of salvation must rest on objective reality and evidence. John also reminds us that there is a subjective aspect of our assurance as well:

"God is greater than our heart, and knows all things. Beloved, if our heart does not condemn us, we have confidence before God" (vv. 20b – 21).

Likewise, the Apostle Peter wrote, "His divine power has given us everything we need for life and godliness through our knowledge of Him who called us by His own glory and goodness. Through these He has given us very great and precious promises, so that through them you may participate in the divine nature and escape the corruption in the world caused by evil desires. For this very reason, make every effort to add to your faith goodness; and to goodness, knowledge; add to knowledge, self-control; and to self-control, godliness; add to godliness, brotherly kindness; and to brotherly kindness, love. For if you possess these qualities in increasing measure they will keep you from being ineffective and unproductive in your knowledge of our Lord Jesus Christ. But if anyone does not have them, he is nearsighted, blind, and has forgotten that he has been cleansed from his past sins. Therefore, my brothers, be all the more eager to make your calling and election sure. If you do these things, you will never fall and you will receive a rich welcome into the eternal kingdom of our Lord and Savior" (2 Peter 1: 10).

Peter is describing the process of gaining biblical assurance of our salvation. He is asking and answering the question, "How do I know that I have been called of God and chosen by God?" "How can I be sure that I am saved and that I will go to heaven?" Notice that the subjective feeling of assurance rests on the ongoing work of the Holy Spirit in one's life. Those who are moving forward in spiritual progress can rest assured that they are children of God and bound for heaven. Through the process the Holy Spirit bears witness with our spirit that we are children of God. It is a process that involves both a personal witness and a practical assurance—by both testifying to our spirit that we are God's adopted children and by taking us to ever-increasing levels of godliness as God's children. This is the Spirit of adoption!

I dare not leave this precious subject of divine adoption without mentioning some of the tremendous benefits that it provides to the believer.

1. First, our adoption shows us the greatness of God's free grace. God was not compelled to adopt anyone. He was under no obligation to save a single sinner much less take them into His family as a child of God. In adoption the sovereign grace of God is clearly displayed. He and He alone chooses if He will adopt anyone and, if He will, who He will adopt. In the ancient world, adoption was the sole prerogative of the father. Adoption, by its very nature, is an act of free kindness.

2. Furthermore, when one adopts another individual that is not the end of the matter. The adoptive parents set about to prove and demonstrate their love and concern for the newly adopted individual. They seek to cultivate a relationship with that individual that will bring about a corresponding or reciprocal sense of love and devotion to them and to their family. The person who adopts wants the one adopted to feel confident and secure in their new

position. They want to cultivate a familial spirit of love and loyalty. Adoption, therefore, is but the starting point of such a relationship. It forms the basis and foundation of a loving relationship which will continue to grow stronger and more vibrant as time goes on. The point I am making, however, is that adoption is a marvelous display of God's free and sovereign grace pointing unmistakably to the fact that God is for us.

All believers are brothers and sisters in Christ. All believers look to God as their Father and to Jesus as their elder brother. The facts point to the reality that our gathering in heaven will be a family gathering. We will be gathered with those that we love with a perfected, familial, love.

The reality of our divine adoption and the fact that all believers are similarly adopted leads us to this conclusion. Heaven will be a time for the spiritual family–the true family of God.

3. Adoption reveals something of the magnitude of the Christian's hope. Our hope is multi fold. It is our certain hope to be eternally secure in heaven and made into the likeness of Jesus Christ our Lord and Savior. It is also our hope to experience the promises of God fulfilled. One of those promises is that we will be coheirs with Jesus Christ.

All that Christ has will be ours as well as His. That is a staggering concept! No wonder John wrote, "What great love the Father has bestowed upon us that we should be called the sons of God; and it does not yet appear what we shall be. Every man that has this hope in him purifies himself even as He is pure" (1 John 3:1 – 3)

The Apostle Peter reminded us that we have an "inheritance" laid up for us, and that there is in heaven, an inheritance awaiting us which is undefiled and never fades away. We are told in the book of the Revelation that we will sit on thrones and rule with Christ. We are told that we will sit with him on His throne. All of this comes about because we have been adopted by God into His family and thereby given all the rights of children. SINCE GOD IS FOR US our divine adoption secures for us eternal treasures.

4. Our adoption also reveals something to us of the work and ministry of the Holy Spirit in the life of the believer. In today's frothy, superficially spiritual culture most people think of the ministry of the Holy Spirit in terms of an explosion of emotion or an overpowering presence that triggers the speaking in other languages, visions, etc.

In Romans chapter eight the Apostle Paul highlights a totally different picture of the ministry of the Holy Spirit. He tells us that the Holy Spirit leads us in our prayer life, leads us to put to death the deeds of the flesh, makes the gospel of the crucifixion of Christ workable for our salvation, and bears witness with our spirit that we are, indeed, children of God.

The Holy Spirit's ministry is to point us to the Lord Jesus Christ and to enable us to be developed spiritually so that we become more conformed to His image. Adoption, therefore, help us to understand the priority and real nature of the ministry of the Holy Spirit.

Charles Wesley was saved on a Sunday in 1738. He wrote many glorious hymns and a good number of them are found in, "The Wesley's Conversion Hymns," Methodist Hymnbook, 361. One of those glorious hymns focuses on the believer's transition from slavery *to* son–ship.

"Where shall my wandering soul begin?
How shall I all to heaven aspire?
A slave redeemed from death and sin,
A brand plucked from eternal fire,
How shall I equal triumphs raise,
Or sing my great Delivers praise?

O how shall I the goodness tell,
Father, which thou to me past showed?
That I, a child of wrath and hell,
I should be called a child of God,
Should know, should feel my sins forgiven,
Blest with this antepast of heaven!

This glorious reality is made possible by the divine adoption by God of every true believer in the Lord Jesus Christ. It guarantees that we will never experience any alienation from God. Hallelujah! Why is this true? SINCE GOD IS FOR US our adoption will always be valid and permanent

God wants His children to be assured of His abiding love and of their absolute security and blessing. Since God is with us and for us, He moved the Apostle Paul to describe our salvation in light of the wonderful truth of divine adoption. The security of adoption and the wonderful and substantial riches that are ours because of our adoption as God's children should assure us and motivate us as we live for God. Since God is for us and with us there is never – ever any alienation!

WHAT A WONDERFUL SALVATION!
WHAT A WONDERFUL SAVIOR!

BRINGING IT HOME

1. How does the Bible deal with the subject of adoption and why do you suppose the Apostle Paul describes our salvation in terms of adoption?

2. What three things does the Holy Spirit do in terms of imparting to us, as genuine believers, a sense and assurance of our adoption?

3. The Holy Spirit leads God's children in a myriad of ways. What are the two principal ways by which the Holy Spirit leads the child of God? What does the Holy Spirit primarily lead the child of God to do?

4. Does God want His children to have an assurance of their salvation or would He rather keep us wondering about whether we will go to heaven or not so that He can keep us on the straight and narrow? How does one gain confidence and assurance regarding their salvation?

WHAT A WONDERFUL SALVATION! –
WHAT A WONDERFUL SAVIOR!

Since God is for us– we will never be alienated from Him

7

Since God is for Us there is

NO (ULTIMATE) FRUSTRATION

No Frustration -In Perpetuity – Romans 8:18 –30

"For I consider that the sufferings of this present time are not worth comparing with the glory that is to be revealed to us. For the creation waits with eager longing for the revealing of the sons of God. For the creation was subjected to futility, not willingly, but because of Him who subjected it, in hope that the creation itself will be set free from its bondage to corruption and obtain the freedom of the glory of the children of God. For we know that the whole creation has been groaning together in the pains of childbirth until now. And not only the creation, but we ourselves, who have the first fruits of the Spirit, groan inwardly as we wait eagerly for adoption as sons, the redemption of our bodies. For in this hope we were saved. Now hope that is seen is not hope. For who hope for what he sees? But if we hope for what we do not see, we wait for it with patience.

Likewise, the Spirit helps us in our weaknesses. For we do not know what to pray for as we ought, but the Spirit Himself intercedes for us with groanings too deep for words. And He who searches hearts knows what is in the mind of the Spirit, because the Spirit intercedes for the saints according to the will of God. And we know that for those who love God all things work together for good, for those who are called according to His purpose. For those whom He foreknew He also predestined to be conformed to the image of His son, in order that He might be the firstborn among many brothers. And those whom

He predestined He also called, and those whom He called He also justified, and those whom He justified He also glorified."

It is said that a man wrote a letter to his insurance company after they had requested additional information regarding a claim that he had made for injuries. He wrote:

"I am writing in response to your request for additional information concerning Block #3 of the accident reporting form. I put "poor planning" as the cause of my accident. You asked for a fuller explanation and I trust the following details will be sufficient.

I am a bricklayer by trade. On the day of the accident, I was working alone on the roof of the new six–story building. When I completed my work, I found I had some bricks left over which, when weighed later, were found to weigh 240 pounds. Rather than carrying the bricks down by hand, I decided to lower them in a barrel by using a pulley which was attached to the side of the building at the sixth floor.

Securing the rope at ground level, I went up to the roof, swung the barrel out and loaded the bricks into it. Then I went down and untied the rope, holding it tightly to ensure a slow descent of the 240 pounds of bricks. You will note on the accident reporting form that my weight is 135 pounds. Due to my surprise in being jerked off the ground so suddenly, I lost my presence of mind and forgot to let go of the rope. Needless to say, I proceeded at a rapid rate up the side of the building.

In the vicinity of the third floor, I met the barrel which was now proceeding downward at an equally impressive speed. This explains the fractured skull, minor abrasions and the broken collarbone, as listed in section 3, accident reporting form.

Slowed only slightly, I continued my rapid ascent, not stopping until the fingers of my right hand were two knuckles deep into the pulley which I mentioned in paragraph 2 of this correspondence. Fortunately, by this time I had regained my presence of mind and was able to hold tightly to the rope, in spite of the excruciating pain I was now beginning to experience.

At approximately the same time, however, the barrel of bricks hit the ground and the bottom broke out the barrel. Now devoid of the weight of the bricks, the barrel weighed approximately 50 pounds. I refer you again to my weight. As you might imagine, I began a rapid descent down the side of the building. In the vicinity of the third floor, I met the barrel coming up. This accounts for the two fractured ankles broken tooth and severe lacerations of my legs and lower body.

Here my luck began to change slightly. The encounter with the barrel seemed to slow me enough to lessen my injuries when I fell into the pile of bricks and fortunately only three vertebrae were cracked. I'm sorry to report, however, as I lay there on the pile of bricks in pain, unable to move and watching the empty barrel six stories above me, I again lost my composure and presence of mind and let go of the rope.

The empty 50-pound barrel, weighing more than the rope I had let go, fell rapidly to earth resulting in the two broken forearms and a broken wrist when I raised my arms to protect myself.

I hope this information satisfactorily fulfills your request for further information."

Life can be frustrating! This colorful and creative story first appeared in a newspaper in 1895 and has resurfaced in various forms down through the years. It serves to illustrate a well-known fact. We have all had times of intense frustration. In fact, as much as I have enjoyed researching the truths of Romans chapter eight I have experienced considerable frustration as I have labored to put my thoughts in print.

A few years ago, I had a stroke which resulted in the impairment of my left side so that I am no longer able to type with my hands. My mobility was also affected and I now walk short distances with considerable difficulty using a cane. My eyesight was also adversely affected by the stroke so that I can read only slowly and with great difficulty with the use of a magnifying glass. I have pastored for 40 years and in that time, I purchased and collected several thousand books in my private library. Since I could no longer read them I made the difficult decision to give most of them away to pastors who are still in the ministry and active in the ministry of the kingdom of God. I continue to be as active as I can be despite my physical limitations. Indeed, I am determined to continue to contribute to the work of God and to finish the race well.

To circumvent the problem of no longer being able to type on my computer, I ordered a program for my computer that allows me to dictate the text. Unfortunately, this program is somewhat intermittent. There are times when the microphone does not work at all. There are other times when the program misunderstands what I'm saying and types something completely different than what I intended. This necessitates going back over all the material and making numerous corrections to the text. Sometimes the program seems to have squirrelly ideas of its own and changes things in the text at its own discretion. I am profoundly thankful to God that I am still able to offer him my service and to contribute my efforts to the kingdom of God. Others, have experienced far worse results from having suffered a stroke. But yes, life can get frustrating.

In Romans chapter eight, however, the Apostle Paul is writing about a particular type of frustration. It is the frustration that we experience as Christians when wrestling against sin. Like tacky glue on sticky fingers we Christians seem to be unable to totally free ourselves from sin. We make progress in holiness and then find that some sin is seeking to threaten our integrity and derail our sanctification.

Sin sticks to us no matter how much we try to rub it off or wash it away. We struggle against it, putting to death the misdeeds of the flesh, but we are constantly surrounded by it while in this world and even the remaining sin in us as Christians cooperates in this effort to keep us from attaining the level of real holiness that we desire. Sin is an inner traitor to our spiritual well-being and seeks to sabotage our sanctification. This ongoing frustrating struggle with sin will go on until finally our bodies are redeemed and the entire world is redeemed and transformed into a perfect realm of righteousness by God.

The frustration that we feel right now might be very real but, praise be to God, it will ultimately come to an end. For the child of God, there is no endless frustration. We are saved in hope. God promises us deliverance from this frustrating experience. When that time comes we will live in a world of unfettered joy, righteousness, and love.

We struggle with remaining sin now and we try every conceivable means to free ourselves from it. We also desperately pray to God for help. We also pray to God in hopes of getting things that we feel that we need to live victorious Christian lives. In fact, sometimes some people resort to unbelievable means to attempt to get God to give them what they desire.

I am reminded of a story about little Benjamin who belonged to a

Roman Catholic family. Little Benjamin sat down to write a letter to God asking for a baby sister. He started the letter out:

"Dear God, I have been a very good boy..."

Benjamin stopped, thinking, No, God will not believe that. He waded up the paper, threw it away, and started again.

"Dear God, most of the time I've been a good boy..." He stopped in the middle of the line, again thinking, God won't be moved by this, and he threw the wad of paper into the trashcan.

Benjamin then went into the bathroom, grabbed a big terrycloth towel off the bar, brought it into the living room and laid it on the couch. Then he went to the fireplace mantle, reached up and brought down a statue of Madonna, the mother of Jesus, that he had eyed many times.

Benjamin placed the statue in the middle of the towel, gently folded over the edges, and placed a rubber band around the whole thing. He brought it to the table, took another piece of paper, and began writing his third letter to God:

"Dear God, if you ever want to see your mother again..."

Benjamin wanted God to act. He wanted Him to act NOW! We get like that sometimes. We want God to come to our aid and to come to our aid right NOW! As we struggle with life's frustrations we are constantly crying out desperately to God and resorting to every conceivable means to get God to help us in our present frustrating situation. Yet, we don't need to resort to such outlandish means to have God help us deal with our frustrations. Frustrations with sin are a present reality and God will certainly help us as we trust Him during our struggle with sin and the problems that sin causes. God has promised to be a "present help in the time of trouble" and God has also promised us a future and full deliverance from our struggles with sin. The hope that we live in light of is the certain hope of complete deliverance from the frustrations that sin causes us. We take heart because God has promised complete conformity to the image of our Lord Jesus Christ. Not only will we, as Christians, be delivered from these present frustrations but the entire world will be redeemed at the same time.

The Present Struggles & Frustrations of Life

A few years ago, on one of the Monday Night Football telecasts, the sportscasters were discussing the great running backs of professional football history, one of whom was Walter Payton of the Chicago Bears. He was the all-time leading ground gainer in the National Football League.

Frank Gifford said, "What a runner! Do you realize that all together, Walter Payton gained more than 9 miles rushing in his career? Just imagine that – more than 9 miles!"

To which the other sportscaster, Dan Dierdorff, responded: "And to think that every 4.6 yards of the way, someone was knocking him down."

What happened to Walter Payton in football, happens to each of us in the "game of life." We would like to move forward unimpeded in our spiritual journey but we keep getting knocked down and frustrated by the trials of life. The body blows caused by sin inflict pain and suffering and take their toll. Bruised and battered we pick ourselves up off the ground and continue our efforts at making forward progress. We are frustrated, at times, because we cannot seem to run forward very far before we are tackled by a number of problems. As Christians, we make progress but it is not nearly as much progress as we would like to make. And so, a life of struggling against sin can at times be a frustrating experience.

It sometimes seems that this sense of frustration of dealing with the constant bombardment of sin will go on forever without end. Suffering is a part of the struggle of life. In this sense, life can, indeed, be frustrating. This frustration, however, will most certainly not persist perpetually and suffering will not always be a part of our experience. When we arrive in glory in our glorified condition there will no longer be any frustration and suffering. That stage of our experience will be entirely over. The new world that we will be introduced to and become a part of will wash away even the memories of that temporary life of frustration that we once lived. This is part of the promise that God makes us in our salvation. Since God is for us He will one day deliver us from this world of frustration, especially the frustration that we feel as we desperately wrestle against our remaining sin and the pressures of sin in this corrupted world.

The Glory

Paul begins this next verse with a direct comparison between the sufferings of this present time and the glory that is to be revealed to us (Romans 8:18), "I consider that our present sufferings are not worth comparing with the glory that will be revealed in/to us." The word, "consider" (Logizomai) refers to a mathematical calculation and is used figuratively to refer to a well thought out, carefully studied process that has led to a clear conclusion. It refers to reasoning and a carefully arrived at conclusion. Paul is saying that any suffering and all suffering for Christ's sake is a small price to pay for the glory that we will ultimately receive from Christ. The sufferings spoken of are sufferings incurred in our present life. The word suffering (pathema) refers in the New Testament to both the suffering of Christ and the suffering of Christians for the cause of Christ. "For it was fitting for Him, for whom are all things, and through whom are all things, in bringing many sons to glory to perfect the author of their salvation through sufferings" (Hebrews 2:10). Christ suffered for us and we, in turn, suffer for Him. His suffering for us was redemptive in nature and our suffering for Him is because we represent Him and reflect Him in this world.

Jesus Christ is the supreme and perfect example of suffering for righteousness sake. Jesus told His disciples, "All this I have told you so that you will not go astray. They will put you out of the synagogue; in fact, the time is coming when anyone who kills you will think he's offering a service to God. They will do such things because they have not known the Father or me. I have told you this, so that when the time comes, you will remember that I warned you. I did not tell you this at first because I was with you" (John 16:1 – 4).

The Apostle Paul wrote to Timothy and said, "In fact, everyone who wants to live a godly life in Christ Jesus will be persecuted, while evil men and impostors will go from bad to worse, deceiving and being deceived" (2 Timothy 3:12 – 13).

The Apostle Peter admonishes his readers to be, "firm in your faith, knowing that the same experiences of suffering are being accomplished by your brethren who are in the world" 1 Peter 5:9. Suffering for righteousness sake is to be expected but it will also be highly rewarded by God. Those who suffer, for whatever other reason, should not expect any spiritual blessing or glory to come from their suffering. It serves no eternal or spiritual purpose. Those, however, who suffer for Jesus Christ, will be richly rewarded and they can know that they are walking the path to glory.

The Heirs of Glory

The emphasis in Romans 8:17–18 on the believer's glory is inseparably tied to their adoption as God's children (versus 14–16). We are heirs of glory. Angels cannot make that claim but rather are ministering spirits, sent out to render service for the sake of those who will inherit salvation (Hebrews 1:14). We, alone, of all of God's creation are described as His heirs – heirs of glory.

The Source of Glory

Romans chapter eight tells us that we are heirs of God. This inheritance is only God's to give, and He sovereignly bestows it on those who become His children through faith in Jesus Christ.

When Jesus described the judgment of the sheep and goats in the last days, He revealed the astounding truth that our inheritance with Him was ordained by God in eternity past! "Then the King will say to those on his right, 'Come, you blessed of my Father, inherit the kingdom prepared for you from the foundation of the world" (Matthew 25:34).

Indeed, we learn elsewhere in Scripture that we were chosen in Christ before the foundation of the world for salvation and marked for eternal glory (Ephesians 1:3–4). We have been loved from all eternity and will be loved for all eternity. The magnitude of God's riches and the majestic presence of God will be ours as heirs of salvation and heirs of God. All of this comes as a source from God alone and is given to us freely, though it cost our Lord Jesus dearly. He paid for our sins and because of Jesus redeeming His people, we are destined for such glory. Hallelujah, what a Savior! All of this powerfully demonstrates to us the fact that God is for us!

The Road to Glory

Believers are destined to glory because of what Jesus Christ did for us on the cross in redeeming us from our sins and preparing us to be fit for heaven. This glory that awaits us does not mean that we will become gods, as some cults teach, but that we will receive a joint inheritance with Christ, we will reap all the blessings and infinite grandeur that God has in store for us. Between our conversion and our ultimate and final glorification struggles and frustrations clutter the road to glory for the believer. That is why the apostle wrote, "If (since) indeed we suffer with Him in order that we may also be glorified with Him" (8:17d). The struggles and difficulties on the road to glory do not actually hinder our progress but they are used of God to promote our spiritual progress and godliness and to display His own glory.

The Incomparable Greatness of Glory

Paul writes, "I consider that our present sufferings are not worth comparing with the glory that will be revealed to us" (verse 18). Again, the word, "consider," is the Greek word *Logizomai* from which our word logic is derived. It refers literally to numerical calculation and figuratively it refers to reaching a conclusion based on careful study and reasoning. You will remember that the Apostle Paul had the unique experience of being caught up into the third heaven and heard things that no other living human being has ever heard. It is this man who categorically affirms that our present sufferings (and in Paul's case those sufferings were many) are not worthy to be compared with the glory that is to be revealed to us. Some translations say, "in us", but the better rendering is, "to us". There is no comparison! Our present sufferings are earthly whereas our glory is heavenly. Our present sufferings are relatively short, whereas our glory will be eternal. Indeed, believers are currently subject to certain frustrations in life but these will be brought to an end, and we will enter glory where there are no frustrations and no difficulties. We will not be subject to frustrations in perpetuity. What a glorious thought! This is so because God is for us.

Illustrating a Sampling of the Common Frustrations & Struggles on the Way to Glory

Frustration is something that we constantly live with, don't we? Frustration is a feeling that we are all too familiar with as we live in this world.

A few years ago, Deborah, my wife, was required to attend an educational seminar for her job. She got the address of the place where the class was to be taught and the time of the class. She left home with time to spare but got backed up in the inevitable snarl of morning traffic. She had left herself enough time to make the trip to the class under normal conditions. That morning, however, for whatever reason, traffic was snarled and backed up more than usual. When she finally reached her destination, she was already late and the parking lot was already filled to capacity. Deborah was forced to park her car in an extremely remote location, somewhere near outer Slobovia! Hurrying from the car to the entrance she arrived only to find the entrance door locked. Not knowing what to do, she frantically searched the perimeter of the facility for another point of entrance. She found one somewhere near the back of the facility.

When she got inside the building, she went to the registration desk to find out what room the class was being taught in. They gave her a room number and when she began to search the large building for the room that she needed she discovered that someone had made paper signs and taped the name of each class over the room number. The room numbers were all concealed and hidden by the paper signs on top of the doors. This made it nearly impossible to see the room numbers over the doors and to navigate her way to the required class. In fact, she had to jump up and down and pull the paper signs back to try to catch a glimpse of the numbers of the rooms so that she could figure out how the rooms were organized.

Hurriedly, she searched the corridors and hallways of the facility, hopping up and down and trying to read the concealed room numbers, until she finally located the proper room. When Deborah entered the room where her class was to be taught, the attendees had already filled the room so that every chair was taken. In fact, the teacher was set to start teaching and my wife nervously looked for someplace–any place to sit. She noticed that there was only one chair left. It was a child's small, plastic chair sitting at the very front of the class room. Swallowing hard, she moved to that chair and took her seat still huffing and puffing from the frantic efforts to find her room and to get situated. She then realized that she did not recall the specific subject which was going to be taught for that required class. Looking around for some clue, she noticed the title of the class written on the blackboard in extremely large, bold lettering. It read, "HOW TO HANDLE STRESS." She couldn't help but laugh. Life can be frustrating – can't it?

The frustrations and groanings that Paul refers to in Romans chapter eight are not mere common inconveniences but they are frustrations due to our innate spiritual weakness and our susceptibility to sin. They far exceed the relatively minor frustrations that Deborah experienced that morning. We, as Christians, struggle to be free of our limitations due to sin like a caterpillar struggles to be free from the cocoon in order to emerge as a beautiful butterfly. These groanings of ours caused by our struggle with sin manifest themselves in different ways.

The Strainings & Groaning of Creation

Notice that Paul speaks of three separate persons or entities as groaning. There is the groaning of creation, verses 19–22, the groans of believers, verses 23–25, and the groans and intercessions of the Holy Spirit, verses 26–27. A groan is a verbal expression of anguish. Sometimes groaning comes because of pain.

Sometimes groaning comes from unfulfilled anticipation. Imagine that it is the bottom of the ninth inning. The home team has the last at-bat and they are losing by one run. There are two outs and there is a runner on third base. Their champion batter comes to the plate. The count is now three balls and two strikes. The opposing pitcher prepares to throw the next pitch. Everyone who is a fan of the home team is sitting on the edge of his seat with fingers crossed, holding his breath, hoping that their champion batter will once again slam the ball and provide a hit which will send the runner on third base home. The pitch comes toward the plate. The champion batter is prepared and begins his swing. With a mighty power he uncoils his muscular, athletic body and whips the bat through the air. Everyone waits with bated breath and then there is the loud pop of the ball striking the catcher's mitt. The mighty champion batter's swing has been executed with all his ferocious might—and yet he failed to make contact with the ball. "Strike three—you are out", cries the umpire! A loud groan emerges from the home fans and from there mighty champion batter. It is a groan of unfulfilled anticipation. What could have been did not happen. In a similar way, the believer experiences the groans of innate spiritual weakness and unfulfilled anticipation. The believer is destined for final and certain glory and freedom from sin but that day has not yet arrived. As long as we are still in this earthly body, our hopes of living free from sin will be unrequited. This groaning is also shared by the creation.

The Apostle Paul wrote, "The creation waits in eager expectation for the sons of God to be revealed. For the creation was subjected to frustration, but not by its own choice, but by the will of the one who subjected it, in hope that the creation itself will be liberated from its bondage to decay and brought into the glorious freedom of the children of God" Verses 18–21.

Actually, the concept of waiting in eager expectation, is a translation of the Greek word "Apokaradokia" which literally refers to watching with outstretched head and suggests standing on one's tiptoes with the eyes fixed intently with expectancy.

Several years ago, I traveled a great deal by air. I would be gone from home for a few days and then fly back into Charlotte, North Carolina. On several occasions Deborah, my wife, would come out to the airport and bring our children with her to greet me when I departed from the airplane. This is before the day of security precautions prohibiting such actions. I distinctly remember leaving the airplane and walking down that deporting tunnel and looking out toward the waiting area. My children would be on their tiptoes, hopping up and down, with eyes fixed intently on the passengers that were disembarking from the plane. They were looking for me. It was heartwarming. That is the concept behind waiting eagerly.

The word, "creation", does not include the heavenly angels, who, although created beings, are not subject to corruption. Neither does it refer to Satan and the host of fallen angels, the demons. They have no desire for being in a godly, sinless condition nor will they ever be. This word is not even referring to believers in the present context because believers are referred to separately in verses 23–25. The only part of creation left is the realm of plants and animals and inorganic matter. What is being said in this verse?

Paul is using a literary device known as personification to convey his point. The Jewish people were familiar with personification because it was used by the prophets in a similar way. Isaiah wrote, "The wilderness and the desert will be glad, and the Arabah will rejoice and blossom" (35:1), and he wrote, "The mountains and the hills will break forth into shouts of joy before you, and all the trees of the field will clap their hands" (55:12). He is ascribing characteristics of personality and personhood to these aspects of creation to make a dramatic point. Just as Paul, in our text, envisions the creation standing on its tiptoes, with eyes fixed intently on its objective.

Paul is drawing attention to the time when creation will be renewed. The Jews were familiar with this well-known concept. Isaiah had written the prediction, "Behold, I will create new heavens and a new earth. The former things will not be remembered, nor will they come to mind" (65:17).

The Determined Termination Point

When will this happen? It will happen when the sons of God are revealed. At that time the creation will be renewed. The word, "revealing", is a translation of, "*apokalusis*" which means to uncover or unveil or reveal. The last book of the Bible is entitled the book of the "Revelation". It reveals Jesus Christ in all His glory and it reveals God's plan at the end of the ages and on into eternity. At the present time, the world may not be able to distinguish clearly between Christians and non-Christians because of a number of reasons but the day will come, when at the appointed time, God will reveal those who are truly His. When that time comes, the renewal of creation will take place.

At the present time, we live in a world overrun by thorns, poisonous plants, bloodthirsty animals, and sinful corruption. Prior to the fall of man such was not the case. After the fall, the original creation suffered frustration and futility because it was subjected to such by the decree of God. Because God is for us, in the world to come, nothing will exist that could cause man misery or harm. Why is the world the way it is today? Paul answers that question by referring to:

The Decree of God

"For the creation was subjected to frustration, not by its own choice, but by the will of the one who subjected it, in hope that the creation itself will be liberated from its bondage to decay and brought into the glorious freedom of the children of God" (8:20–21).

The creation was subjected to "frustration" by the decree of God. This teaches us that God is absolutely sovereign and can do whatever He chooses to do. It also teaches us that God is absolutely holy and must react in a negative way to sin.

The word, "frustration", is a translation of the Greek word, "*Mataoites*" and connotes the idea of being without success or unable to achieve a goal or purpose. It is sometimes translated, "futility". There is a great deal of beauty left in the world even though sin has and is running its course. But everything in the world is dying. Blossoms wither and die. People and animals die. The hope of some environmentalists of preserving the world systems is a vain one. No doubt we should use prudence in the way we handle the environment but this world is destined to corrupt and die. This has been established by the decree of God. The world labors under a sense of frustration because it cannot fulfill its originally designed purpose as it should. It has been invaded and corrupted by sin. It is now subject to a constant degradation of matter and energy resulting in disorder and dissolution. This is known in physics as, "entropy". Creation is not ascending some imaginary scale but is descending into disorder. Not until the sons of God are revealed will this condition be taken away and a new heaven and a new earth will replace the old one. The condition of creation is inseparably linked to the condition of mankind. When man fell into sin, creation was also subjected to the curse of God. Likewise, when God's children are fully liberated from sin, creation will also be fully restored and renewed. The creation will be liberated from this bondage to decay and brought into the glorious freedom of the children of God when those children of God are fully revealed. In the book of the Revelation when John was on the Isle of Patmos he had a vision and "saw a new heaven and a new earth; for the first heaven and the first earth passed away, and there is no longer any sea... And [God] shall wipe away every tear from their eyes; and there shall no longer be any death; there shall no longer be any mourning, or crying, or pain; the first things have passed away. And who He sits on the throne said, "Behold, I am making all things new." And He said, "Write, for these words are faithful and true" (Revelation 21:1, 4–5).

The Deliverance

Jesus referred to this awesome time of deliverance as the "regeneration" Matthew 19:28. Paul tells us that this time of deliverance for the creation will come at the time of the freedom of the children of God. What does the "freedom of the children of God" refer to? It is that time when believers are fully liberated from sin, the frailties of humanness and the flesh and anything else that hinders us, and we are free to glorify God and to share in His glory. John wrote, "How great is the love the Father has lavished on us that we should be called children of God!" And that is what we are! The reason the world does not know us is that it did not know God or the Lord Jesus Christ. Dear friends, now we are children of God, and what we will be has not yet been made known. But we know that when He appears, we shall be like Him, but we shall see Him as He is" (1 John 3:1 – 2).

Until then the creation, "groans." The word "groan" is from the Greek word, "stenazo" which refers to the sounds or utterances of a person who is caught in a dreadful situation and has no foreseeable prospect of deliverance. The Israelites groaned under their bondage in Egypt (Acts 7:34). Here, the groaning is further described as being linked to, "the pains of childbirth" or labor pains.

As you might imagine, I have never personally experienced the pains of childbirth. I have, however, been with my wife as she experienced those pains. I know that childbirth often brings tears of pain but I also know that when the child is born there are tears of joy. The creation is now groaning as in the pains of childbirth and is subjected to sin and frustration, but when the children of God are revealed the frustration and struggles will pass away in the world will dance with delight as it is brought into the glorious freedom of the children of God. Right now, the creation groans in frustration because it cannot fully live up to its original design by God. Though the frustration in this world is real the frustration will not last in perpetuity. Since God is for us, there is coming a day when the frustration will be over and the full renewal of the earth will have taken place.

The Groaning of Believers

Not only so, but we ourselves, who have the first fruits of the spirit, groan inwardly as we wait eagerly for our adoption as sons, the redemption of our bodies" (Romans 8:23).

Not only does the creation groan for deliverance from the destructive consequences of sin but believers also groan inwardly awaiting our full liberation from sin. We are often frustrated by our inability to live as godly as we would like to. Paul's uses the plural pronoun, "we", to indicate that he too shared in the experience that he is describing of all true Christians.

Have you ever committed a sin, confessed it to God and asked for forgiveness and then gone back and committed that same sin again? You feel guilty, ask God for forgiveness again and resolve never to be involved in that sin ever again but you go back and fall into it again–and again–and again. You wrestle with your own sinfulness and guilt and you are frustrated by your inability to live up to what you know you should be living up to. In that sense, we all groan in hope that we will be delivered fully from our sinful self and be made perfectly righteous. There is coming a day, however, when we will no longer have to deal with sin. O glorious day!

Paul describes the believer as, "having the first fruits of the Spirit". He does not mean, "fruit of the Spirit" as in the characteristics described in Galatians 5:22–23. Certainly, every true Christian is indwelt by the Holy Spirit and to varying degrees will manifest the fruit of the Spirit, however, that is not his meaning in this text. He is referring to the Holy Spirit as a kind of first fruit in terms of our salvation. The Holy Spirit is a foretaste of the glory that awaits us in heaven and a guarantee that we will be safely kept by God until the day of redemption. The Apostle Paul wrote to the Ephesians and said, "And you also were included in Christ when you heard the Word of truth, *the* gospel of your salvation. Having believed you were marked in Him with a seal, the promised Holy Spirit, who is a deposit guaranteeing our inheritance until the redemption of those who are God's possession to the praise of his glory" (Ephesians 1:13–14).

The Holy Spirit's work in us and through us is a type of spiritual first fruits. The Holy Spirit enables us to be free of sin's power to a certain and limited degree as we look forward to a full and complete deliverance from sin's power when we are glorified. Until then, we groan within ourselves as we wrestle with sin. This titanic war with sin can be, in some ways, frustrating. Sometimes we are made to cry out, "My sins are ever before me." We are made to cry out, "I do not understand what I do. What I want to do I do not do, but what I hate I do" "for in my inner being I delight in God's law, but I see another law at work in the members of my body, waging war against the law of my mind and making me a prisoner of the law of sin at work in the members of my body. What a wretched man I am! Who will rescue meet me from this body of death? Thanks be to God – through Jesus Christ our Lord." (Romans 7:15–25) (abbreviated by me).

Every true believer experiences this groaning and this frustration over the fact that we are still plagued by sin and longing to be completely free of it. We are saved in hope which means that our full deliverance is still future even though our partial deliverance is in the past and present. The true believer is awaiting his adoption–the redemption of the body. Adoption is something that has already taken place for the child of God, but the final completion and perfection of it is still future. Likewise, the believer is already redeemed but the full perfection of that redemption (the redemption of our bodies) is yet future. We still have unredeemed bodies that make it very easy for sin to harm us and to bring shame and grief to the Lord. In the New Testament the word, "body", often means more than the physical body but also includes the inner person. At the time of our full redemption our physical body and our inner person will be completely perfected and liberated from sin. No doubt, you have wondered what the resurrection body will be like. We know that it will be like the body of Christ in his glorified form. We are also given some general descriptions of what to expect in 1 Corinthians 15:35–41. We cannot, however, possibly know exactly what our glorified body will be like by comparing it to our present body. Further, the Bible tells us very little about the nature of the believer's resurrected body. We are told that our Lord "will transform the body of our humble state into conformity with the body of His glory, by the exertion of the power that He uses to subject all things to Himself" (Philippians 3:21). We simply need trust to God and trust that He will give us a glorified body which is best suited for us in our state of glory. Since God is for us we can be confident that He will do what is best for us.

Indeed, we are saved in hope and that hope is not a mere wishful thinking. It is a certain, bedrock, guaranteed hope that we have in Christ. We are sometimes frustrated by our present spiritual weakness, but that frustration will not be in perpetuity. There is coming a day–o glorious day–when our groanings will cease and glory will begin.

The Groaning of the Holy Spirit

"In the same way, the Spirit helps us in our weakness. We do not know what we ought to pray for, but the Spirit Himself intercedes for us with groans that words cannot express. And He who searches our hearts knows the mind of the Spirit because the Spirit intercedes for the saints in accordance with God's will" (8:26–27).

In the same way, refers back to the groans of the creation and the groans of believers for redemption from the corruption of sin. In the same way that the creation and the believers groan so also does the Holy Spirit groan for us. What an incredibly comforting truth!

Because we are sin laden and susceptible to being led astray and to experience doubts about our salvation the Holy Spirit intercedes on our behalf. This, no doubt, is because of the weakness of our present condition as humans. Even though we are saved we are still spiritually weak in many ways. Any good that we do is because of the Holy Spirit. Since God is for us He gave us the Holy Spirit and the Holy Spirit provides us with everything that we need to be faithful, active, and protected as God's children. We are often perplexed and confused–even frustrated–regarding what we should pray for and how we should pray when we are confronted with the many vicissitudes of life. In addition, because of our innate weakness in the spiritual realm our motives and understanding are not perfect. With these limitations we cannot always pray in absolute consistency with God's will. This is often frustrating to the child of God.

The Apostle Paul experienced this dilemma when God had allowed Satan to afflict him with a "thorn in the flesh". Paul prayed earnestly that he would be delivered from this infirmity. After three concerted petitions, the Lord told Paul that he must be content with the abundance of divine grace that God was giving him to sustain him in the trial (2 Corinthians 12:3–9). Paul learned not only that God's grace is sufficient for every trial but that our prayers sometimes do not correspond to the Lord's will for us at any given time. Even when we do not know what God wants, the indwelling Holy Spirit intercedes for us, and brings our needs before God in a wise and effective manner. Paul is emphasizing that in frustrating times our prayers are helped by the Holy Spirit who intercedes for us. His divine help is personal, direct, and effective. All of this is beyond human comprehension. It is done with "groanings too deep for words".

Paul is not talking about the Holy Spirit enabling believers to speak in unknown tongues or ecstatic utterances as some speculate. On the contrary, Paul specifically says that the groans are not expressible in words–words of any kind. These groans made by the Holy Spirit are profound and specifically designed as divine appeals for the spiritual welfare of each believer. Furthermore, they are specifically described as groanings that cannot be, "uttered."

Since God is for us, both the Lord Jesus Christ and the Holy Spirit are advocates for believers. It is because of that constant intercession and that ongoing intercession for us that we are not engulfed in our sin. Were it not for the redemptive work of Christ and the sustaining ministry of the Holy Spirit on behalf of believers, Satan and his false teachers could easily deceive us (Matthew 24:24) and undermine our salvation. It is this never–ending work of Christ and the Holy Spirit that enables us to move beyond our frustrations in life and secures us in our eternal salvation. Who better to help us than the Holy Spirit? After all, "He who searches our hearts knows the mind of the Spirit..." Here, the Apostle Paul is referring to God the Father who searches the hearts of men. If the Father knows the hearts of men, how much more does He know the mind of the Holy Spirit who is a part of the Trinitarian God? The reason the Father understands exactly what the Holy Spirit is thinking is because the Holy Spirit intercedes for the saints according to the will of God. The Holy Spirit's will and the Father's will are identical because God is one in essence and will with the person of the Holy Spirit. Really, there does not need to be any communication among the members of the Trinity since they are all in perfect agreement. Paul is using this terminology to encourage believers.

Sometimes, matters may seem to have gotten beyond our control and we are filled with frustration but we must remember that they are well in hand with God. They are not out of God's control. In Psalm 41:2 we read,

"The Lord will preserve... The Lord will keep alive... he shall be blessed upon the earth: and you will not deliver him into the hands of his enemies."

Some time ago Vance Havner, speaking at a conference, described the passing away of his wife. Two years before her death they had been visiting in Charleston, South Carolina and he had taken a picture of her standing by the waterfront. He had never finished the role of film. Then one day, long after her death, he thought of it, and finished the role, and had it developed. And there she was, smiling at him out of the past. He said: "Just as that roll of film had lain for a year or so in the darkness of that camera, so her body lies in a quaint little Quaker graveyard in North Carolina. But one of these days the great photographer is going to turn negatives into positives. This mortal will put on immortality and corruption will put incorruption, and death will be swallowed up in victory. That is part of the unfinished work."

It is then that all our frustrations with sin will abruptly and completely cease. They will never again hamper us. What a glorious hope! Until then, be assured, that God has everything well in hand and God is for you.

Believers face many frustrations in life but God has provided everything that we need so that we will not be frustrated in perpetuity. The Lord Jesus Christ and the Holy Spirit are continually guarding us and protecting us. They are continually enabling us so that our ultimate salvation is guaranteed and preserved for us. We are hassled with a myriad of frustrations in our present life but the promise of God is that time will come when we will be completely delivered from all such frustrations. Sin will no longer have access to us nor will it be something that we must constantly contend with. God has determined that we will be totally redeemed from sin and delivered from all frustrations. All of this is a reality since God is with us and for us.

When he was preaching on 1 Thessalonians 1:4 ("Knowing, beloved brethren, your election by God") C.H Spurgeon eloquently expressed this issue:

> "At the very announcement of the text, some will be ready to say, "Why preach upon so profound a doctrine as election?" I answer, because it is in God's Word, and whatever is in God's Word is to be preached. "But," says

the objector, some truths should be kept back from the people lest they make an ill use thereof." That is popish doctrine! It was upon that very theory that priests kept back the Bible from the people. They did not give it to them lest they should misuse it. "But," says the objector, "Are not some doctrines dangerous?" Not if they are true and rightly handled. Truth is never dangerous. It is the error and reticence that are fraught with peril! "But," says the objector. "Do not some men abuse the doctrines of grace?" I grant you that they do, but if we destroy everything that men abused, we should have nothing left... And, besides all this remember that men do read the Scriptures and think about these doctrines and therefore make mistakes about them. Who then shall set them right if we who preach the Word hold our tongues about the matter?" (Cited by H. O. Van Gilder in an unpublished paper entitled "Election," page 8)

SINCE GOD IS FOR US WHAT A WONDERFUL SALVATION WE HAVE!

BRINGING IT HOME

1. What do you find to be "frustrating" as you seek to live a godly life? How do you deal with it?
2. Why is it important to remember that "our present sufferings are not worth comparing with the glory that will be revealed to us"? Who is destined for glory and why?
3. What is the main teaching of this section of Scripture and how does the Apostle Paul drive it home?
4. Do you sometimes feel confused and frustrated in your prayer life? How does the fact that the Holy Spirit is interceding for you impact your thoughts?

8

Since God is for Us there is

NO SITUATION

That can Harm Us Eternally

"And we know that in all things God works for the good of
those who love him, who have been called according to his
purpose. For those God foreknew He also predestined to
be conformed to the likeness of His son, that He might be
the firstborn among many brothers. Those He predestined,
He also called; those He called, He also justified; those
He justified, He also glorified" (Romans 8:28 – 30).

These verses, among other things, underscore the fact that God is
in Sovereign control of all things. Nothing is out of the purview
of God's absolute control be it little or big. No situation arises
that baffles God or that can ultimately hinder and harm God's people.
Since God is for us He is actively at work ensuring that all things will be
worked out for our ultimate good and His purpose in Christ. As we look
at our history books, we are able to clearly see the hand of God in the
situations that occurred. We often say, "I can see God's hand in that."
Consider, for example, one event of the Second World War

On June 22, 1941, Hitler secretly marshals 3 million men, together
with all their weapons and ammunition in a blitzkrieg attack along a vast
front reaching all the way from Poland to the Black Sea at the heart of
Russia. He called it Operation Barbarossa. The fact is, it nearly succeeded.
It was a massive tank warfare utilizing columns of tanks and armor racing
forward, entrapping entire armies of the troops arrayed against Germany

and sweeping away all the opposition before it. It appeared to be invincible. This invading tide reached to the outskirts of Moscow in the north and to Stalingrad in the South. Then it stopped abruptly. What happened? It seems that the German armies had become overcome with exhaustion, stiff resistance had slowed them down, and mud had brought them to a grinding halt—then came the cold and ice and snow. It was colder than the Germans had ever imagined that it could be—four times colder than a meat freezer. Suddenly, the tidal wave of German aggression was stopped.

Historians marvel at how close Hitler came to winning that war. If only Hitler had started Barbarossa 14 days sooner; if only the rains had held off two weeks longer; if only the Germans had attacked when they had originally planned to do so in May instead of in June. If! If! If! But it was not to be. We see God's hand changing the course of history. The psalmist wrote, "His right hand, and His holy arm, has gotten Him the victory" (Psalm 98:1). In the same way God controls every event and situation in life both great and small. God is in Sovereign control of all things and He controls all things in such a way that they work out for the ultimate good of true Christians.

The believer finds this life fraught with many frustrations and unexpected situations but the believer is comforted by the fact that *"We know"* that God is working all things for our good. These words, "we know", convey the idea of absolute certainty and are written by divine inspiration. There is no doubt about it. In fact, "we know". Further, the word in the original Greek conveys the idea of "we can know". Unfortunately, some people doubt that it is possible to know for a certainty that one is a Christian. They say, "The believer can't know for sure". The question of whether or not we can know that we will certainly be going to heaven, however, is answered in this passage as well as in many others. Notice that the Apostle Paul does away with doubt – the doubt of not knowing. In this statement he includes himself when he says "we" know that… He says, "we can—we are able—to know". This passage can be broken down quite easily in the following way: Paul emphasizes several essential things. I will be relatively brief as we examine each of these categories. For the interested Bible student, they are as follows:

- The Core Teaching – the security of the believer

- The Concrete Understanding – "and we know"
- The Continual Working of God – "God works…"
- The Comprehensive Scope – "in all things…"
- The Concerted Goal – "for the good of those who love him, who have been called according to his purpose."
- The Controlling Purpose – "according to His purpose"
- The Complete Plan – "foreknew–predestined–called–justified–glorified"

Let's briefly take a look at them:

The Core Teaching

This is a wonderful passage of Scripture. It addresses both our concerns about the details of life and the possible situations that we as believer's fear may hinder our journey of faith and arrival in glory. It goes far in alleviating the plaguing doubts about whether our salvation is absolutely secure or not. The Apostle Paul deals with the concern about the details of life by reminding us of God's providence and he deals with the doubts about security by reminding us of God's overall plan. There may be frustrations in life but not for perpetuity. These frustrations and situations that seem adverse to us will pass–and yet God successfully addresses our every concern and has safeguarded us in every way in our salvation and journey to eternal glory.

The Concrete Understanding

As has already been stated, the Apostle Paul is writing with the full authority of divine inspiration. His words come from God. They are grounded in a deep knowledge of who God is and what His plan is. It is a knowledge that can be shared by all true Christians hence the word, "we". We can know with certainty and concrete understanding.

The Continual Working of God – "God Works…"

"A new kind of modern airplane was on an experimental flight. It was full of reporters and journalists. A few minutes after the takeoff the captain's voice was heard from the loudspeakers: "I'm delighted to be your pilot, and the captain of this airplane on its first historical flight. I can tell you the flight is going well. Nevertheless, I still need to tell you about a minor inconvenience that has occurred. Passengers that are sitting on the right side can, if they look through the window, see the closest engine is slightly vibrating. That shouldn't worry you, because there are four engines, so you can feel perfectly safe. And we are at the unbelievable altitude of 62,000 feet, flying at the speed of 1,050 mph as planned… but, if you're looking at that engine, you may also notice that the second engine is glowing, or more precisely one can say that it is burning. That shouldn't worry you either, since there are two more engines on the left side, and the altitude and speed are still as planned…

"Those of you that are sitting on the left side shouldn't worry if you notice that one engine that is supposed to be on the left side has been missing for about ten minutes. But, I must ask for your attention concerning one thing that seems to be a little more serious. Along the aisle, all the way through the plane, a crack has appeared. Some of you are, I suppose, looking through the crack and seeing the waves of the Atlantic. Those of you that have very good eyes can notice a small lifeboat on those waves that has been thrown out of the plane. Well, ladies and gentlemen, your captain is speaking from that lifeboat."

There are some situations, I suppose, about which we shouldn't even joke. I couldn't help thinking, however, when I heard that little piece of humor how descriptive it was of the way some Christians view God. As believers, we believe in God but sometimes we tend to think of God as being distant and removed from our immediate situations. Our plane seems to be falling apart, we are slap dab in the middle of a crisis and God is speaking to us from His Word but, somehow, we mistakenly think that God is remote, distant and removed from our actual situation. Nothing could be further from the truth. God is actively working in every situation in our lives to ensure that everything will work out for our ultimate good.

His is a hands-on involvement on behalf of his children. "God is working all things for the good..."

There are some who prefer to believe that God designed and created the universe but now leaves it to operate on its own without divine intervention. This passage should put that lie to rest. God is not an absent landlord. He is deeply involved and active in the affairs of the world and in the affairs of our lives – "God works..." Notice that Paul has previously focused on the work of Christ in our salvation and the work of the Holy Spirit in our salvation. Now he turns his attention and ours to the role of God the Father relative to our salvation.

Dear believer, you should derive great comfort and assurance from the fact that since God is for us He is, even now "working" on your behalf so that all things will ultimately work out for your good. Jesus Christ was incarnated and died to save us from our sin. The Holy Spirit empowers us, leads us, indwells us, intercedes for us, etc. Now, Paul introduces us to the work of God the Father who is ensuring our complete guarantee of eternal glory by His ongoing providential care of believers. The apostle's point is that the entire Trinity is at work on our behalf to secure our ultimate glorification. The Triune God is for us! What a wonderful salvation! Notice also the repeated references to God in this passage. Our salvation is secure because God is at work for us. God's providence is guiding all things so that they are for our good. God's plan involves God foreknowing, God predestinating, God calling, God justifying, and God glorifying His elect. God is at work! God is for us!

This passage is not saying that all things harmful will be kept from believers. He is not saying that since God is for us everything that happens to believers is, in itself, good. He is saying that since God is for us no matter what our situation or circumstances may be our heavenly Father will work with them to produce our ultimate victory and blessing. This ongoing action of God is in keeping with the divine plan to conform believers to the image of Jesus Christ and to secure us in our eternal salvation. Paul is not teaching that all things will work out so that we will be financially secure or materially well-off. He is talking about our ultimate victory and blessing in Christ as we journey toward glory and conformity to the image of Jesus Christ.

Sometimes, to the natural eye things do not seem to be working out for our good. In fact, sometimes doubt creeps in as we try to live by faith clinging to this promise of God. Consider the following words of the poet when you face struggles in this area. I hope these words will strengthen both your faith and your resolve to exercise full confidence in God regardless of life's circumstances.

I WILL NOT DOUBT by Annie Johnson Flint

> I will not doubt, though all my ships at sea come
> drifting home with broken masts and sails;
> I will believe that hand which never fails,
> from seeming evil worketh good for me.
>
> And though I weep because those sails are tattered,
> still will I cry, while my best hopes lie shattered;
> I trust in Thee!
>
> I will not doubt, though all my prayers return
> unanswered from the still, white realm above;
> I will believe it is an all-wise love which has
> refused those things for which I yearn;
>
> And though at times I cannot keep from grieving,
> yet the pure ardor of my fixed believing,
> undimmed shall burn.
>
> I will not doubt, those sorrows fall like rain,
> and troubles swarm like bees about a hive,
> I believe the heights for which I strive
> are only reached by anguish and by pain;
>
> And though I groan and writhe beneath my crosses,
> I yet shall see through my severest losses,
> the greater gain.
>
> I will not doubt. Well anchored in this faith,
> like some staunch ship, my soul braves every gale;
> so strong it's courage that it will not quail,

to breast the unknown sea death.
Oh, may I cry, though body parts with Spirit,
I do not doubt, so listening worlds may hear it
with my last breath

At Valdese Weavers in Valdez, North Carolina yarn is dyed in vibrant colors, and then the yarn is assembled on looms where they will be ultimately woven together into intricate decorative fabrics called jacquards. Like magic, patterns take shape as each added color of yarn intersects with the other colors. Though highly automated today, the weaving process still requires weavers to possess tremendous skill and training. The warp may contain 9,500 individual yarns that are hand tied during loom set up. If in the process of weaving one of the warp yarns breaks the loom automatically stops and the Weaver must locate and repair each thread.

In our lives, God is the master Weaver. His work in our lives is hands-on. He personally puts every thread of our life in its proper place and ensures that the fabric of our lives work out in a beautiful, decorative display of Jesus Christ. Since God is for us He does this for our good and for His glory. Indeed, God works in our lives using the various elements and situations that He has providentially ordered so as to masterfully produce a life for us that is for our good, reflective of the image of Jesus Christ, and a tribute to His glory.

In this passage, Paul is not saying that all things simply fall into place and somehow, all by themselves, mysteriously turn out for the believer's good. No, we are not called upon to believe in some sort of Pollyanna existence. Rather, we are told that, "God (the personal and powerful Almighty God) who deeply loved the works or causes all things to work together for our good..." God is at work and that is our hope and confidence.

To "work together" is a translation of the word "*sunergeo*" from which we derive the word synergism. It means the working together of various components. The combination of various elements can often produce results which are greater than that which can be produced by the individual elements themselves.

This often happens in chemical reactions when two or more elements are joined together so they work in a powerful way to produce a certain result. The combination of elements produces a result that neither of the elements by themselves would produce. The desired result is achieved by combining them properly so that a very specific reaction takes place that otherwise would be impossible. Paul is saying that since God is for us God takes the various elements of life and works them together in a wise and powerful way to produce the desired result of good for His children. The "good" that is referred to refers to this present life as well as our ultimate life to come. God is at work working together all things for our good–particularly as it relates to conforming us to the image of His son Jesus Christ. This keeps us from ultimate failure or catastrophic tragedy. It ensures that everything in our lives will be used by God to produce good for us. What does this include?

All Good Things – God's righteousness, God's power, God's wisdom, God's goodness, God's love, God's Word, etc. are included in this phrase, "all things".

The Holy Angels – The Word of God teaches us that, regarding God's holy angels, they are working for our good. "Are they not all ministering spirits sent out to render service for the sake of those who will inherit salvation?" (Hebrews 1:14). The holy angels are used by God for our good.

The People of God – One of the greatest blessings in life is the fellowship and ministry that Christians have with each other. Christians are to, "stimulate one another to love and good deeds" (Hebrews 10:24). Christians pray for one another. Christians encourage each other. Christians admonish each other. Christians love each other. Christians bear each other's burdens.

It is sad when Christians fail in their responsibility toward each other and it is a joyous, enriching experience to witness Christians lovingly and selflessly serving God and each other. Since God is for us God invariably uses His people to minister to each other to accomplish their ultimate good. Paul wrote to the Romans that he looked forward to not only ministering to them but being ministered to by them. "That is, that I may be encouraged together with you while among you, each of us by the other's faith, both yours and mine" (Romans 1:12).

Bad and Evil Things – It may seem strange, but God can and does use even bad and evil things to accomplish the good of His children. He sometimes uses suffering to make us aware of our frailty and of our need for divine assistance. He uses suffering to sometimes chasten us when we have fallen into sin so that we will be corrected and return to the path of holiness. Since God is for us, God uses suffering sometime to teach us to know Him in a better, more full manner. Job is a classic example of this truth. Though he never lost his faith through a barrage of afflictions he did come to the place where he genuinely questioned the Lord's ways. After a severe rebuke by God and a confrontation with God Job confessed, "I have heard of you by the hearing of the ear, but now my eyes see you; therefore, I retract, and I repent in dust and ashes" (Job 42:5 – 6). The Apostle Paul experienced a thorn in the flesh sent by God. This, "thorn in the flesh", prevented Paul from being unduly proud of his heavenly experiences and it kept him humble and dependent upon God. In this time of suffering Paul learned that God's grace is sufficient in a way that he could not have learned otherwise. (2 Corinthians 12:6–10).

Suffering can teach us sensitivity toward others as well as kindness, gentleness, patience, and compassion. Suffering can cause us to hate sin in ourselves, and in others, when we realize the kind of hurt that it can cause and the damage that it can do. To some degree, suffering can enable us to identify, in part, with the sufferings of Christ. Yes, God uses even our sufferings for our good.

Temptation & Sin – God never causes us to sin but God can use even our sin for His glory and the sin and temptation for our good. This is included in the, "all things" of our text. Sin is never good, but since God is for us it can be used for good by God. When we are tempted to sin, we are often driven to our knees in prayer to ask God for strength to resist that sin. We are made to pray, "Lead us not into temptation, but deliver us from evil (the evil one)". Sin and temptation often drive us to the Word of God. That is why the psalmist wrote, "Your Word I have treasured in my heart that I may not sin against you" (Psalm 119:11). When the believer is tempted he should "flee" the temptation and "resist" Satan's attempts to cause him to sin. Temptation and sin can cause us to hunger and thirst for heaven where there will be no such frustrations and fighting with our inner self. Yes, temptation is difficult and sin is evil but since God is for us both can and are used by God for the good of the believer.

"All things" includes all things. God works in all things for the good of the believer. That is why, as frustrating as life can be, there is comfort in

knowing that God takes, what sometimes seems to be chaos, and wisely turns it into something that serves to produce qualities in us that work out for our ultimate, spiritual good. What a wonderful salvation!

The Concerted Goal

"For the good of those who love Him, who have been called according to His purpose".

We have already dealt with what is meant by the "good". God is working in our lives for our good and for His glory. Paul now addresses exactly who it is that can expect God to be working in all things for their good, and who it is that can rightfully be called a genuine believer.

There are many people who profess to be true believers in the Lord Jesus Christ. Some are, indeed, true believers while others simply do not possess the characteristics of a genuine Christian. In this passage, Paul describes the genuine believer in a twofold way. First, they are those who love God. Second, they are those who have been called according to His purpose. These are the earmarks of genuine believers and recipients of divine providential involvement and the guarantee of spiritual security. The promise is not for everyone but it is solely for God's children.

The children of God love God. This concept of loving God can be subdivided into two parts:

The Primary Evidence – "to those who love God"
The Plural Manifestations

The Primary Evidence

Nothing more characterizes the true believer than a genuine love for God. I once had a conversation with a man who was leading a religious gathering and he told me that he hated God not only before his "conversion" but also after it. He was operating under the popular misconception that a mental acknowledgment of the facts of the gospel coupled with a cursory choice to believe them equated to conversion and salvation. He did not understand that true salvation demanded and produced a true change of heart and disposition toward God.

In the Old Testament, when God gave the Ten Commandments to Israel, He warned them about serving idols and worshiping them and said, "You shall not worship or serve them; for I, the Lord your God, am a jealous God, visiting the iniquity of the fathers on the children, on the third and the fourth generations of those who hate me, showing lovingkindness to thousands, to those who love Me and keep My commandments" (Exodus 20:5–6; cf. Deuteronomy 7:9–10).

In God's eyes, there are only two classifications of people, those who hate Him and those who love Him. Even the foreigner who converted to Judaism was described in terms of serving and loving God, "also the foreigners who join themselves to the Lord, to minister to Him, and to love the name the Lord, to be his servants, everyone who keeps from profaning the Sabbath, and holds fast my covenant" (Isaiah 56:6).

Likewise, the same concept is echoed and stressed in the New Testament. Paul reminded the Corinthians of what was previously written in the Scriptures, "'Things which eye has not seen and ear has not heard, and which have not entered in to the heart of man, all that God has prepared for those who love Him'" (1 Corinthians 2:9; Isaiah 64:4).

Love for God is the primary evidence of genuine faith. Certainly, believers do not love God as deeply and consistently as they should. That is true because of the plague of remaining sin. Nevertheless, they manifest a genuine and abiding love for the one who has loved them from all eternity with an everlasting love. We love God because He first loved us. The love of the genuine believer for God is real and growing. Paul told the Philippians, "And this I pray, that your love may abound still more and more in real knowledge and all discernment" (Philippians 1:9). Do you love God? This is the primary evidence of genuine saving faith.

The Plural Manifestations

The love of God manifests itself in the life of the genuine believer in many ways. As with any true love, godly love causes the genuine believer to desire a personal relationship with God that grows deeper and deeper. The psalmist wrote, "As the deer pants for the water brooks, so my soul pants for you, O God. My soul thirsts for God, for the living God; when shall I come and appear before God?" (Psalm 42:1–2). David prayed, "O

God, You are my God; I shall seek You earnestly; my soul thirsts for You, my flesh yearns for You, in a dry and weary land where there is no water. Thus, I have seen You in the sanctuary, to see Your power and your glory. Because Your lovingkindness is better than life, my lips will praise You" (Psalm 63:1–3). Can you not feel the emotion and detect the love that David had for God?

The true believer is one who loves God and desires an ongoing an ever-deepening relationship with God. The true believer prays to God. He loves God's children and seeks to do them good. He is sensitive to the will of God. He seeks to honor the name of God, and loves the things that God loves. He loves and hates the things that God loves and hates. He obeys God and longs for the return of Jesus Christ our great God and Savior. This love for God manifests itself in a plurality of ways. This love originates from God and we are able to love God only because He has first loved us. John explained, "Love is from God," - it is, "not that we loved God, but that He loved us and sent His son to be the propitiation for our sins" (1 John 4:7, 10, 19).

The Holy Spirit enables the genuine believer to not only have faith but also to love God and that love is a primary evidence that the believer is a genuine Christian and therefore a participant in the divine security that God provides for those that love Him. Before anyone can rightly claim the benefits and promise of this passage of Scripture he must establish the fact in his own mind and heart that he loves God with genuineness. God's promise is only for those who love him.

Do you really love God? What evidence is there in your life that indicates that you genuinely love him? Jesus said, "If you love me, keep my commandments." Does that describe you? God's love is a model for what our love is intended to be. God's love is free, sacrificial, generous, extravagant, patient. Do you have that kind of love for God?

The second way Paul describes the recipients of divine and eternal security is that they are, "called." Just as our love for God originates with God so does our calling into His family. Salvation is the work of God! Lost sinners are hostile to God, "The sinful mind is hostile to God. It does not submit to God's law, nor can it do so" (Romans 8:7). Lost sinners do not of themselves seek God, " There is no one righteous, not even one; there is no one who understands, no one who seeks God" (Romans 3:10 – 11).

How then, is it possible for any lost sinner to reverse this habitual pattern/ scenario and to come to God through faith in Jesus Christ in a saving way?

Thankfully, with God all things are possible. God creates faith where there is no faith and instills within us a desire for Him where previously there was none. God removes the errant sinful hostility and gives the genuine believer a heart of love and acceptance toward Him. The Bible refers to this process as, "calling." Sometimes we think of "divine calling" as it relates to God calling someone to the ministry, to the mission field, etc. But there is a more fundamental calling highlighted in Scripture. It is the calling of lost sinners to become recipients of divine salvation in Christ. This is the calling that the Apostle Paul has in mind in this verse.

At this point, we must distinguish between the general, universal, external call of God in the gospel message and the internal, effectual call of God in the heart of the sinner who is being brought to faith, by God, in the Lord Jesus Christ. When Jesus said that, "many are called, but few are chosen" (Matthew 22:14). He was referring to this distinction. Throughout history, many have heard the gospel message and its call to faith and yet have not embraced it and accepted it. This declaration of the gospel is the external, general, universal call for sinners to come to Jesus Christ freely through repentance and faith.

The terms *called* and *calling* are used in a different sense in the epistles. In the epistles these words refer to the sovereign, effectually powerful work of God which involves convicting the sinner of sin and his lost condition. It also involves the spiritual regenerating of him into new life in Christ. It encompasses all those processes that are necessary to bring the lost sinner into a saving relationship with God through faith alone in the Lord Jesus Christ alone. Divine calling of this nature secures its objects place in the family of God. What do we know, from the Bible, about this "calling?"

First, this is from God alone. This calling is sovereign, unconditional, and effectual. It is not based on who the person is or what they have done but it is based solely on God's grace in Jesus Christ. The Apostle Paul when writing to the Corinthians said, "Brothers, think of what you were when you were called. Not many of you were wise by human standards; not many were influential; not many were of noble birth. But God chose the foolish things of the world to shame the wise; God chose the weak things of the world to shame the strong. He chose the lowly things of this world and the despised things – things that are not to nullify the things that are, so that no one may boast before Him. It is because of Him that you are in Christ Jesus, who has become for us wisdom from God – that is, our righteousness, holiness and redemption. Therefore, as it is written:' let him who boasts boast in the Lord' (1 Corinthians 1:26 – 31).

The divine calling is not based on human credentials, potential, works, etc. it is purely sovereign and based only in God's will and His grace in Christ Jesus. Later in Romans Paul uses the account of Jacob and Esau to illustrate God's sovereign and effectual call. "For the twins were not yet born and had not done anything good or bad, in order that God's purpose according to His choice (election) might stand, not because of works, but because of Him who calls, it was said to her 'the older will serve the younger.' Just as it is written,' Jacob I loved, but Esau I hated'" (Romans 9:11 – 13). God's divine calling is personal and sovereign as well as effectual. Effectual means that it will always accomplish its intended end. Notice that in our text in Romans chapter eight that everyone who is called is predestinated and everyone who is predestinated is justified and everyone who is justified is glorified. There is perfect precision and effectiveness in this plan.

I once heard a theologian say that the Bible did not teach effectual calling anywhere. He must have never studied Romans chapter eight where the truth of God's effectual call is crystal clear. God accomplishes what He intends to accomplish by His divine call. Divine calling can sometimes relate to offices of service, as well. For example, Paul was "called as an apostle of Jesus Christ by the will of God" (1 Corinthians 1:1). What did he mean when he referred to being called? In another place, Paul described himself as being, "laid hold of by Christ Jesus" (Philippians 3:12). This calling was powerful, sovereign, personal, and effectual. Paul also referred to all Christians as, "those who are the called, both Jews and Greeks" (1 Corinthians 1:24). When writing to the Romans he said, "and you also are among those who are called to belong to Jesus Christ. To all in Rome who are loved by God and called to be saints: Grace and peace to you from God our Father and from the Lord Jesus Christ" (Romans 1:6 – 7).

God's calling is also personal. Someone may suggest that God calls all people in some sort of indiscriminate manner and only some respond properly to this calling and are thus saved. This, however, is not true in any sense. First, not all people have heard the gospel message and, therefore, they could not have received the external call of God. I suppose one could say that they have seen the evidences of God in the created world and therefore, in that sense, they have received a revelation from God calling them to faith in Him. But in terms of hearing the gospel message not all people have been privileged to hear the good news and therefore, in that sense, have not experienced the external call of God. Second, our text clearly teaches that all those who are called of God, in the sense that we have been describing, are ultimately justified and glorified. No one is called of God who does not come to faith in Jesus Christ (justification) and who will not ultimately be glorified in heaven. This demonstrates that the call of God, in this sense, does not extend to each and every person or else each and every person would be saved and heaven bound. The call of God never fails! It always secures the salvation of the one to whom it is extended. Regarding those who accept the call of God to salvation, they could only do so if God granted them the gift of faith and repentance brought about by the new birth. Otherwise, "none seek God" and "all men have not faith."

Furthermore, all lost sinners are, "dead in trespasses and sins." In fact, responding to Jesus Christ in repentance and faith is impossible apart from the powerful drawing of God and the life-giving enablement that comes from God. Jesus said, "No man can come to me except the Father who sent me draws him, and I will raise him up at the last day" (John 6:44).

Notice, the vital necessity of the calling or drawing of God and the absolute certainty that those who are so drawn by God to Christ will be resurrected at the last day to be glorified. This describes God's effectual and personal call of some lost sinners to Jesus Christ for salvation.

Some wonder, if this call of God can be rejected. As for as rejecting the call of God is concerned, that is true of all lost sinners until God secures their cooperation by working in their hearts to cause them to love Him. Ultimately, the divine call of God to salvation is effectual and irresistible. This is part of the powerful, personal calling of God. Certainly, lost sinners may struggle with coming to faith in Jesus Christ when called of God but God so powerfully moves in the heart of these sinners as to warn them and woo them and move them successfully in such a way that they ultimately are overjoyed at the prospect of trusting in Jesus Christ as their Lord and Savior. The divine call of God is personal.

The Divine calling of God is permanent - Romans 11:29. In one sense, the divine calling is once and for all but in another sense, it continues in an ongoing way until the genuine believer is finally glorified. The Apostle Paul understood that he had been called of God both to salvation and apostleship. He also understood, however, the ongoing nature of his calling. He wrote, "I press toward the mark of the prize of the upward call of God in Christ Jesus" (Philippians 3:14). God initiates and controls the processes of the salvation of the genuine believer to secure his or her ultimate safety and glorification. He does so, however, by utilizing the Holy Spirit to cause the true believer to exercise faith and perseverance in the path of salvation. Paul wrote to the Philippians, "being confident of this, that He who began a good work in you will carry it on to completion until the day of Christ" Philippians 1:6. God's calling is permanent and ever present in terms of its perpetual power and effectiveness thus rendering the believer absolutely secure in his salvation. The Apostle Paul wrote, "For the gifts and calling of God are without repentance" (Romans 11:29). That is, God does not change His mind and withdraw His calling and gifts. God is for us!

God's calling is purposeful. We have already touched on this subject. God's intention in calling the sinner is to remove them from the realm of sin with all its negative consequences and to place them into the body of Christ and ultimately glorify him with all its attendant blessings and this is all done for the glory of God. There is a very precise purpose behind the calling of God.

God's divine calling is personal, it produces its desired effect, it is powerful, it is purposeful, it is permanent, it is purely sovereign, etc. since God is for us His call of us to salvation is perfect achieving its intended end.

God's calling utilizes participants. Though the call of God is divine in every way God does choose to use human agents when making this call effective to the salvation of sinners. "How then shall they call upon Him in whom they have not believed? And how shall they believe in Him whom they have not heard? And how shall they hear without a preacher?" (Romans 10:14). God uses human agents in this wonderful work of calling lost sinners to salvation. He is pleased to use human agents to share the message of the gospel and pray for the salvation of the lost. Ultimately, their salvation can only be accomplished by the work of the ministry of the Holy Spirit. He must grant salvation by divinely calling the person.

We have looked at the core teaching of this passage (security), the concrete understanding, the continual working of God ("God works..."), the comprehensive scope of God's working ("all things") and the concerted goal ("for the good of those who love him, who have been called according to his purpose.") There remain two other aspects of the passage that we need to deal with; first, the Controlling Purpose and second, the Complete Plan. I will close this chapter by touching on the first of these and will focus on the second ("the complete plan") in the next chapter.

The Controlling Purpose

"According to His purpose" (8:28d). The reason God causes all things to work together for the good of His children is because it is according to His divine purpose. Paul helps us to understand the meaning of God's "purpose" in verses 29–30 which we will discuss in the next chapter. Suffice it to say that God's purpose is to glorify Himself by securing the salvation of those whom He has called and "predestinated to become conformed to the image of His Son" (Romans 8:29). One might question why God selectively calls some and not others in this internal, powerful and effectual manner. It is here that one's sense of "fairness" encroaches on the Bible's teaching regarding God in salvation. God is sovereign–absolutely sovereign. This same objection could be raised regarding why God selected to bless the nation of Israel while bypassing the other nations. Moses addressed this issue by writing, "The Lord did not set His love on you nor choose you because you were more in number than any of the peoples, for you were the fewest of all peoples, but because the Lord loved you and kept the oath which He swore to your forefathers, the Lord brought you out by a mighty hand, and redeemed you from the house of slavery, from the hand of Pharaoh king of Egypt" (Deuteronomy 7:7–8).

God did not choose Israel based on who they were or what potential they had. His choosing of Israel was solely based on His divine will and purpose. His choosing and calling of believers is also exclusively based on His divine will and purpose. There is a great mystery in all of this. It should produce great humility in every believer and great gratitude in every believer toward God. We escape what we rightly deserved and receive the treasures of eternal salvation. We are no longer separated from God but we are permanently placed in the family of God. God is actively working in all things for our good and He has called us and secured us by His divine will and power in His gracious love through Christ Jesus our Lord. Since God is for us all of this will be done for us by God himself.

When we think of the myriad of details in life that could possibly derail us in our journey of faith we must remind ourselves that in all things (excluding nothing) God is actively at work to ensure that these details will work out for our good. We are sometimes frustrated by the frantic pace of life and the monotonous plodding of life. We sometimes wonder how our circumstances can be of any good. But God is not only working out life's situations for our ultimate good, but He is working in our lives in such a way as to make us useful for His Kingdom and glory and to conform us to the image of the Lord Jesus Christ. Or on the other hand we may wonder whether we have the strength and resolve to continue until the end.

There is a beautiful, although fictitious, story of three trees that grew together on a lovely hillside with a beautiful view. As they grew, they did what many young people do, they imagined what they would do when they were full grown. One tree said to the other two. "What I want more than anything in the world is to be important. I want people to acknowledge my importance and to bow before me."

The second tree said, "What I want more than anything in the world is that wherever I go in the world people will recognize me and will receive me gratefully and will be glad that I have come."

The third tree said, "What I want more than anything in the world is to help people be connected, to be in fellowship, to love one another."

The time came for the mature trees to be cut down and be made useful. The first tree was selected by a master carpenter, and much to the disappointment of the tree, was made into a shed and feed trough for the animals. But the three came to understand that God had other ideas because it was that shed that became a shelter for Mary and Joseph in the manger of the baby Jesus.

The second tree was selected by a mariner who transformed the wood into a sturdy workboat. The second tree was also disappointed. It was not what it had wished. But it was that boat that Jesus got into to go to the other side of the Sea of Galilee and it was that boat which became His pulpit and people were glad to see the boat.

The third tree was cut down by a Roman crew who used, it as rough as it was, for an execution cross. Again, it also felt bitter disappointment, and sadness that it was to be the instrument of the death of Jesus. But after that use, he was placed across the stream, and people used it to cross over to a place of worship and fellowship. (From a sermon by Norman Lawson)

An old Spiritual speaks of crossing the river Jordan to get to the "Promised Land." The cross of Jesus Christ is that bridge. There is no other. He paid the price that we might reach God. Once we reach God through Christ there is never, again, any alienation from Him for the true believer.

Be assured dear believer that as mysterious as life may be to you it is no mystery to God. God is for you and is actively at work for you. God has called you personally, powerfully, purposefully, and permanently. You are in God's hands and on His heart. You are secure. You are loved. You may experience frustration from time to time but you will not have frustration in perpetuity. There is coming a time—O glorious time—when our salvation will be completed and we will be with God forever.

WHAT A WONDERFUL SALVATION! WHAT A WONDERFUL GOD WHO IS ALWAYS FOR US!

BRINGING IT HOME

1. Are all things working for the good of all people? What are the two distinguishing characteristics given of true believers in Romans 8:28? Examine yourself in light of these two characteristics.

2. Is God at work today or did His work cease after the week of creation? If you think that God is still at work today name some things that God is at work doing.

3. Name and describe some characteristics of God's calling of believers to salvation.

4. Do you have a solid sense of security in terms of your salvation? Why or why not?

9

Since God is for us, there is

NO ELIMINATION

Not one of his chosen children will be lost. Everyone who God begins to save will be ultimately saved. No one is eliminated along the way.

> "For those God foreknew He also predestined to be conformed to the likeness of His son, that He might be the firstborn among many brothers. And those He predestined, He also called; those He called, He also justified; those He justified, He also glorified." Romans 8:29 – 30

We are now entering into a particularly glorious section of Scripture. Unfortunately, this section of Scripture has also been viewed as being controversial by some and they have suggested repeatedly that preachers and Christians should steer clear of teaching these biblical truths because they might be misunderstood, abused or even found to be offensive to some who hold to an alternative doctrinal position. The Apostle Paul begins this section of Scripture by dealing with God's "foreknowledge," God's calling sinners to salvation, God's predestination of those who are elected by Him for eternal salvation, etc. I want to encourage you, the reader, to focus your *entire attention on the explanation of this wonderful section of* Scripture. The story is told of a man who showed up at church with his ears painfully blistered. After the service, is concerned pastor asked, "What in the world happened to you?" The man replied, "I was lying on the couch yesterday afternoon watching a ball game on TV and my wife was ironing nearby. I was totally engrossed in the game when she left the room, leaving the iron near the phone. The phone rang and keeping my eyes glued to the television, I grabbed the hot iron and put it to my ear." "So how did the other ear get burned?" The pastor asked. "Well, I had no more than hung up and the guy called again." (*Country*, October – November 1994, page 45, "overheard at the Country Café," Bill Teweles) Now there, my friend, is a man who was focused. The best way to understand this section of Scripture is to focus your whole attention on it. Rivet your thinking to the specific revelation that the Apostle Paul gives us and you will come away with a clear understanding of this precious part of the perfect package of salvation that God has constructed for us. Furthermore, you will discover it to be a spiritual truth that you will greatly rejoice in.

When he was preaching on 1 Thessalonians 1:4 ("Knowing, beloved brethren, your election by God") C.H Spurgeon eloquently expressed this issue:

> "At the very announcement of the text, some will be ready to say, "Why preach upon so profound a doctrine as election?" I answer, because it is in God's Word, and whatever is in God's Word is to be preached. "But," says the objector, some truths should be kept back from the people lest they make an ill use thereof." That is popish doctrine! It was upon that very theory that priests kept back the Bible from the people. They did not give it to them lest they should misuse it. "But," says the objector, "Are not some doctrines dangerous?" Not if they are true and rightly handled. Truth is never dangerous. It is the error and reticence that are fraught with peril! "But," says the objector. "Do not some men abuse the doctrines of grace?" I grant you that they do, but if we destroy everything that men abused, we should have nothing left. And, besides all this remember that men do read the Scriptures and think about these doctrines and therefore make mistakes about them. Who then shall set them right if we who preach the Word hold our tongues about the matter?" (Cited by H. O. Van Gilder in an unpublished paper entitled "Election," page 8)

Gene Ruyle in his book, *Making a Life,* tells a story about Eliazar Hull, the captain of a whaling ship, who sailed from the ports of New England in the early 1800s. It seems that Eliazar had the astounding ability to be able to sail out farther, stay out longer, and, to come back with larger catches than anyone else. Meanwhile, the owners of the fleet, were always concerned to insure their ships against damage or loss at sea so they required all ship captains to be instructed in the latest navigational techniques of the day.

Eliazar, like the other ship captains, went off for training and the instructors of the training school, who had long since heard of his amazing sailing prowess, questioned him about how he was able to navigate the vast distances of the ocean without losing his way. Eliazar said, "I go up on deck at night, and I look at the stars, and I listen to the wind and the rigging's, and I checked the drift of the seas, and then I set my course." When Eliezar had completed his course of study in the science of navigation, he returned home and resumed his maritime location.

Sometime after that the instructors visited Eliazar and once again ask how he navigated his great ship. "Exactly like you taught me," he responded to everyone's surprise, "I use the sextant to shoot the angle of the sun at midday. After fixing my longitude and latitude on the charts, I get out my compass and other instruments to plot my course. And then, "he continued, "I go up on deck at night and I look at the stars and listen to the wind and the rigging's, and I check the drift of the seas... And go back down to correct my calculations." (New York: Seabury Press, 1983).

God gave us brains. He meant for us to use them. Sometimes we must unlearn or ignore the prevailing teaching on any given subject and trust in what we know to be true and workable. The best source of accurate, spiritual truth, of course, is the Bible. In this chapter that we are now engaged in it will be necessary for you, the reader, to use your brain and perhaps even ignore and disregard things that you may have heard or read about this section of Scripture in the past. Let the passage speak for itself. Put your thinking cap on and reason with the Apostle Paul as he explains these wonderful truths to us.

There is a hilarious story about a country preacher who announced that he would preach on Noah and the Ark on the following Sunday. He gave the Scripture reference for the congregation to read ahead of time. A couple of mean boys noticed something interesting about the placement of the story of the flood in the pulpit Bible. They slipped into the church and glued two pages of the pulpit Bible together. On the next Sunday the preacher got up to read his text.

"Noah took himself a wife," he began, "and she was..." He turned the page to continue,"... 300 cubits long, 50 cubits wide and 30 cubits high." He scratched his head, turned the page back and read it silently, then he turned the page and continued reading. When he looked up at the congregation he said, "I've been reading this old Bible for nigh on to 50 years, but there are some things that are hard to believe."

There are some sections of the Bible with which we struggled even without someone gluing the pages together. Some people struggle with the doctrines of divine foreknowledge, divine calling, and divine predestination. When we examine these truths carefully, however, and prayerfully we can understand what God teaches about them and find them to be thrilling and comforting to we who are Christians.

In his classic book, *Evangelism and the Sovereignty of God*, J. I. Packer points that out that, in reality, all Christian people believe in election and God's sovereignty in salvation, even if they deny that they do.

> "Two facts show this. In the first place, you give God thanks for your conversion. Now why do you do that? Because you know in your heart that God was entirely responsible for it. You did not save yourself; He saved you. There is a second way in which you acknowledge that God is sovereign in salvation. You pray for the conversion of others. You ask God to work in them everything necessary for their salvation. So, our thanksgivings and our intercessions are proof that we believe in divine sovereignty. On our feet we may have arguments about it, but on our knees, we all agree."

(J. I. Packer, evangelism in the sovereignty of God, (Downers Grove, Illinois, InterVarsiy Press, 1961), page 17)

Can a believer lose his salvation? People have differing opinions on the subject. Some of these people are sincere Christians but I think they would be well served to spend time studying and contemplating the passage of Scripture now before us. It is my belief, based on Scripture, that every person who is genuinely saved will remain saved for all eternity. Why do I say that? Are we not all weak in many ways and prone to wander? Are we not still plagued by sin, tempted by the world, accosted by Satan? Then why would I emphatically believe that all genuinely saved people will persevere in their salvation and be eternally saved? This passage addresses that issue head on and it is a great comfort to the true believer. In it Paul reveals just how secure God's salvation of His children is because God is for us. He describes it piece by piece as an unbroken chain of grace. He envisions salvation as a great panoramic picture stretching from eternity past into eternity future and encompassing all those who are the recipients of that salvation. Everyone who is in the beginning of the process is ultimately glorified as a finished product of the process—there is no leakage in terms of people. Since God is for us there is no loss of salvation for anyone who trusts in Jesus Christ by faith alone. No one who is involved in this process of salvation at the beginning will be eliminated along the way. All will be glorified because God is for us.

It was mid-August and the Florida heat was almost unbearable. Not only was the temperature hovering around 95° but the humidity was so thick that it made the air heavy and wrapped you up in a wet blanket of atmospheric misery. The football coaches were yelling out directions, cajoling, berating, and insisting on additional effort. The calisthenics were long since over, the wind sprints seemed to be without end, the hard-hitting—teeth-jarring football collisions were underway. We were engaged in summer training with two four-hour sessions scheduled each day. The ordeal was grueling but anyone who wanted to play football during the season had to prove his worth to the coaches during this "boot camp" type of experience. Many prospective players competed for the coveted position of being accepted on the team. Many were eliminated. Each Friday evening the coach would post a renewed list of the players who were still in contention for the team. Those whose names were not on the list had been eliminated/cut from contention. I remember that I would anxiously check the list each time it was posted to make sure that I had not been eliminated/cut. Those who were eliminated were no doubt disappointed and would never know the joy and sense of being part of the team. Such is the nature of elimination. I was thankful that my name continued to appear on the coach's listings and that I was privileged to play on the team as a member that had paid his dues – I was not eliminated.

We have all watched game shows where a panel of contestants started out in competition with one another only to watch one contestant after another be eliminated from contention until a single winner emerged.

Sometimes elimination can be self–induced. Perhaps the most rigorous and demanding military training in the world is that of the United States' S.E.A.L.S. During the course of their training to see who will and who will not be accepted into this elite military unit, the instructors are constantly harassing each individual, pressuring them to remove themselves from competition by simply stepping forward and ringing a bell signifying that they want to be eliminated from any further training and return to their former station in life. The reason for this is that only those who have the strength of will to endure incredible hardships and still persevere are desired as part of this elite unit of fighting men.

Elimination (whether imposed by another or self–induced) is the process by which some who begin a process or course of action are removed from consideration and contention.

This passage before us deals with the blessed reality that no single believer will ever be eliminated from the process of salvation. The passage can be easily broken down into three parts:

The Purpose of Salvation
The Preeminence of Christ
The Plan of God for Securing the Salvation of His People

The Purpose of Salvation

I will not spend a great deal of time here on this first point because, to a large extent, this has already been dealt with previously. God's immediate purpose is to glorify Himself by causing all things to work together for good to those who love God, to those who are called according to His purpose and thus conform these individuals to the image of His son, Jesus Christ. God, Himself, prepares the sinner and makes him receptive to faith and the Divine call. He enables and encourages the lost sinner to turn from his sin and to trust in Jesus Christ by faith alone. God, then, actively works in all the circumstances and details of the believer's life so that He ensures that all things will work out for the good of the believer. This means that nothing can ultimately harm the believer or keep him from being glorified—God ensures it.

These are immediate purposes for God's salvation in Christ, but then Paul directs our attention to the ultimate purpose and that is to promote the preeminence of Christ for the glory of God. In keeping with this theme, Paul tells us that God's ultimate purpose is to make believers into the likeness of His Son (Romans 8:29). God intends for believers to be like Jesus Christ and for Jesus Christ to be the ultimate leader of all believers. We are being conformed to the image of His Son in order that He might be the firstborn among many brothers. The concept behind, "firstborn", is not chronological birth but it is preeminence. To be the "firstborn" is to be the leader and chief person. God is redeeming for Himself an eternally holy people who are like Christ and who are willingly subject to the authority of Jesus Christ. These people, as a race of people, are to be brothers and sisters (citizens) in His divine kingdom.

Is the Believer in Jesus Christ Secure in Salvation?

For a believer to lose their salvation would mean that God had failed in His divine purpose. Those He elected before the foundation of the world He could not save. Those He chose for heaven would end up in hell. It would mean that the divine seal of the Holy Spirit could not secure the salvation of the believer and that the divine indwelling of the Holy Spirit was impotent to keep the believer from losing his salvation. It would mean that the divine promises of God rooted in the new covenant were pointless and that God's assurances of ultimate salvation for all believers would be meaningless. God would be proven to be a liar or merely unwise and impotent. Such scenarios are unthinkable and impossible! No, "there is now no condemnation for those in Christ Jesus." There will never be any condemnation—it has utterly ceased. It has been taken care of by the perfect propitiatory substitute of Jesus Christ and His payment for our sin on the cross. Everyone who is in Christ will ultimately be glorified.

They will be ultimately conformed to the "image" of Christ. None will be eliminated–since God is for us, all will ultimately be saved.

Some contend that a person can remove themselves from salvation by committing some heinous sin. Others believe that some previous sin may come back to haunt them and disqualify them from salvation. Some even argue that their "free will" got them into salvation, so they conclude that their "free will" can also be instrumental in choosing to take them out of salvation. This type of argument hinges on the false belief that the sinner both initiated and consummated his own conversion. To such people it seems logical that if salvation was accomplished by act of their own will then by another act of their will they can also choose to exit salvation in the same fashion that they entered it. The problem with these erroneous concepts is that they are totally without biblical foundation. God, and not man, initiates and consummates true salvation. Furthermore, no genuinely saved sinner will commit a perverted act of sin like desiring to escape salvation. He would not so jeopardize his salvation since the Holy Spirit who indwells him is powerfully and effectually leading him in the path of righteousness and sustaining him in the way of faith.

Concerning the matter of entering salvation by an act of "free will," that too, is without biblical foundation. It is true that a person chooses freely and, in that sense, has a free will. The problem, however, is that a person also has a mind and emotions as well as a volitional capacity. Sin has adversely affected the mind, the emotions, and the will. These faculties have been so corrupted by sin that they no longer are able to operate rightly in the spiritual realm. The lost sinner evaluates spiritual things incorrectly. He responds emotionally to spiritual things in a negative fashion because they seem repulsive and odious to him. Consequently, the will acts in lockstep concert with that information that it derives from the sinfully twisted, distorted, and corrupted mind and emotions. The result is that the will, following the lead of the mind and emotions, bucks up in defiance at the things of God. The lost sinner chooses freely but that choice is made in an errant way because the will is chained to the sinful mind and sinful emotions. In fact, when addressing the subject of salvation and the human will the Bible clearly says that the human will is not the cause behind our new birth: "He came to his own, and His own people did not receive Him. But to all who did receive Him, who believed in His name, He gave the right to become children of God, who were born, not of blood nor of the will of the flesh nor of the will of man, but of God" (John 1:1–3). This passage clearly teaches that the new birth is brought about by the will of God rather than the will of man.

Along this line of thought, the Apostle Paul wrote to the Corinthian church "The natural person does not accept the things of the Spirit of God, for they are folly to him, and he is not able to understand them because they are spiritually discerned" (1 Corinthians 2:14). Notice, that this verse teaches that "the natural person" not only does not accept the things of the Spirit of God but he is not able to even understand them properly.

In an extended argument declaring God's sovereignty in electing grace Paul concludes by writing, "So then it depends not on human will or exertion, but on God, who has mercy" (Romans 9:16).

Our transformation into the likeness of Jesus Christ will be completed and it will be successful for every single sinner who God has foreknown in pre-ordaining love. Because God is for us we will ultimately even have a body like the body of Christ. One day the Lord will, "Transform the body of our humble state into conformity with the body of His glory, by the exertion of the power that He has even to subject all things to Himself" (Philippians 3:21). We look forward to our total transformation into the likeness of Jesus Christ, "For if we have become united with Him in the likeness of His death certainly we shall be also in the likeness of His resurrection (Romans 6:5). Since God is for us, we will be a race of glorified people able to give fullness of glory to God our Savior. Jesus Christ will be the undisputed King and we will be like Him.

In his letter to the Philippians, Paul described the reason that our future in Christ is *secure,* "Therefore God has highly exalted Him and bestowed on Him the name that is above every name, so at the name of Jesus every knee should bow, in heaven and on earth and under the earth, and every tongue confess that Jesus Christ is Lord, to the glory of the Father" (Philippians 2:9–10). The one who died for us has all authority in heaven and in earth and is preeminent in all things. Because of that, our Lord lovingly secures the total salvation of each of His sheep. To the Colossians Paul wrote that Christ is presently "the head of the body, the church. He is the beginning, the firstborn from the dead, that in everything He might be preeminent" (Colossians 1:18).

So, our Lord Jesus Christ who loved us and gave Himself for us is in total charge and He is for us. Regarding the salvation of the believer and his ultimate glorification, the immediate purpose of God is to ensure that the lost sinner designated for salvation comes to faith in Jesus Christ and that all things are worked out for his ultimate good. The ultimate purpose is to ensure that every believer will be ultimately conformed to the image of Jesus Christ and that our Lord will be the undisputed King of every glorified believer. Jesus Christ will have the preeminence.

The Plan of God for Securing Our Salvation

The Apostle Paul explains the panoramic view of God's salvation by describing it in five separate steps or phases. Perhaps, no other teaching in Scripture is more comforting and instructive than what Paul is about to say. The reader who gives himself to fully understand this teaching and its ramifications will be greatly benefited.

When it comes to the doctrine of "foreknowledge" there are those who insist that the meaning is "before the world was created God foresaw who was going to believe in Him and who would not. So, on the basis of that foreseen faith, He decided to elect to salvation those good people who were going to exercise faith in Him.

This concept of foreknowledge is generally accepted today by the average Christian but it cannot be the correct one for at least two reasons:

1. Our passage teaches that the object of God's foreknowledge is not the action of certain people but the actual people themselves. It is not what these people do but who these people are.

2. If God predestinated people because they were going to believe, then the ground of their salvation is in themselves and their merit and not in God and his mercy. The theologian, John Murray, expressed this concept in the following way: "Even if it were granted that "foreknew" means the foresight of faith, the biblical doctrine of sovereign election is not thereby eliminated or disproved. Indeed, it is certainly true that God foresees faith; He foresees all that comes to pass. The question then becomes: Wence precedes this faith, which God foresees? And the only biblical

answer is that the faith which God foresees is the faith He Himself creates (f. John 3:3–8; 44, 45, 65; Ephesians 2:8; Philippians 1:29; 2 Peter 1:2). Hence, His eternal foresight of faith is preconditioned by His decree to generate this faith in those whom He foresees as believing." (John Murray, the Epistle to the Romans, (Grand Rapids: William B Erdman's, 1968), 316).

I will address this matter in fuller detail momentarily.

"For Whom He Foreknew" (8:29a)

The first step in Paul's description of God's salvation of sinners is described as "foreknowledge". God's plan of redemption began with God's foreknowledge. Salvation is not initiated by a sinner's decision but it is initiated by the action of God's foreknowledge. Certainly, a sinner's repentant faith is necessary for salvation, No one should doubt that. But repentant faith does not initiate salvation. In fact, in this passage Paul is describing salvation from God's perspective and saving faith is not even mentioned though it comes as a response to one's, "calling". Paul's point is that God is for us and has taken the initiative to bring about our ultimate salvation.

The whole of redemptive history is about the Father seeking a bride for His Son. The Father loves the Son perfectly. His desire is to give the Son a unique gift of love. That gift will be a redeemed humanity that constitutes a loving bride–a loving, submissive, joyous, holy, bride. And so, all through redemptive history, the Father is seen as drawing the bride and preparing the bride for His Son. Even when we get to heaven, the New Jerusalem is called the Bridal City.

In ancient times, the bridegroom had to pay a price for his bride. Following that pattern, the church is the bride and Jesus Christ is the bridegroom. The price that He paid for his bride was His own life. As Peter says, the price for our salvation was not paid in silver or gold but with the precious blood of the Lord Jesus Christ (1 Peter 1:19). When we get to heaven the bride is brought to the Bridal City. It is the time when the bride is complete and redemptive history ends with her gathering around the Son. She will love Him, adore Him and worship Him as she shares in

His image. This is the purpose of redemptive history. In all of this, God displays the fullness of His attributes and His glory. In the end, we will give all glory to Christ. We will cast our crowns at His feet and confess that He is the preeminent Lord. After that, Christ will take Himself and the bride and return them all to the Father in an act of reciprocal love.

If this is the purpose of salvation, how does it progress to that end? Clear insight into this matter is laid out for us by the Apostle Paul in verses 29 and 30. These verses describe the whole panoramic view of salvation in a nutshell. Paul gives us the comprehensive, all-inclusive picture of the process of salvation and describes the wide focus plan of God for the salvation of His people.

According to Scripture the process of salvation begins with God's foreknowledge. But what does it mean that God "foreknew"? As I said, for some people this is a choking point for accepting the sovereignty of God in salvation. Some make the erroneous assumption that this "foreknowledge" is referring to God's omniscience (His prescience). They think it is referring to the fact that God knows the end from the beginning and therefore can foresee before-hand who will and will not believe. There is no doubt that God does know the end from the beginning (God knows all things) but that is not what Paul is talking about when he uses the word, "foreknew/ foreknow" in this context.

If one were to be able to gaze into the future and see who would and who would not believe in the Lord Jesus Christ by their own power of choice or their own exercise of faith, the sight would be distressing. The psalmist wrote, "The Lord looks down from heaven on the sons of men to see if there are any who understand, and any who seek God. All have turned aside, they have together become corrupt; there is no one who does good not even one" (Psalm 14:2–3). The Apostle Paul quoted this passage in Romans 3:10–12 in his description of the utter lawlessness and corruption of mankind.

Because of man's deep depravity he rejects and will always reject the righteous claims of Jesus Christ and will not come in submission and faith to Christ. Jesus Christ said that men loved darkness rather than light because their deeds are evil. Paul said, "The man without the Spirit does not accept the things that come from the Spirit of God, for they are foolishness to him, and he cannot understand them, because they are spiritually discerned" (1 Corinthians 2:14). He wrote again, "The sinful mind is hostile to God. It does not submit to God's law, nor can it do so" (Romans 8:7).

Those who envision sinners coming to repentant faith in the Lord Jesus Christ for salvation (without divine aid) do not understand the depths of depravity and sin that sinners are trapped in. They do not understand the addiction sinners have to sin and the love that they have for it. Sinners are enslaved in the chains of sin and infatuated with the lure of sin. They do not understand that the sinner is dead in trespasses and sins. Sinners fully believe that they are the living epitome of freedom. There is absolutely nothing in man's carnal nature to move him to trust in God against whom he is actively rebelling. The Bible teaches that the lost sinner will not seek God because his nature is to lust after sin and reject righteousness. The Bible also teaches that a lost person, apart from the powerful work of the Holy Spirit, does not even have the capability of seeking after God (he cannot do so) (1 Corinthians 2:14).

This passage does not mean that God foreknew (in the sense of foreseeing) who would ultimately come to faith in the Lord Jesus Christ. Keep in mind that if God looked ahead He would have seen that no person would choose to believe and therefore, apart from his intervention on their behalf, all people would go to hell. Why then, did God go ahead and create those people who would not be saved? Do you see the reason some people postulate the idea that foreknowledge means foreseeing? It is an attempt to try to get God off the hook—to save Him from a supposed bad reputation. By interpreting God's foreknowledge as mere foresight and by attributing some supposed innate ability to sinful men, enabling them to desire and decide to trust in Christ, they then seem to clear God of any responsibility in the matter of some being saved and some not being saved. They want to exonerate God from being responsible for people's salvation or lack thereof. But, once again, why would He create people who He knew were going to hell? Somehow, all of this, mysteriously works together to accomplish God's purpose and His glory. But how?

Keep in mind that the words faith and believe are not even used in the passage. I mention this because some people try to insert those words into this passage so that the passage is supposed to be saying, "For whom He foresaw would repent and believe He did predestinate..." But that is not what this passage of Scripture says at all and to insert any word into a given passage is to tamper with and distort the passages' meaning. Yet, there are those who persist in doing so in order to reconcile this passage with their predetermined doctrinal system. As far as faith is concerned, it does not come up in this passage but if it did we must remember that even faith does not originate with the believer but with God, "For by grace you have been saved through faith; and that not of yourselves, it is the gift of God; not as a result of works, that no one should boast" (Ephesians 2:8–9).

This entire section of Scripture focuses our attention entirely on God's will, God's purpose, God's plan, etc. The point is that our salvation is secure in an absolute and guaranteed way because it is entirely in the hands of God and God is for us.

Furthermore, regarding the personal choice of coming to Christ, the Lord Jesus often invited sinners to come to Him for salvation but He reminded them, "No one can come to Me, unless the Father who sent Me draws him" (John 6:44).

Again, I affirm to you, God's foreknowledge is not a reference to His omniscience or prescience but to His foreordination. It does not mean that God knew what would happen and then he just reacted to it. The reason that God can see faith in some is because He ordains it in advance. Peter had this same concept of divine foreknowledge in mind when he wrote of Christians as those, "who are chosen according to the foreknowledge of God the Father" (1 Peter 1:1–2). Note that Peter used the same word "*foreknowledge*" again, in the same chapter when he wrote that Christ "was foreknown before the foundation of the world" (1 Peter 1:20). The word means the same thing in both places. It is saying that believers are foreknown in the same sense as Christ was foreknown. "Foreknowledge," cannot mean merely foreseen, but must refer to a predetermined choice by God.

This is not a new concept in Scripture. On the day of Pentecost, Peter declared of Christ: "This man, delivered up by the predetermined plan and foreknowledge of God, you nailed to a cross by the hands of godless men and put Him to death" (Acts 2:23). In this passage the word, "predetermined", is from *horizo* from which we get our English word horizon. It describes the outer limits of the earth that we can see from a given vantage point. The basic idea of the Greek word refers to setting the boundaries or limits. The word, "plan", is from *boule* which was used in classical Greek to refer to an officially convened, decision-making council. Both words highlight the idea of deliberate intention. "Foreknowledge", is from the noun form of the verb translated foreknow in our passage. According to the Granville Sharp's rule of Greek grammar, if two nouns of the same case (in this instance, "plan" and "foreknowledge") are connected by the Greek word kai ("and") and have the definite article (the) before the first noun but not before the second noun, the nouns refer to the same thing (H. E. Dana and Julius R. Mantey, *A Manual Grammar of the Greek New Testament* [New York: Macmillan, 1927], page 147). In other words, Peter is equating God's predetermined plan (God's foreordination) with God's foreknowledge.

Another aspect of foreknowledge has to do with loving in an experiential, intimate way before–hand. The word, "foreknew" is from *proginosko*. This is a compound word made up of two parts. The first part (pro) carries with it the idea of before–hand or prior. The second part (ginosko) is a very special word denoting a particular kind of knowledge. It usually denotes an intimate, experiential kind of knowledge such as a loving relationship. For example, "Cain *knew* his wife and she conceived" (Genesis 4:17). Some translations use the phrase, "Cain had relations with his wife" speaking, of course, of conjugal relations. When Joseph found out that Mary was pregnant the Bible tells us that he did not "know" her. That is, there were no conjugal relations. He kept her a virgin. Jesus also used this word. He warned, "Then I will declare to them,' I never knew you; depart from Me, you who practice lawlessness" (Matthew 7:23). He is obviously not saying that He was unaware of their existence or behavior because He specifically identifies their practice of lawlessness. He is saying that He never "knew" them in an intimate, saving manner. The Apostle Paul uses this word when writing to Timothy. Paul says, "The Lord "knows" those who are His" (2 Timothy 2:19). Again, this is not suggesting that God has some lapse in knowledge regarding those who are not His but it is stating that He has a special, loving relationship with those who belong to Him.

Galatians 4:9 speaks of salvation this way: "Now you have come to know God, or rather to be known by God." This obviously means more than mere cognitive knowledge. It describes a love relationship. In Romans 11:2 Paul writes, "God has not rejected His people whom He foreknew."

What does that mean? Does it not mean that God has not rejected His people whom he foreknew or predetermined to love from among the nation of Israel?

On the day of Pentecost, Peter was preaching concerning Christ and he talked about Christ's death and the people nailing Him to a cross, but he says that Christ was delivered over to you to be crucified by the predetermined plan of God. Another way to say the same thing is that God destined, purposed, planned, pre-decided what would happen to the Lord Jesus Christ. Foreknowledge and foreknowing are best understood as a foreordination (a determined, willful choice before–hand) and as a setting of God's special love on the future subjects of salvation. That is why the Apostle Paul begins the description of our security in salvation with the foreknowledge of God. What does God do for those that He has foreordained to salvation and loved before–hand (before the foundation of the world) to ensure our ultimate glorification and our ultimate security? This takes us to Paul's second step in his description.

Predestination

Foreknowledge and predestination are not the same. Predestination means to "predetermine". In the case of salvation, it is to predetermine someone's destiny. It might be likened to an airline flight to heaven. Election is God deciding who gets on the plane bound for heaven. It is like God making up the passenger list. Predestination is His taking care of all the arrangements necessary for the flight to be successful; Each route the plane will take, issuing the boarding passes, establishing the timing of departures and landings, ensuring that all supplies that would be necessary for the flight are on board the plane so that it will make the trip successfully and the passengers will arrive safely, etc. In election God is responsible for deciding who will fly on the plane as a passenger. In predestination God is responsible to make sure that each passenger who has been chosen to make the flight boards the plane and has the necessary boarding pass of faith, in hand, to gain access to the flight to heaven and that every other need is met in order to make the flight successful.

Foreknowledge is God focusing His intimate and deep love on the elect and ordaining that they will ultimately be saved completely and eternally.

Predestination is ensuring that the elect will fulfill their destiny. Whereas the doctrine of election points out that God chooses the recipients of salvation, the doctrine of foreknowledge underscores that God intimately and sovereignly loves these that he has chosen and predetermined so they will be saved. John Stott wrote:

> "Clearly then, a decision is involved in the process of becoming a Christian, but it is God's decision before it can be ours. This is not to deny that we "decided for Christ", and freely, but to affirm that we did so only because He had first decided for us." Actually, this choice was made in eternity past."

(John R. Stott, "Men Made New: An Exposition of Romans 5–8," (Grand Rapids: Baker Book House, 1984), 101).

Some, objecting to this doctrine, have employed an argument against the doctrine of election which might be called the "apathy argument." It goes something like this "If God is sovereign in salvation, then we have no responsibility to evangelize the lost. Loraine Boettner addresses this argument by saying:

> "The decree of election is a secret decree. And since no revelation has been given to the preacher as to which ones among his peers are elect and which are non-elect, it is not possible for him to present the gospel to the elect only. It is his duty to look with hope on all those to whom he is preaching and to pray for them that they may each be among the elect. In order to offer the message to the elect, he must offer it to all; and the Scripture command is plain to the effect that it should be offered to all."

(Loraine Boettner, The Reformed Doctrine of Predestination, (Grand Rapids: William Burban's Publishing company, 1954), 285.)

Still others have argued against this biblical doctrine from the standpoint that the doctrine of election supposedly destroys man's freedom and therefore his sense of responsibility. Sinclair Ferguson points out, however, "the clearest example we have of both election and freedom residing in the same man, is the man Jesus Christ. No one's life was more predetermined than His, yet He was the most free man who ever walked on the earth."

("Predestination in Christian History," Tenth: An Evangelical Quarterly, (October 1983), 7.)

Isn't it strange how this word predestination has received such bad treatment in some Christian circles? In fact, when rightly understood, it is a comforting reality for the true believer. From foreknowledge we are introduced to the doctrine of God's electing love. Paul, then, moves on to talk about the results of that choice–the plan that leads to salvation. So, whoever God foreknew, He predestined. Those He loved before–hand and ordained before–hand He predestinated. Foreknowledge stands at the beginning of God's first act in our salvation. Paul then declares that God has *predetermined* the destiny of every person who will believe in Him. He refers to this by the word predestination, which is a translation of "proorizo," which literally means to mark out, appoint, or determine beforehand. It was often used of ship captains who would mark out on their sea charts the course that they intended to take. That is, they would determine beforehand the route that their ship was to follow. God has pre-determined or predestinated every believer to salvation through the means of the redeeming work of Jesus Christ on the cross.

When Paul addressed the Ephesians, he wrote that God "chose us in Him before the foundation of the world, that we should be holy and blameless before Him. In love He predestined us to adoption as sons through Jesus Christ to Himself, according to the kind intention of His will" (Ephesians 1:4–5). Not only were we predestinated by God to adoption and to ultimate salvation but even the Lord Jesus Christ and His work on our behalf was predestinated by God.

In the immediate aftermath of the crucifixion and resurrection of Jesus Christ a group of believers in Jerusalem, in the early church, gave praise to God for His sovereign power declaring, "For truly in this city there were gathered together against Your holy servant Jesus, whom You anointed, both Herod and Pontius Pilate, along with the Gentiles and the peoples of

Israel, to do whatever Your hand and Your purpose predestined to occur (Acts 4:27 – 28).

So much of contemporary Christianity emphasizes the role of the individual sinner, particularly that person's "deciding for Christ." While it is true that the lost sinner must choose to turn from his sin and to trust in Jesus Christ by faith, we must remember that the sinner can only choose Christ because God first chose him. The Apostle Paul drives home this point, "We have obtained an inheritance, having been predestined according to his purpose who works all things after the counsel of his will" (Ephesians 1:11). We should, therefore, place more emphasis on the will and work of God in salvation and less emphasis on the so-called ability of man to initiate salvation. We must give God the glory. We must trust in the security that God provides and rejoice in the grace and love that God shows us in Christ. This leads us to step number three in Paul's description of God's salvation of his people.

Calling

The general, external call of the gospel is like advertising for the trip to heaven that is being freely offered to all who will respond by repentance and faith. God's people are to get the Word out to the whole world and make sure the invitation is extended. The Word of the gospel is to be shared with the unsaved encouraging them to embrace it personally, freely, and immediately. (Illustrations for Biblical Preaching, editor. Michael Green, (Grand Rapids, Michigan: Baker Book House, 1982), 117.)

When one considers carefully how the Apostle Paul depicts salvation, it is clear that salvation is God's work. The longer we are Christians and the more we study the Word of God the more we become increasingly aware of the fact that we had very little to do with our salvation. That biblical truth becomes immensely clear. C. J. Vaughn emphasizes this truth:

> "Everyone who is eventually saved can only ascribe his salvation, from the first step to the last, to God's favor and act. Human merit must be excluded; and this can only be by tracing back the work far beyond the obedience which evidences, or even the faith which appropriates, salvation;

even to an act of spontaneous favor on the part of that God who foresees and foreordains from eternity all His works." (Cited by John Stott, page 250).

The young, untaught Christian sometimes fails to understand that the real work of salvation has been done for him by God. He thinks that he has somehow believed on his own to receive salvation. I am reminded of an interesting account that I once read.

"A little nine-year-old boy got tired of practicing the piano. His mother heard that the great Paderewski was coming into town to do a concert and she thought that by hearing him her son would be motivated to continue with his piano lessons. She bought two tickets, one for herself and one for her boy. She dragged him along, set him down by her in his little tuxedo, and she began visiting with her friends. Then, she looked up on the platform and there was this giant, ebony black, Steinway concert grand piano. The keyboard was lifted and the leather bench was there. Her darling little boy he had seen it as well. The little boy looked at this piano, popped his knuckles, and said to himself, "oh, man, I would like to play that."

So, he slipped down the aisle, walked across the front of the concert all, ascended the steps to the stage, sat down, and started playing "Chopsticks."

Well, the people down front said, "Who... Who is...?" "QUIT!" "Hey, kid, stop!" "Where's his mother?" Of course, she was embarrassed beyond words.

The great Paderewski, who was back stage fixing his tie, heard what was going on, so without the boy seeing him, he slipped out onto the stage and came in behind the little boy, reached around him and improvised a beautiful medley to go with "Chopsticks." Then he said to the boy,

"Keep playing. Don't quit. Don't stop." (D. H. DeHaan,
Windows on the Word)

I'm sure it would not have been long before the young boy realized that
the real music being created was being created by the great Paderewski and
not himself. At the first, however, he probably thought that he was actually
creating the music. When we become Christians as a result of the effectual
calling of God, we need to realize that the real "miracle" of our salvation
was created in us by God Himself. It is God that changes the music of
our soul. It is God who gives us the desire for salvation and the ability to
believe in Jesus Christ. Everything is a work of God.

In God's divine plan of salvation, predestination leads to calling. It
is one thing to predetermine what will happen but it is another thing
altogether for God to actually make it happen in time and in real life. It is
at the point of our calling that God's predetermined plan intersects with
our lives. I have already touched on this subject of calling in an earlier
chapter so I will restrict my remarks somewhat in this section.

Chapter X of the 1647 Westminster Confession of Faith describes the
effectual call of the unsaved sinner by God to salvation: "The effectual
call" is God's sovereign drawing of a sinner to salvation. The effectual call
extended to a sinner overwhelms his natural inclination to rebel against
God and causes him to willingly trust by faith in Jesus Christ." Some people
refer to the effectual call of God as irresistible grace. This effectual call
from God calls the unsaved person out of worldliness and slavery to sin. It
calls the unsaved sinner to faith in Christ, holiness of life, and ultimately
to eternal glory. The unsaved person's initial resistance to this powerful,
effectual call of God to salvation by the Holy Spirit is eventually overcome
so that the subject of call is made to come by faith through Jesus Christ to
God willingly and joyously. The calling of God is irresistible and effectual.

Those who are called are those in whose hearts the Holy Spirit works
effectually to lead them to saving faith in Christ.

If there is one doctrine that Satan would like to distort, it is the
doctrine of salvation. Satan would love to confuse people about God's
salvation in Christ and how it operates. He wants to keep lost sinners under
his bondage, blinded by his lies, blockaded from the door of salvation,
and laboring under the burden of divine judgment. He uses both religious

and nonreligious means to accomplish his ends. In the realm of religion, whether primitive religions or liberal, unbiblical religion, Satan often fills religion with meaningless pageantry. In addition, Satan convinces people that their salvation is dependent to some extent on their own works or personal contributions in addition to whatever God may provide in Christ. Any such notion, of course, distorts the real message of Gospel salvation and throws the monkey–wrench into the gears of true salvation. True salvation is by God's grace alone!

Perhaps no doctrine better captures this concept than the doctrine of divine calling. Divine calling means much more than a mere invitation or summons. Perhaps no example of divine calling is better suited to illustrate this concept that salvation is all of God than the divine calling of Abraham to salvation.

The Apostle Paul asks this question: "What then shall we say that Abraham, our forefather according to the flesh, has found? For if Abraham was justified by works, he has something to boast about; but not before God" (Romans 4:1 – 2).

Paul is making the point that Abraham was not justified by works and therefore had no grounds for boasting before God. The apostle goes on to say: "For what does the Scripture say? 'And Abraham believed God and it was reckoned to him as righteousness' (Romans 4: 3). Paul's point here is that Abraham was saved by faith alone – not by works of any kind.

The Bible goes on to describe the kind of faith that Abraham possessed. It was a faith which believed in God and obediently acted upon the directions of God. It was a faith that looked forward to receiving an inheritance beyond this world–whose architecture and builder is God. But how did Abraham, come to possess this faith and believe in God? This brings us into the realm of divine calling.

Like all "Christians," Abraham was sovereignly and directly chosen by God. The divine call is a gracious call. It is a call that singles out a sinner to become the object of salvation and divine blessing. It is a call of God grounded in His foreknowledge/foreordination and carried out by the Holy Spirit in the full scope of regeneration. It is an internal call, a mighty, effectual work of God that results in the salvation of the one called. Paul wrote to the Romans (1:7), "To all who are beloved of God, called to be saints." He wrote to Timothy (1:9) "who saved us and called us with a holy calling." Paul wrote to the Thessalonians (2:13) and reminded them that God had chosen them for salvation and then he added these words, "We should always give thanks to God for you, beloved by the Lord, it was for this He called you through our gospel that you may obtain the glory of the Lord Jesus Christ." The fact that we are beloved by the Lord refers to our election and foreknowledge. It is another indication in Scripture that God is for us. God set his love upon us before we were ever born or created. God chose us to be the recipients of salvation from the beginning. That is why Paul is giving thanks to God for the salvation of the Thessalonians. Paul, himself, was called of God to salvation even though he was not at the time seeking God.

Abraham, like the Apostle Paul, was not searching for God when he was divinely called. While Paul was well-versed in the Old Testament details about God, Abraham had probably never heard of the true God. Abraham was raised in idolatrous paganism where he lived in the Ur of Chaldee (Genesis 11:31; 15:7). This was a purely pagan and idolatrous city. Archaeologists estimate that it probably had 300,000 inhabitants during Abraham's time. So, Abraham was a city dweller in an important pagan commercial city located in Mesopotamia on the lower Euphrates River, a little more than 100 miles northwest of the Persian Gulf. The people of that region were reported to be highly educated and accomplished. They were polytheistic, having a multitude of gods, the chief of which was called Nanna, the moon God. Abraham's father was an idolater (Joshua 24:2) and Abraham was, no doubt, raised in paganism.

When God called Abram (later to be named Abraham) He gave no reason for selecting that particular pagan from the millions of others in the world. God chose Abraham because it was His divine will to do so and the Bible never attempts to explain or justify God's decisions. In fact, God chose Israel from among the nations in the same manner. God chooses some sinners for salvation from among the host of lost humanity in exactly the same manner.

God's call of Abraham was attended by the power of God to enable him to respond properly in faith. The call of God is not only sovereign, but it is more than a mere summons. It is a divine summons accompanied by the attendant power to enable the person called to comply with the divine call and to be willing to do so in eager faith.

God told Abraham to leave his homeland and family and go to a place where God would show him a new land that he would possess. Abraham obeyed God only partially. He left his homeland but he took some of his extended family with him. This indicates to us that even some of those who are divinely called of God do not always obey God perfectly. Abraham faced many trials and pressures in life but his faith was a resilient one. He learned that God's promises can only be fulfilled by God's power. He learned that God's protective hand is upon those who are His own. Abraham lived a good life but he did not live a perfect life and he revealed certain spiritual imperfections throughout his life—but Abraham always returned to the Lord in faith.

The divine calling of God is not only sovereign and powerful but it sustains and perpetuates the believers continued compliance with God throughout his life. God's divine calling of the lost to salvation always accomplishes His intended end. That is why Paul could write, "and whom He predestined, these He also called; and those whom He called, these He also justified..." (Romans 8:30)

Notice that everyone who is called is also justified (declared by God to be righteous in His sight and free from the penalty of sin). This is also why Paul could write to the Philippians (1:6), "He that began the good work in you will continue it until the day of Jesus Christ." Divine calling is sovereignly selective, strong and powerful, and sweetly brings the sinner to the place of saving faith. Justification is by faith alone. Paul wrote, "Therefore having been justified by faith we have peace with God through our Lord Jesus Christ" (Romans 5:1). This faith, by which the lost person is justified, is a gift of God.

It should be strongly emphasized, however, that Scripture nowhere teaches that God chooses unbelievers to condemnation. That may seem like the logical corollary to what we have been studying about divine calling but that is nowhere taught in Scripture.

In truth, God's ways are far above our ways and His thoughts are far above our thoughts so that we may be incapable of fathoming how all of this works in every detail. We are merely to study what God says about divine calling and believe it. Scripture teaches many truths which seem to be paradoxical. Is Christ human or divine? The answer is "yes." Did men write the Scriptures or did God write the Scriptures? The answer is both. We cannot always understand every nuance of detail but we can understand what God has revealed to us and believe it.

If a person goes to hell, it is because he rejects God and God's way of salvation. If a person goes to heaven it is because of God. The Apostle John declared in his Gospel that believers are saved and made children of God, "Not of blood, nor of the will of the flesh, nor of the will of man, but of God" (John 1:13). This all has to do with God's divine calling of people to salvation both immediate and ultimate.

This matter of divine calling is constantly recognized and emphasized by the biblical authors. The Apostle Paul wrote, "We received grace and apostleship to call people from among all the Gentiles to the obedience that comes from faith and you also are among those who are called to belong to Jesus Christ." – "to all in Rome, who are loved by God and called to be saints" (Romans 1:5b–7). The same apostle wrote to the Corinthians: "God, who has called you into fellowship with His Son Jesus Christ our Lord, is faithful" (1 Corinthians 1:9). Paul wrote to the Galatians and said: "I am astonished that you are so quickly deserting the one who called you by the grace of Christ and are turning to a different gospel" (Galatians 1:6). He wrote to the Ephesians: "As a prisoner for the Lord, then, I urge you to live a life worthy of the calling you have received" (Ephesians 4:1). When the Apostle Peter preached on the day of Pentecost he said: "Repent and be baptized, every one of you, in the name of Jesus Christ for the forgiveness of your sins. And you will receive the gift of the Holy Spirit. The promise is for you and your children and for all who are far off–for all whom the Lord our God will call" (Acts 2: 38–39). Peter also wrote: "Therefore, my brothers, be all the more eager to make your calling and election sure" (1 Peter 1:10a).

Divine, effectual calling to salvation is emphasized throughout Scripture just as it is in Romans chapter eight. Divine calling leads the sinner to the place where they can and will believe on the Lord Jesus Christ and be justified. Divine calling, like all the other components of this chain of salvation, is entirely the work of God. It is precisely because these things are the work of God and not dependent upon us in our human frailty that our ultimate salvation is so secure. This gives the insightful believer real reason to have absolute assurance and confidence in his ultimate salvation and to be convinced, as well, of the passionate commitment of God toward us. God is for us. The next link in the chain of salvation that the Apostle Paul gives us in Romans chapter eight is:

Justification

"And whom He called, these He also justified" (Romans 8:30b).

Notice that all who are divinely called to salvation are also justified. Justification is referring to that aspect of divine calling that is effectual and declarative in nature. It always secures the legal salvation of the one who is called. To grasp the concept of justification one might want to envision a courtroom scene. The judge pronounces the accused criminal innocent. That act does not change the criminal's character but it does clear the accused criminal of any legal culpability. The difference between justification and sanctification is significant. Sanctification might be pictured as a scene in a surgical operating room. The surgeon *actually* changes something in the patient. Sanctification *actually* changes the believer in an ongoing way causing him to become more conformed to the image of Jesus Christ. Justification, on the other hand, is a declarative act of God whereby He declares us (true believers) to be righteous based on the imputed righteousness of Jesus Christ and received by faith alone.

Notice also that just as foreknowledge, predestination, and calling are the exclusive works of God, so is justification. In Romans chapter eight the Apostle Paul is focusing on the divine side of salvation to ensure his readers of their absolute security in salvation. Paul does not even mention any human contribution to salvation but solely focuses the reader's attention on the fact that everything regarding salvation is being handled by God Himself. God is in charge. God is controlling the entire process for the security and well-being of those who love Him. God is underwriting our security. God is for us!

Note also that the Bible is extremely clear about the basis for justification. For example, the Apostle Paul has already taught the Romans about justification in chapter 4 of the book of Romans: "What then shall we say and that Abraham, our forefather according to the flesh, has found? "For if Abraham was justified by works, he has something to boast about; but not before God" (Romans 4:1–2). Paul is saying that Abraham was not justified by works. Then he adds: "For what does the Scripture say?' And Abraham believed God, and it was reckoned to him as righteousness.' Now to the one who works, his wage is not reckoned (counted) as a favor, but as what is due. But to the one who does not work, but believes in Him who justifies the ungodly, his faith is reckoned (counted) as righteousness." (Romans 4: 4). Paul cites the same verse in Galatians when talking about justification and the writer of Hebrews also uses the same verse when underscoring the place of faith in our justification (Hebrews 11:8–10).

The idea behind "reckoning" or "counting" is the legal meaning of crediting something to another's account. It is from the Greek word, "*logizomai*". The only thing that God received from Abraham was his imperfect faith (even that was a gift from God), yet God in grace and mercy counted it to Abraham's spiritual account as righteousness. The same thing occurs when God calls each and every sinner that He intends to save. God enables that sinner to believe and even though the faith of the sinner is imperfect and to some extent flawed (though not fatally) God counts it or reckons it to the sinner's spiritual account as righteousness. That is why the Bible can declare that God "justifies the ungodly."

According to the Oxford dictionary, to "justify" means to make a "pronunciation" or to declare or make righteous in the sight of God." The word is used in common English in much the same way. We often say, "The end does not justify the means." Literally, the end does not make the means used to accomplish that end right. To be justified, then, means to be declared righteous in the sight of God by God. It is the term related to declaration and to making a statement regarding one's legal standing. As I have stated, in a theological sense, justification does not make the sinner righteous but declares the sinner to be righteous based on the imputation of the sinner's sin to the Lord Jesus Christ and the reciprocal imputation of the righteousness of Christ to the sinner. This swapping of accounts is the basis for the divine justification of the believing sinner–it is received by faith alone.

What a deal for the unbeliever! He is offered the opportunity to give Jesus Christ all his sin along with its penalty and in exchange receives the righteousness of Jesus Christ with all its benefits and rewards. Humanly speaking, why would anyone reject such a wonderful proposition? But sin runs deep. God has so designed salvation that our justification cannot be accomplished by ourselves or by some other mere human on our behalf but rather He/God has accomplished it for the ungodly through His perfect Son, Jesus Christ. In this way, God receives all the glory.

That is why justification is based on faith. The Apostle Paul writes about this: "God made Him who had no sin to be sin for us, so that in Him we might become the righteousness of God" (2 Corinthians 5:21). God does not leave us, as believers, in an ungodly state but God declares us righteous based on faith in the Lord Jesus Christ alone. Subsequent to this justification, is the inevitable process of sanctification. Sanctification is inevitably and powerfully worked out in the believer's life by God through the ministry of the Holy Spirit. Justification is by grace through faith. It is not based on human works to any degree at all. Those who are called by God are brought to the place of faith in Jesus Christ (His person and redeeming work) whereby they are then declared by God to be righteous (justified). Paul explains this process in clear detail in Romans 4 and then in Romans 5:1, he writes, "Therefore, since we have been justified through faith, we have peace with God through our Lord Jesus Christ, through whom we have gained access by faith into this grace in which we now stand" (Romans 5:1–2a).

Abraham was not justified before God by his works (though in a sense his declaration of faith in God was justified in the eyes of other human beings by his actions) but Abraham was justified by God through God's grace and through faith alone. Some have wrestled with this concept because they have misunderstood the focus of passages dealing with justification. For example, James writes about justification from the perspective of our faith being justified in the eyes of other human beings (James 2). On the other hand, Paul writes about justification from the perspective of our justification in the eyes of God (Romans 4). What seems like contrasting messages regarding justification can actually be shown to be compatible when the context, purpose, and focus of these passages is clearly understood.

In terms of one's justification before God, those who are divinely and effectually called are also justified (declared by God to be righteous) by God's grace through faith in Jesus Christ alone. Furthermore, all of those who are called are justified.

The faith of the one justified includes an understanding of the facts of the gospel and an agreement with those facts, an internalization of those facts, and a complete trust in the person and work of Jesus Christ that those facts describe. It embraces these facts but more than that it embraces the person of the Lord Jesus Christ in his redeeming and reigning work. This faith is transforming. It is a repentant faith and a motivating faith. It is a faith which draws one closer to God in submission and obedience as well as in wonder and amazement while it causes the believer to turn away from sin. It is a divine gift enabling the unsaved sinner to trust in Jesus Christ as one's Lord and Savior and thus be justified by God. Dear reader, do you clearly see and understand that since God is actually for us He has carefully taken care of every need that we have for our salvation to be guaranteed and divinely secured with an unshakable and absolute security in Christ?

Glorification

"And whom He justified, these He also glorified" (Romans 8:30c).

Paul expresses our glorification as Christians in the past tense. He says we have been "glorified" already. Actually, glorification, as we know, is yet future but Paul wants to express to his readers the absolute certainty that if they are in the Golden chain of divine salvation described in verses 29–30 then their glorification is guaranteed and certain. Griffith Thomas writes:

> "The tense in the last word is amazing. It is the most daring anticipation of faith that even the New Testament contains." (Griffith W. H. Thomas, "St. Paul's Epistle to the Romans, (Grand Rapids: William B Erdman's Publishing Company, 1946), 226.)

As with each of the steps or the successive links of salvation that Paul has been describing (foreknowledge, predestination, calling, and justification) glorification is exclusively a work of God. Note that no one who begins this process of salvation is lost – all are ultimately glorified. Our ultimate glorification is the very purpose for which we are redeemed, "It was for this He called you through our gospel, that you may gain the glory of our Lord Jesus Christ" (2 Thessalonians 2:14).

The promise of glory is not in the least an uncertain hope. It is the promise of being perfected in the perfect image of Christ and taken to be with God and other believers to live in the perfect and joyous world of heaven for eternity. As I have noted, our glorification is a sure thing. Paul even declares the ultimate glorification of the believer as something which has already (in the mind of God) occurred. Again, he uses the past tense, *"these He also glorified."* The security and ultimate glorification of the believer is absolutely certain because God designed it and ensures that it will come to pass. What a wonderful salvation! What a wonderful Savior! Since God is for us eternal glory awaits us as believers (2 Timothy 2:10).

In describing the experience of salvation, the Apostle Paul writes, "Therefore, since we have been justified through faith, we have peace with God through our Lord Jesus Christ, through whom we have gained access by faith into this grace in which we now stand. And we rejoice in the hope of the glory of God" (Romans 5:1–2).

Believers are the heirs of glory (Romans 8:17a) and God is the source of glory (Romans 8:17b). Regardless of what a believer suffers in this life it does not begin to compare with the glory that awaits us in the life to come and the rewards to come will make present sufferings all worthwhile. "For I consider that the sufferings of this present time are not worthy to be compared with the glory that is to be revealed to us" (Romans 8:18).

Everyone who is justified by God will also be glorified by God. What does this say about the erroneous teaching of some that one can lose his salvation? How can this truth bring immense comfort to that one who is plagued by a reoccurring doubt regarding his security in salvation? Can any truth bring more confidence and boldness to the believer?

Does this truth not kindle an even greater passion for God within you? You, dear believer, are secure and on your way to experience an eternity of glory with God. Nothing and no one can prevent this from happening. Like David who faced off against the giant Goliath, we should have a burning passion for God and, also, be completely persuaded that God is with us and for us. Paul will further address this aspect of the believer's security in the next section of Romans chapter eight but this is enough for now. It is enough to know that God is in absolute control of guaranteeing the security of our ultimate salvation as believers in Christ. All of this is a glorious reality because GOD IS FOR US!

BRINGING IT HOME

1. Describe the steps or links in the salvation process that Paul addresses in this section of Romans chapter eight.
2. What does Paul mean by, "foreknow"?
3. Is God active or passive in our salvation? How does this make you feel?
4. What is God's purpose in our ultimate salvation? Will it be accomplished? How does this make you feel?

WHAT A WONDERFUL SALVATION!
WHAT A WONDERFUL SAVIOR!

10

NO TREPIDATION

Since God is for Us the Believer does not have to Worry about and Fear (experience trepidation) the Future

"What then shall we say to these things? If God is for us, who can be against us?" – (Romans 8:31).

NO TREPIDATION – THE ABSOLUTE
CONFIDENCE OF GOD'S SUPPORT

The Pennsylvania denominational executive tells of his family's stay in a dilapidated hotel one summer while on vacation. They had made reservations long in advance, sight unseen. Upon awakening the morning after their arrival, they heard what they thought was the sound of a wrecking ball working very close to them. The thuds kept getting closer and closer. Suddenly, they realized that the huge wrecking ball was hitting the very building in which they were housed. They went out into the hall and looked out the window. The hotel was being torn down around them. (Herb Miller, ACTIONS SPEAK LOUDER THAN VERBS, (Nashville: Abingdon Press, 1989). As Christians, we need not fear nor have trepidation regarding our salvation. God will not allow our spiritual "house" to be torn down around us. We are completely safe in the protective care of God who loves us and has everything under perfect control for our good and for His glory.

Think of the last time you were in attendance at a July 4th fireworks display. The crowd had gathered and was spending time enjoying each other's company while waiting for the fireworks to begin. Perhaps some martial music was being played with a patriotic theme to set the mood for the festive fireworks. When the fireworks finally began, after the skies were dark, the crowd "ooed and ahhed" as they witnessed each explosion of light and color as they gazed expectantly into the heavens awaiting the next burst of light and sound. The fireworks went off with precision and perfect timing. Each new burst of colorful explosion brought a gasp of wonder and amazement from the appreciative onlookers. Then came the grand finale! Suddenly, the skies lit up with an unbelievable eruption of a kaleidoscope of color and crescendo of sound. Everything prior to this was but a prelude to the grand finale. This was the main event.

In a sense, that is where the Apostle Paul is now taking us. In the eighth chapter of Romans we are brought to the place by Paul where we will ultimately stand in utter awe and in amazement at the grand display of God's provision of the loving and guaranteed security for the believer. The final section of this chapter has not yet come but Paul, at this point, continues to deal with the enormous benefits of the substitutionary death of Jesus Christ for believing sinners. After this, the apostle leads us in a hymn of confident, joyous, security as we praise God in a prophetic declaration of God's grace. The believer will rejoice in this grace throughout all eternity. In a sense this passage of Romans chapter eight that we are about to deal with is the beginning of the beginning of the grand finale. The final fireworks and crescendo will soon be coming but here Paul begins to tune up for what is yet to come.

I have chosen to call this section, "No Trepidation." You may have heard someone say that they are approaching a particular situation or challenge with, "fear and trepidation." You know what "fear" is but what is "trepidation?" The word has its root in Latin and actually means to quiver or shake. In some ancient astronomy texts, the stars were referred to using this word because they appeared to quiver or shake in the heavens.

We sometimes refer to them as twinkling. It is similar to the kind of sensation a speaker might feel before he gets up in front of an audience. He feels a surge of nervousness in his stomach and his hands shake due to the fear of standing up in front of this audience and addressing them.

Sometimes believers cast a wary eye toward the future horizon of their lives and respond with fear and trepidation. They think about their own innate weakness, the long road which presumably lies ahead filled with unknown problems and obstacles, the enormity of the power of the forces of evil aligned against them, etc. and they feel trepidation as they consider the prospects of their safety and security in their salvation. Some even imagine that, in standing before God, they will be found out to be less than what God requires…weighed in the balance and found lacking. Such real and imagined thoughts can cause great trepidation to the sincere believer. Such fear can also create a paralyzing of the believer in terms of their spiritual walk. It can overwhelm and intimidate the believer and rob him of all spiritual joy.

To minimize and even illuminate all worry and fear regarding our salvation, the Apostle Paul takes decisive action. In Romans chapter eight Paul spends considerable amounts of time underscoring the absolute perfection of our salvation. Paul declares that there is no need at all for the true believer to feel fear and trepidation concerning the security of their salvation. The basic and fundamental reason that he gives the reader to eliminate all trepidation is simply, "If/since God is for us, who can be against us?" (Romans 8: 31b)

To fully appreciate the impact of this statement/question we need to understand the context in which these words were written. Right now, however, I would like to begin to unpack the passage step-by-step. First, notice:

The Reality of God's Being *For Us* Affirmed – "Since"

The Reality Affirmed– The word "if" in the Greek text of this verse is not a word that denotes a question but rather it affirms a declaration. It means, "If this is true *and it most certainly is*. It is a construction in the Greek that expects a positive affirmation. For English readers, it could better be translated, "since." In other words, the Apostle Paul is saying that based on the aforementioned participation of God on our behalf in our salvation it is clear, therefore, that God is with us and for us. So, Paul begins with this assumption, "Since God is for us…

Before we proceed any further, one might first ask the question, why did Paul write Romans chapter eight? What is the context of this chapter? Would it not be helpful for us to understand what the Apostle Paul's purpose was in penning this passage if we are to understand the specific teaching of the passage?

Paul's Purpose in Writing Romans Chapter Eight

The answer to the question is quite simple. In a very real way, in Romans chapter eight Paul is going back to pick up the theme that he was pursuing in Romans chapter 5:1–11. It was there that he began to emphasize the absolute security of the true believer in Christ because of the grace of God. In the following chapters after Romans 5 (chapters 6–7) the apostle took up and answered some possible objections which might naturally arise from his teaching. This caused him to become temporarily distracted from pursuing his main theme of the believer's absolute security and assurance in Christ because of the grace of God.

Then in Romans 7, Paul had raised the question, "Is the law sin?" (Romans 7:7) He raised this question because he had pointed out previously that not only could the law not save the sinner but it was used by God to stir up sin in the sinner and to expose his sin (v8). So now, he asks the question, "If that is what the law does "is then the law sin?" Paul's statement regarding the fact that the law is a source of stirring up or inciting sin in that it foments what it forbids, requires Paul to entertain this possible objection. After all, the law serves to so stir up the "sinful" nature to disobey God so that the more a man sets himself to keep the law the more he finds himself rebelling against it and transgressing it – thus increasing his sin. Sin is like a bear that has been hibernating and sleeping all winter and then it is suddenly prodded awake by someone poking it with a stick. In this case, the stick is the law of God. Paul even used his own personal experience to demonstrate to his readers the experiential reality of what he was teaching regarding the law of God and sinful behavior. He wrote, "Apart from the law, sin lies dead. I was once alive (or appeared to be so) apart from the law, but when the commandment came, sin came alive and I died. (Paul is speaking of his gaining of a conscious reality of his sinfulness). Paul also wrote that he could "will" what is right but did not seem to be able to perform what is right. Why? Because of Paul's indwelling sin. His efforts at obedience to the law of God were being hampered and sabotaged by his sinfulness. Paul wrote that he became so animated about this titanic and fierce personal struggle with sin that he cried out, "Wretched man that I am! Who will deliver me from this body of death" (Romans 7:24)? The question was, no doubt, very real in terms of the apostle's experience but he is also using it in a dramatic and somewhat rhetorical way in this chapter to underscore the reality of his struggle with sin outside of Christ (Paul knew that total deliverance from sin would come through Christ but that it would be in the future and not in the present, total deliverance from sin will come through "the redemption of our body") (8:23).

Outside of Christ before his conversion, Paul was left to fight the bitter struggle of trying to overcome sin and live in obedience to God's law—by futilely relying on his own strength and determination.

Having made his point about the fact that the law cannot save us, and the way the law of God reveals our sin and even stirs it up causing us to feel guilt and a sense of failure, Paul now wants to move on to a more positive perspective so that his readers will not be gripped by gloom and pessimism. That is where we are in Romans chapter eight. Now you understand the context of the passage.

In that light, Paul now returns to the theme of Christian assurance and security and he does so in a strong and forceful way. He begins Romans chapter eight with a confident declaration that there is "no condemnation" for the true believer in Jesus Christ (all condemnation is permanently removed) and Paul concludes the chapter with a confident declaration that there is "no separation". Christians still must wrestle with their imperfection of sin which the law sniffs out, stirs up and condemns but they now have the enormous help of the Holy Spirit grounded on the perfect work of Christ and the will of the Father to ensure that the true believer will be absolutely secure in his or her salvation—all the way to glory. We have all this because GOD IS FOR US!

As someone has observed, Romans chapter eight falls into two parts of unequal length. The first 30 verses set *forth the total sufficiency of the grace of God* to deal with a whole series of predicaments and possibilities for the believer—"the guilt and power of sin (verses 1 – 5); the fact of one's mental state and how it relates to life and death (verses 6 – 13); the distinguishing evidence of being a child of God-being led by the Holy Spirit (verse 14); the believer's struggle with assurance and the Holy Spirit's ministry (verse

15-16); the believers need for a glorious hope in Christ (verse 17); weakness and frustrating struggles in the face of sin's continued presence (verses 18–25); the struggles of the believer in prayer (verse 26); the concern to know how salvation is designed and implemented (verses 28–30).

Paul addresses these areas by dwelling on the fact that God completely forgives us and grants us a perfect righteousness from Jesus Christ. This is the "good news" message of the gospel of grace–there is "no condemnation" (verse 1). The second real benefit to the believer is that the Holy Spirit is given to help us and enable us to live for God even in a world of sin (versus 4–17). The third is sonship–adoption into the divine family in which the Lord Jesus is the firstborn (verses 14–17, 29). The fourth is that we are secured, now and forever (verses 28–30). This composite endowment is more than enough to support a Christian in whatever his trouble may be.

Then in verses 31–39, the Apostle Paul calls on his readers to react to what he has said. "What then shall *we say* to these things?" (Verse 31). In this latter part of Romans chapter eight the apostle shifts his focus from the sufficiency of the grace of God to *the sufficiency of the God of grace*. In this section the focus moves from the gift to the giver. It highlights the fact that God is all that we need as believers. It is as if God is saying to us what he said he would be to Abraham. "Your shield and your exceeding great reward" (Genesis 15:1).

In this section of Romans chapter eight, the full spotlight is put on God – the God of our salvation. This has been true throughout the chapter but becomes more prominent in this last portion of Romans chapter eight. The believer's response to God, in light of all that God has done, is doing, and will do for him in salvation combined with the amazing and perfect character of God's person is intended to overwhelm the reader with the clear evidence that God is for us.

It is the true believer's reaction to God that Paul highlights in this section of Romans chapter eight that we are now dealing with. The Apostle Paul asks a series of powerful rhetorical questions which are geared to elicit the believer's response to the truths being taught. Paul is reminding and reaffirming to the believer that, in fact, God is with us and for us. That is an undisputed reality!

This truth is only powerful and encouraging, however, for those who realize who God really is. If God is of an anemic nature, a God who is tottering in old age and weakness, a God who is filled with good intentions but is powerless to bring them about, a God whose love is fickle and a God who is prone to abandon His people in times of trouble, a God who is not all wise, etc., Such a God cannot be of great comfort to the believer but if God is a God who is the God described in the Bible then that God can, indeed, bring us great comfort. Simply by knowing that the biblical God is with us and for us adds a powerful dimension to our confidence and comfort as Christians. It is vital to realize and understand something of "who" the true God – the God of the Bible is, in order to derive strong encouragement and increased strength from the truth that He is with us and for us. So, the apostle begins this verse underscoring that God is for us. *The reality of that fact is affirmed.*

The Rudimentary Characteristics of His Readers Examined

Remember, that the Apostle Paul is writing this letter to people like us. The Apostle Paul wrote, "(If) Since God is for *us*" and, "What then shall *we* say to these things?" The "us" and "we" are important. Here Paul is not referring to all people in a general sense but rather to those who have trusted in Jesus Christ for their salvation. In effect, he means to say to fellow Christians, "As a Christian, I know what I will say to these things; will you say it, too?"

In asking his readers to speak, he asks ("*what shall we* say *to these things?),* Paul first calls on them to think and then to respond. He wants them to think like Christians and to apply what he has just taught them. He wants them to apply what they now know (based on the teaching of Romans chapter eight) of God's involvement in their salvation (to their present state and to their ultimate salvation).

Remember, that the apostle does not actually know his readers personally (because he had not yet traveled to Rome) and for that matter, neither could he know us who read his writings in the 21st century. What Paul does know is that there are two critical factors common to all Christians everywhere in every age and that these two factors characterize those Christians to whom he is writing.

First, he knows that they (all Christians), because of Divine regeneration, have a commitment to righteousness and are yielded to God as "slaves of righteousness" (Romans 6:13, 18; 8:31 – 39). In other words, they are sincerely seeking to do the will of God wholeheartedly. That is one clear mark of genuine Christianity. If one does not have a personal commitment to righteousness that person has yet to come to know the Lord Jesus Christ in a saving way. God saves us from sin to righteousness. Paul wrote of the sacrifice of our Lord Jesus Christ to the Galatians: "Who gave Himself for our sins_*to deliver us from the present evil age, according to the will of our God and Father, to Him be the glory forever and ever. Amen*" (Galatians 1: 4).

It is this present evil age that Jesus died to deliver us from as well as from eternal perdition. As the Apostle John wrote:

"No one who abides in Him keeps on sinning; no one who keeps on sinning has either seen Him or known Him. Little children, let no one deceive you. Whoever practices righteousness is righteous, as He is righteous. Whoever makes a practice of sinning is of the devil, for the devil has been sinning from the beginning. The reason the son of God appeared was to destroy the works of the devil. No one born of God makes a practice of sinning, for God's seed abides in him, he cannot keep on sinning because he has been born of God. By this it is evident who are the children of God, and who are the children of the devil: whoever does not practice righteousness is not of God" (1 John 3:6 – 9).

So, Paul knows that those Christians to whom he wrote had a real and ongoing commitment to genuine righteousness. This is the earmark of all true Christianity.

Second, all true Christians are also constantly exposed to a plethora of perpetual pressures and hardships in this world. For example, Romans 8:31–39, treats material hardship and human hostility as the common experiences of Christians. This is all encompassed in Paul's reference to the "we". He is writing to Christian people who may be troubled by a personal moral lapse, people who may have lost a job or a friend because of their faith, Christians who are struggling with loneliness or financial problems, Christians who are taking care of an aging, senile parent, or are wrestling with the heartbreak of a rebellious child, etc. He was writing to real people who were being opposed because of their faith and often persecuted and being made to suffer simply because they were believers in Christ and pursuing righteousness. He is writing to people like us and he is imploring them and us to think deeply as we answer the question "What shall *we* say to these things?" *We* are going to have to face many of "those things" – those hardships of life, but the Apostle is calling upon us to think now about "these things" set out in verses 1–30 before we find ourselves consumed by and enmeshed in the difficulties of life that are the common lot of Christians.

Think Now So That You Can Properly Respond Later

Paul doesn't want us to wait until we are already neck deep in life's problems and then just instinctively react blindly so that we are merely thinking under pressure and emotionally. Rather, Paul wants us to spend time right now, before hand, understanding and applying the things that he has previously taught us to be thoroughly prepared to think clearly when "those things" (the difficulties of life), come our way. As one writer put it, he is calling upon us to think against our feelings and to reason ourselves out of the grip of gloom, fear, disillusionment and despair that "those things" tend to bring with them. He wants us to take ourselves in hand and to think about what we already know of God through the gospel and then apply this understanding to our current situations. Paul wants us to tear our eyes away from a fixation on our problems, and focus them instead on the person of God, and his provisions, for us as believers. He wants us to talk to ourselves and think like Christians instead of being driven mindlessly by our emotions.

A wonderful study of this same process can be achieved by a careful examination of the Psalms of David. David is often beset by enemies and other problems that would normally be bewildering and disillusioning, however, David exhibits a clear understanding of his difficulties while at the same time taking himself in hand and forcibly turning himself to the solid truths of Scripture and to the unimpeachable character of God. By this means, David deals with his difficulties successfully and reasons himself, by faith, out of his gloom and doom. That is exactly what Paul is after for his readers in Romans chapter eight.

Paul begins his therapy for Christians by asking the rhetorical question, "What then shall we say to these things?" Paul will follow-up with several other pertinent thoughts that are framed as questions as well and are calculated to cause people to think. Paul is going to present these thoughts in the form of questions because that is best suited to stir the thinking process in people. In fact, Paul will combine questions one after the other in a staccato, rapid-fire fashion so that in considering the answers to these questions he can employ them to overwhelm his readers with the rich reality of how strong their security is in Christ and to bolster their faith and encouragement. Since God is for us we have every reason to have a certain and confident hope.

The first question that Paul asks is this, "If God is for us, who can be against us?" Again, the thought here is NOT that there will be no one against us but that no opposition can finally crush us, destroy us, win against us, or do us irreparable damage. Why? Because, Paul says, God is our sovereign, loving, omnipotent protector and He is determined to honor and uphold His covenant commitment to us to ensure our salvation.

For this question to mean anything to us we must ask and answer the question, "Who is God?" Why should the fact that "God is for us" give us comfort and encouragement?

Later, in a crescendo of questions and answers the Apostle Paul leads us to gaze at the grand finale of chapter eight of Romans. But He first begins with the question: "What, then, shall we say in response to this?" (Romans 8:31a). The "this" to which he is referring is the plurality of details and doctrinal, practical, spiritual truths that he has already shared with the reader regarding the security of the believer. These truths are found in Romans chapter eight. Or, it is possible that the apostle may, in fact, be referring to the content of the entire letter of Romans up to this point. At any rate, he wants his readers to digest and directly apply the truths previously revealed to them regarding their salvation.

Many fearful believers have doubts about their security and false teachers stand ready to exploit those doubts. To give such believers the assurance that they need, the apostle concludes this chapter by answering the very important question: Can any person or can any circumstance cause a believer to lose his salvation? Since God is for us, we need to think through the implications of that fact and apply this truth to our situations in life.

Let's consider, for a moment who this God is that Paul is referring to. We have noted (1) the reality of the fact that God is with us – affirmed, and (2) the rudimentary characteristics of those encompassed by the reference to "we" and "us". Now, we will focus on who this God is that Paul says is for us. I am calling this, "The right portrayal of God."

The Right Portrayal of God

Knowing the true God is incredibly important. Many people who claim to believe in God believe in a self-made idol that they have constructed in their minds and dubbed with the name "God." We sometimes think of idolatry in terms of wild natives dancing around a totem pole or cultic priests pursuing religious rituals in the name of a supposed "god." The truth is, however, there are far more subtle forms of idolatry that are practiced faithfully by many modern people.

Sometimes the god that is constructed by such people retains some of the elements of the God of the Bible while eliminating others. Sometimes it is a self-made or imagined god who has certain of the true God's attributes, yet they are distorted and exaggerated out of their proper proportion relative to His other attributes. All such twisted perspectives, regardless of how sincere and well-intentioned, are but forms of idolatry and are categorically condemned by the God of Scripture.

The priority established at the beginning of the Ten Commandments: When examining the Ten Commandments, we find that the second commandment states, "You shall not make unto you any graven image, or any likeness of anything that is in heaven above, or that is in the air beneath, or that is in the water under the earth: you shall not bow down yourself to them, nor serve them: because I the Lord your God am a jealous God…" (Exodus 20:4).

This second commandment is not a mere repetition of the first commandment for that would be redundant and make it totally unnecessary. Rather, in this second commandment God is pointing us to the principle as Charles Hodge writes, "idolatry consists not only in the worship of false gods, but also in the worship of the true God by images." God is concerned that we have no errant concepts of what He is like. Any statue, picture, or visual representation of God can only partly and imperfectly capture a portion of one dimension of His unfathomable character. Thus, God forbids any such attempts at representing Him because all attempts to do so would be flawed and be a misrepresentation of Hm. Such flawed representations of God lead the practitioners (worshipers) subconsciously into a worship of a caricature of God rather than the true God.

The Self-Revelation of God

That is precisely why God demands that we derive our entire image of Him from His self–revelation in the Word of God and He prohibits us from any human effort, no matter how well-intentioned, to portray Him otherwise. God wants us to understand that He is transcendent, mysterious, and inscrutable, beyond the scope or range of any human imagination or philosophical speculation.

We are to humble ourselves and learn of Him only from the written Word of God alone. We must rid ourselves of all the beggarly and limiting views of God that we may have accumulated in one way or another from our life journey. Then we must install in our minds and hearts the proper view of God as revealed in the Bible.

For example, we have a striking picture of God given to us in Isaiah chapter 40. Read this chapter and consider the things that He (the true God) has done. In Isaiah chapter 40, the prophet speaks on the subject in verse 12. The prophet speaks to people whose mood is the mood of many Christians today–despondent, despairing, distracted, dumped on by the world, disillusioned, fearful of the future. What does he say to these people to encourage, strengthen and embolden them in their faith?

Isaiah, speaking on behalf of God and by infallible inspiration reveals how God tells them to look at *His_works*, and to ask themselves, "Could you do that?" "Could any man do them?" For example, God describes Himself as the one, "Who has measured the waters in the hollow of His hand and measured out the heavens with the span, and comprehended the dust of the earth in a measure, and weighed out the mountains in scales, and the hills in a balance" (verse 12). God is posing the question, "Are you wise enough, and powerful enough, to do things like that? But I am; or I could not have made this world at all." – "Behold your God!"

These verses are describing God relative to His creation. It is clear from Genesis chapter 1 that God created all things in the space of six days. Theologians refer to this creative act as *Ex Nihilo* (Latin for "out of nothing") and as a "fiat" creation (a creation accomplished by merely speaking it into existence). God said, "Let there be…" and the vast creation sprang into existence.

Consider for a moment the magnitude and intricate details of this divine creation that we call the universe. For example, we all learned in school that light travels at the speed of 186,000 mi./s. That equates to 6 trillion miles per year. Let's imagine that a light beam is sent out by you during your lunch break. It is sent out at 12:00 noon and by 12:08 PM the light beam is passing the earth and heading out toward the edge of the solar system. After you eat your lunch and order dessert your waitress brings you dessert and coffee at 12:45 PM. By now the light beam is passing Jupiter. By midafternoon the light beam is passing Pluto traveling at 186,000 mi./s. Let's fast-forward five days. It is now the weekend and that little light beam is leaving our solar system. In just a few months this beam of light will have finally reached the nearest star to our sun, Proxima Centauri (which is a conflux of several stars). Fast-forward again seven years and our little light beam has only passed 20 stars. By now our sun appears as a rather bland, yellowish, blurry star which is disappearing into the Galactic darkness. Let us suppose that this little beam of light has been heading out into the constellation Sagittarius. On this path, it will be headed for the center of the Milky Way galaxy. Our little light beam must travel 32,000 years at 6 trillion miles per year before it reaches the center of our galaxy. When it reaches the center of our galaxy is still needs to travel another 50,000 years at 186,000 mi./s just to get to the other side of the Milky Way. When it finally arrives at the other side of the Milky Way it will have passed 100 billion stars. Remember, the Milky Way galaxy is only an average sized galaxy and there are at least 50 billion galaxies in the known universe (according to information derived by the use of the Hubble telescopic cameras).

Now, our little light beam needs to travel another 80,000 years at 6 trillion miles per year to reach the nearest galaxy to our Milky Way. It must also travel through 1.8 million years of empty space before it reaches the end of the Andromeda galaxy. From there it must travel another 20 billion years before it reaches the edge of the known universe. By then it will have passed through 50 billion galaxies containing 100 billion stars in those 50 billion galaxies. Our light beam, at this point, has only seen the work of

God's fingers (Psalm 8:3; Job 26:14), "Behold these are the fringes of His ways and how faint a word we hear of Him."

If we turn our eyes away from the Galactic world to our own surroundings, we could focus on the tiny atom. The atom is mostly empty space. It is invisible without the use of powerful electronic equipment. Atoms are so small it takes three atoms to make up one water molecule. If you were to take every water molecule in one single drop of water and enlarge them so that each molecule was the size of a grain of sand, you would have enough grains of sand to make a road 1 foot thick and ½ mile wide that would extend from Los Angeles to New York City. Remember, these are the molecules in a single drop of water and for every molecule there are three atoms.

Does this not give you an added appreciation for the magnitude and power of our Almighty God? Stand and wonder in awe-Behold your God!

Think of these kinds of things when you consider the import of the phrase "Since God is for us..."

Then Isaiah says to look now at the *nations*, (as the prophet continues): the great national powers, which seem invincible and which you stand in awe of and are afraid of because of their powerful armies, evil intent, and vast resources. But consider how God relates to these "so-called" mighty empires and national forces which you are so intimidated by. "Behold, the nations are as a drop of the bucket, and are counted as the small dust of the balance... All nations before Him are as nothing; and they are counted to Him less than nothing, and vanity (empty)" (verse 15). Have you ever dropped a single drop of water in a galvanized bucket? It is hardly noticeable and who concerns themselves with the incidental light dust on a merchant's scales? Compare these insignificant things to God almighty. Do you realize how much more powerful and mighty the true God is than even the combined forces of all the nations of the earth? They are nothing before him – "Behold your God!" It is this God that Paul wants us to think about when he writes, "Since God is for us..."

What about *the world and the physical universe?* We have touched on this but we are sometimes awed by the sheer size of it, the intricate complexity of it, the vast population of it, the various and diverse cultures and variety of it, etc. We can sometimes seem like insignificant ants by comparison with the whole planet on which we live!

Consider this: The earth is 25,000 miles in circumference and weighs 6,586 sextillion tons and yet it hangs in empty space spinning at 1,000 mph while maintaining perfect balance. At the same time, it is spinning at 1000 mph it is also moving through space around the sun at 1,000 mi./m in an orbit of 580 million miles. It does all of this while perched at a perfect angle set to create the seasons and to sustain human life.

Yet, look at a comparison of this "so-called" mighty planet with God. "It is He who sits upon (above) the circle of the earth and the inhabitants of it or as grasshoppers; He stretches out the heavens as a curtain, and spreads them like a tent to dwell in"(verse 22). We may seem like gnats or tiny dwarf–like creature's as we compare ourselves to the world but, then again, the world dwindles into insignificance when compared to Almighty God. The world is referred to as His mere "footstool". Behold, your God!

Consider also *the great men of the world* with their governments, fortunes, laws, and policies that manage the lives of millions and millions of people. Some of these people are so powerful that they could easily plunge the entire globe into catastrophic warfare or financial confusion. How does God compare to the world's great men? The prophet answers, "He brings the princes to nothing; He makes the judges (the rulers) of the earth as nothing (emptiness/vanity) (verse 23) – "Behold your God!"

Now, consider *the celestial heavens*. Again, I have made some pertinent remarks already about the size of the universe. Nothing is geared to create awe in man like the universal experience of standing alone on a clear night under the boundless canopy of billions of stars. I have already described a slice of these celestial heavens. Do you want to feel little, powerless, remote and insignificant? Then stand and gaze into the star filled sky for a while and contemplate the billions of galaxies and the billions of light years that it would take to travel across this vast space even if we could somehow move at the speed of light. Our minds cannot even comprehend or begin to grasp the enormity of space and the universe – but what is this to God? "Lift up your eyes on high, and behold who has created these things, that one who brings out their host (the stars) by number: He calls them all by name by the greatness of His might, for that He is strong in power; not one fails (v 26). Behold, your God!"

God created every star and placed it where He chose for it to be. He is their maker and master and controls the universe with an unimaginable power. As we used to sing, "He has the whole world in His hands" – "Behold your God!" This gives added insight into the phrase "Since God is for us..."

As Isaiah the prophet applies these biblical doctrines of the majesty of God in chapter 40 he asks three pointed questions.

"To whom then will you compare Me, that I should be like him? Says the Holy One" (verse 25). He's really saying that we suffer from not having large enough thoughts of God. We need to learn to think of Him in the unlimited fashion that the Bible describes Him. God is not like we are, only bigger. He is incomparable and unimaginable in His majesty and might.

Isaiah continues, "Why are you saying, O Jacob, and speaking, O Israel, my way is hid from the Lord and my judgment is passed away from my God?" (verse 27). This verse rebukes and reminds us of the truth that God has not abandoned us nor does He ever abandon any one on whom He has set His love. God does not lose interest in us nor does He leave us high and dry. Such thoughts of God are not only wrong but they are dishonoring to our great God and Savior.

Then, Isaiah adds "Have you not known? Have you not heard, that the everlasting God, the LORD, the Creator of the ends of the earth, does not faint, neither is he weary?" (verse 28). It is as if God is rebuking us for even entertaining the thought that he has grown old and tired. In fact, God is saying, "Has nobody ever told you the truth about me? Don't ever think of me in that fashion again.

A Picture of God Through the Eyes of the Psalmist

While we're considering the subject of who God is, let us reflect on the thoughts of the psalmist in Psalm 139. Here the psalmist meditates on the infinite and unlimited nature of God's presence, knowledge, and power in relation to men. The psalmist tells us that man is always in God's presence. You can become a hermit, cut off from other human beings but you cannot get away from your Creator. "You hem me in, behind and before, and lay your hand upon me. Such knowledge is too wonderful for me; it is high; I cannot attain it. Where shall I go from your Spirit? Or where shall I flee from your presence? If I ascend to heaven, you are there! If I make my bed in Sheol, you are there! If I take the wings of the morning and dwell in the uttermost parts of the sea, even there your hand shall lead me, and your right hand shall hold me." The psalmist is saying, If I go up to heaven (the sky), or down into hell (i.e., the underworld), or away to the world's end, I still could not escape from the presence of God – "behold, you are there" (verse 5). Even the darkness which may normally hide a person from human sight cannot begin to shield one from God's gaze (verse 11).

Not only are there no bounds to God's presence with men, there are no limitations to His knowledge of men – to make it personal, there are no limitations to God's knowledge of you and me. I never ever go unnoticed or unknown by God. The psalmist says God has searched me and known me. He further states that, "You know when I sit down and when I rise up; You discern my thoughts from afar (our imaginations, our plans, suspicions, desires, fears, etc.) You search out my path (my actions, habits, wanderings, etc.) and my lying down and are acquainted with all my ways. Even before a word is on my tongue, Behold, O Lord, you know it all together." (Parentheses mine)

In other words, I cannot escape God or hide anything at all from God. I cannot deceive God with my words because He knows my mind and sees through me. God knows me as I really am. He knows me better than I know myself. Living in light of this kind of God becomes an awesome business. The Latin phrase Coram Deo conveys the idea of living before the face of God continually. For the Christian it is extremely comforting to know that God who loves us knows everything about us and is always with us—yes, and He continues to love us and will always love us and He is for us. In fact, "nothing will ever separate us from the love of God in Christ Jesus." He knows every imaginable obstacle in our way and has provided for our success. He knows and has fashioned even my body when I was still in my mother's womb to be what He wants it to be. What a God we serve! "Behold your God!"

And, by the way, I would urge the reader to consider the fact that we have only begun to scratch the surface of who God is. Scripture speaks of the God of the Bible and the gospel saying, the Lord Jehovah, "A God merciful and gracious, slow to anger and abounding in steadfast love and faithfulness" (Exodus 34:6). Concerning God, "the only begotten Son, who is in the bosom of the Father, has declared" (John 1:18). The sovereign God says, "I am God, and there is no other; I am God and there is no one like of me, declaring the end from the beginning, and from ancient times things not yet done, saying "my counsel will stand, and I will accomplish all my purpose" (Isaiah 46:9). This is the God who "committed His love toward us, in that, while we were yet sinners, Christ died for us" (Romans 5:8). This is the God who calls, justifies and glorifies those that He has set His love upon from all eternity. Those that He "predestined to be conformed to the image of His Son" (Romans 8: 29) will, in fact, attain that ultimate objective. This is the one living and true God, everlasting, infinite in power, wisdom and goodness; He is the maker and preserver of all things both visible and invisible. BEHOLD YOUR GOD! This is the God that is for us!

We have been spending time establishing a right portrayal of the God that Paul is referring to and reiterating that this one true and living God is for us. Now, that we have begun to look at God with a more clear, biblical eye, we are somewhat better prepared to ask and answer the question that the Apostle Paul poses, "If God"– this God – "is for us"– what does that mean to us? We have already noted the reality of this fact affirmed in this text ("since"). We've also noted the right portrayal of who God is (the biblical God). Now it is time to move our focus to the relationship focused on that we as Christians have with this God.

The Relationship on Which We Are Focused

The Apostle Paul begins by asking, "What shall WE say to these things?" "Since God is for US who can be against us?"

The identity of the *US* and the *WE*, is incredibly important to understand. *WE* are those who have trusted in Jesus Christ alone by faith alone for our salvation. *WE* are God's elect (His chosen ones) as Paul will refer to the Christian in the next verse. *WE* are those who have been predestinated to be conformed to the image of God's Son. *WE* are those who have been called, justified and who are protected by God's ongoing providence so that He is working all things out for our good as we journey toward our ultimate glorification. *WE* are those who have been adopted by God as His sons and daughters. *WE* are those who have been indwelled by the Holy Spirit. Paul is asking his readers to think deeply about their secure position with God in Christ considering what they have learned.

Consequently, he is saying, "What shall *WE* say to these things," "If God is for US who can be against *US*?

A Covenant Committment

The phrase, *"is for us,"* is declaring God's covenant commitment to His people. The goal of saving grace is to create a love–relationship between God and we who believe, the kind of relationship with God that man was first made for in the Garden of Eden. This is the bond (unbreakable bond) of fellowship by which God binds Himself to us in His covenant. To accomplish this goal God needed to save us from sin and to secure us on a path of sanctification leading to glory. This covenant is not dependent on us to achieve its ends, rather it is a unilateral promise made by God like the covenant made with Abraham in Genesis 17: "I am the Almighty God... I will establish my covenant between me and you and your seed... To be a God to you, and to your seed after you... I will be their God... He shall keep my covenant therefore..." (verses 1, 7).

In Galatians, the Apostle Paul tells us, that as believers, we are considered to be the seed of Abraham–a part of the covenant company. If the covenant and its fulfillment is dependent upon us then certainty and security would not be possible since we are still plagued by sin and subject to weakness. Paul's point is that our security and the certainty of our salvation rests entirely in the hands of the Almighty God. That's why it is so encouraging to the believer to read and understand, "Since God is for us..."

God is not merely for us like we are for our home team cheering from the bleachers and hoping that all will turn out successfully, but unable to influence the actual game itself. God is for us in a very active, deliberate, all-powerful, loving involvement in our salvation. To use a sports colloquialism, it is God who goes to bat for us.

In Psalm 56 we read the words of the psalmist, "God *is for me*" (verse 9). In this Psalm, the psalmist is perpetually surrounded by and being attacked by his enemies. In a very real way his back is against the wall. Rather than giving up in despair, however, he turns toward God and reminds himself that God is for him. He recounts in the Psalm how carefully and thoughtfully God has taken note of his every stress and sorrow (verse 8). He reminds himself of the promises of God on his behalf.

Finally, he says, "When I am afraid I put my trust in you... In God I trust without a fear. What can flesh (man) do to me?" (verse 4).

Surely, his enemies could do him damage from the outside but in the deepest sense they could not touch him, because his real life was in the inward life of fellowship with the loving God, a covenant keeping God who will preserve his (the psalmist's) ultimate life regardless of what happens.

In What Ways is God for Us?

Now, the question that we need to ask ourselves is, "In what ways is God for us?" There are a number of ways that we can look at this question and answer it. God is for us:

In a purely sovereign way – That is to say, God chose us to be his own special possession in a totally unconditional manner. In John 15:16 the Lord Jesus Christ said to his apostles, "You did not choose me, but I chose you and appointed you..."

Now, it is certainly true that these 11 men chose to follow Jesus Christ. The point that Jesus is underscoring, however, is that the reason they chose to follow Him is because He had already chosen them. Ultimately and originally it was the purely sovereign choice of them by the Lord Jesus that caused them to become His followers. Jesus was "for them" in a purely sovereign way.

An old hymn contains the lines: "I sought the Lord and afterwards, I knew, He moved my soul to seek Him seeking me."

This same reality is true of Christians in salvation. We are chosen by God for salvation in its present and ultimate state purely out of God's sovereign will without any regard for either our character or conduct in terms of recommending us to Him for that choice. It is an unconditional election.

Sovereignly Chosen

On one occasion during the ministry of the Apostle Paul as he carried on his mission work, the Jewish leaders in a certain location rejected the gospel that he preached. Paul responded by turning the focus of his gospel preaching toward the Gentiles. The Gentiles responded enthusiastically and in faith to Paul's gospel. In Acts 13:48 we read, "And when the Gentiles heard this, they began rejoicing and glorifying the Word of the Lord, and as many as were appointed to eternal life believed." These people chose to believe the gospel because they had been chosen/ordained (appointed to eternal life) by God. Nor is this concept a rare thing to read in Scripture. Consider the Apostle Paul's words to the church at Thessalonica, "But we ought always to give thanks to God for you, brothers beloved by the Lord, because God chose you as the first fruits to be saved, through sanctification by the spirit and belief in the truth." (II Thessalonians 2:13).

This is why, when Jesus encountered the bitter, critical, murmuring of some to whom He had preached, we read that He said, "Do not grumble among yourselves. No one can come to me unless the Father who sent me draws him. And I will raise him up on the last day" (John 6:43b–44). Coming to Jesus Christ for salvation requires the purely sovereign and powerful drawing of the sinner by God the Father.

In Ephesians chapter 1, the Apostle Paul wanted to highlight the absolute enormity of the spiritual riches and the eternal security of the true believer. There he noted that everything that we have, as believers, is "in Christ." In this first chapter of his letter to the Ephesians, Paul provided them with a comprehensive and panoramic view of their blessings in Christ. He went back as far as his mind could go (before the foundation of the world) and as far forward as his mind could go (the fullness of time). Paul boldly declared that God "has blessed us "in Christ" with every spiritual blessing in the heavenly places even as He chose us in Him before the foundation of the world, that we should be holy and blameless before Him. In love He predestined us for adoption as sons through Jesus Christ, according to the purpose of His will, to the praise of His glorious grace, with which He has blessed us in the beloved." Once again, the Apostle Paul is pointing out that "God is for us" in a purely sovereign way.

The Christian's Comfort

As Christians, we ought to rejoice in this fact because nothing we do and nothing that is done to us can keep God from ultimately saving us. Why? Because He has sovereignly placed His love upon us and determined that we should be His forever. God is for us sovereignly! In addition, God is for us:

In a Personal Way – God told the prophet Jeremiah, "Before I formed you in the womb I knew you, and before you were born I consecrated you..." (Jeremiah 1: 5a). In John 10, Jesus describes Himself as the "good shepherd," and He says, "I am the good shepherd. I Know my own and my own know me, just as the Father knows me and I know the Father; and I lay down my life for the sheep. And I have other sheep that are not of this fold. I must bring them also, and they will listen to my voice. So, there will be one flock, one shepherd" (Verses 14–16)

God knows us and is for us in a personal way. We belong to Him and He is our "Father" and we are His "children." Just as a father on earth is for his children in a personal way so is God the Father for US in a personal way. To give insight into how the Apostle Paul viewed a father's relationship to his children as personal and intimate we read his words to the Thessalonian church:

"For you remember, brothers, our labor and toil; we worked night and day, that we might not be a burden to any of you, while we proclaimed to you the gospel of God. You are witnesses, and God also, how holy and righteous and blameless was our conduct toward you believers. For you know how, like a father with his children, we exhorted each one of you and encouraged you to charge you to walk in a manner worthy of God, who called you into His own kingdom in glory" (1 Thessalonians 2:9 – 12). Our Father God is for us in a personal way.

God is also for us:

In a Passionate Way – God loves us so much that He intervened for us to the extent that He gave His only begotten Son to be the sacrifice and substitute for our sins. We are the, "Apple of His eye." That one who touches us to do us harm is striking out at God and God who is for us takes these slights and attacks personally. He will react toward them in a passionate way. The Apostle Paul wrote to the Thessalonians who were being persecuted for their faith and reminded them of what it will be like when Jesus Christ returns. He wrote to those who were suffering: "Since indeed God considers it just to repay with affliction those who afflict you, and to grant relief to you who are afflicted as well as to us, when the Lord Jesus is revealed from heaven with His mighty angels in flaming fire, inflicting punishment on those who do not know God, those who do not obey the gospel of our Lord Jesus Christ. They will suffer the punishment of eternal destruction, away from the presence of the Lord and from the glory of his might, when he comes on that day to be glorified in his saints, and to be marveled at among all who have believed, because our testimony to you was believed" (2 Thessalonians 1:6–10). God is for us passionately.

God is also for us:

In a Permanent Way – The Lord Jesus Christ, by the will of God the Father, died and was resurrected to give us everlasting/eternal life. Further, the Apostle Paul will tell us at the end of Romans chapter eight that nothing "can separate us from the love of God which is in Christ Jesus." God is for US in a permanent way. God is also for us:

In a Practical Way – God understands and lovingly provides everything that we need or will need so that our every need will be fully met in a practical way. Do we need fellowship with others? God will provide it. Do we need comfort, admonition and correction, guidance, instruction, a sense of a purpose for our lives which is greater than ourselves, an assurance of being loved deeply, healing, protection, etc.? God is for us in every practical way. God understands far better than we do what we need and He provides it in a practical way. Our God is for us!

God is for us in a Patient and Tenderly Merciful Way – we read in Matthew 12:20 that our Lord Jesus Christ said, "A bruised reed shall he not break, and smoking flax shall he not quench."

C. H. Spurgeon commenting on this passage wrote,

> "What is weaker than the bruised reed or the smoking flax? *A reed* that grows in the fen or marsh, bent and bruised because the wild duck lights upon it, and it snaps; (or the foot of some man brushes against it, and it is bruised and broken; every wind that flits across the river moves it to and fro. You can conceive of nothing more real or personal, or whose existence is more in jeopardy, than a

bruised reed. Then look at the smoking flax—what is it? It has a spark within it, it is true, but it is almost smothered; an infant's breath might blow it out; nothing has a more precarious existence than its flame. *Weak things* are here described, yet Jesus says of them, "the smoking flax I will not quench; the bruised reed I will not break." Some of God's children are made strong to do mighty works for Him; God has His Samsons here and there who can pull up Gaza's gates, and carry them to the top of the hill; He has a few mightys who are lion—like men, but the majority of His people are a timid, trembling race. They are like starlings, frightened at every passerby; a little fearful flock. If temptation comes, they are taken like birds in a snare; if trial threatens, they are ready to faint; their frail skiff is tossed up and down by every wave, they are drifted along like a sea bird on the crest of the billows—weak things, without strength, without wisdom, without foresight. Yet, weak as they are, *and* because they are so weak, they have this promise made especially to them. Herein is grace and graciousness! Herein is love and loving kindness! How it opens to us the compassion of Jesus—so gentle, tender, considerate! We need never shrink back from *His* touch. We need never fear a harsh word from *Him*; though He might well chide us for our weakness, it is not rebuke. Bruised reeds shall have no blows from Him, and the smoking flax no damping frowns." (C. H. Spurgeon, *Morning and Evening,* McDonald Publishing Company, McLean Virginia 22102, page 403.)

Dear ones, God is for us in a patient and tenderly loving way even despite or because of our weaknesses and frailties.

I could easily go on to describe how God is for US in a powerful way and a perfect way, etc. The point, however, has been made clear – GOD IS FOR US. He is always for us.

It is not merely that God has been for us in the past or will be for us in the future. Both of those things are true. But it is also true that God is for us right now in the present. He is actively for us, intimately for us, effectively for us, unashamedly for us, etc.

It is in this wonderful light that the Apostle Paul poses the obvious question, "Since God is for us, who can be against us?" (Romans 8:31).

In reality and truth, there are many who are against us. Satan, our adversary, is against us–like a roaring lion seeking whom he may devour. The world system is against us seeking to tear us away from God and to totally absorb us into its sinful ways and thoughts. The ideology of the world, the culture of the world, the values of the world, the desires of the world, the educational system of the world, the religions of the world, etc. These are all against us as true believers in Christ. Our sinful flesh is also against us. "For the desires of the flesh are against the Spirit, and the desires of the Spirit are against the flesh, for these are opposed to each other..." (Galatians 5:17). The lusts, sinful pleasures, sinful habits, etc. of the flesh war against we who are pursuers of holiness and true righteousness. There are many forces arrayed against us but the Apostle Paul's point is that when compared to the reality and undeniable fact that the Almighty God, Himself, is for us then the combined forces of our enemies' amount to nothing and pose no lasting danger to those loved by God and those who are under the protective umbrella of the fact that GOD IS FOR US. For all practical purposes, who then or what then can be against us successfully? What a wonderful reality!

Think about the following:

Can any person cause a believer to lose his or her salvation?

"What, then, shall we say in response to this? If God is for us, who can be against us? He did not spare his own son, but gave Him up for us all – how will He not also, along with him, graciously give us all things? Who will bring any charge against those whom God has chosen? It is God who justifies. Who is he that condemns? Christ Jesus who died – more than that, who was raised to life – is at the right hand of God and is also interceding for us" (Romans 8:31b–34).

The Apostle Paul begins with an all-encompassing rhetorical question: "If God is for us, who can be against us?

First, note again, that the word "if" translates the Greek conditional particle "ei", signifying a fulfilled condition and not a mere possibility. It could be translated, therefore, "since" or "because." "Because God is for *us...*" This word is not calling in question the possibility that God is not for us but is establishing the reality that He is, indeed, for us. Note also, that the apostle is not implying that there will not be those who oppose us as Christians. Certainly, as we have already stated there are many who oppose the child of God. The apostle is calling the reader to ponder the implications of God being for us and to realize that were anyone able to rob us of salvation they would have to be greater than God Himself. Is there anyone who is greater than God–the creator, life giver, sustainer, and sovereign ruler? The answer is obviously, "No." Hence, the crux of Paul's point is that God is for us so it really doesn't matter who is against us.

Katharina von Schlegel's beautiful hymn, "Be Still, My Soul," captures and expresses the confident hope of every believer.

> Be still my soul: the Lord is on my side Bear patiently the
> cross of grief or pain,
> Leave to thy God to order and provide;
> In every change He faithful will remain.
> Be still, my soul: thy best, thy heavenly Friend
> Thro' thorny ways, leads to a joyful end.
>
> Be still, my soul: thy God doth undertake
> to guide the future as He has the past.
> Thy hope, thy confidence let nothing shake,
> All now mysterious shall be bright at last,
> Be still, my soul: the waves and winds still know
> His voice who ruled them while He dwelt below.
>
> Be still, my soul: the hour is hastening on
> When we shall be forever with the Lord,
> When disappointment, grief, and fear are gone.
> Sorrow forgot, loves purest joys restored.
> Be still, my soul: when change and tears are past,
> All safe and blessed we shall meet at the last.

Why are these things so? Because God is for us! God is for us all the time in every way. God is for us powerfully and personally and practically.

God is for us in wisdom and in love. God is for us in our good times and in our bad times. God is for us unflinchingly and without limitation. God is for us faithfully, perpetually, irresistibly. Dear Christian, take heart, when all is against you God is still for you.

He cannot be defeated nor outwitted. He cannot be deterred or distracted from your cause. God cannot and will not stop being with you and for you. Your ultimate safety, security, and success are underwritten and guaranteed because God is for you.

Expanding on this thought a bit, C. H. Spurgeon commenting on the biblical phrase, *"Thy Redeemer"* (Isaiah 54:5) wrote:

> "Jesus, the Redeemer, is altogether ours and ours forever. All the offices of Christ are held on our behalf. He is King for us, Priest for us, and Prophet for us. Whenever we read a new title of the Redeemer, let us appropriate Him as ours under that name as much as under any other. The shepherd's staff, the Father's rod, the Captain's sword, the priest's mitre, the prince's scepter, the prophet's mantle, all are ours. Jesus has no dignity which He will not employ for our exaltation, and no prerogative which He will not exercise for our defense. His fullness of God is our unfailing, inexhaustible treasure–house. His manhood also, which He took upon Him for us, is ours in all its perfection. To us our gracious Lord communicates the spotless virtue of a stainless character; to us He gives the meritorious efficacy of a devoted life; on us He bestows the reward procured by obedient submission and incessant service. He makes the unsullied garment of His life our covering beauty; the glittering virtues of His character our ornaments and jewels; and the superhuman meekness of His death our boast and glory. He bequeaths us His manger, from which to learn how God came down to man; and His Cross to teach us how man may go up to God. All of His thoughts, emotions, actions, utterances, miracles, and intercessions, were for us. He trod the road of sorrow on our behalf, and has made over to us as His heavenly legacy the full

results of all believers of his life. He is now as much ours as heretofore; and He blushes not to acknowledge Himself "our Lord Jesus Christ," though He is the blessed and only Potentate, the King of kings, and Lord of lords. Christ everywhere and every way is our Christ, forever and ever most richly to enjoy. O my soul, by the power of the Holy Spirit: call Him this morning "thy Redeemer." (C. H. Spurgeon, *Morning and Evening*, McDonnell Publishing Company, McLean Virginia 22102, page 340)

Indeed, not only is God the Father for us but so are the other members of the Trinity for us. What an overwhelming and encouraging truth. God is for us! The one true Almighty God of the Bible is for us!

Consider the Wonderful Implications

With God for us, consider the following questions:

- Can other people rob us of our salvation?
- No, no one can deprive us of our salvation.
- Can a believer put themselves out of God's saving grace by committing some heinous sin?

Some believers are fearful that they might not be trustworthy and might fall into some kind of gross sin which will sever their saving relationship to Jesus Christ. Unfortunately, some churches teach that the loss of salvation is possible. But, consider the fact that, if we were not able by our own power or effort to save ourselves from sin and to bring ourselves to God for salvation at the outset or beginning of our relationship with God—how could it then be possible that by our own efforts we could cancel out the work of God's grace that He has already accomplished in us and is accomplishing in us? We must remember the words of Scripture, "Being confident of this, that He who began a good work in you will carry it on to completion until the day of Christ Jesus" (Philippians 1:6).

Is it possible that God will take away our salvation? Is it possible that God will stop loving us?

To answer that question, we must remember the condition that we were in when God loved us and gave His son to be our Savior. *"You* see, at just the right time, when we were still powerless, Christ died for the ungodly" (Romans 5:6a).

God already knew every flaw in us and that we were ungodly yet He still loved us in Christ. Scripture points us in a different direction than doubting whether God will continue to love us and provide for our safety and security in salvation: "He who did not spare His own son, but gave Him up for us all—how will He not also, along with Him, graciously give us all things?" (Romans 8:32)

Paul is assuring us that God's love is not fickle and that He will not cease loving us. Our salvation is secure in the love of God and there is no deprivation for God's children regarding salvation. In this passage, Paul is arguing from the greater to the lesser. He is saying that God has already given us the greatest gift (His Son) and therefore He will not deprive us of anything else that we need to secure our salvation. There is no deprivation. God will freely and graciously give us all things that we need. The word, "graciously," is a translation of the Greek word *charizomai* which means to bestow graciously or out of grace. In addition, the Apostle Paul's other letters the same word carries the idea of forgiveness (2 Corinthians 2:7, 10; 12:13; Colossians 2:13).

Where You Are standing Can Make a Difference

The place where we stand and the convictions which compel us to stand there are altogether important. Imagine a soldier with his fellow soldiers who strays into a minefield without realizing it. Suddenly, one of the soldiers in his platoon spots a half covered explosive mine and yells out for everybody else to stop in their tracks. To extricate themselves from the dangerous, life-threatening minefield without harm or death they carefully retrace their footsteps in reverse. In this scenario, where you stand makes all the difference in the world.

I heard a story some time ago about a local pastor who visited one of his very ill parishioners in the hospital. When the pastor entered the hospital room he was a bit taken back by the number of tubes and wires connected to the patient. On a mission to be encouraging, however, he proceeded to the side of the patient's bed, took his hand, and spoke encouragingly to him. The patient had been intubated and could not speak to reply to the pastor. Instead, he pointed to a pad of paper on the table next to the bed and indicated to the pastor that he would like to write something to him. The pastor gave him the pen and paper and the patient began to write but at just that exact point in time alarm bells began to go off and nurses began to flood into the room to attend to the patient in crisis. The Pastor thought it best to leave the room and to make space for the medical personnel to minister to the patient. Unfortunately, and sadly the medical personnel were unable to save the patient and the patient passed away.

The deceased person had attended the pastor's church so the pastor was asked to conduct the funeral service for him. As the pastor began to address those people gathered for the funeral he commented on the good character of the one who had passed away and then he remembered that when he was in the hospital room and the patient was still alive that the patient had written him a brief note just before all the alarms started going off. The pastor had merely folded the paper and put it into his coat pocket not giving it another thought until that very moment. He mentioned this to the gathered congregation and said that just prior to his passing the patient had written him a note which he had just remembered and that he had put it in his pocket. He took the note out in front of the congregation and was going to read it to them—until he saw the message. It said, "You are standing on my air hose!" Sometimes it really matters where you are standing.

It was April 18, 1521. Martin Luther had been summoned to the Imperial Diet in Worms to defend himself and his teachings. Toward the end of his defense he said, "Since your most serene Majesty and your highness require of me a simple, clear and direct answer, I will give one, and it is this: I cannot submit my faith either to the Pope or to the Council because it is clear as noonday they have fallen into error and even into glaring inconsistency with themselves. If, then, I am not convinced by proof from holy Scripture, or by cogent reasons, if I am not satisfied by the very text I have cited, if my judgment is not in this way brought into subjection to God's Word, I neither can nor will retract anything., For it cannot be either safe or honest for a Christian to speak against his conscience. Here I stand: I cannot do otherwise, God help me! Amen."

Martin Luther felt compelled to stand on the truth and promises of God's

Word and that made all the difference in the world. The Christian must be careful to stand by faith and conviction on the truth of God as revealed in His Word. He must stand completely trusting in the work of Jesus Christ as Lord and Savior. He must stand on the promise that GOD IS FOR US.

Dear Christian, think about the fact that God is for you–think deeply about this wonderful reality. In a figurative sense, close your eyes and place your hand in His mighty hand. Feel the strength of His almighty being standing with you and engaged for you. Now, look into His eyes of love and wisdom and be comforted because He is for you. When you take on some mission or project and others are hoping that you will fail know that God is for you–He is always for you. When you stray from the path and God must come and restore you and sometimes even chasten you always remember that God is for you. Goliaths may rise up from time to time to oppose you but God is for you. Friends may forsake you and betray you, loved ones may misunderstand you and distance themselves from you but God is for you. God is always for you!

BRINGING IT HOME

1. What proof has Paul given us that God is for us as believers?
2. Describe some of the attributes and characteristics of the true God of the Bible. How does an understanding of these encourage you and give you boldness in your Christian walk?
3. What specific group of people is the Apostle Paul including in the assertion that, "God is for us?"
4. Describe some ways in which God is for us – as believers.

11

Since God is for Us there is

NO DEPRIVATION

"What then shall we say to these things? If God is for us, who can be against us? He did not spare his own son but gave them up for us all, how will he not also with them graciously give us all things?" (Romans 8:31 – 32).

Complete deprivation of all sensory perception is what is promised by the promoters of an isolation tank or a sensory deprivation tank. It is an enclosed tank made soundproof and filled up to 10 inches with a high Epson salt (magnesium sulfate) and saltwater solution warmed to skin temperature and created so that, as a person floats, they are cut off from all sensory perception. The promoters tout the supposed neurological and health benefits of this device. Allison P. Davis wrote an article in August 20, 2015 describing his experience with the deprivation tank. He entitled it, *I Survived My Terrifying Hour in a Sensory–Deprivation Tank.*

Some participants describe experiencing intense relaxation and a state of semi–consciousness. Others say they experience hallucinations and "out of body" experiences. The first commercial "float spa" opened in 1979 in Beverly Hills, California. The inventor Dr. John C Lily developed the first consumer–friendly tank. It was called "Samadhi"-Sanskrit for higher consciousness. Actually, the very first use of such tanks began in 1954 in psychiatric experimentation.

He who volunteers to experience the deprivation tank is instructed to get naked, scrub clean, and use Vaseline on any open wounds. Then he is led to the float tank through a door that looks like a door to a shell, or a wood-fired Kiln. Initially, the person immediately feels the sting of the

Epson salt concoction as it makes contact with any blisters, scrapes, etc. The subject is settled down in the 10 inches of water and given an inflated pillow to rest his head and neck on while the water cradles his floating body in a lukewarm embrace of liquid. The ceiling of the tank is covered with tiny LED stars imitating stars of the sky at night. Some subjects in the deprivation tank report that at first one's body relaxes in a feeling of complete contentment. When the person decides to turn off all the lights and experience full sensory–deprivation mode that is when a real change occurs.

Lying in the complete darkness, the person can't see anything or hear anything except his own breathing and the draft of the tank's filter system. He often starts to experience weird feelings and a loud voice from somewhere in his brain which comments on his thoughts while he lays there. Participants report that it is like your brain neurons seem to be firing off with warp speed. You become disoriented and can't figure out how many minutes or hours you have been in the tank. Then a measure of fear almost to the point of panic comes on the person. Just about that time the soft sound of music can be heard. This is the signal that one's time in the tank is almost over. The attendants finally open the hatch to the tank and help the person to get out. The individual is usually standing on wobbly legs very glad to be finished with the experience.

Deprivation can be serious. It has been proven medically by studies done in European countries that babies who are deprived of nurturing care even though they are faithfully fed and changed regularly, do not develop as well as babies who are nourished, loved, and touched by their mothers. Deprivation is harmful to them.

Some years ago, I was receiving my accreditation for scuba diving and one of the requirements was to descend to 65 feet and kneel before the instructor. He then turned off the breathing regulator which normally allowed oxygen to flow through the tubes. We had been previously instructed to ascend slowly to the surface (without the use of artificial air) while gradually letting our own air out of our lungs. The point was to simulate a time when we might be deprived of the regular oxygen flow from our scuba tanks and to teach us the proper method of ascending to the surface without panic and in a way which would not rupture our lungs. Many scuba accidents and deaths occur when there is a certain deprivation of oxygen and panic ensues. Deprivation can be dangerous.

Alexander Haro wrote an article on Monday, May 29, 2017 entitled, *"New Study Finds that Sleep Deprived Brains Literally Eat Themselves."* Most of us have experienced sleep deprivation. Chronic sleep deprivation, however, evidently makes the brain become cannibalistic.

Our brains need rest—the kind of rest that only comes from good sleep. When we sleep the microglia cells and the astrocytes ingest waste products from the nervous system, gobbling up the cellular debris of worn-out and dead cells. In effect, these things are tasked with "pruning unnecessary synapses." The study that found that the brain literally eats itself was recently published in the *Journal of Neuroscience.* Neuroscientist Michelle Bellesi explained this process to *New Scientist.* She wrote, "We show for the first time that portions of synapses are literally eaten by astrocytes because of sleep loss." Evidently, sleep deprivation can be hazardous in a number of different ways.

The last several years I have had to go to hemodialysis due to my failed kidneys. One of the side effects of this treatment is that it tends to cause you to have extremely restless legs. At times, it feels like I'm going to come out of my skin. You can imagine trying to sleep when that is going on. Consequently, I lose a great deal of sleep. If the scientists are correct concerning the negative effects of sleep deprivation then one day in the future my brain should be the size of a peanut. Perhaps, some would contend that it already is.

One can see the damaging effects of water deprivation when plants, crops, and grass are exposed to the burning rays of the sun and yet are deprived of water due to the lack of rainfall or proper irrigation. Water deprivation will bring about death if it is not alleviated.

Deprivation is, "the damaging lack of material benefits considered to be basic necessities in a society; the lack or denial of something considered to be a necessity." Synonyms of deprivation might be destitution, privation, disadvantage, distress, hardship, etc.

The verse we are now considering in Romans chapter eight clearly teaches that God will not deprive us of anything that is necessary to secure our ultimate salvation. On the contrary, God will give us all those things that we may need to be successful in our spiritual journey. In many ways, it is a corollary to Psalm 84:11, "For the LORD God is a sun and shield, the LORD bestows favor and honor, no good thing does He withhold from those whose walk is blameless (upright)." There are no exceptions and no limitations on this promise.

I have met those who grew up in abject poverty but now make a good income. Sometimes they say, "I am not going to deprive myself of anything—any pleasure, any form of entertainment that I enjoy—no, not anything. I know what it is not to have anything and I am determined not to deprive myself now that I can have what I want. Sometimes, that kind of attitude, though somewhat understandable, can be dangerous as well.

The Powerful Argument

The promise of Divine provision for our eternal security is here given to all true believers. When you pack for a vacation or camping trip you try to think through all the things that you may need while you are going to be away from home. With that in mind, what are some of the things that you think you might need for your spiritual journey through this world? Allow me to suggest some of them:

1. Spiritual Guidance
2. Spiritual Nourishment
3. Faith
4. Hope
5. Spiritual Companionship
6. Encouragement
7. Strength
8. Proper Perspective and Purpose in Life
9. Joy
10. Love
11. Humility
12. Intimacy
13. Assurance
14. Material Resources
15. Cleansing, Forgiveness and Peace
16. Correction & Discipline
17. Courage

Even when you try to anticipate and plan for everything that you might need for a trip invariably there will be something that you forget to consider. Some circumstances will arise that you had not planned for. Thankfully, God in His infinite knowledge and wisdom knows everything that we will need on our journey to heaven and has willingly promised to give us those things. He will freely give us all things in order, to ensure that, our salvation is airtight and that we are completely outfitted for our successful journey as pilgrims of faith.

The previously stated list could go on and on and on and on. God will give us all those things that we need to be successful and safe in our spiritual journey toward heaven. Since God is for us He will provide everything that we could possibly need. Why? Because God is for us!

Is God sufficient in resources to provide everything that we might need as Christians in our salvation?

Charles Haddon Spurgeon was riding home one evening after a heavy day's work. He was feeling weary and depressed when the verse came to mind, "My grace is sufficient for you."

In his mind he immediately compared himself to a little fish in the Thames River, apprehensive less drinking so many pints of water in the river each day he might drink the Thames dry. Then father Thames says to him, "Drink away, little fish. My stream is sufficient for you."

Next, he thought of a little mouse in the granaries of Egypt, afraid lest its daily nibbles exhaust the supplies and cause it to starve to death. Then Joseph comes along and says, "Cheer up, little mouse, my granaries are sufficient for you."

Then he thought of a man climbing some high mountain to reach its lofty summit and dreading lest his breathing there might exhaust all the oxygen in the atmosphere. The Creator booms His voice out of heaven, saying, "Breathe away, oh man, and fill your lungs. My atmosphere is sufficient for you!"

God has unlimited resources and He stands ready to give His children whatever they need. He is sufficient for every and all needs that we might encounter and since God is for us He has committed Himself to giving us whatever we may need, as His children, to successfully persevere in our salvation so that we will be guaranteed to spend eternity in heaven with our glorious Savior. Furthermore, He has given us the most valuable and greatest gift already in the person of His Son. It only follows that He will also give us all things that we need as His children. We will never suffer deprivation when it comes to having those things that we need to be secure in our salvation.

Sometimes the believer may be concerned that his heart will grow hard toward God as he lives out life here on earth. He fears that the fires of spiritual passion will burn themselves out and that his sensitivity and submission to God along with his passion for Him will dissipate due to a hardening of his heart.

Personally, God has wired me in such a way that I tend to concentrate on some new project or interest with a high degree of intensity and thoroughness only to find that once I have explored and experienced that which I focused on, I start to lose the intensity of interest in it and move on to something else which now occupies my full attention. In a fashion, my heart is relatively hardened to the old while it is awakened to the new.

In the Bible, we find that God sometimes hardens the hearts of individuals. In fact, God hardened the heart of Pharaoh in Egypt during the days of the Exodus. The Apostle Paul commenting on this as an example of God's dealings with men wrote, "Therefore He has mercy on whom He will have mercy, and whom He wills He hardens" (Romans 9:18).

Is it possible that God does this by a direct act of His will? If He were to do so, it is His right since He is absolutely sovereign. It is also possible however, that, at times, God hardens men's hearts in another way. Living in North Carolina I am in clay country. In fact, clay and the pottery that is made from it form a major industry in our state. Imagine that I were to take a lump of moist clay and set in on a rock during the heat of the summer. Then, I was to take great care to continually moisten the clay. It would then stay moist and pliable. If I were, however, to take that same lump of moist clay and place it on the same rock exposed to the heat of the summer sun and not moisten it at all, it would then quickly grow hard and brittle and no longer be pliable.

God sometimes hardens men's hearts in this fashion. For an individual's heart to remain soft and pliable toward God he must be constantly cared for by God's grace so that his heart remains soft, "moist" and pliable. If God merely withholds His tenderizing blessings from an individual that individual's heart will grow hardened by its constant exposure to sin.

God's promise to us, as believers, is that He will not withhold anything that we need to continue successfully in our spiritual journey and achieve our goal of ultimate salvation. He will continue to ensure that our hearts do not grow cold and hard toward Him. His mercies are constant and given to us copiously out of His great heart of love for us. Since God is for us He will give us all good things that we need.

During the days of the great California gold rush some prospectors discovered a very rich mine. "We've got it made," they said, "As long as we don't tell anybody else before we stake our claims." And they made a vow of secrecy.

But they had to go into town for provisions and tools. When they left the town, a great host of people followed them. Why? Their "secret" was written all over their faces. It was impossible for them to hide what they had found.

A gifted speaker was asked what his most difficult speaking assignment was. He said that it was an address he gave to the National Conference of Undertakers entitled "How to Look Sad at a $10,000 Funeral."

I'm sure you have observed the unique demeanor of two young people who have fallen in love and are looking forward to marriage. They seem to be filled with a type of joy that cannot be concealed.

When we think of the biblical reality that God has wisely and abundantly provided for our salvation and we embrace that indisputable fact by faith, it will fill us with exuberant joy and mountains of confidence. When we understand, in our souls, that we, as believers, will never suffer any serious or detrimental deprivation that threatens our ultimate salvation, we will not be able to mask our joy in God.

For some reason people tend to feel like Christians should merely sit quietly and contain their feelings. At one time, one of America's favorite and most vocal humorists was Erma Bombeck. In one of her columns she told about the little boy who was sitting in front of her in church. He was just as quiet as could be and certainly wasn't bothering anyone, but every occasionally, he would turn around and smile happily at everyone behind him. He did this several times to the pleasure of everyone who could see him. Suddenly, his mother jerked him around and told him in a loud whisper to stop grinning – he was in church. Then, when the tears came to the little fella's eyes, his mother said, "That's better." I'm not advocating that children should become a distraction or the center of attention in church services. I am merely pointing out that Christians could use an added measure of joy in their lives. When we contemplate seriously the words of Paul in the conclusion of Romans chapter eight regarding the fact that God will always love us – always, and that he will not deprive us of anything that we need but will graciously and generously bless us with all things, then we will certainly feel the exuberant waves of joy washing over our souls. (J. Ellsworth Kalas, THE POWER OF BELIEVING, (Waco, Texas: Word Books, 1987).

What a wonderful God! What a wonderful promise! What a wonderful salvation! God is For us!

BRINGING IT HOME

1. What has God already given us?
2. What is Paul's main point in this passage of Scripture? How does that main point comfort you and encourage you as a child of God?
3. What are some of the things that you think you might need to successfully and securely finish your journey of faith and safely arrive in heaven? Explain why you think that you might need them.
4. Try to imagine how much God gave up for us when "He spared not His own son but delivered Him up for us all." Meditate on this and utilize it as a means of worship and gratitude to God.

What a wonderful comfort and encouragement this promise is to the child of God. What reassurance and what a confident hope and trust we can have in our loving, powerful, and all sufficient giving and gracious God. NO DEPRIVATION! God is for us!

12

Since God is for Us there is

NO ACCUSATION –

Romans 8:33 – 34

"Who shall bring any charge against God's elect?
It is God who justifies. Who is to condemn? Christ Jesus is
the one who died more - than that, who was raised - who is at
the right hand of God, who indeed is interceding for us."
An Admission of Reality

I t is Christ who died." "It is God who justified." God is a demanding judge who, because of his nature, must judge sin. He cannot overlook even one sin because of His infinitely holy and just nature. The story is told of an ongoing exchange between former Secretary of State, Henry Kissinger and his biographer. Sometime after the author submitted his first draft to the former cabinet member Kissinger asked, "Is this the best you can do?" The biographer replied, "Henry, I thought so, but I'll try again." So back he went to craft his work returning in a few days with another draft. Kissinger called the author in the next day and said, "are you sure this is the best you can do?" "Well, I really thought so, said the biographer. "But I'll try one more time." This very same exchange went on eight times, eight drafts, and each time Kissinger asked, "is this the best you can do?" Finally, the author submitted his ninth draft and was called into Kissinger's office the next day. Again, Kissinger asked the same question. Exasperated, the author replied, "Henry, I've beaten my brains out – this is the ninth draft. I know it's the best I can do. I can't possibly improve even one more word." Kissinger then looked at his biographer and said. "In that case, now I'll read it."

God requires that we keep his law perfectly. We may have tried to comply with that command but inevitably we fall short of perfection. We try and try again but each time we fall short. In the illustration that I used Kissinger was very demanding and held up a high standard but eventually he was content to accept "the best the author could do." God, however, is not content to accept the best that the sinner can do. In truth, sinners do not actually give God their best in obedience but even if they did do so their obedience would still fall short of the standard of perfection. For that reason, out of His abundant grace and mercy God gave us the Lord Jesus Christ to be our perfect substitute and sacrifice to meet God's perfect standard for salvation. The believer can now rejoice that Christ has died and that God is satisfied with His sacrificial death. Based on this, God now declares believing sinners to be justified (righteous before His eyes).

Have you ever been accused of something that you were not guilty of? It hurts, doesn't it? Such accusations are often unexpected and shocking. They sting and wound. Sometimes they discourage. Sometimes they arouse anger. Sometimes they place the accused person on the defense, provoke arguments, destroy relationships, and mar testimonies.

Because of accusations some people are driven to excessive self-examination. Unnecessary self-examination can drive a wedge between two people in a relationship producing resentment and destroying trust.

Over the years, I have been personally accused of things that I not only did not do, but I had never thought of doing. Sometimes the accusations are leveled because of misunderstanding and at other times out of a malicious intent. Often such false accusations can cloud the air concerning a person's sterling reputation. They cause people to question whether there is some remnant of truth to the accusation even though the person may be completely upright and innocent. People think, "Where there is smoke, there must be fire." This is especially so if the accusations are repeated over and over so that they take root in the minds of those infected by the false claims. False accusations are evil. False accusations are hurtful.

What is also hurtful is when accusations are made that are founded in truth. You made a mistake. You spoke in haste – in anger – untruthfully. You acted in an unchristian manner whether deliberately and willfully or because of some emotional knee-jerk reaction. Either way, what you did was wrong and the accusation leveled against you (regardless of the motive) is correct and true.

You know that you have done wrong and you feel the weight, guilt and the truthfulness of the accusation. The Apostle Paul teaches us that we have a conscience that accuses us when we have done wrong. "For when Gentiles, who do not have the law, by nature do what the law requires, they are a law to themselves, even though they do not have the law. They show that the work of the law is written on their hearts, while their conscience also bears witness, and their conflicting thoughts accuse or even excuse them…" (Romans 2:14 – 15).

Satan is described as "the accuser of the brethren" (Revelation 12:10). The book of Job depicts him clearly in that role:

"And the Lord said to Satan, "Have you considered my servant Job? For there is no one like him on the earth, a blameless and upright man, fearing God and turning away from evil." Then Satan answered the Lord, "Does Job fear God for nothing? Have you not made a hedge about him and his house and all that he has, on every side? You have blessed the work of his hands, and his possessions have increased in the land. But put forth your hand now and touch all that he has; he will surely curse you to your face" (Job 1:8–11).

Even though Job was guiltless, Satan accused Job. Later, in the New Testament, we read that Satan sought to "sift" the Apostle Peter like wheat. He also accuses Christians of every age in the same fashion. Satan, our adversary, brings charge after charge against us when we slip and walk unworthy of our calling as children of God. The accusations made against believers by Satan and the unbelieving world are not always false. The fact is we are still sinners not yet having been perfected. But even when a charge or accusation against us is true, it is never sufficient grounds for our damnation because all our sins–past, present, and future–have been paid for by the blood of Jesus Christ and we are now viewed by God in the perfect righteousness of Christ.

Count Zinzendorf was inspired by this truth to write the great hymn, *"Jesus Thy Blood and Righteousness,"* which was translated into English by John Wesley. One line of that hymn reads:

"Bold I shall stand in that great day,

For who ought to my charge shall lay?
Fully absolved through Thee I am
From sin and fear, from guilt and shame"

He was poetically expressing the same concept that the Apostle Paul taught when he wrote, "*Who shall lay anything to the charge of God's elect?*"

Being accused is a very real reality. Jesus our Lord was accused of wrongdoing. Recall that false witnesses were solicited to testify against him. The Apostle Paul was accused by his enemies of wrongdoing. The truth is, the world is sitting on ready looking to bring some accusation against God's people.

The early church was accused of idolatry because they had no visible images of their God. They were accused of immorality because they greeted each other with a holy kiss, usually met at night due to the fact they worked all day, and participated in "love feasts." They were accused of being rebels to the government and enemies to the King because they taught that Jesus was King. They were accused of cannibalism due to a misunderstanding of eating the body and drinking the blood of the Lord Jesus Christ symbolically in the Lord's Supper.

The accusations and charges against the early church and against the church today are legion. That is why the Apostle Peter counseled Christians, "For this is the will of God, that by doing good you should put to silence the ignorance of foolish people" (1 Peter 2:15). There is no shortage of ignorant people who stand ready to make foolish accusations and charges against God's people. We must be honest and truthful in making the clear admission that Christians will be accused and charged in every conceivable way. It is not unusual to hear the unsaved person accuse Christians of being hypocritical and un-Christlike (again, this is sometimes founded in truth and other times it is purely fabricated).

We know then, that our earthly enemies will accuse us as Christians. We know that Satan will and does accuse us as Christians. We know that our consciences will sometimes accuse us as Christians. We know that sometimes these accusations are founded in truth while at other times they are fabricated with a malicious intent. So, let us admit that we, as Christians will be accused continually. Accusations and charges are inevitable. How then, can the Apostle Paul honestly ask the question, "Who shall bring any charge against God's elect?" (Romans 8:33a).

The truth is, many are standing in line ready to charge God's people with any number of accusations. What then, does the Apostle Paul mean and how does his statement buttress and support the Christian's sense of absolute security in his salvation? We must understand that the Apostle Paul does not intend to deny that Christians will be accused from a number of different areas but his point is that God (the final and absolute judge) is fully aware of any and all accusations and charges against the Christian and yet has, Himself, declared the Christian to be totally without guilt/justified through the work of Jesus Christ on the Cross. The Christian is viewed by God as "in Christ" and therefore justified completely and freed from all guilt due to sin. His sins have been completely paid for in a totally satisfactory way so that God now declares that no charges or accusations will be considered against the true Christian.

The ADAMANT CHALLENGE

The Apostle Paul is in effect issuing a challenge. He is asking, "WHO" will bring any charge against God's elect? There are three things that we need to understand about this passage at this point to fully appreciate what Paul is trying to teach us.

> The Context
> The Community of People in View
> The Confidence and Assurance Exhibited

The Context

The clear context of Romans 8:34 is that of Jesus Christ and his work of salvation for sinners. Our certain hope is that we are standing in Jesus Christ our refuge and protector and defender. It makes a great deal of difference where one stands. In the first Psalm, the psalmist describes the blessedness of the man who does not, "stand in the way of sinners."

I feel certain that when Noah heard and felt the great roar of rushing water that would ultimately cover the earth flooding and destroying all human life outside of the ark that he felt deeply grateful to God to be standing in the ark of safety. Likewise, the believer stands in Jesus Christ who is our refuge and place of safety. It does not matter who accuses us or what they accuse us of so long as we are standing in the ark of Christ.

Every Christian who desires assurance, confidence, and a sense of security in their salvation must also resolutely be committed to stand on the Word of God as it is in Christ Jesus. The Word of God tells us that Jesus died, was buried, was raised, and is now in heaven interceding for believers to ensure their absolute safety and full acceptance with God.

Romans chapter eight is an exceedingly beautiful and comprehensive treatment concerning the absolute security and guaranteed salvation of the true Christian. Romans 8:1–30 highlights the fact that the grace of God is currently active and sufficient to deal with a whole series of predicaments that we might find ourselves in as Christians in our journey of faith. Since God is for us, God's grace meets our every need and supplies that which is required to ensure our guaranteed security in Christ. Then in verses 31–39 Paul calls on his readers to respond to these truths. He begins by saying, "What then shall we say to these things?" (Verse 31). Whereas in the first 30 verses of this chapter Paul is highlighting the sufficiency of the grace of God, now he shifts his focus and begins to highlight the sufficiency of the God of grace.

In this first verse the Apostle Paul highlights three specific aspects of the work of Jesus Christ whereby He secures our complete and ultimate salvation. Those three areas are:

1. The substitutionary sacrifice of Jesus Christ on behalf of believing sinners. "Christ is the one who died…"
2. The resurrection of Jesus Christ from the dead. – "More than that, who was raised"
3. The intercession of Jesus Christ for believers. – "Who is at the right hand of God, who indeed is interceding for us."

THE CONTEXT: The Death of Jesus Christ

The Apostle Paul draws our attention to the substitutionary sacrifice of Jesus Christ on behalf of His people who will ultimately become believers. In the context, the apostle is reemphasizing that which he has previously said in Romans 8: 1–4 about the fact that no one and no thing can bring the believer back under a state of condemnation again because Jesus Christ has eternally ensured our freedom and deliverance from condemnation by his substitutionary death and resurrection. Moreover, our Lord Jesus Christ is now at the right hand of God interceding for us based on the never diminishing merits of his perfect sacrifice on our behalf.

Concerning the death of Christ, recall that the Word "Christ" is synonymous with the Old Testament word, "Messiah." It refers to one who is anointed by God for a specific task. It ultimately came to be understood as referring to the one great Savior who would be anointed by God to save His people. In His work as our Messiah/Christ, he paid for every one of our sins. They (our sins) have been fully judged and successfully dealt with by Jesus our Lord. As genuine believers, He paid the full penalty for all the sins of His redeemed people. That is why the writer of Hebrews could write:

"But this man, after he had offered one sacrifice for sins forever, sat down on the right hand of God; from henceforth expecting till his enemies be made His footstool. For by one offering He has perfected forever those that are sanctified" (Hebrews 10:12–14).

This is also why the Apostle Paul wrote: "Who shall bring any charge against God's elect? It Is God who justifies. Who is he who condemns? Christ Jesus is the one who died—more than that, who was raised—who is at the right hand of God who indeed is interceding for us" (Romans 8:33–34).

In this context, the Apostle Paul cites the realities that safeguard our salvation in Jesus Christ. First, he says that, "Christ Jesus… died." In His death Jesus took upon Himself the full penalty of our sins and bore our condemnation rendering us forever free from it (Romans 8:1). By His stripes we are healed—through His death He abolished death in the ultimate sense and brought life and immortality to light through the gospel (2 Timothy 1:10). Jesus died for us (His elect) as the perfect and sinless sacrifice.

He died for us willingly and voluntarily. He loved us and gave Himself for us. Jesus died for us vicariously as our substitute taking the full weight of God's wrath due to us on Himself and therefore He served as our propitiation or propitiatory sacrifice satisfying the righteous wrath of God against our sin. Jesus died for us purposely. His intention was to save His people from their sins (Matthew 1:21). Jesus died for us effectually in that His death on the cross actually accomplished our salvation. It accomplished the complete salvation for all of those for whom it was intended. He did not die for us merely in a potential/provisionary way to merely hold out the possibility of salvation but He died for us to really pay for and procure our actual salvation. Nowhere in Scripture is the death of Christ pictured as a provisionary payment for sin or a mere possibility regarding salvation. The death of Christ is the full and actual payment for the sins of His people. When our precious Lord exclaimed on the cross, "It is finished!" our sin-debt to God was actually paid in full at that point by the efficacious death of our Lord Jesus Christ.

Jesus did not die for us as a mere martyr or example of selflessness but as an acceptable substitute and an approved propitiatory sacrifice to God on our behalf. "For our sake He made Him to be sin who knew no sin, so that in Him we might become the righteousness of God" (2 Corinthians 5:21). The Apostle Paul described the salvation which was achieved for believers by our Lord Jesus Christ in the following way:

"And are justified by His grace as a gift, through the redemption that is in Christ Jesus, whom God put forward as a propitiation by His blood to be received by faith" (Romans 3:24–25a).

The word, "redemption," describes the purchase of something, particularly in the culture of this day the purchase of a slave and the freeing of that slave. It is the buying of the slave out of his bondage and thus setting him free from his slavery. The word, "propitiation," describes a sacrifice that satisfies the wrath of God against sin. Our Lord Jesus Christ by his death is not only our Redeemer but our propitiation. Our Lord Jesus Christ died for us with a certain hope and inner joy. When Jesus died on the cross for us he looked forward with joyous anticipation to the time when all His, "ransomed church," would be saved and safe through His sacrificial work for them.

"Looking unto Jesus the author and finisher of our faith; who for the joy that was set before him endured the cross, despising the shame, and is set down at the right hand of the throne of God" (Hebrews 12:2).

Jesus died on the cross obediently to carry out God's will and to bring glory to God's name. In the garden of Gethsemane Jesus prayed, "Not my will, but your will be done." Our Lord Jesus Christ said, "For I came down from heaven, not to do my own will, but the will of Him that sent me. And this is the Father's will which has sent me, that of all which He has given me I should lose nothing, but should raise it up again at the last day" (John 6:38–39). The death of Jesus Christ our Lord was in keeping with the will of God and it was ordained by God.

In the early days of the church, Peter and John were arrested and interrogated for preaching the gospel. After spending the night in jail and on the next day answering the questions of the Jewish leaders both Peter and John went back to their friends and reported what the chief priests and the elders and said to them. Luke wrote:

"And when they heard it, they lifted their voices together to God and said, "Sovereign Lord, who made the heaven and the earth and the sea and everything in them, who through the mouth of our father David, your servant, said by the Holy Ghost 'Why did the Gentiles rage, and the peoples plot in vain?' The kings of the earth set themselves, and the rulers were gathered together, against the Lord and against his anointed. For truly in this city there were gathered together against your holy servant Jesus, whom you anointed, both Herod and Pontius Pilate, along with the Gentiles and the peoples of Israel, *to do whatever your hand and your plan had predestined to take place*" (Acts 4:24-28).

Our Lord Jesus Christ died in accordance with the will of God. He came to, "give his life as a ransom for many" (Mark 10:45b). Jesus shed his blood to purchase/obtain the salvation of the church of God (Acts 20:28). The Apostle Peter wrote, "Knowing that you were ransomed from the futile ways inherited from your forefathers, not with perishable things such as silver or gold, but with the precious blood of Christ, like that of a lamb without blemish or spot" (1 Peter 1:18–19). "He Himself bore our sins in His body on the tree, that we might die to sin and live to righteousness. By His wounds you have been healed" (1 Peter 2:24).

Jesus Christ our Lord died for us personally. He knows each of His sheep intimately and perfectly. He calls them by name in a personal way. He had us in mind personally when He died on the cross on our behalf. Not only so, but Jesus Christ died victoriously. When the soldiers were led to Jesus in the garden of Gethsemane by the traitor Judas, Jesus asked them who they were seeking. They said that they were seeking Jesus of Nazareth. To that He replied, "I am." At that point the entire entourage of soldiers was knocked to the ground by an overwhelming display of supernatural power emanating from Jesus. Jesus was going to go with His captors but He was making it clear that He had the power over them if He chose to use it. He was going willingly as a victor and He died on the cross as a means of defeating Satan. His death on the cross sealed the fate and future of Satan's kingdom. Jesus accomplished his mission. He was successful and victorious. He could say to the Father, "I have finished the work which you gave me to do." So much more could be said about the fact that Christ died. He died literally/physically. He died painfully. He died submissively. Paul's main point, however, is to point out that through the death of Christ we are freed from divine condemnation forever and secured in salvation forever. No accusation can never be leveled against us that will stick.

It is not enough that one merely believes in the "historical" Jesus as He is defined by the world. It is not enough to merely be enthralled with the moral teachings of Jesus. These things, alone, are not enough for a lost sinner to be saved. One must believe in the crucified Jesus. It is Christ who died…Paul declares that Jesus Christ was also "raised" from the dead.

THE CONTEXT: The Proof Underscored by the Resurrection

The commentator John Phillips wrote a dramatic and personalized description of being at the tomb of Jesus on that resurrection morning. He wrote: "We creep toward the sepulcher in the gloom of that Saturday night. There they are, the ironclad soldiers of Rome, pacing up and down before the solid stone that seals the rich man's tomb. Upon that tomb is the seal of Empire. Who would dare tamper with that seal? Who could brave those marching men, the merest tip of mighty Caesars finger?

Suddenly the tough troopers stand still in their tracks. All about them is the stillness of the night. The first faint blush of dawn is in the sky and there is the merest glint of light upon the tomb. Then of its own accord and without touch of human hand, the Caesars seal cracks wide. Then slowly, airily, and likewise of its own accord, the great stone begins to roll. First it shows but a crack, then firmly and forever back it rolls. The hair stands up on the soldier's necks. They stare in horror. The tomb is empty.

But wait, what's this? Into the growing morning twilight comes a shining one, his face ablaze with the glory of God and his garments shining the light of another world. It is an angel come down from heaven to take charge of that empty tomb. With one wild whale of terror, the keepers fling down spear, shield, and sword and flee headlong from the scene." (John Phillips, *Exploring the Psalms*, II, (Loizeaux Brother: Neptune, New Jersey, 1988), page 20 – 21.)

Can you imagine that scene? Can you get a sense of the feeling of that supernatural moment? A miracle had occurred! The resurrection of Jesus Christ from the dead was now a reality! This event changed everything. Death had been defeated, sin had been successfully paid for, God had been satisfied, the resurrection proved that the believer has a glorious future as he trusts God in Christ. Because of the resurrection of Jesus Christ, the believer is now able to face the future with hope and confidence. He can look forward to victory after victory as he follows the directions of the resurrected Christ. A poet of old wrote:

> "And I said to the man who stood at the gate of the year;
> "Give me a light, that I may tread safely into
> the unknown!"
> And he replied:
> "Go out into the darkness and put your hand
> Into the hand of God.
> That shall be to you better than light and
> Safer than a known way."
> So, I went forth and finding the hand of God
> Trod gladly into the night.
> And he led me toward the hills and the
> breaking of the day in the lone East.

Because of the resurrection of Jesus Christ, the believer does not need to fear anything. He merely needs to put his hand of faith into the hand of the God who has conquered death on his behalf and trust this God completely to lead him and to save him.

The physical and very real resurrection of Jesus Christ proved that He had triumphed over sin and over the penalty of death. It verified the veracity of His claims and His teaching. It demonstrated God's acceptance of our Lord's sacrificial death.

In his sermon on the day of Pentecost (at the initial founding of the church) Peter declared the awesome fact of the resurrection of Jesus Christ from the dead. The grave, Peter said, "could not hold Him." Peter reasoned from Scripture with the Jewish people that he was preaching to and pointed out to them that the resurrection of Jesus Christ from the dead was predicted by David (Acts 2:22–35). The hymn writer wrote, "Up from the grave he arose with a mighty triumph o'er his foes." The resurrection of Jesus Christ from the dead signals His conquest over death, God's acceptance of His sacrifice on our behalf, and paves the way for our justification before God. As Paul had stated earlier in Romans, Christ "Was delivered up because of our transgressions, and was raised because of our justification" (Romans 4:25).

The death of Christ without the resurrection of Christ would be incomplete and insufficient. That is why the New Testament writers constantly stressed the importance of the resurrection of Christ. By His crucifixion and resurrection Jesus destroyed him who had the power of death (the devil) (Hebrews 2:14). Jesus destroyed the power of death and the grave (1 Corinthians 15:19 – 22, 49 – 58) and opened the way for eternal life. In addition, because He was raised as the first fruits we will also be raised from the dead by the empowering work of God. Because of the resurrection of Jesus Christ from the dead true believers have a living hope of the hereafter.

At the very beginning of his first letter the Apostle Peter burst forth into a mighty and magnificent doxology. After a brief salutation he immediately began exuberantly praising God. This is not unusual for the biblical writers. In Paul's letter to the Ephesians, he does the same thing. In the very beginning of his letter after his salutation. Paul writes "Blessed be the God and Father of our Lord Jesus Christ, who has blessed us with all spiritual blessings in heavenly places in Christ" (Ephesians 1:3). Paul continues this doxology of praise to God all the way through the 14th verse of that wonderful chapter.

THE CONTEXT: The Manner of True Christianity

One great characteristic of true Christianity and of the New Testament and of the early church is that it was characterized by praises to God and by a sense of joy. This same attitude or spirit characterized the times of revival that the church has experienced down through its history. Why has the church felt this way? Why was Peter so filled with praises for God that he began his first letter with a doxology to Him? Peter wrote: "Blessed be the God and father of our Lord Jesus Christ, which according to His abundant mercy has begotten us again unto a living hope by the resurrection of Jesus Christ from the dead, to an inheritance incorruptible and undefiled, and that does not fade away, reserved in heaven for us, who are kept by the power of God through faith unto the salvation ready to be revealed in the last time" (1 Peter 1:3–5).

Let's see if we can understand the secret of why Peter felt that way and what caused him to burst forth into this mighty, joyous, and grateful adoration, and thanksgiving to God. To understand why Peter felt as he did we will need to meditate for a few minutes on what Peter refers to as the, "living hope." Peter is praising the God and Father of our Lord Jesus Christ, which according to His abundant mercy has begotten us again into a *living hope.* But, exactly how has all this been done? Peter answers, "By the resurrection of Jesus Christ from the dead." Here we have the core truth and the foundation of the whole passage. It is the controlling principle of Peter's thinking.

THE CONTEXT: The Resurrection & the Living Hope

Apart from the resurrection there can be no true Christianity and certainly no living hope. The resurrection of Christ is vital; it is absolutely essential. If the resurrection of Jesus Christ had not taken place, the Apostle Peter could never have written about the living hope. After the crucifixion of Jesus Christ His followers were dejected, downcast, depressed, despondent, and despairing. All seemed lost. Peter even went back to fishing. What was it that changed these frightened and forlorn followers of Christ into a band of enthusiastic ambassadors"? It was this, the resurrection!

Paul wrote to the Corinthians concerning the resurrection of Jesus Christ from the dead, "and if Christ has not been raised, then our preaching is in vain and your faith is in vain" (1 Corinthians 15:14). Furthermore, he wrote "and if Christ has not been raised, your faith is futile and you are still in your sins" (1 Corinthians 15:17).

The truth of the resurrection of Jesus Christ from the dead then is basic and foundational. If one does not believe in the resurrection of Christ, whatever else he may believe, he is not really a Christian. The Apostle Paul wrote to the Romans and said: "If you confess with your mouth that Jesus is Lord and believe in your heart that God raised him from the dead, you will be saved" (Romans 10:9).

The great message that the apostles preached was, "Jesus and the resurrection." Their messages are found throughout the book of Acts. The resurrection of Jesus Christ from the dead is taught and explained in the epistles. Without the resurrection they really had no message but because of the resurrection of Jesus Christ from the dead their hearts were filled with enthusiastic hope and confident joy. They understood that the resurrection of Jesus Christ from the dead was planned by God and brought about by the power of God for their salvation and it was a harbinger of the future resurrection of every true believer. Because of this they were filled with praises to God and filled with joy regarding the living hope which God had provided for them. This was the "manner" (the characterizing perspective) of the early church, the early apostles and the church during its most spiritual times of revival. It can also be the "manner" of our own individual Christianity today.

THE CONTEXT: Focusing on the Living Hope

Why is the resurrection, according to Peter, so central and foundational to vibrant Christian living? Why is it the occasion for such praise to God? What is it that the resurrection does?

According to Peter the first thing that the resurrection does is that it gives us a "living hope." This "living" hope is in contrast with the vague, shadowy speculations of unsaved people. This living hope is not uncertain but it is a dynamically charged reality based on the real, objective resurrection of Jesus Christ from the dead.

But there is more involved in the "living hope" than this simple contrast. The living hope is something substantial, certain, vibrant with both life and power to transform the believer's attitude and actions. The great thing about this hope is that it enables us to live–really live, as vibrant Christians. The Apostle Peter was writing this letter to people who were experiencing a very hard time: "though now for a little while, if necessary, you have been grieved by various trials," That is the background of Peter's first letter. In every chapter of his first letter, he refers to this time as the time of adversity, trials, and hardships for the saints.

In the second chapter Peter tells his readers that though they are experiencing hard times for their faith they were, in fact, following in the steps of their Lord Jesus Christ who also was mistreated horribly (2:22–23a). In the fourth chapter, Peter again refers to adversity but this time with reference to the time of Noah and the few godly people left alive in that godless age. Also, in the fourth chapter, the apostle tells them to not think it strange concerning the fact that they were experiencing "fiery trials" (4:12). In the final chapter of this first letter Peter ends his letter with a glorious doxology but he includes a stark statement of reality – "after you have suffered a while." (5:10)

For people facing perpetual suffering and the prospect of possible death for their faith, the "living hope" of a better, more joyous, and eternally enduring future is a bright ray of sunshine in a context of dismal darkness.

The New Testament never sugar coats the Christian life. It is honest, personal, and practical. It does not minimize difficulties, problems, and severe trials. It does, however, reveal to us as believers that regardless of how dark, ugly, and cruel the times are in which we live we still have an unquenchable, undefeated "living hope" that can motivate us and sustain us as we not only endure the trials but emerge from the fray as "more than conquerors" with a certain hope of heaven and holiness. All of this is possible because God is for us.

In Romans 8:36b–37, the Apostle Paul says basically the same thing. This "living hope" enables the believer to not only endure whatever trials he is called upon to face but also to do so with assurance and with a sense of triumph. This world of difficulties is not all that there is. We have been begotten again unto "a living hope."

But how does the resurrection accomplish all this? And, are you experiencing this sense of confident triumph in your heart when you deal with the trials that you face? During the trials, are you able to say with genuine authenticity, "Blessed be the God and Father of our Lord Jesus Christ?" Do you have this "living hope?"

When Jesus was raised from the dead He was raised in a literal sense and literally came out of the grave that had held his body. This was the same body that had been crucified on Friday and then placed in a borrowed sepulcher. The empty tomb is the foundation and basis of all our hopes. That, of course, assumes that the resurrection of Jesus Christ from the dead literally took place. When Jesus emerged from the tomb it was not merely a testimony to His survival but He arose from the dead victorious over Satan and sin. He arose with the approval of God. He arose as King – the Prince of life with all authority in heaven and in earth entrusted to Him. Through His resurrection following His crucifixion our Lord destroyed our enemies and His. We no longer need to fear anyone or anything (even death) because our Lord Jesus Christ has triumphed, on our behalf, completely crushing all opposition.

THE CONTEXT: The Meaning
& the Importance of the Resurrection

Our text in 1 Peter 1 tells us that Christ was raised by God the Father. The one who is the eternal Son of God, the second person in the blessed holy Trinity experienced human life, death, and resurrection from the dead. From all eternity He had been in the bossom of the Father possessing eternal existence in that realm of glory. At a given point, however, He entered into time and took upon Himself our human nature. He stepped into a world of sin and death and according to the Apostle Paul "was made of a woman, made under the law." He did not cease to be God but He also became man, a complete and perfect man. He identified Himself with us fully.

All the opposition of the world and the devil (with his malignant hatred) was unleashed upon Him and amassed against Him with the intended purpose of destroying Him to thwart the whole purpose of God connected with His coming. Ultimately all the forces arrayed against Him as the Son of God forced Him to be led to the Cross, there to be crucified, and to die for us.

Little did the forces of evil realize, that they were actually accomplishing what God had purposed beforehand and they were helping to seal their own defeat and damnation. On the cross all the righteous demands of God's law were being fulfilled and the consequences of sin were being poured out upon our Lord Jesus Christ. Sin was the cause of His crucifixion and He was the solution for sin's curse. He shed His blood for the remission of sins Hebrews 9:22b. And so, he died. His body was taken down and buried in the grave. Then came that momentous moment when the resurrection of Jesus Christ took place. This is the truth, says Peter, that thrills me and grips me, moving me to exclaim with wonder and adoration the blessedness of God who caused all of this to happen. Christ did not remain in the grave. He was raised from the grave on the third day as a conquering Savior. After appearing to certain of his chosen followers He ascended into heaven and again took His seat in the everlasting glory.

But what does all this mean? The Apostle Paul explains it to us in Romans 6. He wrote, "Christ being raised from the dead, dies no more; death has no more dominion over him. For in that he died, he died in to sin once; but in that he lives, he lives unto God (6:9–10). Notice the word, "once." "In that He died, He died once." Paul then says that now, "death has no more dominion over Him." Once, when He was on earth, death did have dominion over Christ but not any longer.

While on earth our Lord never sinned nor was He sinful, but as part of His identification with us (we who are all sinners) He took his place as our substitute. He placed Himself under the law that condemns and the law condemned Him because of our sins. "He died to sin once." He died once but never again. The resurrection is God's great announcement of the glorious fact that Christ has finished the work He came to do. It is over. He is no longer "under the law," He is back in glory. Sin and death have been conquered! The resurrection demonstrates that He has conquered death and has gone back into the realm above and beyond sin and beyond death. Since we are identified with Him we too are conquerors—no, we are "more than conquerors" through Him who loved us. That is the meaning of the resurrection of Jesus Christ.

THE CONTEXT: The Identification With the Living Christ

The resurrection of Jesus Christ is glorious but the Apostle Peter says that because of what happened to Him on the cross and because of His resurrection from the dead you and I have this "living hope." The apostle wrote, "Blessed be the God and Father of our Lord Jesus Christ, which according to his abundant mercy has caused us to be born again to a living hope through the resurrection of Jesus Christ from the dead, to an inheritance that is imperishable, undefiled, and unfading, kept in heaven for you." In 1 Peter 1:2-4, Peter uses exactly the same word: "*being born again,* not of perishable seed but of imperishable, through the living and abiding Word of God;" What does it mean to be born again?"

To be born again means that the Christian is a person who has not only believed in Christ as the Son of God and believes that He was raised from the dead (certainly, every Christian must believe that) but the Christian is also a person who knows that he has been regenerated (given new life) or born again unto a living hope. The Christian has "new life" from God. In fact, it is this infusion of new life from God during the process of the new birth that enables the unsaved person to see spiritual things with a clear perspective and to trust in Jesus Christ alone, by faith, for salvation. The natural or unsaved person does not have this hope because he has never received the new birth with its attendant enablement. He is without Christ, "having no hope, and without God in the world" (Ephesians 2:12c). You will never have this living hope unless you are born again/regenerated by God. The only person who has this living hope is the one who has been regenerated/ born again and this spiritual new birth activates all his spiritual desires and faculties in a correct, godly fashion. This takes place by the agency of the Holy Spirit through the medium of Christ's resurrection from the dead. In this fashion Christians are born again unto a living hope!

How does all this come about? It comes about when the Holy Spirit secures our union with Christ. We are then one with Him. What happened to Him happened to us. In Romans 6, the Apostle Paul raised the question, "What shall we say then? Are we to continue in sin that grace may abound? By no means! How can we who died to sin still live in it? Do you not know that all of us who have been baptized into Christ Jesus were baptized into his death? We were buried therefore with Him by baptism into death, in order that, just as Christ was raised from the dead by the glory of the Father, we too might walk in newness of life. For if we have been united with Him in a death like His, we shall certainly be united with Him in a resurrection like His (Romans 6:1–5).

The apostle goes on with this line of reasoning: "We know that our old self was crucified with Him in order that the body of sin might be brought to nothing, so that we would no longer be enslaved to sin. "So, you must also consider yourselves dead to sin and alive to God in Christ Jesus" (Romans 6:9, 11).

This truth is found everywhere in the New Testament. Consider Colossians 3:3, "You are dead and your life is hidden with Christ in God." Also in Ephesians: "You has He made alive, who were dead in trespasses and sins... But God, who is rich in mercy... Even when you were dead in sins, has made you alive together with Christ... And has raised us up together and made us sit together in heavenly places in Christ Jesus" (Ephesians 2:1, 4–6).

This, then, is how a person gets the living hope. He receives it from God because he is joined to Christ. In this light, whatever happened to the Lord Jesus also happens to the believer. Christ and his people are one. For the Christian, death has no more dominion over him, just as it has no more dominion over Christ. Because of his union with Christ the believer is alive with Christ, now and forever more. The believer has been "begotten again/regenerated into a living hope by the resurrection of Jesus Christ from the dead."

THE CONTEXT: The Meaning of the "Living Hope"

The living hope that the believer has is "an inheritance that is imperishable, undefiled, and unfading, kept in heaven for you" (1 Peter 1:4). The believer's hope is not merely surviving past the grave but it is the resurrection of the body, and also a receiving of the glorious incorruptible, perpetual inheritance that God has reserved for us in heaven. It is to be like Christ and to be with Christ in holiness and genuine love and joy.

We as believers are already renewed in our spirits which will one day be perfected in the image of our dear Lord and Savior. But, we also look forward to the resurrection of our bodies which will be made like his glorious body. God saves the whole man, body, soul, and spirit and grants us an everlasting inheritance in heaven. This is the believer's living hope and it is made possible by and secured by the resurrection of Jesus Christ from the dead. Instead of struggling endlessly in a world of sin and corruption we are promised, by God, another world which is totally incorruptible, undefiled, and never fades away. This future existence is held out to us by God who cannot lie and we are, having been begotten again, filled with this living hope.

Not only does the Apostle Paul point to the death and resurrection of Jesus Christ but he also reminds us of the present work of Christ which is that He is interceding on our behalf.

THE CONTEXT: The Intercession of Christ

Third, Christ is now, "at the right hand of God." The "right hand" is the designation for a place of exaltation and honor. We read that because, "He humbled himself by becoming obedient to the point of death, even death on the cross. God highly exalted him, and bestowed on him the name which is above every name" (Philippians 2:8–9). In the Old Testament Temple, there were no seats since sacrifices made there by the priest were never finished. The writer of Hebrews explains that, "every priest stands daily ministering and offering oftentimes the same sacrifices which can never take away sin. But by way of contrast the writer of Hebrews points to Jesus and wrote, "He offered one sacrifice for sins for all time, *and sat down at the right hand of God*" (Hebrews 10:11 – 12). Our Lord Jesus Christ is seated at the right hand of God and all authority in heaven and in earth has been given to Him.

Not only has Christ died and then been raised from the dead and is seated at God's right hand but He "also intercedes for us." What is He doing there? Among other things, He is interceding for His people to ensure their safety and security and He will do so without interruption until every redeemed soul is safe in heaven. The writer of Hebrews tells us that Jesus Christ, "is able to save to the uttermost those who draw near to God through him, since he always lives to make intercession for them" (Hebrews 7:25).

When we sin, even after we are saved, our Lord intercedes on our behalf and comes to our defense protecting us in His everlasting love.

Christ intercedes for us in both a preventive and remedial way. A loving mother prevents her children from going out in the cold without proper clothing and she is also careful to ensure that they do not play in dangerous places lest they have a possible accident and get hurt. She takes these preventive steps to protect her children from that which would harm them. Likewise, our Lord Jesus Christ intercedes for His children in a preventive way to keep them from falling into sin and in a remedial way when, in fact, they do stray into sin. The term "intercession" referring to the fact that Jesus Christ intercedes on behalf of believers could identify a great deal of His present work of mediation in heaven. Fundamentally, however, the Bible uses this term more specifically as it relates to the life and work of Christ on behalf of the believer's weakness and temptation.

Please note that Christ intercedes for us Himself. It is personal. He does not leave the task to another but is concerned to carry it out Himself. Since He knows each of His sheep intimately He knows best how to pray for us for our well-being.

Jesus Christ also intercedes for us perpetually. This work of intercession is not a once and for all event, but it continues perpetually. The writer of Hebrews wrote, "He ever lives to make intercession for them" (Hebrews 7:25). The Apostle Paul, in Romans 8:34, is pointing out the fact that since God is for us this perpetual intercession for us is carried out personally, passionately, purposely, perpetually, and perfectly (effectually) by Christ.

Many parents will teach their children to pray certain prayers at bedtime. They are taught to pray for others as well as themselves. Often these prayers can become mere recitations and ritualistic. Later in life as they mature, as they come to know Christ personally in a saving way through faith, and as they face the rigors of living and are exposed to the difficulties of life there will be a transformation in the kind of praying that they do. No longer will they merely recite memorized prayers but now they will become more fully engaged in their hearts as they pray for themselves and as they intercede for others.

The intercessory prayers of Christ are not mere recitations of the prayer list but are, in fact, an expression of the heart of God. Jesus, in His earthly mission, was, "moved with compassion" (Matthew 9:36). When He asked His disciples to intercede for the world, the biblical record states, "When He saw the crowds, He had compassion for them, because they were harassed and helpless, like sheep without a shepherd. Then He said to his disciples, "The harvest is plentiful, but the laborers are few; therefore, pray earnestly to the Lord of the harvest to send out laborers into His harvest" (Matthew 9:38). When Jesus prays for us He becomes actively involved in helping us. The writer of Hebrews wrote that we do not have a high priest who cannot be touched with the feeling of our weaknesses but He was tempted in all points like we are yet without sin. He then urged us to come boldly to the throne of grace to receive grace and mercy to help in times of need. Jesus feels for His children like a parent feels for his child when that child is going through difficult times. He intercedes for us from the heart with an active intercession. Jesus is concerned for our ongoing well-being. He told His disciples, "I will pray the Father and He shall give you another Comforter, that He may be with you forever" (John 14:16).

The intercession of Jesus for us is specific and relates to the specific needs and weaknesses in our own lives. Jesus knows us better than we know ourselves and He knows what is around the bend in our lives whereas we cannot know. In great love and with penetrating insight and wisdom Jesus faithfully prays for each of His followers in a precise and specific way suited for that believer.

The intercession of Jesus for believers is also preventive in nature. God does not delight in our failure. In the ministry of Jesus Christ as our intercessor He works in cooperation with the work of the Holy Spirit and Scripture to prevent us from sinning. After all, He died for us to deliver us from this present evil world and to sanctify us. David wrote, "I have stored up your Word in my heart, that I might not sin against you" (Psalm 119:11). Jesus intercedes for us in that same spirit with the intent of preventing us from falling into sin. "He leads us in paths of righteousness for His namesake" (Psalm 23:3b).

The intercession of Jesus for us is effective. The Bible teaches that, "The effectual, fervent prayer of a righteous man avails much" (James 5:16). We often use this passage as the means of encouragement in our own prayer life but it can also be applied to the prayer life of Christ. Certainly, no one is more righteous than Christ. Certainly, no one is more fervent in prayer than Christ. We can conclude, therefore, that His intercession for us is effective.

What happens when we fall into sin? And we all do, due to remaining sin. One of the most famous backsliders in the history of the church was Simon Peter. This man, who had followed Jesus faithfully for three years ultimately denied Him when Jesus made that final journey to the cross. Peter publicly and boldly denied that he had ever known Jesus of Nazareth. Is there any hope for such a man – for such a sinner?

Thankfully, we can easily answer that question because we have the biblical record of Jesus forgiving Peter of his sin and restoring him. Why did Jesus do that? In Luke 22:31–34, He does so because He is for us.

We have the biblical record of Jesus predicting Peter's denial. Jesus said, "Simon, Simon, indeed, Satan has asked for you, that he may sift you as wheat, but I have prayed for you, that your faith should not fail; and when you have returned to me, strengthen your brethren." Jesus knew that the time was coming when Simon Peter would buckle under pressure and temptation in a desperate move to save his own skin and in doing so would deny his Lord. Even knowing this Jesus comforted Peter by assuring him that he would not lose his faith. Why? Because Jesus was praying for him and interceding for him. We, too, can be confident of our salvation because of Jesus's promise, "I will pray for you."

We also have a record in the Bible of our Lord's intercessory prayer. It is recorded in John 17. In this prayer, Jesus prays for the safety and spiritual security of His followers (and for those who would come to believe through their ministry).

In this prayer, Jesus reveals that He is keenly aware of the difficulties facing His followers in this sinful world. He also reveals that one of His primary priorities is for His followers to be sanctified through the truth of God and so He prays for that reality (John 17:17). It is interesting as one reads this 17th chapter of John's Gospel containing the intercessory prayer of Jesus Christ that our Lord clearly states that He is not praying for the world but rather is praying for His followers. Such is still the case. Jesus is exclusively interceding for those who have embraced Him by faith and are following Him in obedience.

Not only has Christ died and secured our salvation, but He has been raised giving us a living hope and He has ascended to the right hand of God and is perpetually making personal, effectual, and passionate intercession on our behalf. What a glorious salvation! What a wonderful Savior! What a solid foundation we have for our confident assurance and sense of security as believers all because God is for us!

Can you begin to see just how perfect this salvation which God has given us is? Can you begin to understand what it means to be absolutely 100% secure in your salvation? Do these truths help you to get a better sense and perspective on the nature of the heart of God and how passionately

He loves us and is for us? Do these truths stir and enlarge your passion for God?

Such is clearly the context of the Apostle Paul's statement in this passage of Scripture. No one can successfully bring a charge or accusation against the true believer in Christ that would in any way jeopardize his salvation and security. Why? Because Jesus Christ, by His death, has satisfactorily paid for all our sins and God is fully and completely propitiated. God has already declared us to be justified through faith in Jesus Christ. Thus, despite what we may have been and done in a sinful way, God declares us to be completely righteous in Christ. Our sins have been placed upon Him and He has borne the penalty for them. His righteousness has been imputed to us (put to our account):

"For our sake He made Him to be sin who knew no sin, so that in Him we might become the righteousness of God" (2 Corinthians 5:21).

The accusations and charges of the naysayers are really of no relevance. They cannot be counted against us. Our salvation is perfect and complete because a perfect priest has offered a perfect sacrifice to provide us with a perfect salvation so that one day we will be perfect in a perfect world. Our salvation in Christ is eternal and never perishing. Through the resurrection of Jesus Christ, we have a living hope and a lasting inheritance that never fades away. Our salvation is impervious to the accusations and charges that might be brought against us since no charge or accusation "will stick." What a wonderful realization! Such is the context of Paul's statement. God is for us!

The Community of the Blessed Ones That Are in View

The Apostle Paul refers to the specific individuals or community of individuals who enjoy this freedom from any damaging accusations or charges by identifying them. He writes, "Who shall bring any charge against GOD'S ELECT." Who is this community of people to which he is referring? What does it mean to be "GOD'S ELECT?"

THE COMMUNITY: Elect

The word, "elect," in this context means, "to choose or pick, or select from out of a greater number." It has reference to a selective process whereby some individuals are chosen from among others. The people who are in view in this text are called the, "elect" (the chosen). The subjects of election do not include everyone, but only those whom God chose, hence the import and meaning of the word. Those whom God chooses are those whom He has declared holy and those He chose to be holy before the foundation of the world (Ephesians 1:4). These are those who come to be identified with His Son Jesus Christ by faith.

Being a Christian is a result of having been chosen by God to be His child and to inherit all things through and with Jesus Christ (Ephesians 1:4). In the Old Testament God chose the nation of Israel in a special way over and above the other nations of the earth to be the special recipients of divine blessings and protection. Moses reminded the Jewish people of this fact and consequently of God's special love for them and their special place among the nations. We read:

THE COMMUNITY: The Divine Election of Israel

Moses' message to Old Testament Israel reads: "For you are a holy people unto the Lord your God: the LORD your God has chosen you to be a special people unto Himself, above all people that are upon the face of the earth." He went on to write, "The Lord did not set His love upon you, nor choose you, because you were more in number than any people; for you were the fewest of all people: but because the Lord loved you, and because He would keep the oath which He had sworn unto your fathers..." (Deuteronomy 7:6 – 8a).

Not only did God choose Israel, He did so unconditionally (not based on anything in the nation itself) and He did so for special blessings. But not every Israelite was chosen by God in a spiritual and eternal way. God also sovereignly and freely chose a number of people within the nation of Israel to be recipients of eternal salvation. In the book of Romans, the Apostle Paul explains in detail the gospel of salvation and in doing so he also mentions that since the Jewish people sinfully rejected their Messiah/ the Lord Jesus Christ that they had been temporarily cut off by God, as a nation, from the blessings of salvation.

The question Paul is now forced to ask and answer is, whether or not this temporary disciplining/judgmental action on God's part calls into question the trustworthiness of God's promises toward Israel. In other words, has God abandoned Israel in terms of salvation? Has He failed to keep His Word? In his answer Paul will go on to show how Israel's chastisement by God in being temporarily removed from the path of salvation is just that–it is temporary and that they will be restored to their place of divine blessing in the future. Furthermore, Paul writes that this divine judgment/chastisement on the nation of Israel does not prohibit individual Jewish people from being saved in the present time. Quite the contrary. After all, Paul himself was a Jew and he was graciously saved by God unto eternal life through faith in Christ. The Apostle Paul teaches this truth very clearly in Romans 11:1–6a. There we read:

> "I say then, has God cast away His people? God forbid. For I also am an Israelite, of the seed of Abraham, of the tribe of Benjamin. God has not cast away His people which He foreknew. Do you not know what the Scripture says of Elijah? How he made intercession to God against Israel, saying, "LORD, they have killed your prophets, and destroyed your altars: and I am left alone, and they seek my life. But what was the answer of God to him? "I have reserved to myself 7000 men, who have not bowed the knee to the image of Baal. Even so at this present time also there is a remnant according to the election of grace. And if by grace, then it is no more of works: otherwise grace is no more grace. But if it is of works, then it is no more grace: otherwise work is no more work. What then? Israel has not obtained that which he seeks after; but the election has obtained it, and the rest were blinded" (Romans 11:1 – 7).

THE COMMUNITY: Election in
Other Old Testament Passages

Notice, that God's "election of grace" was operative in the days of Elijah just as it was in the days of the Apostle Paul. It has always been God's operative principle. It is still God's operative principle today. It was because of divine election, by God, that certain individuals (including Paul) were saved. Paul wants to make sure that his readers understand that God has not changed His ways (God has always operated in keeping with this process of election). God has not failed to uphold His Word – nor will He do so. He writes concerning this truth:

"But it is not as though the Word of God has failed. For not all who are descended from Israel belong to Israel, and not all are children of Abraham because they are his offspring, but, "through Isaac shall your offspring be named." This means that it is not the children of the flesh who are the children of God, but the children of the promise are counted as offspring. For this is what the promise said: "About this time next year I will return, and Sara shall have a son. And not only so, but also when Rebecca had conceived children by one man, our forefather Isaac, though they were not yet born and had done nothing either good or bad – in order that God's purpose of election might continue, not because of works but because of Him who calls–she was told, 'the older will serve the younger.' As it is written "Jacob I loved, but Esau I hated:" (Romans 9:6 – 13)

I hope you see the clear truth that God has always operated by utilizing the practice of election? It is not for us to question why God has chosen to operate in this manner. God is sovereign. He can operate in any way He chooses to and it will be right. It is for us to study the Word of God and discern, from it, what it teaches and to embrace that teaching as the Word and truth of God.

The Apostle Peter in his first epistle wrote to Christians and said, "But you are a chosen race, a royal priesthood, a holy nation, a people for His own possession, that you may proclaim the excellencies of Him who called you out of darkness into His marvelous light" (1 Peter 2:11). Consider also the Apostle Paul's words justifying God's action in election, "There is no injustice with God, is there? By no means!! For he says to Moses, I will have mercy on whom I have mercy, and I will have compassion on whom I have compassion." So, then it depends not on human will or exertion, but on God, who has mercy" (Romans 9:14–16).

THE COMMUNITY: Election is Unconditional

Again, let me stress that God's election of individuals is entirely unconditional. That is, it is not based upon the character of those chosen or on any meritorious conduct or foreseen faith on their part. It is an election of free and sovereign grace.

Specifically, we need to understand this in light of the preponderance of erroneous teaching current in contemporary Christianity about this subject. What is often taught today is that divine election is based on foreseen faith. This concept has taken root because of a weak understanding of the biblical doctrine of man's total depravity (sinfulness) and total inability. It has blossomed in the soil of the culture that treats man as the center of all things and minimizes the role of God and the impact of sin on the individual sinner. Technically, we are inundated in a culture of man centered humanism rather than a biblical, theocentric perspective.

The fact that the biblical teaching regarding unsaved man's spiritual deadness and depraved twistedness is not understood or is denied produces the false notion that it is within unsaved man to (in himself) desire salvation and to comply with the commands of God to repent and savingly believe in Jesus Christ. The Bible is clear that man has no appetite, in his sinful, unsaved condition for holiness and the things of God. Furthermore, the unsaved man cannot discern spiritual things. Because he is "dead in trespasses and sins" he is incapable of responding to spiritual stimuli or overtures apart from the new birth which comes from God alone.

Not only so, but, as has been previously stated, this weak, superficial understanding of the Scriptures has led many to assume that when the Bible says that Christians are "Elect according to the foreknowledge of God" that this "foreknowledge" is equivalent to God "foreseeing" the future (prescience). While it is true that God sees all things from beginning to end, that is not the biblical meaning of the term, "foreknowledge." There is no dispute that in His omniscience God is certainly able to look to the end of history and beyond and to know in advance the minutest detail of the most insignificant occurrences. That is how some interpret the word, "foreknowledge." But, it is both unbiblical and illogical to argue from the truth of God's omniscience that the Lord simply looked ahead to see who would believe and then chose those particular individuals for salvation.

If that were true, not only would salvation begin and be initiated by man's faith but it would also make God obligated to grant salvation (since man has already believed) and therefore remove divine grace as the cause of salvation. It would also deprive God of his glory as the sovereignly powerful savior of sinners. It is clear, however, from Scripture that saving faith does not originate with the sinner but with God and that God's grace is the moving cause behind the salvation of the individual sinner. "For by grace you have been saved through faith; and that not of yourselves, it is the gift of God; not as a result of works, that no one should boast." Interestingly, the Apostle Paul continues this passage by stating "FOR WE ARE HIS WORKMANSHIP, created in Christ Jesus unto good works, which God has before ordained that we should walk in them" (Ephesians 2:8–10). The words "workmanship" and "created" are extremely significant. "Workmanship" literally means masterpiece and refers to something which has been produced which is of significant worth and beauty. The word "created" reveals that just as God created the universe out of nothing by the Word of His power so has He created "new creatures in Christ" by his same creative power. This, again, underscores the fact that salvation is the work of God alone. It is not the work of man or the work of God and man combined.

Concerning the unsaved sinner's salvation, the Apostle Paul wrote to the Corinthians and said:

"For God, who commanded the light to shine out of darkness, has shined into our hearts to give the light of the knowledge of the glory of God in the face of Jesus Christ." (2 Corinthians 4:6).

Again, the apostle likens salvation to the original creative acts of God. He is saying to us that just as God created light out of abject darkness and nothingness in the original days of creation so does He create completely new spiritual creatures in Christ in divine salvation. Both are totally the workmanship of God alone. God is for us in that He created us anew in His own likeness.

God's foreknowledge has been dealt with in a previous chapter entitled "no situation." Suffice it to say, at this point, that foreknowledge is not a reference to God's omniscient foresight but to His foreordination and to His loving, intimate knowledge of certain sinners beforehand (before the foundation of the world). God ordains whatsoever comes to pass beforehand and therefore sees it clearly with a full knowledge of all the details. In Isaiah we read:

"Remember the former things of old: for I am God, and there is no one else; I am God, and there is no one like me. Declaring the end from the beginning and from ancient times the things that are not yet done, saying, "My counsel shall stand, and I will do all my pleasure." (Isaiah 46:10).

Even in the trials and crucifixion of Jesus Christ, the sinless one, God's foreordination was mysteriously but unmistakably at work bringing to pass the events that took place.

Divine "foreknowledge" carries with it two specific ideas. First, it has to do with "foreordination." Second, it has to do with an intimate loving relationship–beforehand.

Sinful man has no inclination toward or ability to savingly believe in Jesus Christ. Why? Because faith is a gift from God resulting in salvation (Ephesians 2:8–9) and without this sovereignly bestowed gift of faith sinful man inevitably and continuously refuses to seek God. God does not merely give sinful man the potential to believe but when He saves him He gives him the faith to believe with. The Apostle Paul makes this clear in his indictment of sinful man in Romans 3. This is a universal reality for all sinful, lost and unsaved men. We read: "As it is written, there is none righteous, no, not one: there is none that understands, there is no one that seeks after God" (Romans 3:10–11).

Sinful man in his depraved condition does not seek after God for salvation and, in fact, cannot do so. Cannot? Consider the words of our Lord *Jesus* Christ who said: "All that the Father gives me shall come to me; and he that comes to me I will in no way cast out" "No man can come to me except the Father which has sent me draws him; and I will raise him up at the last day." (John 6: 37, 44)

Notice that our Lord Jesus Christ stated that no one CAN come to him unless he is drawn by God the Father to Him and that everyone who is so drawn will come to Jesus and Jesus will raise him up at the last day. Further elaborating on sinful man's INABILITY to understand and seek salvation through faith in Christ, the Apostle Paul wrote:

"But the natural person does not accept the things of the spirit of God, for they are folly to him, and he is not able to understand them because they are spiritually discerned" (1 Corinthians 2:14).

According to Scripture, the natural or unsaved sinful man does not have the ability to know or embrace spiritual things nor does he have lying dormant within him saving faith that merely needs to be activated or exercised by him if he so wills.

The ancient heresy of Pelagianism is the belief that original sin did not drastically damage human nature and that the mortal will is still capable of choosing good or evil without special divine aid. This heresy derives its name from a British or Irish lay monk who made his way to Rome during the time of Augustine and taught in the fifth century Roman Catholic Church. His teaching stressed the freedom of the human will and the ability of the human spirit to respond to the things of God and to spiritual truth.

Growing out of this heresy of Pelagianism is what might be called semi—Pelagianism. It is rampant in today's church. It too, stresses the freedom of the human will and, contrary to Scripture, teaches that God so influences the human being by the Holy Spirit that he is brought to a state of virtual neutrality (it's sort of spiritual limbo) and then, the unsaved sinner is given the choice and the ability to discern spiritual truth and to positively respond in saving faith and to the gospel. This limbo – like state is thought to give every human being the equal opportunity to cooperate with God in his own salvation. Nowhere is such a doctrine taught in the Bible. Quite the contrary. The Bible always teaches that salvation is a divine work of God alone.

The Apostle John wrote, "He (Christ) came to His own, and His own people did not receive Him. But to all who did receive him, who believed in his name, he gave the right to become children of God, *who were born, not of blood nor of the will of the flesh nor of the will of man, but of God*" (John 1:11–13). (parentheses mine)

Notice that John is stressing the fact that our new birth and our ability to respond properly to God is a divine gift. It is attributable to God alone. This would be in keeping with our Lord Jesus Christ's comments to Nicodemus when he described the spiritual new birth as something which is brought about entirely by the Holy Spirit. It is not something which sinful man causes to happen.

Again, in 1 Corinthians 1 the Apostle Paul is defending his presentation of the gospel message and is refusing to alter it to suit the desires of his hearers. Paul goes on to state that some will reject the message of the cross but that those who are "called" by God respond personally and properly to the one true gospel while their peers often continue to reject it out of prejudice, pride, or preconceived notions that militate against the truth of God. In concluding his discussion on how salvation is made effectual to those who are called by God the Apostle Paul wrote, *"and because of Him* (God) you are in Christ Jesus, who became to us wisdom from God, righteousness, and sanctification, and redemption: so that, as it is written, "Let the one who boasts, boast in the Lord" (1 Corinthians 1: 30-31).

Here again, the Apostle Paul is underscoring that salvation is entirely a work of God on behalf of unsaved sinners.

He makes the same point when writing to the Ephesians believers. He reminds them that, "He (God) has chosen (elected them) us in Him (Christ) before the foundation of the world, in order that we should be holy and without blame before Him in love: having predestinated us onto the adoption of children by Jesus Christ to Himself, according to the good pleasure of His will, to the praise of the glory of His grace, wherein He has made us accepted in the Beloved" (Ephesians 1:4–6). (parentheses mine)

In this passage in Ephesians 1:4, the apostle identifies the time of our election (before the foundation of the world), the purpose of our election (that we should be holy and without blame before Him), and the results of our election (the elect are predestinated to be adopted as children by Jesus Christ), and He underscores the motivation behind our election (according to the good pleasure of His will and to the praise of the glory of His grace – in Christ).

I have heard some say that God does not choose people to salvation but only to service. It is true, that there is a sense in which there is an elective process regarding God's selection of certain people to certain spheres of service. But this does not mean that the concept of election is totally relegated to the realm of service and not the realm of salvation. The best way to respond to such reasoning is by consulting the Word of God. The Apostle Paul wrote, "But we ought always to give thanks to God for you, brothers beloved by the Lord, because God chose you as the first fruits to be saved, through sanctification by the Spirit and belief in the truth. To this He called you through our gospel so that you may obtain the glory of our Lord Jesus Christ" (2 Thessalonians 2: 13–14).

No, election is not confined to the area of service but it also extends to the area of salvation. Nor is Paul shy about speaking of our "election" by God in the normal course of his writings. When he wrote to his protégé, Timothy, and encouraged him to faithfully persevere in the face of hardships for the gospel he used his own experience as an example of doing so:

"For which I am suffering, bound with the chains of the criminal. But the Word of God is not bound! Therefore, I endure everything for the sake of the elect, that they also may obtain the salvation that is in Christ Jesus with eternal glory" (2 Timothy 2:9 – 11).

The Lord Jesus Christ also freely used the terminology of "divine election." In describing the time of the Second Coming He said, "And he will send out His angels with a loud trumpet call, and they will gather his elect from the four winds, from one end of heaven to the other" Matthew 24:31. In describing the horrific conditions of the Great Tribulation our Lord Jesus Christ said, "For then there will be great tribulation, such as has not been from the beginning of the world until now, no, and never will be. And if those days had not been cut short, no human being would be saved. But for the sake of the elect those days will be cut short" (Matthew 24:21 – 22).

"Election" is a concept that permeates the Bible and it is completely and freely God's sovereign choice apart from anything in the one elected. It occurred before the foundation of the world Ephesians 1:4, and pertains to a group of people chosen to be the recipients of divine salvation purely for the glory of God and as a tribute to His sovereign grace in Jesus Christ. These people can rightfully and truly say, "God is for us!"

As I have already indicated, in addition to the idea of foreordination, the term, "foreknowledge," also emphasizes the idea of an intimate love for its object. God not only has a predetermined plan for those He intends to save, but He also has a predetermined divine love for them as well. This understanding of, "election," gives real force and meaning to the words of the Apostle Paul when he wrote, "Who shall lay any thing to the charge of God's elect? It is God who justifies" (Romans 8:33).

The venerable hymn writer, Isaac Watts, expressed these biblical concepts with his usual poetic eloquence. Note the words of stanzas two through four in light of what we have been studying:

How Sweet and Awful is the Place

How sweet and awful is the place
With Christ within the doors,
While everlasting love displays
The choicest of her stores.

While all our hearts and all our songs
Join to admire the feast,
Each of us cry with thankful tongues,
"LORD, why was I a guest?

Why was I made to hear Thy voice
And enter while there's room,
When thousands make a wretched choice
And rather starve than come?

'Twas the same love that spread the feast
That sweetly drew us in,
Else we had still refused to taste
And perished in our sin.

Pity the nation's, O our God,
Constrain the earth to come;
Send thy victorious Word abroad
And bring the strangers home.

We long to see Thy churches full
That all the chosen race,
May with one voice and heart and soul
Sing Thy redeeming grace."

While everything we have said thus far about God's unconditional election of sinners unto salvation is absolutely biblical, true and vitally important, we must also balance this truth with the biblical teaching of man's responsibility to properly respond to the gospel message.

Once our Lord Jesus Christ was attending a banquet and, as usual, He used the occasion to teach spiritual truths. During the course of one of His teachings we read:

"When one of those who reclined at table with Him heard these things, he said to Him, "Blessed is everyone who will eat bread in the kingdom of God!" But He said to him, "A man once gave a great banquet and invited many. And at the time for the banquet he sent his servant to say to those who had been invited, "Come, for everything is now ready. But they all alike began to make excuses. The first said to him, "I have bought a field, and I must go out and see it. Please have me excused." And another said, "I have bought five yoke of oxen, and I go to examine them. Please have me excused." And another said, "I have married a wife, and therefore I cannot come." So, the servant came and reported those things to his master. Then the master of the house became angry and said to his servant, "Go out quickly to the streets and lanes of the city, and bring in the poor and crippled and blind and lame." And the servant said, "Sir, what you commanded has been done, and still there is room." And the master said to the servant, "Go out to the highways and the hedges and compel people to come in, that my house may be filled. For I tell you, none of those men who were invited shall taste my banquet" (Luke 14:15–24).

While I understand that parables teach one specific lesson there are, however, many insightful observations that we could make from this parable. Some of these insightful observations were noted in a sermon by my pastor (Dr. Lee Pigg of Hopewell Baptist Church, Monroe, North Carolina).

The full provision and invitation of the master – (notice that the master was involved personally and that the open invitation was extended to many).

The false excitement – the parable is preceded by the excited exclamation of one who professes enthusiasm about eating bread in the kingdom of God. There are many who have a superficial enthusiasm regarding the things of God but that enthusiasm is shallow and evaporates quickly. They are like emotional sparks that are extinguished and burned out in short order.

The foolish excuses – people make all kinds of excuses for why they will not respond to the Masters invitation. Those excuses cover a wide range of flimsy reasons which are intended to mask the real reason that they do not respond properly to the master – they simply do not want to. Unsaved sinners make continual foolish excuses for rejecting the gospel and the master's overtures. They simply want nothing to do with the master.

The further enticements – not only did the master invite and include those in his banquet that would normally never entertain the idea of being invited into the master's house, but he also sent his servant out again to, "compel people" to come in and partake. This word, "compel," carries with it the idea of pleading and doing whatever is necessary to ensure the compliance of those that are invited. It is clear that the master is greatly concerned that people respond properly to his invitation.

The final declaration – the excuses of the ones who were originally invited and their rejection of the master's invitation angered the master. His final declaration was that none of those who rejected his invitation would taste of his banquet.

God has invited people to partake of salvation – a salvation which has been freely provided by Him. People continue to make foolish and fateful decisions to reject this gracious invitation. The most needy and infirmed are invited to come and partake freely. Those, however, who choose to reject the master's gracious invitation and provisions will never taste of His banquet and they have no one to blame for this fact but themselves.

While divine election is a biblical reality, human responsibility is also a biblical reality. God does not tell us how the two truths mesh harmoniously but simply presents them as facts. He, and perhaps He alone, understands exactly how these truths work together.

The emphasis of the Apostle Paul in Romans 8:33 is focused on the work of God in Christ in securing our salvation. He has loved us and chosen us before the foundation of the world in Christ, He continues to love us in Christ and to powerfully meet our every need in the present, and He will always love us for all eternity. Our Lord Jesus Christ has secured us and made it possible for us to be justified before God. We give evidence that we are God's elect if we have trusted by faith alone in Jesus Christ as our Lord and Savior. We simply trust in Christ to save us from sin to holiness. The Apostle Peter exhorts us as Christians to live in such a holy and biblical way that we "confirm" our calling and election" (2 Peter

1:10b). The community of people that Paul has in view, in our text, is the company of the "elect." Truly, it can rightly be said of each of God's elect that God is for us.

We must never forget, that God's elect are chosen in Christ alone. Jesus Christ is central to everything in the believer's salvation.

Concerning the centrality and vital importance of Jesus Christ as the means of our salvation and the basis of our assurance of salvation C. H. Spurgeon wrote the following when commenting on Hebrews 12:2, *"Looking unto Jesus."*

He wrote:

> "It is ever the Holy Spirit's work to turn our eyes away from self to Jesus; but Satan's work is just the opposite of this, for he is constantly trying to make us regard ourselves instead of Christ. He insinuates, "Your sins are too great for pardon; you have no faith; you do not repent enough; you will never be able to continue to the end; you have not the joy of His children; you have such a wavering hold of Jesus." All these are thoughts about self, and we shall never find comfort or assurance by looking within. But the Holy Spirit turns our eyes entirely away from self: He tells us that we are nothing, but that "Christ is all in all." Remember, therefore, it is not thy hold of Christ that saves us–it is Christ; it is not thy joy in Christ that saves thee–it is Christ; it is not even faith in Christ, though that be the instrument–it is Christ's blood and merits; therefore, look not so much at thy right hand with which thou art grasping Christ, but to Christ; look not to thy hope, but to Jesus, the source of thy hope; look not to thy faith; but to Jesus, the author and finisher of thy faith. We shall never find happiness by looking at our prayers, our doings, or our feelings; it is what Jesus is, not what we are, that gives rest to the soul. If we would at once overcome Satan and have peace with God, it must be by "looking unto Jesus." Keep thine eye simply on him; let His death, His sufferings, His merits, His glories, His intercessions, be

fresh upon thy mind; when thou wakest in the morning look to Him; when thou liest down look to Him, He will never fail to give you rest for your soul. If we would once overcome Satan and have peace with God, look to Him.

Oh! Let not thy hopes and fears come between thee and Jesus; follow hard after Him, and He will never fail thee."

"My hope is built on nothing less
Than Jesus' blood and righteousness,
I dare not trust the sweetest frame
But wholly lean on Jesus name."

(C H Spurgeon, *Morning and Evening, McDonald publishing, McLean Virginia, 22102)*

So far, we have noted the context of this passage which is rooted in the saving work of Jesus Christ. We have noted also the community of people in view in this passage–the elect. Finally, let us take note of:

The Confident Assurance Exhibited

In this verse, it is as if the Apostle Paul is boldly throwing out an open and confident challenge to anyone and everyone regarding God's elect. "WHO" shall bring any charge against God's elect? "WHO" is to condemn? Paul then points to the perfect, finished work of our Lord Jesus Christ in saving us the propitiation of His death on the cross. He also points us to the powerful proof that His sacrifice was accepted by God as seen in his resurrection from the dead, and then he underscores the ongoing perpetual intercession of Jesus on our behalf. On what basis does our Lord Jesus Christ intercede for us? His intercession for us before God is based on the merits of His saving work on our behalf. "He has paid it all, all to Him we owe." He intercedes for us feelingly, lovingly, effectually, perpetually and personally based on His love for us and based on what He has accomplished for us – our Lord Jesus Christ is for us.

"Since then we have a great high priest who has passed through the heavens, Jesus, the Son of God, let us hold fast our confession. For we do not have a high priest who is unable to sympathize with our weaknesses, but one who in every respect has been tempted as we are, yet without sin. Let us then with confidence draw near to the throne of grace, that we may receive mercy and find grace to help in time of need" (Hebrews 4:14 – 16).

Paul's point in Romans 8:33 is to underscore the absolute confidence and assurance that we should have in our God-given, perfect, guaranteed salvation in Christ as God's elect. We are absolutely and eternally safe and secure because God is for us.

But, someone may say with Job, "How many are my iniquities and sins?" (Job 13:23). Job was intimidated and overwhelmed with a sense of his own mountain of iniquities and sins. How could he hope for a holy God to be for him when he was such a sinner in God's eyes? C. H. Spurgeon commented on this passage and said:

> "Have you ever really weighed and considered how great the sin of God's people is? Think how heinous is your own transgression, and you will find that not only does a sin here and there tower up like an alp, but that your iniquities are heaped upon each other, as in the old fable of the giants who piled Pelion upon Ossa, mountain upon mountain. What an aggregate of sin there is in the life of one of the most sanctified of God's children! Attempt to multiply this, the sin of one only, by the multitude of the redeemed, "a number which no man can number," and you will have some conception of the great mass of the guilt of the people for whom Jesus shed His blood. But we arrive at a more adequate idea of the magnitude of sin by the greatness of the remedy provided. It is the blood of Jesus Christ, God's only and well–beloved Son! Angels cast their crowns before him! All the chorus symphonies of heaven surround His glorious throne. "God over all, blessed forever. Amen." And yet He takes upon Himself the form of a servant and is scourged and pierced, bruised and torn, and at last slain; since nothing but the blood of the incarnate Son of God could make atonement for our offenses. No human mind can adequately estimate the

infinite value of the divine sacrifice, for as great as is the sin of God's people, the atonement which takes it away is immeasurably greater. Therefore, believer, even when sin rolls like a black flood, and the remembrance of the past is bitter, can you stand before the blazing throne of the great and holy God, and cry "Who is he that condemns?" It is Christ that died; yes rather, that has risen again." While the recollection of sin fills him with shame and sorrow, he at the same time makes it a foil to show the brightness of mercy–guilty as the dark night in which the fair light of divine love shines with serene splendor." (C. H. Spurgeon, *Morning and Evening*, McDonald Publishing Company, McLean Virginia 22102, page 377.)

THE CONFIDENT ASSURANCE: The Force & Future Implications of the Resurrection

The Apostle Peter wrote, "Blessed be the God and Father of our Lord Jesus Christ! According to His great mercy, He has caused us to be born again to a living hope through the resurrection of Jesus Christ from the dead, to an inheritance that is imperishable, undefiled, and unfading kept in heaven for you, who by God's power are being guarded through faith for a salvation ready to be revealed in the last time" (1 Peter 1:3 – 5).

What a wonderful reality! If God is for us (and He most certainly is) who then can be against us? Who can level a charge against us that will stick? Who will condemn us in light of the immeasurably great and perfect sacrifice that has been given for our sins? We can have absolute confidence and assurance in our salvation as God's elect–as those who are trusting in Jesus Christ for our salvation. Since God is undoubtedly for us, in so many ways, our confident assurance in our salvation can be absolute and our passion for the God that we love is continually being enlarged and expanded in ever deepening ways.

So then, in this verse we have noted:

The Context – The sacrificial death and resurrection of Jesus Christ coupled with His ongoing intercession for those He came to save and who are trusting in Jesus Christ alone by faith alone for their salvation.

The Community of People in View – God's elect, those He foreknew (foreordained/foreloved), predestinated to be saved, and redeemed by the blood of His only begotten Son.

The Confident Assurance Exhibited –Since God is for us who then can be against us, who can successfully charge us with any sin, etc. Indeed, for the true child of God no accusation brought against us will stand.

SINCE GOD IS FOR US WHAT A WONDERFUL
SALVATION WE HAVE AS BELIEVERS
IN JESUS CHRIST! God is for us!

BRINGING IT HOME

1. Do you ever worry that some accusation or charge might be brought against you when you stand before God that has slipped through the cracks in terms of being paid for and that you will surprisingly find yourself still guilty of that sin? Why can or cannot this happen?

2. What does the resurrection of Jesus Christ from the dead prove and what does it pave the way for?

3. What is Jesus Christ doing at the right hand of God at the present time?

4. Why is it important to understand the doctrine of, "election," and "foreknowledge?" Can you describe what each of these means?

5. Does God want you to be confident and assured regarding your security in salvation? How do the truths of Romans 8 relate to this subject?

13

Since God is for Us there is:

NO SEPARATION

Romans 8:35 – 39

"Who shall separate us from the love of Christ? Shall tribulation, or distress, or persecution, or famine, or nakedness, or danger, or sword? As it is written, "For your sake we are being killed all the day; we are regarded as sheep to be slaughtered." "No, in all these things we are more than conquerors through Him who loved us. For I am sure that neither death nor life, nor angels nor rulers, nor things present nor things to come, nor powers, nor height nor depth, nor anything else in all creation, will be able to separate us from the love of God in Christ Jesus our Lord."

The Apostle Paul has been telling us in a variety of different ways that as Christians we are loved by God beyond our most creative and expansive imagination and that our identity as a child of God in Christ is secure – because of God's good grace. In effect, he has been stressing to us that our God is a, "good, good Father" and that our good, good father is for us as our Father. He has taken care of and will take care of all our needs and has secured for us eternal life in heaven with absolute certainty. God will always love us. God will never abandon us. God will always protect us. God will always provide for us. We can rejoice in the fact that we have a "good, good Father." Consequently, we have a salvation given to us by God the Father that is secure and unshakable. Since God is for us it is ironclad and guaranteed. Furthermore, this sense of absolute security and confidence that God has so richly blessed us and is with us and for us forms the basis of a life that is free to stand up and step forward to promote and defend the cause of God with champion like courage. Like David, our increased knowledge of the person of God and his loving commitment to us serves to immeasurably increase our spiritual passion for God. From our study of Romans chapter eight using the book "Since God is for us," we have discovered the detailed proves of all the various ways that God has demonstrated that he is both for us and with us. We are thus equipped with a rock-solid confidence that since He is with us it does not matter who stands against us. Fueled with these two essential ingredients of biblical understanding we are, then, fully equipped to be David-like champions for our God. We are now ready to stand strong and courageous against the giants of life that oppose us.

To add to these wonderful truths of God's commitment to us, the Apostle Paul adds the crowning touch to this chapter by assuring believers, in unmistakable terms, that God loves us and that we cannot be separated from the wonderful love of God in Christ Jesus.

The hymn writer of yesteryear pondering the Words of God recorded in the Old Testament, wrote on this very theme applying the same truth to the people of God in the church. No doubt, the passage that had captured his attention and his heart as he wrote was Jeremiah 31:3, "I have loved you with an everlasting love; I have drawn you with unfailing kindness." He wrote:

> "Loved with everlasting love,
> Led by grace that love to know;
> Spirit, breathing from above,
> You have taught me it is so.
> What a full and perfect peace
> Joy and wonder all divine!
> In a love which cannot cease
> I am His, and He is mine.
>
> Heaven above is softer blue
> Earth around his richer green
> Something lives in every hue,
> Christless eyes have never seen:

Songs of birds in sweetness grow,
Flowers with deeper beauties shine,
Since I know, as now I know
I am His, and He is mine.

His forever, His alone!
Who the Lord and me shall part?
With what joy and peace unknown
Christ can fill the loving heart!

Heaven and earth may pass away,
Sun and stars in gloom decline,
But while Christ and I shall be:
I am His, and He is mine. (Author: Wade Robinson, 1842)

Take a moment and mentally review the exciting and wonderful journey that we have taken in Romans chapter eight guided by the book "Since God is for us." The Apostle Paul began the chapter with the confident concept THAT GOD IS FOR US and showed how He accomplished salvation for us so that for those who are saved through faith in Christ, "There is therefore now:

NO CONDEMNATION – The Apostle Paul's meaning is that, for believers, we are delivered forever from condemnation (v 1). In a very real way the rest of the chapter is a systematic unpacking and application of this important truth. Never again will a true believer in Christ ever be exposed to the possibility of condemnation. We are forever delivered from the threat of condemnation because of the grace of God sending His own Son as the full payment for all our sins. Furthermore, since God is for us there is also:

NO DOMINATION – Paul went on to emphasize that those who are freed from condemnation are also inevitably changed inwardly in their natures by the powerful work of the Holy Spirit and that they can now never be dominated by sin again in terms of an overall lifestyle – never again (Romans 6:14, 8:4 – 8). This, of course, does not mean that the believer is freed from struggling with sin and at times can temporarily be overcome by it. What it does mean, however, is that the believer's fundamental character and nature is so dramatically changed by the work of the Holy Spirit that he now wants to be free from sin and its contamination/control and eagerly desires righteousness. Furthermore, God graciously causes this to happen in the life of the Christian. This is true of all genuinely saved people. "Blessed are they who hunger and thirst after righteousness: for they shall be filled… Blessed are the pure in heart: for they shall see God" (Matthew 5:6, 8). Because God is for us, He forever and powerfully delivers us from the reign and domination of sin over us. The true believer is, thereby, freed from the dominion of sin. In addition, since God is for us there will be:

NO ISOLATION – (Romans 8:9 – 11) – God has provided for the believer in such a way that he will never be isolated and left alone to fend for himself in this world which is hostile to holiness and filled with corruption and sinfulness. Our loving God has graciously caused each believer to be indwelt perpetually, powerfully, personally, practically, and permanently by none other than the Almighty person of the Holy Spirit. The Holy Spirit is the divine, "earnest," (foretaste, and guarantee from God of our eternal inheritance.) By the Holy Spirit the believer is sealed, identified and secured until the day of redemption. *Since God is for us,* the Holy Spirit is our constant protector, guarantee, teacher, encourager, guide, enabler, etc. The believer is never isolated, therefore, but is always indwelt by the Holy Spirit – the third member of the Trinity. Furthermore, in this wonderful salvation that God has powerfully and graciously blessed us with the believer's sense of debt and obligation has drastically changed. Now, there is:

NO OBLIGATION (to continue in sin) – (Romans 8:1–14). Whereas, when the sinner was yet unsaved, his masters (Satan, the sinful flesh, the sinful world system) demanded obedience, in the area of sinfulness. Unsaved sinners felt a compulsive need to obey the dictates of the sinful. The unbeliever felt compelled to comply with these dictates. Indeed, the unsaved person has a nature that delights in and thirsts for sin. Now, however, having been saved, the believer is no longer disposed to or obligated in any way to continue in sin. Rather, because of God's great grace in saving us by grace through faith we owe our entire allegiance to God in Christ to live for Him. "For the love of Christ controls us, because we have concluded this: that one has died for all, therefore all have died; and He died for all, that those who live might no longer live for themselves but for Him who for their sake died and was raised" (2 Corinthians 5:14–15). There is more. Since God is for us there can be:

NO ALIENATION – (Romans 8:14 – 17). Because the believer has been graciously adopted by God he has been given the Spirit of adoption as a child of God and has been granted the privilege of being a coheir with Jesus Christ. The Apostle Paul chose to employ the metaphor of adoption because adoption in the Roman culture was nonreversible. In other words, once adoption was consummated legally it was binding forever. Not only is the believer made secure by this gracious transaction but he is granted a work of the Holy Spirit which causes him to more fully understand and deeply appreciate that the act of divine adoption has, indeed, taken place for him. The Holy Spirit also testifies powerfully with our spirit that we are indeed children of God. There is never any alienation from God for the true believer. And yes, there is even more to ensure our absolute security in our salvation. Since God is for us there is:

NO FRUSTRATION (in perpetuity) – This is not to say that there are not present frustrations as we live the Christian life in a world contaminated by sin, and as we live in bodies still plagued by remaining sin. What is true is that present frustrations will not endure forever and we will ultimately receive that which we eagerly long for in terms of complete freedom/ deliverance from sin and its effects (Romans 8: 18–30). The frustrations that we sometimes feel as believers in struggling with sin and its temptation are very real. So are the frustrations during those times when we do not know what to pray for as we ought to. We also experience those times when the excruciating experience of frustration overtakes us because we are trying to reconcile the seeming bad things that are happening in our lives with the fact that God loves us, has promised to work these things out for our ultimate good and that He will eventually save us for all eternity. These frustrations are very real but they are only temporary, and even in those times of frustration, God's truth and the Holy Spirit help us and comfort us. We are taught that God is working in all things for our good and that everyone who has been foreknown by God (fore–loved and foreordained) will ultimately be glorified. All frustrations will one day be removed and God provides help and insight to aid us in dealing with present frustrations. Then, too, thankfully, *since God is for us* there will be:

NO ELIMINATION – No one who is foreknown/foreordained by

God in eternity past will ever be lost. God has predestinated that each one of these people will be called, justified, and ultimately glorified. Not one of them will be eliminated from salvation but all will be securely kept by God's grace, love, and power in Christ. And it should be stressed that though each one of us will be forced to face uncertainties and difficulties as we move along in our journey toward our future home in heaven, since God is for us, there needs to be:

NO TREPIDATION – (Romans 8:31) The true believer need never fear or be intimidated by anything whatsoever since, "God is for us." The Apostle Paul is making the assertion that it really doesn't matter who or what stands against the believer and tries to prevent the believer from being eternally secure because God is with us – then, "Who can be against us?" At least, who can be against us successfully and effectively? There is no one and no thing that can compete with God or thwart the will of God and since God is with us there will also be:

NO DEPRIVATION – The believer will never be deprived of anything that he needs to successfully be eternally saved (Romans 8:32). God as our gracious and faithful benefactor has already demonstrated the great links to which He will go in securing our eternal salvation. He has already given us His own Son as a sacrifice for our salvation. It is therefore, inconceivable that God will not also give us everything and anything we need to be eternally saved and secure. For the believer, there will never be any deprivation!

In addition, the all-knowing and infinitely just God has declared us to be righteous in his eyes because we have been relieved of our own unrighteousness and given the righteousness of Jesus Christ. This has all been accomplished in the will of God. Therefore, since God is for us there can be:

NO ACCUSATION – (Romans 8:33–34) The Apostle Paul issues an open challenge to anyone who thinks he may be able to accuse or charge God's elect with an accusation that will stick and that will render the Christian guilty before God. Paul's argument is that Jesus Christ our Lord has paid in full, by the sacrifice of Himself, for every single sin of God's elect. Furthermore, His sacrifice was fully received and accepted by God. This has been demonstrated by the physical resurrection of Jesus Christ from the dead. In addition, our Lord Jesus Christ is actively interceding for the believer based on the infinite merits of His finished work on their behalf. It is therefore impossible for anyone, at any time, in any sphere to bring an accusation or charge against God's elect which has not already been dealt with in a final and complete way. Thus, for the believer, there is no accusation.

This leaves us with the final declaration of the Apostle Paul regarding God's perfect work in guaranteeing the ultimate assurance of our eternal salvation. It is the last and final stop on the tour of Romans chapter eight – Romans 8:35–39. In this final section, the Apostle Paul ends this chapter with a crescendo of praise and confidence in God. Specifically, he says that in addition to all the other enormous blessings that the believer has through faith in Christ and by God's grace, since God is with us there is also:

NO SEPARATION – (Romans 8:36–39) - Nothing will ever separate us, as believers, from the love of God which is in Christ Jesus. In Jeremiah 29:11 God said to Israel, "For I know the thoughts that I think toward you, says the LORD, thoughts of peace, and not of evil, to give you an expected end (a certain hope)." (Parentheses mine) In as many words, God says the same thing to believers in the New Testament.

Throughout the eighth chapter of the book of Romans God has revealed His thoughts toward we who are His people–thoughts of peace and not of evil. Further, God has promised us present help and safety as well as a successful and glorious future in heaven. We are saved "in hope" (Romans 8:24a). The Apostle Peter also emphasized this biblical truth when he wrote of the fact that we, as believers, are spiritually born into a living hope and that we are guaranteed an eternal, never fading inheritance in heaven. Moreover, Peter ensures us that we are being "kept" or guarded in our salvation during our present life on earth (1 Peter 1:3–5).

I am sure that at some point in time you have observed a tiny baby who was so attached to his mother that he cried frantically and uncontrollably when separated from her? This is referred to as, "separation anxiety." Perhaps, you have also observed or personally experienced the heartfelt separation when servicemen/women are deploying to a foreign field for military service. Often, they are being placed in harm's way. The military person will be in harm's way and separated from their loved ones for months at a time. The sense of heightened emotions at the time of their departure and deployment is very real and dramatically strong. Separation can be very difficult and emotional.

I once had a job that required me to travel away from home for five days per week. I had never been forced to be away from my wife and children before and I had been married for over 20 years at the time. I was accustomed to being in my home with my family in a familiar and comfortable setting every night. It was secure, warm, and loving. I vividly remember the awful feeling of homesickness and the dread of being separated from my family that I experienced during those times of travel and separation. I had never really known that kind of inner pain could be caused by such times of separation. No doubt, many readers of this book can identify with the rigors and emotional struggles caused by separation.

These illustrations are common experiences in our world. We are even familiar with the universal experience of being separated in a dramatic fashion from our loved ones when they die.

Though these examples of separation remind us that such times are often painful, there remains the bond of enduring love when distance and even death separate individuals. It would be horribly tragic, however, if someone who deeply loved us and someone we trusted completely would, for some reason, stop loving us altogether. That is, it would be tragic if the fire of love utterly died and was extinguished and quenched so that not even a smoldering ember of the previous love remained.

Just Imagine

Imagine a good, loving father, a good provider and a committed protector of his family. Imagine this loving father who delighted in each member of his family and embraced them with loving warmth and loyalty. Picture this father who always promoted the best interests of each family member with tenderness and thoughtfulness nurtured by deep love. Then, imagine that this same father who is the idol and stalwart of his children and the tender, loving companion of his wife suddenly loses all love and affection for them. He walks away from the family as if he never had a relationship with it. He leaves the children to fend for themselves and to protect themselves and to live in a world where they are no longer loved nor cared for. He abandons his wife and acts as if she never even existed in his life. Sadly, in a world that has been corrupted and twisted by sin this sometimes occurs but it cannot and will not take place with God and His children. Nothing can separate us from the love of God which is in Christ Jesus! Dear Christian, does that not comfort your heart and cause you to love God even more passionately than you ever have before? Hallelujah! God is and will always be for us.

The Apostle Paul has been assuring the believer in Christ, in Romans chapter eight, that God is in complete control of his salvation and is ensuring and will ensure his absolute security in Christ. No truth could more strongly drive this point home to the reader than to know that, in Christ, nothing and no one can ever separate us from God's love for us and from Christ's love for us. In this section of Romans chapter eight the Apostle Paul ends this chapter with a crescendo of glorious praise and confidence declaring that for the believer in Christ there is NO SEPARATION from the love of Christ and from the love of God.

AN OPEN CHALLENGE: A Declaration of Confidence

The Apostle Paul puts his imagination to work and rhetorically shoots out question after question regarding every conceivable person or circumstance that might be thought as threatening to the permanence of God's love for the believer. He keeps asking, "WHO or WHAT shall separate us from the love of God in Christ Jesus?"

Difficult and dangerous circumstances can sometimes detrimentally influence the faith and endurance of believers. Although, even in those difficult circumstances God, in His grace, powerfully and mysteriously works "all things" for the good of His elect (those who are called according to his purpose). Can these difficult circumstances sever a believer from the love of God by causing him to sin himself out of salvation and God's favor? Here, Paul anticipates and refutes the idea that any circumstance (in the present or in the future, in this world or the next) will be able to cause a believer to lose his salvation and cease being loved by God.

The apostle references both the, "love of Christ," and the, "love of God in Christ Jesus." Can anything cause Christ to turn his back on the believer? Can anything cause God to stop loving the believer? Paul cites several threatening circumstances in the concluding verses of Romans chapter eight and confidently asserts that NOTHING will ever separate us, as believers, from God's love in Christ.

Two Things Needed

To fully appreciate the magnitude and meaning of what the Apostle Paul is teaching here in this section of Romans chapter eight we need to do two things. They are:
1. Establish a clear understanding of God's love
2. Embrace a joyous and confident assurance of the permanence of God's love for us

Apart from understanding what God's love is, we cannot fully appreciate or embrace, with joy and confidence, the awesomely glorious fact that He will always love us. At this point, one might be tempted to think that such a full knowledge of and complete trust in God must surely be something only, "Super–Saints" or saints like the early apostolic saints could enjoy. Yet, such is not the case. All of this is available to every saint.

Commenting on this truth from the biblical phrase, *"Called to be Saints"* (Romans 1:7), Spurgeon wrote:

> "We are very tempted to regard the apostolic Saints as if they were "Saints" in a more especial manner than the other children of God. All are "Saints" whom God has called by His grace, and sanctified by His Spirit; but we are apt to look upon the apostles as extraordinary beings, scarcely subject to the same weaknesses and temptations as ourselves. Yet in so doing we are forgetful of this truth, that the nearer a man lives to God the more intensely he has to mourn over his own evil heart; and the more his Master honors him and his service, the more also does the evil of the flesh vex and tease him day by day. The fact is, if we had seen the Apostle Paul, we should have thought him remarkably like the rest of the chosen family: and if we had talked with him, we should have said, "We find that his experience and ours are much the same. He is more faithful, more holy, and more deeply taught then we are, but he has the selfsame trials to endure. Nay, in some respects he is more sorely tried than ourselves. "Do

not, then, look upon the ancient Saints as being exempt from infirmities or sins; and do not regard them with that mystic reverence which will almost make us idolaters. Their holiness is attainable even by us. We are "called to be Saints" by that same voice which constrained them to live in faithfulness to God. It is a Christian's duty to force his way into the inner circle of saintship; and if the Saints were superior to us in their attainments, as they certainly were, let us follow them; let us emulate their ardor in holiness. We have the same light that they had, the same grace is assessable to us, and why should we rest satisfied until we have equaled them in heavenly character? They lived with Jesus, they lived for Jesus, therefore they grew like Jesus. Let us live by the same Spirit as they did, "looking unto Jesus," and our saintship will soon be apparent." (C. H. Spurgeon, *Morning and Evening*, McDonald Publishing Company, McLean Virginia 22102, page 374.)

God Wants You to Know His love & Rejoice In It

Dear reader, I want you to know that God wants you to understand and experience these precious truths of Romans chapter eight (including His never-ending love for you) and He wants you to understand and experience them at the highest level. Such confidence in God, such assurance in the security of our salvation, such appreciation for the magnitude of God's love, grace, wisdom, and power on our behalf in Christ Jesus is attainable and assessable by every true Christian. Moreover, God delights in our appreciative reveling in His love for us as His children. We, too, can be assured that nothing and no one will ever separate us from the love of God which is in Christ Jesus.

It is vitally important that we get our minds and hearts around this concept that God is love and that He loves us as believers in Christ. To help you, the reader, do so I would like to approach our investigation of the love of God in the following way:

The Establishment of a Clear Understanding of God's Love

The powerfully clear biblical assertion that "God is love" is a good place for us to start our investigation of God's love.

Fundamental to our understanding of God's love is the Apostle John's thrice repeated statement, *"God is love"* (1 John 4:8, 16). These statements have terrific import but they are also terribly misunderstood by many. Many have assumed that because, "God is love," this must mean that He is benevolently disposed toward every person and therefore will "lovingly" receive every person into heaven when they die. These people assume that because, "God is love," that He will deliberately overlook any misbehavior of human beings except perhaps those of the most radical and inhumane. These errant beliefs are born and bred from the misunderstanding of the Bible's meaning or the deliberate twisting of the Bible's meaning when it declares that, "God is love." One thing is certain, however, and of that there can be no argument and that is that the Bible definitely and deliberately asserts the undeniable truth that, "God is love."

Since this statement is clearly made in the Bible regarding the God of the Bible, let us do a quick survey of some of the particular deeds and actions of this biblical God who is described as, "love." This survey of God's actions as recorded in Scripture will help us to avoid embracing a wrong idea of the fact that "God is love."

The Particular Deeds and Activities Ascribed to God in the Bible – God made the world in creation and it was all divinely declared to be very good. He lovingly provided for Adam and Eve in a most generous manner. But, then He destroyed the great bulk of mankind from the face of the earth by the universal flood killing all but eight people because of their sinfulness. When He was finished with His destruction of mankind you could have seated the entire remaining population of the earth around an average dining room table.

God not only created mankind but He also graciously chose and established the nation of Israel as His own. He loved them and provided unique and gracious blessings to them. Beginning with Abraham and eventually, through Moses, God gave them a law to keep with the divine promises of both a positive and a punitive nature. When Israel disobeyed God and rebelled against Him God severely chastened His Old Testament people by causing them to be defeated by their enemies. Depriving them of freedom He caused them to become captives, and He also exiled them from their land and from the place of divine blessing.

Later, in love God sent His Son into the world, through the nation of Israel, to save sinners. In love he provided Jesus Christ to be the savior of believing sinners. But when the Lord Jesus Christ was utterly rejected by Israel God temporarily severed the unbelieving nation from the place of divine blessing and caused the devastating and total destruction of the city of Jerusalem.

It is this God, says John, who is "love." Certainly, there are many examples of God's rich goodness and mercy and of His loving benevolence. We find them everywhere in the biblical record. I have chosen to highlight these other particular activities of God, however, to demonstrate that the fact that "God is love" does not negate His other attributes and consequent activities. In fact, God's love can be a very stern love:

"My son, do not regard lightly the discipline of the LORD, nor be weary when reproved by Him. For the Lord disciplines the one He loves, and chastises every son whom He receives" (Hebrews 12:5–6).

God's love is perfectly balanced and harmonized with all His other attributes. It is not the entire picture of who God is. It would be a great mistake to pretend that the fact that, "God is love" dwarfs the rest of His being or somehow means that God will only act benevolently.

Thankfully, all of God's attributes are expressed in divine love toward His children. His justice is satisfied when He lovingly gave His Son to be the sacrifice for our sins. His mercy is highlighted in love when He stooped to deliver us from our guilt and misery. His omniscience and power is utilized to provide for and protect His elect. The same could be said of His grace, His justice, His wisdom, etc. Each and every attribute of God is exercised in love for the welfare of the believer in Christ. Even God's wrath in some ways is a demonstration of His love as He repays those who mistreated His children.

The Plethora of Biblical References That Describe God's Essential Character – The Bible tells us that, "God is Spirit" (John 4:24). This statement was made by none other than our Lord Jesus Christ and it occurs in His conversation with the Samaritan woman at the well. She wanted to debate Him about the proper place to worship God (was the proper place the mountain in Samaria where her people worshiped or Mount Zion in Jerusalem). Jesus proceeded to tell the woman that God is more concerned with our hearts than He is where our feet stand. He is not confined by a location but is much larger and different than she may have believed. Jesus said, "God is Spirit," which means, in context, that He is non-material and non-localized. The essence of the true worship of God is to worship Him in spirit as well as in truth. God's spirituality means many things but it certainly dramatically transcends any preconceived ideas that she may have had regarding a God who was only localized or sovereign over a region. The fact that God has no physical body puts Him in a dimension that is free from physical limitations.

The Bible goes on to tell us that God is perfect. That He is a jealous God. It tells is that He is a God that shows mercy, "to thousands – generation after generation", that He is all-powerful, all-knowing, altogether worthy of the worship of His creatures - that He independently exists and is dependent upon no one or thing. He is so infinitely glorious no human being has ever seen Him in all His glory. He is invisible yet totally real. He transcends the world and yet is everywhere present at the same time. God is not subject to, fluctuating emotions that men often experience. God's whole being is firmly fixed and is without vicissitudes, inconsistencies and imperfections. He lacks nothing of any worth and possesses everything that is good and righteously divine. These are but a few of the many self-revelations that we have of God recorded in the Bible. It would be very easy to go on citing the many and varied aspects of God's character. For example:

Not only does the Bible declare, "God is Spirit," but the Bible also says that "God is light," (1 John 2:7–11, 3:10). When we read that God is light in the context of 1 John, "darkness," refers to moral sinfulness and "light" refers to God's holiness and righteousness. John's point in the passage under consideration is that those who "walk in the light", seeking to please God and to be like God in the area of holiness and righteousness of life rather than continuing to walk in the normal, worldly, path of sin (darkness) are the true children of God. God intends for believers in Christ to be holy and righteous. "But as He who called you is holy, you also be holy in all your conduct, since it is written, "You shall be holy, for I am holy" (1 Peter 1:15–16). He, God chose us for that purpose (Ephesians

1: 4). He has caused us to be indwelt by the HOLY Spirit. God's Word (The Holy Bible) has been given to us so that we can be made more holy through reading and obeying it (John 17:17). We are children of light, born in God's image to be living creatures of holiness and when the Bible tells us that, "God is light," we must remind ourselves that this light/holiness is part and parcel of everything that God is just as surely as God's love is part and parcel of everything that He is and just as surely as the numerous other attributes of God are part and parcel of everything that He is. In other words, God loves because He is "love," and He does so with a holy love. Likewise, He is "light"/holy. His judgment is a holy judgment. Salvation is rooted in and geared to produce holiness in its objects. The point that I am making is that God's love must be understood in the total, overall context of who God is in all His fullness. God is "love" but He is much more than that.

The glorious truth is that the full beam of God's infinite love shines upon those who are believers in Christ. All His other attributes are exercised in love toward believers. They, His elect, are the, "apple of His eye," and His most precious possession, and His covenant people. Since God is for us, God's love forever belongs to us as His covenant people.

We have looked at the powerfully clear biblical assertion that, "God is love," the particular deeds and activities that are ascribed to God in the Bible and a sampling of the plethora of other attributes ascribed to God in the Bible. We have noted that all the various attributes of God are interdependent and woven together in a perfect harmony. Our focus now, at this point, is on the fact that God's love is especially evident in a saving way toward those who are believers in Christ Jesus. That is a major portion of the import of the Apostle Paul's words in this passage of Scripture.

The Special Recipients Who Know That God Loves Them

It will be beneficial if we learn from the Bible exactly who is privy to this insight that God loves every believer with an overwhelming and purposeful love. God loves His own, in an extremely personal way, and God wants believers to know that He loves them so that they can be encouraged and spiritually strengthened with full assurance of this fact.

This leads us to examine: The *people* who are privileged to personally know and understand that God loves them.

A good place to investigate this truth is Romans 5:1–5.

A Quick Survey

The Apostle Paul, in Romans, had been establishing the clear need that sinners have for the righteousness of God. Unsaved men/women are exposed to the certainty of the wrath of God. It "is revealed against all ungodliness and unrighteousness of men..." (Romans 1:18). They stand in need of a perfect righteousness to be accepted with God. This revelation of the wrath of God is true in a present, ongoing manner as well as a future manner. The Apostle Pau has declared that, "None is righteous, no, not one....", "Both Jews and Greeks, are under sin", and "the whole world" is accountable to God (Romans 3:9,10, 19). Next, Paul explains how God set forth His Son as a propitiatory sacrifice (satisfying God's righteous wrath toward law–breaking, rebellious sinners). Paul underscores the fact that lost sinners are not saved through the law but rather by Jesus Christ. Paul's next step in the book of Romans was to explain that sinners receive God's righteousness through faith alone in Jesus Christ alone (Romans 4).

Security

When Paul continues his explanation of salvation in Romans 5 his purpose is to demonstrate that those in Christ by faith alone now have peace with God and full assurance that God will ensure their ultimate salvation. The question is, however, "Will God actively ensure and guarantee the salvation of true believers even in the face of life's inevitable hardships and struggles?" Remember, in the world and culture in which Paul wrote Christians could expect to suffer hardships and hostility even to the point of death. Paul assures his readers, however, that the difficulties of life for a Christian will only be used by God to further confirm the believer's assurance of salvation. These difficulties will not threaten the believer's salvation but will, in fact, further enhance and grow it (Romans 5:1–5). After chapter 5, Paul will temporarily digress from his main theme of the absolute assurance of the believer's salvation to answer possible objections to his teaching, but the reality of the confident assurance of the believer and his ultimate salvation will be Paul's continuing overarching theme. Salvation, and a full assurance of salvation, because of God's grace and power in Christ, is where he begins in Romans chapter five. This section of Romans is dealing with the confident assurance of true believers in the ultimate success of their salvation. It begins in Romans five and concludes at the end of Romans chapter eight. The Apostle Paul begins this section as follows:

"Therefore, since we have been justified by faith, we have peace with God through our Lord Jesus Christ. Through Him we have also obtained access by faith into this grace in which we stand, and we rejoice in hope of the glory of God. More than that, we rejoice in our sufferings, knowing that suffering produces endurance, and endurance produces character, and character produces hope, and hope does not put us to shame, *because God's love has been poured into our hearts through the Holy Spirit who has been given to us*" (Romans 5:1–5) (emphasis mine).

Paul's intention is to acknowledge that believers will not only successfully endure sufferings, but that because of God's grace and power those sufferings will not deter the believer or destroy his faith and salvation. On the contrary, the believer "stands" in grace and will be spiritually profited by the process of struggles that God allows him to endure.

Paul highlights this process in the passage just quoted. Moreover, the Apostle Paul states that the believer will personally experience the hand of God in his life causing these seeming negative experiences to further mature him in the faith. When the believer realizes, by experience, this fact he will be increasingly filled with hope rather than being demoralized and fearful as he faces the unknown and uncertain future. Why? Because this whole process indicates that God is for the believer and is actively working in the believer's life to move him forward progressively in his salvation. Further, the believer is made to understand that this whole process which serves to further the believer's spirituality and to confirm the believer's assurance of salvation is because God loves him, "because God's love has been poured into our hearts through the Holy Spirit who has been given to us" (Romans 5:5).

Interestingly, the Apostle Paul begins this section of Romans (dealing with the believer's assurance of salvation) and he stresses the fact that God has poured his love into our hearts as true believers to confirm to us that He is for us. By this reference to love Paul is referring to God's love for us, not our love for him. God's love for us is always fixed, profuse, and perfect. Our love for him is sometimes fluctuating, lukewarm, distracted, etc. The fact is that our personal experience with God as we persevere through life's problems will indicate that God is for us and that God loves us.

When the apostle concludes this major section dealing with the absolute assurance of salvation for the believer (Romans 8:35 -39) he, once again returns to the same theme of God's love for the believer. He declares that nothing shall be able to separate us from the love of God which is in Christ Jesus our Lord. Paul concludes Romans chapter eight by acknowledging and enumerating various trials and sufferings that the believer may endure but in doing so he, again, firmly assures the believer that none of these trials will be able to destroy their faith and salvation. Instead, the apostle focuses on the ongoing certainty of God's love for the believer. Since God is for us – "Nothing shall separate us from the love of God which is in Christ Jesus."

So far, we have circumscribed the truth of, "the love of God." We have demonstrated, from Scripture, its reality and shown in general terms how and when it operates. Now, we need to deal with this awesome subject in more precise terms. What essentially is the love of God? We ask, how should we define and understand it?

Dr. J. I. Packer in his excellent book, *Knowing God,* (InterVarsity press, Downers Grove Illinois 60515, 1978) sets forth a conception of God's love which is as follows:

> "God's love is an exercise of His goodness towards individual sinners whereby, having identified Himself with their welfare, He has given His Son to be their Savior, and now brings them to know and enjoy Him in a covenant relation." (Page 111)

I would like to follow the definition as well as the example of Dr. Packer by examining each part of his proposed definition of "God's love." As we examine the constituent parts of this excellent definition of God's love the precise nature of His love will be seen with a clearer focus. For example:

God's love is an exercise of his goodness – when the Bible speaks of God's goodness it is making reference to his overall generosity. This is that attribute in God which prompts Him to deal bountifully and kindly with all his creatures.

Within this general category of God's goodness, the love of God shines most brightly. James Orr wrote that love,

> "is that principle which leads one moral being to desire and delight in another, and reaches its highest form in that personal fellowship in which each lives in the life of the other, and finds his joy in imparting himself to the other, and in receiving back the outflow of the others affection to himself." (*Hastings Dictionary of the Bible, volume III, page 153*)

That's a pretty good description of the nature of true love and a good description of God's love.

God's love is an exercise of His goodness, "towards sinners." This means that God's love includes His grace and mercy to those who are undeserving, corrupt in His sight, rational creatures who have deliberately disobeyed His law and defied His authority and who deserve only condemnation and eternal judgment. There is nothing in the sinner that would appeal to God. There is nothing in the sinner that would form the reason for why God would love him. The very opposite is true. The corruption of the sinner would naturally elicit the negative response of a Holy God, yet God chooses to love sinners. What a staggering concept! Paul wrote, "God commended His love towards us, in that, while we were yet sinners Christ died for us" (Romans 5:8).

God's love is an exercise of His goodness towards, "individual sinners." God's love is not some sort of vague, watered down, sentiment of goodwill toward mankind in general. God's love is intensely personal, intimate, purposeful and practical. His love prompted Him to choose particular individuals for salvation Ephesians 1:4 God's love planned and secured the ultimate salvation of those individual sinners from the very start. Paul wrote to the Thessalonian Christians, "But we ought always to give thanks to God for you, brothers beloved by the Lord, because God chose you as the first fruits to be saved, through sanctification by the Spirit and belief in the truth" (2 Thessalonians 2:13).

God loves individual sinners and purposes to bless them with His abundant goodness in spite of the fact that they are unworthy and undeserving of such love. God's love for these individual sinners prompts him to take great care to ensure their ultimate salvation and well-being. He knows His sheep by name and He has loved us from before the foundation of the world. As a believer, I can rejoice in the fact that God loves me in a personal way even though I am a sinner. Again, Paul wrote, "But God shows His love for us in that while we were still sinners, Christ died for us" (Romans 5:5).

God's love to sinners involves His identifying Himself with their welfare. That's what love does. In fact, it is the test of whether love is genuine or not. Love cannot stand by without seeking to help. There is no sacrifice too great for love. Love will go to any length and do whatever is necessary for the well-being of the one loved. Love rejoices in the well-being of its object and is deeply moved by the hurt and hardships encountered by its object. Love, by its very nature, demands that one identifies with the welfare of the object of love.

God's glory is always to be the paramount consideration but God's, "gladness," is impacted by the improved welfare of those He loves. That explains why there is joy, "in the presence of the angels," when a sinner repents (Luke 15:10). That being the case and considering the multitude of biblical evidence testifying to the fact that God loves the believer we can conclude that, God identifies with us and secures our welfare. This is nowhere clearer than in the fact that Jesus identified with those He came to save to secure their welfare. The writer of Hebrews wrote:

"For it was fitting that He, for whom and by whom all things exist, in bringing many sons to glory, should make the founder of their salvation perfect through suffering. Since, therefore, the children share in flesh and blood, He Himself likewise partook of the same things, that through death He might destroy the one who has the power of death that is the devil, and deliver all those who through fear of death were subject to lifelong slavery. For surely it is not angels that He helps, but He helps the offspring of Abraham. Therefore, He had to be made like His brothers in every respect, so that He might become a merciful and faithful high priest in the service of God, to make propitiation for the sins of the people. For because

He Himself has suffered when tempted, He is able to help those who are being tempted" (Hebrews 2:14 – 18). Since God is for us, God identifies with His people to ensure their welfare.

God's love to sinners was expressed by the gift of His Son to be their Savior. Love can be measured by how much it is willing to give and the measure of God's love is that he was willing to give His only Son to be made a man, to die for sins, to painfully and yet successfully secure our salvation by bringing us to God and making us acceptable to Him. The songwriter seeking to express the magnitude of God's love wrote:

> The love of God is greater far
> Than tongue or pen could ever tell
> It stretches to the highest star
> It reaches to the lowest hell.
>
> The guilty pair, bowed down with care
> God gave His Son to win.
> His erring child, He reconciled,
> And pardoned from his sin.
>
> Were all the sky of parchment made
> And every stalk on earth a quill
> To write the love of God abroad
> Would drain the ocean dry
> Nor could the scroll contain the whole,
> Though stretched from sky to sky.

There is no limit to the love of God for believers. The Apostle Paul speaks of the love of God as being "great," and passing knowledge (Ephesians 3:19). This great love of God for His people is itself the guarantee of every other blessing promised and the assurance of the believer's ultimate salvation.

God's love to sinners reaches its objective as it brings them to know and enjoy Him in a covenant_relationship. The covenant relationship that believers have with God has been designed and set up by Him. It has been ratified by the death of Jesus Christ. It is permanent and unbreakable. It is received through faith alone in Jesus Christ alone. It is rooted in God's promise to Abraham when He promised, "to be a God unto you" (Genesis 17:1, 7). This same promise is given to all true Christians (Galatians 3:15, 29) who are, in fact, the spiritual seed/children of Abraham.

In this promise God is binding Himself and all that He is to us for our ultimate welfare. His grace continues to provide for us in a never-ending supply of goodness. His power protects us and provides for us. His wisdom directs us. His love envelops and undergirds us. His sovereignty controls all things for our well-being. In this covenant relationship that we have with God through faith in Jesus Christ the great God of the universe pledges Himself, "to be a God unto us." Indeed, God is for us!

When we love someone, we do the best for them that we can and this is what God does for those He loves – the best He can. Is there anything too great for God to deal with? How blessed we are as believers to be the objects of such great love for now and for all eternity! Since God is forever for us, we are forever loved.

Now that we have a better understanding of the nature of God's love, we are ready to examine more fully Paul's statement in Romans 5:5. As we examine Romans 5:5, "God's love has been poured into our hearts by the Holy Spirit" there are four specific things that we need to understand.

First, notice the *profuseness* indicated by the passage. The verb translated "shed abroad" or "poured into." This verb literally means to pour copiously and plentifully. It is the same word used of the "outpouring" of the Holy Spirit Himself in Acts 2:17, 33; 10:45 and Titus 3:6. The conscious fact that God loves us as believers is abundantly poured out into our hearts by the Holy Spirit. It is not dribbled out but is copiously poured out in abundance.

Second, notice the fact that the tense of the verb is in *the perfect tense* which implies a completed past action with continuing results. Not only has the love of God flooded our hearts in the past when we were originally converted, as believers, but it continues to fill our hearts now thus providing us with a strong remaining sense of God's ever-present love for us. That is, because of the ministry of the Holy Spirit, the believer is made to understand that God's love for him is abundant and ongoing.

Third, notice *the part played by the Holy Spirit*. This filling of the believer's heart with the conscious realization of God's love for him is a ministry of the Holy Spirit provided for every believer. This is not something reserved for only a few Christians but is something which is enjoyed and experienced by every true Christian.

We must, of course, be careful when we refer to believers as "in Christ." As our Lord Jesus Christ indicated, not everyone who says to Him "LORD, LORD," is a true Christian/believer. In fact, according to a miscellaneous author citing a recent Barna Survey of "born-again Christians," it found that only 78% say God is the "all–powerful, all–knowing Creator of the universe who rules the world today." The rest believed something demonstrably non-biblical. Amazingly, 40% said Satan is not a living being but (merely) a symbol of evil." 58% agreed to or somewhat agreed that the Holy Spirit is, "a symbol of God's power and presence but is not a living entity. 22% believe Jesus sinned while on earth; only 46% – less than half – said He did not.

There are certain biblical truths that are absolutes for every genuine believer in Christ. These are nonnegotiable and must be believed wholeheartedly by the genuine Christian. They include such doctrines as the virgin birth, the deity of Jesus Christ and His sinless character and life, the substitutionary sacrifice of Jesus Christ on the cross, the resurrection of Jesus Christ from the dead, the ascension of Jesus Christ into heaven, the future coming of Jesus Christ, salvation from sin through faith alone in Jesus Christ alone, the Trinity.

These general statements of faith must be embraced by every true believer. Not only does the true believer hold to these truths but he has obediently surrendered to the Lordship of Jesus Christ as an ongoing way of life, is trusting by faith alone in Jesus Christ alone for his complete salvation, and loves God and the things of God.

Certainly, this summary of a statement of faith is not complete but at a very minimum the true believer must believe in the essential and cardinal truths of Orthodox Christianity These are some of the doctrines that must be held and embraced by faith by all true Christians.

The Purpose – Why did the Apostle Paul choose to interject the idea and certainty of God's love for believers at this juncture in his discussion? It is precisely because the apostle wants the believer to recognize the personal and practical reality of God's love for him and to take comfort and encouragement from that truth even in the most adverse circumstances of life. He is saying, "consider your own experiences in life and reflect upon the fact that these negative experiences did not destroy your faith but actually were used by God to help build up your faith" and to mature you and strengthen you as a Christian. Not only did you endure the trials but you were spiritually profited by them. How could this be possible? It is a clear and personal demonstration that God loves you and is taking care of you. That is Paul's purpose. Hence, we are more than conquerors through him who loved us - and continues to love us – and will always love us.

So far, we have looked at the profuse pouring out of, "the love of God," by the Holy Spirit into the heart of every true believer. We have noted the fact that the verb is in the perfect tense indicating that this copious outpouring of God's love took place in the past (probably at conversion) and continues to fill the believer's heart in an ongoing way with the conscious realization that God loves us in the present just as he has loved us in the past. Third, we noted that this profuse and personal outpouring of, "the love of God," in the believer's heart is the ministry of the Holy Spirit. This ministry of the Holy Spirit is exercised toward all true believers. Finally, we have noted that the Apostle Paul's purpose in revealing this precious reality at this point in his discussion in Romans is to further buttress the reality of the believer's security and personal assurance of their perfect salvation by appealing to the believer's personal experience of God's love evidenced by God's taking care of them in the face of difficult and sometimes overwhelming problems.

Having established these facts about, "the love of God," toward believers, let us dig just a little deeper. What, exactly does it mean that God loves believers?

There are all kinds of loves. Our text, however, speaks not of romantic or sensual love, but of God's very special kind of love for us. Whereas our love for God wavers and fluctuates because we are not yet made perfect, God's love for us is always fixed and settled, sacrificial, intense, intimate, personal, perpetual and practical. The love of God for His children/ believers in Christ is something altogether different than worldly love. I have already quoted the best definition that I have ever found for the love of God. It was written by Dr. J. I. Packer in his excellent book, *Knowing God. (InterVarsity press, Downers Grove Illinois)*, page111.

To appreciate and experience the enjoyment and assurance of the permanence of God's love for those in Christ we need to investigate three additional areas. They are:

The Foundation Laid for Understanding the Love of God
The Faith That We Need to Exercise in the Love of God
The Fullness That We Can Come to Appreciate About the
Love of God

The Foundation Laid for Understanding the Love of God

Upon what does a believer base his trust that God loves him and will always love him? The answer is very simple. The true believer's faith rests on the foundation of the inspired Word of God. Some will say that they do not believe that the Bible is the Word of God. Very well, they have their right to be wrong, but they do so at their own peril. In this study we do not have the time and space to devote to the many clear arguments for the fact that the Bible is the Word of God and is both infallible and inspired. I am assuming that the great majority of the readers of this book believe that the Bible is God's Word and trust its teachings. God's Word clearly teaches that He loves His children.

We have previously discussed the nature of the love of God and we have pointed out, from the Bible, the awesome fact of God's sovereign love for His elect. We need not therefore, repeat what we have already examined. The saving love of God is a function of omnipotence, goodness, faithfulness and many other facets of God's holy character and it has at its heart an almighty, sovereign purpose to bless those in Christ – a purpose which cannot be thwarted.

Open or Off Limits

This saving love of God is off limits and unknowable to those outside of Christ. No one should suppose that this saving kind of divine love embraces him unless he has come as a sinner to Jesus by faith alone and has learned to say to Jesus from the heart, "My Lord and my God." The saving love of God is the Christian's privilege, and the Christian's alone. It belongs to the Christian alone to know for certain that God loves him savingly, immutably, and that nothing can at any time part him from that love, or come between him and the final enjoyment of the eternal fruits of salvation. That is the foundation upon which the believer must base his faith.

Since God Is for Us

373

Thankfully, in God's immeasurable grace through faith in Christ, all lost sinners are invited to come and partake of this wonderful salvation, secured by God through Christ, enabling the believing sinner to experience the everlasting love of God.

Since God is for us, God loves us and will always love us. The Bible tells us so. And that makes all the difference.

I'm sure that you get the wonderful and biblically revealed point. God's love never fails, it never runs out on us. God's will and purposes are always accomplished. God's children are always secure and loved. Nothing can separate us from the love of God which is in Christ Jesus.

The Faith That Needs to be Exercised in the Love of God

The fact of God's love for His people is a glorious reality but it can only be fully enjoyed and appreciated when faith is exercised by the child of God. Consider Paul's words in Romans 8:38 in which the language of faith and full assurance is heard. I paraphrase his words but essentially, he wrote, *"I am convinced (persuaded)"* that there is nothing in death or life, in the realm of the spirits or superhuman powers, in the world as it is or the world as it shall be, in the forces of the universe, heights or depths—nothing in all creation can separate us from the love of God in Christ Jesus our Lord.

In this passage, Paul is countering fear of the unknown and fear of the things of this world. He is countering the fear of our own weaknesses and fear of our enemy's strengths and strategies as well as fear of pain and fear of loss. Paul's focus on facing fearful beings and circumstances has to do with the effect these things might have on one's relationship and fellowship with God, by overwhelming our reasoning ability and thus sucking the very life out of our faith. Paul is telling the Christian that we must fight this fear knowing that literally nothing can separate us from the love of God in Christ. No matter what may happen to us we are still safe in the arms of God because of His unbreakable and inseparable love for us. In fact, Paul declares, "in all these things we are more than conquerors through Him that loved us" (Romans 8:37).

An Honest Assessment of a Difficult Journey

This list of frightening things listed by the Apostle Paul was not mere speculation and hypothetical theorizing. Quoting from the Septuagint, (Greek Old Testament) version of Psalm 44:22, Paul wrote, just as it is written, "for your sake we are being put to death all day long; we are considered as sheep to be slaughtered." The Apostle Paul knew by personal experience what it was to suffer intensely for the cause of Christ and to face, daily, the very real possibility of death. He wrote to the Corinthian church and said, "We are troubled on every side, yet not distressed; we are perplexed, but not in despair; persecuted but not forsaken; cast down, but not destroyed; always bearing about in the body the dying of the Lord Jesus, that the life also of Jesus might be made manifest in our body. For we which live are always delivered unto death for Jesus sake that the life also of Jesus might be made manifest in our mortal flesh" (2 Corinthians 4:8 – 11). His multiple stoning's, beatings and imprisonments, etc., made Paul keenly sensitive and personally aware of the dangers facing true believers in their faithful pursuit of Christ in this world.

Augustus Toplady in a hymn called, *"Full Assurance,"* penned the following words which describe what is involved in our assurance of God's love and our salvation even in the face of the harsh realities and difficulties of life:

"A debtor to mercy alone, of covenant mercy I sing;
Nor fear, with thy righteousness on, my person and offering to bring.
The terrors of law and of God with me can have nothing to do;
My savior's obedience and blood hide all my transgressions from view.

The work which His goodness began,
The arm of His strength will complete,
His promise is yea and amen,
And never was forfeited yet;
Things future, nor things that are now,

Not all things below or above
Can make Him His purpose forgo
Or sever my soul from his love.

My name from the palms of his hands
Eternity will not erase,
Impressed on his heart it remains!
In marks of indelible grace
Yes, I to the end shall endure,
As sure as the earnest is given,
More happy, but not more secure,
The glorified spirits in heaven!

This is what the believer must embrace by confident faith exercised in the person and promises of God. Paul, when writing to his young protégé (Timothy) encouraged him to persevere in the work of the ministry despite the hardships and sufferings that he might have to endure. Paul mentioned the fact that he too was suffering and then stated, "But I am not ashamed, for I know in whom I have believed, and I am convinced that He is able to guard until that day what has been entrusted to me" (2 Timothy 1:12).

We must, by faith, stand boldly on the truth of God's Word and proclaim, "I am convinced/persuaded" that nothing will ever separate me from the love of God in Christ Jesus. Such an attitude and disposition calls for the faith of the believer to be firmly and resolutely exercised.

We have now noted the biblical foundation which must be laid to embrace this truth of God's perfect, never ending love. It is the unerring and clear teaching of the Word of God that God loves his children. We've also noted the fact that His love must be embraced by an exercise of the believer's faith. Now, finally we note the:

The Fullness of God's Love Appreciated

The cost of faithfully following God has always been high. Jesus declared, "He who loves father or mother more than Me is not worthy of Me; and he who loves son or daughter more than Me is not worthy of Me. And he who does not take up his cross and follow after Me is not worthy of Me. He who has found his life shall lose it, and he who has lost his life for my sake shall find it" (Matthew 10:37 – 39).

The Apostle Paul reminded his dear son in the faith (Timothy) that, "All who desire to live godly in Christ Jesus will be persecuted" (2 Timothy 3:12). Jesus constantly warned those that He evangelized to, "count the cost," before deciding to follow Him.

Luke gives us an account of three men who are, no doubt, representative of many others, who professed an allegiance to Jesus but were unwilling to submit to His Lordship. In so doing they demonstrated their lack of saving faith. The first man identified by Matthew as a scribe (Matthew 8:19) promised to follow Jesus wherever He went. Jesus, however, knowing the man's heart responded to him accordingly. Jesus said to him "The foxes have holes, and the birds of the air have nests, but the Son of Man has nowhere to lay his head" (Luke 9:57 – 58).

When the Lord called the second man, this man asked permission to first bury his father. He did not mean that his father had just died but rather that he wanted to postpone his personal commitment to Christ until after his father did eventually die, at which time the son would receive his family inheritance. Jesus said to him, "Allow the dead to bury their own dead; but as for you, go and proclaim everywhere the kingdom of God" (Luke 9:59 – 60).

In other words, let those who are spiritually dead take care of their own carnal interests. The third man wanted to follow Jesus after he said goodbye to those at home. To him the Lord replied, "No one, after putting his hand to the plow and looking back, is worthy of the kingdom of God" (Luke 9:61 – 62).

We are not told what any of these three men eventually did regarding following Christ but the implication is that they all considered the cost of discipleship which involves submission to the Lord Jesus Christ as too high a cost for them. This same scenario is played out in our Lord's words to the rich young ruler (Matthew 19:22). The cost of discipleship seemed too high a price for him and he decided not to follow Jesus.

The parable of the sower also describes those who seem to show spiritual promise at the beginning, but ultimately fall by the wayside when trials, the deceitfulness of riches, the cares of the world, and temptations overtake them. The danger is very real. The cost of discipleship is very real. The difficulties and losses and frightening circumstances facing Christians can seem daunting and beyond their ability to cope with and remain faithful. Paul is coming alongside the believer and with a realistic perspective of life's possible difficulties. He, nevertheless, encourages the believer by assuring him that God will always love him and be with him ensuring his ultimate success and safety.

In Romans chapter eight, the Apostle Paul is not merely theorizing about the many difficulties that a Christian may be called upon to endure. He himself constantly faced those hardships and many more as he recorded in 2 Corinthians 11. True Christians don't successfully persevere in faith because of their exceptional strength but they persevere because God and His love is engaged for them. God's love supplies all their needs and ensures their ultimate faithfulness. We hold fast to God because He holds fast to us. We hold on to God because He holds on to us. Because of God's love for us we are "more than conquerors". The word literally means to be an overwhelming conqueror and one who is supremely victorious in overcoming everyone and everything that threatens him. Because God has His hand on us and His heart is with us we not only survive the hardships on the road of faith but, we are made spiritually stronger and more mature and drawn closer to God through the very things that would seem to threaten our security. In that light, we are overwhelmingly conquerors. Why? Because God loves us with an inseparable love, an unquenchable love, an unlimited love, an everlasting love, and a practical and reassuring love. Since God is for us, His love for us ensures that we will ultimately succeed in our pilgrimage of faith and be eternally secured and saved finally reaching and occupying our home in heaven.

If God Loves us, Then Why the Difficult Trials

But, one might ask, "Why does God allow the believer to go through these difficult circumstances in the first place?" This question has puzzled many people. Some have asked, "Why does God let bad things happen to good people?" Well, in reality, there are no perfectly good people. All people are sinners and we live in a world which has been inundated by and thoroughly infected with the toxin of sin. Because of that bad things are inevitable. Only when we are safely situated in God's coming kingdom will we be totally free from the adverse effects and sufferings caused by sin.

Some Possible Reasons

We have already noted some of the reasons why God may allow the Christian to experience difficult trials Still, there are some other, very practical, reasons why God allows Christians to feel the discomforts and suffering in this world.

First, God allows bad things to happen to His people to test the validity of their faith. Certainly, God knows the condition of every person's heart. Sometimes, however, the individual may not really know the condition of their own heart. Proverbs 17:3 states, "The Lord tests hearts." God spoke to Israel through Moses and said, "The Lord your God has led you in the wilderness these 40 years that he might humble you, testing you, to know what was in your heart, whether you would keep His commandments are not" (Deuteronomy 8:2).

The Apostle Peter wrote to Christians who were suffering for the faith and said, "In this (salvation) you greatly rejoice, even though now for a little while, if necessary, you have been distressed by various trials so that the proof of your faith being more precious than gold which is perishable, even though tested by fire, may result in praise and glory and honor" (1 Peter 1:6 – 7).

These tests and trials are not for God's sake since He knows every person's heart. Instead, these trials reveal to those tested whether their faith is real. The faith of the true believer will not be ultimately destroyed no matter how severe the trial. In Matthew 24:13, in the parable of the sower, our Lord Jesus Christ described four different results from sowing the seed (of the gospel). Some did not respond to the gospel at all. Others responded with a seeming positive response to the gospel only to encounter hardships of one type or another and fall by the wayside withered and dead. Only one of the four responses to the sown seed produced fruit and continued to prosper. Our Lord was saying that the disciples should expect various responses from the preaching of the gospel. Some would be disappointing and yet some would receive the Word/gospel in a saving way with lasting results. Only the latter ones (those who were not overcome by trials or drawn away from the faith by the lure of the world) were true believers/ Christians. Difficulties and trials, therefore, help the professing believer to test the validity of his faith thus reassuring him that it is real or else awakening him to the reality that it is not a saving faith.

You will recall from the Scriptures that Job was a godly man. You will also recall that Job experienced incredible suffering and trials. I would remind you, as well, that Job struggled under the confusion and pain of his problems and sometimes even waivered in his faith concerning what God was doing in his life. Yet Job's faith continued to follow God throughout his entire ordeal. In Job 13:15, he confidently declared, "Though He slay me, I will hope in Him." Job went on to see something of God's glorious, majestic holiness that he had not seen or known before and he repented of the fact that he had had doubts during his difficulties. Job is a shining example of the fact that true saving faith demonstrates itself in the crucible of trials and sufferings by persevering.

Second, God allows the difficulties of trials to wean his people from the world. The believer is sometimes influenced and allured by the enticements of the world and its many empty promises. Difficulties are sometimes used by God to instill within them a longing for heaven. He sometimes places us in difficult circumstances so that we will be forced to look to Him alone for the answers and resources that we need to deal with the difficulties that we face and to look beyond them to a world of perfect peace and joy.

God also allows the believer to experience difficulties to cause us to evaluate what we really love. Do we really love God supremely or do we love the world? When God calls us to give up something or someone that we cherish (for His sake) our response will indicate whether we truly love Him or whether we love the world.

God brings difficulties into our lives to instill within us a longing for heaven and a desire to be free of this world.

Third, God allows bad things to happen to His people to teach them obedience. The psalmist wrote, "Before I was afflicted I went astray; but now I keep your Word. It is good for me that I was afflicted, that I may learn your statutes" (Psalm 119:67, 71).

Fourth, God allows His people to experience trials and difficulties so that He might display His compassion and mercy towards them in helping them and demonstrating His grace and sufficiency in the real-world problems and trials. By experiencing God's practical goodness in these circumstances, the believer is strengthened for greater usefulness.

Paul learned this lesson when he was afflicted by a messenger from Satan. He prayed three times to be delivered from whatever this problem was but God's answer to Paul was different that he might have expected. Instead of delivering Paul from the problem He would give him grace sufficient to deal with the problem successfully. God said, "My grace is sufficient for you, for my power is made perfect in weakness" (2 Corinthians 12: 9). When a believer learns that God will comfort them and that God will give them grace to successfully deal with the difficulties of life they will then be encouraged, emboldened, and enraptured by the love and goodness of God to them. Meanwhile, the on–looking world will witness the supernatural strength and comfort which the believer experiences in the problems he faces. Through this God is magnified and glorified.

Fifth, God sometimes uses bad things and difficult times to humble the believer or to keep the believer from becoming proud. This was Paul's testimony in 2 Corinthians 12, when he described his supernatural experience of being caught up into paradise and hearing things that are unlawful for man to share with others. He said that for him to keep from being conceited and proud God allowed a messenger of Satan to buffet him, trouble him, and keep him humble. Pride in a believer is deadly to their spiritual walk and usefulness. God resists the proud and gives grace to the humble. Sometimes bad things and severe trials are used by God to ensure the believers humility.

Sixth, God fashions difficulties and trials for the believer to cope with so that they can be encouraged by the several and varied encouragements that God employs to help them persevere in those difficult times. These trials are often necessary to equip God's children to be able to help others who experience similar or identical problems in their lives. Jesus said to Peter, "Simon, Simon, behold, Satan has demanded permission to sift you like wheat but I have prayed for you, that your faith may not fail, and you, when once you have turned again, strengthen your brothers" (Luke 22:31 – 32).

These are but a few of the possible reasons why God allows bad or difficult things to happen to His children. I'm sure that there are many possible other reasons that only God knows in the depths of His wisdom. I'm indebted to Dr. John MacArthur who cited some of these reasons in one of his sermons.

Thankfully, we know from Scripture, that in all things God is working for the good of those who love Him and are called according to His purpose (Romans 8:28).

Since God Is for Us...Who or What Can Separate Us from the Love of God?

The Apostle Paul, in Romans 8:31–39, discusses persons who might seem to threaten our security and circumstances that might seem to threaten our security in Christ as believers. Can anyone or any situation separate the true believer from the love of God in Christ Jesus? First of all, it should be noted that, "the love of Christ" does not refer to the believer's love for Him but rather to His love for the believer. In this context, "love of Christ" represents that salvation which God has lovingly provided for the believer in Christ and which He will never take away.

Paul proposes a sample listing of threatening circumstances that might seem to threaten this saving love relationship between Jesus and His children. He mentions "tribulation." Again, this word is from the Greek Apostle JohnSpirit *thlipis* and carries the idea of being squeezed or placed under pressure. In the context it has the idea, most probably, of severe adversity.

Paul's conclusion is that no one or any circumstance can separate us from the love of God in Christ Jesus our Lord regardless of how much pressure these things are able to exert on the true Christian.

His sample listing of possible dangers to our saving love relationship with God includes "tribulation." He then uses the word "distress." This is from the compound Greek word "stenochoria" which means narrow place. This is similar to the meaning of the previous word. Have you ever felt squeezed and confined by your circumstances? Locked in and being squeezed under a terrific burden of pressure? Paul goes on to refer to, "persecution," "famine," "nakedness," "peril," and the "sword."

These are not theoretical situations as far as the apostle was concerned. The Apostle Paul experienced these kinds of difficulties in his own ministry and he, quoting Scripture, said that, "*We are* considered as sheep for the slaughter." Paul uses the word, "we," to indicate that he personally shared in the difficulties and dangers that his readers might well face. Paul quotes the Septuagint (Greek Old Testament version of Psalm 44:22.) He says, just as it is written, "For your sake we are being put to death all day long; we are considered as sheep to be slaughtered."

Paul's conclusion is that though these circumstances are very real and possible, nevertheless, they cannot begin to separate us from the love of God which is in Christ Jesus.

To try to cover every contingency the Apostle Paul writes, "neither death, nor life, nor angels, nor principalities, nor things present, nor things to come, nor powers, nor height, nor depth, nor any other created thing, shall be able to separate us from the love of God which is in Christ Jesus our Lord." (Romans 8: 38–39).

The apostle is stating categorically that no circumstance or person in any dimension, occupying any position, in any time zone will be able to separate us from God's love for us in Christ Jesus our Lord.

What About Death?

One critical circumstance and event is, perhaps, most frightening and daunting to many people. That is the time and event of one's death. The book of Job referred to death as, "the King of terrors." The Bible clearly teaches that many people experience the fear of death (Hebrews 2:15) and everyone who is outside of Jesus Christ as an unbeliever should, in fact, be terrified at the thought of their death and the horrors that they will face in a Christ–less eternity. Each sinner should make it their first order of business to trust in the Lord Jesus Christ and surrender to Him by faith alone. That is the only place of safety and the only ground of real assurance and security as one faces the inevitable time of death. Yet Paul confidently writes that, for the genuine believer, even death cannot separate us from the love of God in Christ Jesus. The apostle wrote to the Corinthians and assured them that death had been conquered by Jesus for believers in Christ. In 1 Corinthians 15:54–57, Paul wrote to Timothy his son in the faith and reassured him that our Savior Christ Jesus abolished death and brought life and immortality to light through the gospel (2 Timothy 1:10). That is, Jesus has destroyed and negated the power of death for those who are trusting in Him alone for their salvation.

Donald Grey Barnhouse told a personal story that beautifully illustrates death's powerlessness over Christians. When his wife died, his children were still very young and Dr. Barnhouse wondered how he could explain their mother's death to them in a way that their childish minds could understand. As they drove home from the funeral, a large truck passed them and briefly cast a dark shadow over the car. Immediately he had the illustration that he was looking for to help his children understand the passing of their mother. He asked the children, "Would you rather be run over by a truck or by the shadow of a truck?" They replied. "That's easy daddy, we would rather get run over by the shadow, because that wouldn't hurt." Their father then said, "Well, children, your mother just went through the valley of the shadow of death, and there's no pain there, either."

For the true believer, there is *no separation from God.* Nothing shall separate us from the love of God which is in Christ Jesus our Lord. Why? Because God is for us!

Benjamin Reaves tells about a little fellow whose mother had died. His father was trying hard to be both mom and dad under difficult circumstances. The father had scheduled a picnic for the two of them. The little fellow had never been on a picnic. He was excited – so excited that he couldn't sleep. Soon there was the patter of little feet down the hall to where his father was sleeping. He shook his dad who would have responded gruffly except he saw the expression on his little son's face. "What's the matter, son?" He asked. The little fellow said, "Oh, daddy, tomorrow is going to be so wonderful. I just can't sleep I'm so excited."

The father laughed and said, "Son, it won't be wonderful if we don't get some sleep. Now you go back to your bedroom and try to sleep."

A little while later the ritual was repeated. The father was already sleeping soundly, and the boy placed an excited hand on his shoulder. "What do you want now?" His father asked.

"Daddy," said the boy, "I just want to thank you for tomorrow."[1]

God not only loves us now but he will love us tomorrow and forever. He will continue to love us in the great tomorrow which will last for all eternity. Perhaps our prayer should be, "Father, I just want to thank you for loving me and for tomorrow."

---

[1] PREACHING TODAY

BRINGING IT HOME

1. What does it mean when we say that God loves someone savingly? Please explain.
2. Certainly, God's love is universal but how is this distinguished from God's saving love? How do you know that God loves you savingly?
3. How permanent is God's love for genuine believers? What difference does it make?
4. What does it mean to be more than a "conqueror"– as a Christian? How does this happen?

WHAT A WONDERFUL SALVATION! – WHAT
A WONDERFUL SAVIOR! SINCE GOD IS
FOR US THERE IS NO SEPARATION.

Conclusion

I began this book by citing a quotation from a historical biblical commentator. Allow me to paraphrase his remarks one more time. He said that if all the Bible were a ring the book of Romans would be the diamond in the setting and the eighth chapter of the book of Romans would be the sparkle on the diamond. In studying Romans chapter eight, I hope that you have come to appreciate its precious value. It teaches us that since God is for us everything regarding our salvation will work out perfectly for our security and welfare.

Speaking of diamonds, in November 2015 a Hong Kong billionaire named Joseph Lau of Property Firm Chinese Estates Holdings purchased the most expensive diamond in the world (sold at auction) for his seven-year-old daughter. Back in 2009, Lau purchased a 7.03–carat blue diamond for $9.48 million. He named it, the "Star of Josephine" in honor of his daughter. Last November, he purchased a 9.75 carat blue diamond for $32.6 million, calling it "The Zoe Diamond" as well as a Burmese ruby and diamond brooch weighing 10.10 carats for $8.43 million naming it "The Zoe Red."

According to Forbes, Lau is the 114ᵗʰ richest person in the world with an estimated net worth of $9.8 billion.

According to Sotheby's auction, Lau shelled out $48.5 million for the 12.03 carat diamond which is the world's most expensive diamond and he renamed it, "The Blue Moon of Josephine." Josephine, again, being his seven-year-old daughter. This diamond sold for over $4 million per carat. As you might know diamonds are judged by four C's: Clarity, Color, Carat, and Cut. The most expensive diamonds by color are the crystal clear or blue diamonds. The most expensive diamonds by cut are the emerald diamonds. Diamonds are placed face down for examination. The clarity of a diamond is judged on a scale ranging from D (the most clear) to Z (the least clear). A1–C3 are not used since many diamond stores use these designations as part of their in-house classification. The carat, of course, having to do with the weight of the diamond. Diamonds are renowned for their beauty and worth. Lau's "The Blue Moon of Josephine" is the most expensive diamond ever sold at auction.

Diamonds may also be valued for their purpose and for the person who gives them. When we were young and already very much in love (which we still are) I asked my wife (to-be) to marry me and when she said, "Yes," I gave her a diamond engagement ring to wear as a token of my love for her and as a token of the promise that we would be married. Deborah wears that small diamond ring with immense pride and joy. The diamond is not huge and probably is not noteworthy in terms of dollar value. The value of that diamond is to be found in the purpose for which it was given and in the person who was giving it.

In this light, God Himself gives us the diamond engagement ring of the Holy Spirit. In the present ministry of the Holy Spirit in our salvation He is referred to as the, "guarantee of our inheritance." (Ephesians 1:14). God gives us this *guarantee* because He loves us and has every intention of making our relationship one of perpetual love for all eternity. Not only is there great intrinsic value in the wonderful salvation that He gives us but there is also an intimate love relationship with the triune God signified by the giving of this token of our permanent loving relationship.

This special diamond sparkles with eternal glory and it is given by God who has eternal unsurpassed love for us in Christ. Since God is for us we need never fear.

As incredible as the diamond Mr. Lau purchased for his daughter no doubt was, it pales into utter insignificance when compared to the great riches that are ours, as believers, in Christ. The book of Romans is the depiction of the diamond of our salvation in Christ. The eighth chapter of the book of Romans is the sparkle on the diamond. It radiates with beauty and staggers one with its worth.

Were one to have a bushel basket full of the valuable diamonds like that which Mr. Lau purchased for his seven-year-old daughter, Josephine, they would not even be considered rubbish next to the wonderfully rich salvation that our Lord Jesus Christ purchased for us on the cross. Since God is with us and for us, ours is a treasure that has great present value and immense eternal value beyond our wildest imaginations.

Hold this diamond that God has given us up to the light and marvel at the sparkle that emanates and radiates from it. As you do, remember that God has given it to you because of His great love for you and His promise of ultimate salvation which He will one day bestow upon you. Since God is for you it is all yours – yours by free and abundant grace.

How can we be certain that it will always be ours? The Apostle Paul answers that question emphatically by declaring, "If/since God is for us, who can be against us?"

Young David stood up and walked out to face Goliath – the intimidating and frightening warrior/giant. David was consumed with a passion for God and could not stand by while God and the armies of Israel were being humiliated by the pagan Philistines. David's heart was for God. David would have identified with the spirit of the psalmists. Some of the Psalms said that, "As the deer pants after the water brook, so my soul pants after God." Again, another Psalm exclaims, "Whom have I in heaven but you and there is none on earth that I desire beside you." And again, "My soul thirsts for God, for the living God." "Because your lovingkindness is better than life my lips will praise you." "One thing have I desired and that will I seek after that I may dwell in the house of the Lord forever."

David shared this same burning passion for God. He was a man after God's own heart. David was extremely jealous for the glory of God. His soul exulted in God and his entire being was caught up in a burning passion for God.

Second, David was persuaded with absolute confidence that God was with him and for him. His confidence was rooted in his anointing by God's prophet Samuel (which carried with it the weight of God's authority and His revealed will) and it was reaffirmed by God's continual protection of him and empowering of him. David felt that God was for him and so it really did not matter who tried to stand against him. God being for him gave David an absolute sense of confidence. Since God is for us we, too, can have great confidence

Fueled by these two strong beliefs, David was motivated to stand up and step forward in the defense of the cause of God. David did so against what appeared to be overwhelmingly bad odds. By God's grace, however, David was spectacularly victorious.

Every champion for Christ must follow this same pattern. In Romans chapter eight, the Apostle Paul has taken us on a grand biblical tour of a dazzling display of God's grace, power, love, and victorious goodness toward we who are His children (His elect, true believers in Christ). Paul has proven beyond a doubt that God is for us. Paul has shown us God in all His loving glory and His sovereign determination so that we, as believers, may be able to understand something of His passion for us and, in turn reciprocate with a corresponding passion for God.

Fueled with these strong beliefs we are not only comforted and confidently assured of our continued and ultimate security and safety in our salvation but we are also encouraged and emboldened to stand up and step forward to promote and defend the cause of God against the braying spiritual giants that oppose Christianity. We are enabled to be champions for Christ since God is with us and for us. May God help us to do so! Remember the wonderful truth, *"Since God is for us, – we are more than conquerors through him who loved us.*

As the song writer wrote, "When we all get to heaven what a day of rejoicing that will be!"

And, may I add:

Soli Deo GLORIA

One Final Appeal

I would be remiss if I did not address the unbelieving reader one last time. Perhaps you have been reading this book and God has spoken to you telling you that you are not saved and that you are still under the condemnation of God and a stranger to the glorious and powerful working of God in salvation. If that is the case, I urge you with all urgency to come to Jesus Christ trusting in Him by faith. Acknowledge that you are accountable to God your Creator. Furthermore, acknowledge that you are a sinner in your heart by nature and that you have sinned against the one true and righteous God thus you have incurred His wrath upon you. Acknowledge that you cannot save yourself from this dire predicament or even prepare yourself to be saved. You need to understand your just condemnation before God as a sinner, and yet also understand that God in His rich love and mercy has graciously provided for your salvation through the sacrifice of His Son Jesus Christ. Jesus Christ died as a substitute for believing sinners. Furthermore, you need to believe that God raised Jesus Christ from the dead on the third day after His burial as a proof that the sacrifice of Jesus Christ had been fully accepted and effective. Considering these truths, you must now personally come to Jesus Christ trusting Him alone by faith alone as your Lord and Savior (from sin and from sin's condemnation). I invite you to do so. Then, you too, will be able to revel in the fact that God is for you and that you are saved and secure for all eternity.

Indeed, you will most certainly be welcomed with open arms and gracious, forgiving love by our wonderful Lord and Savior. Come now without delay–come wholeheartedly–come taste and see that the Lord is good! Then you, too, will be able to face the difficulties of the journey of faith on the road to heaven with joyous confidence saying, "SINCE GOD IS FOR ME," who can successfully stand against me?

About the Author

Born in Waycross, Georgia, Dr. Randall Odom grew up in the Palm Harbor area of the Gulf Coast of Florida. It was there that he met and later married his childhood sweetheart, Deborah Seiver. Happily married for over 46 years, they have two grown, married children who are also Christians, and three grandchildren.

Having pastored churches for 40+ years, Randall is now retired, living in Monroe, NC and teaching a discipleship class and a men's mentoring program at Hopewell Baptist Church in Monroe, where he and Deborah are members.

In addition to pastoring, Dr. Odom has pursued several interests including beekeeping, Bass Masters competitive fishing, woodworking, gourmet cooking, traveling, writing poetry and a weekly newspaper article. He also loved motorcycle riding, sailing and scuba diving. As an extension of his time in the pastorate he was involved in book publishing, as a conference speaker, seminary professor and writing books. An avid student of History, particularly the American Civil War, Randall has led several 3-day bus tours for 45 men each time, teaching the on-site history of the battles and highlighting the Christian character, Christian principles and leadership of certain Civil War personalities.

Dr. Odom's primary passion in life is to glorify God, to build the kingdom of God through evangelizing the lost, and discipling Christians in the truths of Scripture. In his highly informative, encouraging, inspiring and deeply practical book, Dr. Odom leads his readers through the core teaching of the Biblical truths of Romans chapter eight written by the Apostle Paul. "Since God Is For Us," Christians are absolutely secure in Christ and are "More Than Conquerors" through Him who loved us!

Printed in the United States
By Bookmasters